FLOREAT LANDUBRIENSE

FLOREAT LANDUBRIENSE

celebrating a century and a half
of education at Llandovery College

compiled by
R. BRINLEY JONES

THE TRUSTEES OF LLANDOVERY COLLEGE
1998

First Impression—March 1998

ISBN 0 9507636 1 6

© The Contributors and The Trustees
of Llandovery College, 1998

All rights reserved. No part of this book may be reproduced, stored in a retrieval system, or transmitted in any form or by any means, electronic, electrostatic, magnetic tape, mechanical, photocopying, recording or otherwise, without permission in writing from the publishers.

*Printed in Wales at
Gomer Press, Llandysul, Ceredigion*

CONTENTS

Foreword
   Sir John Dillwyn-Venables-Llewelyn *Bart. M.A.*
   Chairman of the College Trustees   7

Preface
   R. Brinley Jones   9

Section I   THE TIME AND THE PLACE:
               a taste of Llandovery College   13

Section II   VOICES FROM WITHIN:
               reminiscences 1848-1997   23

Section III SPORT AT LLANDOVERY COLLEGE:
               prepared by David I. Gealy   239

Section IV IN HONOREM LANDUBRIENSIS ACADEMIAE:
               celebrations 1848, 1898, 1949, 1998   273

Appendices
   The Endowment Deed   321
   Greetings from the Borough of Llandovery   326
   Carmen Landubriense   327
   Pen-pictures of the founding 'Fathers':   328
      Thomas Phillips, Founder
      Connop Thirlwall, Bishop of St. Davids, Visitor
      Lady Augusta Hall (Lady Llanover)
      William Rees
      The Reverend Joshua Hughes
      The Reverend Thomas Price
      John Jones, Cefnfaes
      The Venerable John Williams, Warden

Rules and Regulations	344
Record of an early Trustees' meeting: minutes of 11 August 1852	345
Trustees of the College 1847-1997	346
'An Heritage they must maintain'—The Dillwyn-Llewelyn connection of a century and more	348
The Wardens of the College 1847-1997	351
Trustees, Staff and Prefects 1997-98	356
Selection from the Yearbook (1997-1998) of the Headmasters' and Headmistresses' Conference	358
'Take one long look before you go': a pictorial pilgrimage	360

Foreword

Llandovery College was founded by a wise and enlightened patriot whose aims were clearly stated in the founding deed: then, as now, education was at the forefront of national debate and the preservation of the Welsh language and culture was a major concern. That Thomas Phillips' foundation has succeeded over a period of 150 years in remaining true to the spirit of his wishes is indeed a tribute both to his foresight and to the learned men who have served it as Wardens over that long and turbulent period. The influence of Llandovery College on Welsh life and culture has always been out of all proportion to its physical size; the number of pupils has never greatly exceeded 300 at any one time and in earlier days was often below three figures; yet its reputation has been carried to great heights by former pupils as diverse and colourful as an early missionary to Korea and a famous jazz musician. Therefore as the Sesquicentenary approached, it was obvious to the Trustees that a new book should be commissioned to supplement the existing *History of Llandovery College* which had been written by W. Gareth Evans in 1981. That volume is excellent and essential to those who want to know the facts, but there is so much more to the life of the College than could be contained in such a slender tome that a completely new approach was needed. Debates in Trustees' meetings are often lively and intense—perish the thought that we should ever descend to mere argument—but when the name of Dr R. Brinley Jones was put forward as prospective author acclaim was immediate and unanimous. The qualities required for the task were seen to be scholarship, originality, and humour. In all these Dr Jones excels, additionally he brings a wealth of experience not only of Llandovery College, where his Wardenship is increasingly seen as one of the most notable of recent memory, but as a writer and publisher of true distinction. His recent appointment as President of the National Library is a reminder of our exceptional good fortune in securing his agreement to undertake the task. On behalf of the Trustees, I thank him for the warmth of his friendship for the College, for the wisdom he shares so generously, and above all for the way in which he has accomplished this onerous mission.

January 1998   John Venables-Llewelyn
                                                                                           Chairman of the Trustees.

Preface

When the Trustees invited me to write the story of Llandovery College to mark its sesquicentenary in 1998 I consulted the notes I had collected during my twelve years' wardenship and proceeded to examine the background of nineteenth century Welsh education and the prevailing social conditions. I read, avidly, the records of other similar establishments. I collected details of the careers of those who had served and those who had been educated at the College. I knew, well, the splendid *History* by W. Gareth Evans published in 1981 and still in print: it was I who encouraged the Trustees of the time to publish it as the first full record of the history of the institution. I was also acquainted with *Llandovery's Achievements*, a short but fascinating account which appeared in 1961. I read all the *School Journals* and other 'inside' material that was available. Mine seemed to be the straightforward task of collecting, digesting and supplementing with new-found material and bringing the story up to date.

Then, in November 1996, when I was working on my draft 'history', I was elected President of the National Library of Wales. (The first President, Sir John Williams *Bart, M.D.*, Court physician and principal founder of the National Library had been chief guest at the Annual Distribution of Prizes at the College in 1894 when he remarked that 'Llandovery was a young school . . . yet still it . . . had made its position, and a very high one among educational institutions.') My new appointment afforded me with a fine opportunity of searching the Llandovery College archive deposited there. Among the papers was a significant collection from the Llanbadarn Chest and a substantial amount of correspondence to Daniel Lleufer Thomas, Old Llandoverian, distinguished public servant and one of the founding fathers of the National Library. (It is a happy coincidence that he and I shared Rhondda connections, as we did Llandovery ones . . . that we were both at Jesus College Oxford and both closely associated with the National Library). A hundred years ago he had solicited Old Llandoverians to record their recollections: hardly any of them ever saw the light of day. I decided to supplement these from my own readings from newspapers and autobiographies and biographies . . . and by my own commissioning of reminiscences. Remembering Dr Gareth Evans's fine historical study it seemed to me that a personal anthology of recollections would be more appropriate than a revised 'history' to celebrate the one hundred and fiftieth anniversary.

Intentionally I selected, rigorously, memories of the later years. I had noted what one correspondent, the Reverend John Price of Brecon, had written to Lleufer Thomas in 1898 *'I have read your accounts of Llandovery School in the "Western Mail" and must confess to feeling a wee bit hurt at no mention of my name: I went to Clare Coll. when he went to Caius . . .'*. I realise that there may well be some 'a wee bit hurt' at not being included or mentioned: the omission is mine, *mea culpa*. A view of my own days at Llandovery was published in 1992 under the title *Prize Days: A headmaster's view of his school 1976-1987* and Lt. Colonel J. R. Evans recorded his account in *Llandovery College: Building for the future 1982-1992*, published in 1994.

For this present volume I have composed a short essay, 'The Time and the Place' as a brief introduction. The Appendices are included to indicate the uniqueness of the institution together with some up-to-date information and a pictorial 'reminder'. Llandovery College is, after all, very much a living organism. I might have included whole sections on Music, Drama, the Visual Arts, Science, Religion, Welshness . . . at Llandovery: the list is illimitable. But I opted for one on Sport. It is difficult to imagine any Llandoverian who has not, in some way, been touched by it. And its rugby remains remarkable—to say the least. I invited my friend and former colleague Mr David Gealy to contribute this section. (I recalled the comment in the School Journal of May 1957, forty years ago: '. . . D. I. Gealy, our captain, was a brilliant fly-half and can be rated as ranking with the greatest players the School has produced.') His very considerable sporting talents, not only in rugby, and his intimate knowledge of the school as pupil and master made him the obvious choice.

The method I have adopted results, inevitably, in some repetition. I hope that it emphasises, as it has for me, the extraordinary history of this place. I did not count it necessary to list a Bibliography since the core of the volume derives from sources which are identified. Neither have I provided an Index. I trust that their omission will not cause inconvenience. This is a book, first and foremost, for Llandoverians.

I owe a special debt of gratitude to editors of the School Journal over the years and I must mention, in particular, those whom I have known—the late Mr D. Joshua Evans who gathered *so* much information, and more recently Mr John Jenkins, Mr Randall Jones and Mr J. H. Thomas. I acknowledge the great help I have received from my colleagues at the National Library of Wales and the permission of the Librarian, Dr Lionel Madden, to reproduce material.

I wish to record my thanks to a host of friends—Sir John Venables-Llewelyn, Dr Claude Evans, Dr Gareth Evans, Mr D. I. Gealy, Mr O. M. R. Howell, Dr

Huw Bowen and Mr Huw Lewis. Mr Philip David supplied me with invaluable information regarding his uncle, the late Major D. D. Pole Evans MC, Old Llandoverian. I am grateful to all who responded to my quests and commissions. It gives me pleasure to acknowledge the kindness and great skill of Mr Barrard Lynas who, at my request, took so many photographs. I acknowledge, too, the photographs I have borrowed from Miss Esther Poole-Hughes, Mr Gealy, Mr Jackie Morris, Mr Dewi James and Mr John Morgan. And it is more than a convention that I make special mention of the forbearance and help of my wife Stephanie and my son Aron Rhys for their part in this undertaking.

I wish to thank Mr Jonathan Lewis for his guidance on printing and presentation and to the staff of Gomer Press for all their kindness, expertise and patience.

Above all I must pay tribute to the late Sir Daniel Lleufer Thomas for his labours a century ago, 'Eraill a lafuriasant a minnau euthum i mewn i'w llafur hwynt'. But for him so much would have been lost. I dedicate this work to his memory and to all Llandoverians—past, present, future.

Gyda diolch am y fraint o fod yn rhan o'r sefydliad unigryw yma. Boed llwyddiant!

Floreat semper nostra sedes

October 1997 R. Brinley Jones

Sir Daniel Lleufer Thomas M.A., LL.D., F.S.A.,
1863-1940
'Old Llandoverian'
(Bronze by A. Bertram Pegram, 1939, in the National Library of Wales).

[Abbreviations used throughout are D.N.B. (Dictionary of National Biography), D.W.B. (Dictionary of Welsh Biography) N.L.W., D.LL.T. (National Library of Wales, Daniel Lleufer Thomas Papers.]

SECTION I

THE TIME AND THE PLACE:
a taste of Llandovery College

In 1847 an old man shared a dream about Welsh education. Thomas Phillips, born 6 July 1760, a London Welshman of Radnorshire parentage, surgeon of the East India Company, shrewd businessman, discerning book purchaser, sometime benefactor of Saint David's College, Lampeter, demonstrated his enormous generosity by endowing a 'Welsh School in the Diocese of St. David's'. The Foundation Deed stated that it should provide, within a Christian framework, 'a good, sound classical and liberal education, fitting for young men destined for any liberal profession or scientific pursuit' and should give encouragement to the Welsh language and the study of Welsh history and literature. It would be concerned 'especially for young men desirous of qualifying themselves to be efficient Ministers of the Church in (the) Principality'. The dream was realised with the help of a distinguished group of Trustees appointed in August 1847—Lady Hall (later Lady Llanover), John Jones, Cefnfaes, Radnorshire, William Rees, Tonn, Llandovery, the Reverend Joshua Hughes, vicar of Llandovery and the Reverend Thomas Price (Carnhuanawc). It was agreed that Llandovery was the town which combined 'the greatest number of advantages'—its central position, its history, its culture, its flourishing trade and the enthusiastic support for the endeavour which was locally available. There were other reasons too: Warden John Williams in June 1848 was to refer to 'the great beauty and healthiness of the locality and the absence of manufacturing industries'. Llandovery was a town of some one thousand nine hundred people and three hundred and ninety dwellings. The original name of the establishment was to be the 'Thomas Phillips Foundation': later, it was called the 'Welsh Educational Institution', the 'Welsh Collegiate Institution'—the 'Insti' for short—and later still 'Llandovery College'. Thomas Phillips, who died in 1851, had provided for it with £140 p.a. to pay the salary of the Master/Warden and £12,300 as an endowment for masters' salaries. The cost of the buildings and their upkeep were matters for others to address.

The school's first home was in a building near Llandingat Church known as the Depot, latterly used as a National School and previous to that as the armoury of the Carmarthenshire Fusiliers. It was opened, appropriately, on St. David's Day 1848, the year of revolutions in Europe. In France it was the year of the Third French Revolution: there were insurrections in Italy, Spain, Germany and Austria: Marx and Engels had published the Communist Manifesto . . . and in Wales reverberations were being felt from the publication in 1847 of *The Blue Books*, reports commissioned by the Government on the state of education in Wales, reports which triggered religious controversy, patriotic feelings and which left an indelible mark on political and cultural consciousness in Wales. The time was ripe for revolutionary ideas: Llandovery College was a new concept, radical and challenging. Though it was not part of the wider educational movement, it channelled for itself a furrow that would irrigate so many aspects of life in Wales and beyond.

When the Trustees had considered the appointment of a 'Master', the advertisement stipulated 'a Clergyman of the Established Church, in full orders, thoroughly acquainted with the Welsh Language in its colloquial as well as literary use, and competent to impart a sound Classical Mathematical and General Education'. They canvassed competent opinion, including that of John Williams, Rector of the Edinburgh Academy: he offered himself for the post and the Trustees accepted with alacrity. John Williams, son of John Williams sometime headmaster of Ystrad Meurig School, was born in 1792, graduated at Oxford as an outstanding student from Balliol College in 1814. Another remarkable student of that year, three years Williams' junior, was Thomas Arnold who, as headmaster of Rugby School, was to become the legendary figure associated with the reform of the public schools. Williams taught at Winchester, was ordained and in 1820 followed Eliezer Williams in the living of Lampeter and continued his predecessor's notable work as headmaster of the school which Eliezer had opened. There is no doubt that John Williams exercised considerable influence in the establishment of the Divinity School, to become St. David's College at Lampeter: he was eligible for the principalship but was not offered it. In 1824 he was appointed Rector of the Edinburgh Academy: in 1827 he was elected Professor of Latin in London University but resigned nine months later. He had been made Archdeacon of Cardigan in 1833. In November 1847 he was appointed to Llandovery and in 1848 saw the first of the Free Scholars, Owen Jones of Defynnog enter his school. Williams remained until 1853 when he retired owing to ill health.

By 1 May 1851 the school had left the old Depot and moved to the new splendid Gothic buildings specially designed and built by Thomas Fuller and William Gingell of Bristol, on a field known as Caebrenin. John Williams was there to witness a dream come true: he had enjoyed a distinguished classical education and his publications bear witness to his scholarship. But he had gained a considerable reputation as a teacher, too; his friend Sir Walter Scott—at whose funeral at Dryburgh Abbey in 1832 John Williams delivered the oration—had described him as a 'heaven-born teacher'. In his inaugural address on 1 March 1848 spoken at Llandingat Church Williams invoked 'God to visit with his blessing the work which we have this day commenced, to ask him to regard with his favouring eye the Founder, the Trustees, the present and all future Teachers, and above all those young Christians, whose minds will have to be formed, and intellects cultivated, and pray that they may be sent forth from the Institution into the world, full of Christian zeal and Christian principles'. It was an auspicious beginning to a unique Welsh institution.

Over the years the 1851 building presented its problems: there were structural difficulties and with time it was inadequate, too. The Taunton Report of 1861 had referred to it as 'neat externally and internally well arranged': by 1875 a good deal of repair was necessary. The increased numbers of students, the phasing out of the lodging system, the new demands of curriculum and interests—and far, far later, in 1968, the admission of girls—all these considerations meant that new buildings were needed and adaptation required. In response to appeal after appeal, and due to the munificence of former pupils, wardens, trustees and other benefactors, Old Llandoverians and The Parents' Association, the challenges were met. There were new buildings, substantial refurbishment, purchase of town properties and land. During the last few years there have been new and imaginative uses of space . . . new lighting, new heating, new amenities. The splendid paintings and portraits—all of them due to the largesse of the friends of the College—hang from the walls of the Dining Room and Library, adding charm and dignity to the old school buildings.

Embellishments were unlikely to be derived from the profits on school fees. In 1865 the tuition fees were eight guineas a year, the boarding fees £31-£42 a year: lodging in town was cheaper at £20-£25 a year. There was little increase during the first half century. From the fees the Warden paid his staff and met the bills for the running costs of the school. Such revenue was dependent on numbers, and *these*, over the century and a half have fluctuated both with the reputation of particular periods and more so because of the economic conditions of the time. In 1854 there were 20; in 1861, 70; 1875, 27; 1880, 178. There was a boom in 1980-81 with 297 names on the register.

There is no doubt that the success of the school depended on the leadership of the Warden, the enlightened support of the Trustees and the calibre of the Masters. There were lean years as when there was no Trustees' meeting between 1920 and 1928 *and* when the early Trustees appointed the Reverend Dr James as second Warden, a man whose scholarship was suspect (to the discerning eye of the classicist Dr Thirlwall, Bishop of St. Davids and Visitor to the School). Of James it was said that he was 'an excellent after dinner speaker and the best judge of Baltic timber and Canadian pine in the country . . .

but he never got through the Latin grammar'. He had composed a best-seller (to Protestants) on *The Pope's Supremacy Disproved*—but after a year of wardenship he was 'convinced that his true vocation was that of a parish priest and not a leader of education, being never happier than when ministering to his congregation and comforting the sick and dying'. But it would be fair to say that most appointments to the wardenship were from those of distinguished academic attainment and experience. And despite the trials and uncertainties of the years, Wardens and Trustees held firm to the independence of the Institution even when the economic pressures were daunting and even when the Welsh Intermediate Act was threatening.

Masters came and went but they were chosen with discrimination and in the first half of its existence Llandovery attracted a veritable cluster of young promising—many outstanding—Oxbridge graduates who responded well to the community they found and to the Llandovery environs. Despite the fact that before the mid 1840s there was no notion of a professional teaching body or training towards it, most of the appointees seem to have coped well. It was to the School's good fortune that it had attracted minds of the calibre of Coulton, Hartwell Jones, Stenton and Powys even though their stay was short. Others, of course, came and stayed. The names of some of those who made their mark are noted in the section 'Voices from Within'. Among them is a lady: Miss Ada Mary Smit was to serve the school for fifty-six years as teacher of Music to the boys and secretary to successive Wardens—and confidante to both.

One of the drawbacks of the influx of so many from outside Wales was to dilute the Founder's intention of nurturing Welshness within the Institution . . . though maybe it was the conscious policy of the Wardens of one period in its history to do so: for them Llandovery was a public school of the English tradition grafted on to Welsh soil. There were those who shared the opinion of the Newcastle Commission of 1861 'the language of the past and not of the present'. In such circumstances it is extraordinary, and telling, that two of the seven founding members (D. Morgan Jones, D. Lleufer Thomas) of the Oxford University Welsh Society 'Cymdeithas Dafydd ap Gwilym' founded in 1886 should be Llandoverians: it was a society described by the eminent scholar Sir Thomas Parry as 'a nursery of giants'. By the end of its first term of existence, W. Llewelyn Williams, Llandoverian—who later was to campaign against monoglot English judges in Wales—was also to join it. Later the psychoanalyst Ernest Jones was to deplore the lack of Welsh at the School. Indeed the question of the status of the language at Llandovery even reached debate in the House of Commons. Not until the appointment as warden of the very distinguished scholar, Gwilym Owen Williams, a double first of Oxford and later Archbishop of Wales, did the School in the last hundred and twenty years pay due respect to the intentions and idealism of the early Trustees. Whatever else its strengths—and there are very many—Welshness remains Llandovery's essential and unique quality.

The years to 1914 were remarkable in academic success. Precisely one hundred years ago ten pupils proceeded, in the same year, to Oxford or Cambridge. Classics, Mathematics, Medicine, Divinity, Law—those were the disciplines which Llandoverians pursued. Of course the school curriculum was circumscribed though the Aberdare Report of 1881 details that all 178 of the pupils were studying Greek, 120 Geometry, Algebra or Higher Maths, 80 Natural Science and 70 were studying French. A School advertisement of 1894 claimed that it offered 'classical and modern sides, drawing, shorthand, penmanship, book-keeping, business correspondence, commercial geography, elocution'. Llandovery was adjusting to the call of the times. By now Computing and Design Technology, Business Studies, Photography, Spanish, for example are set side by side with the old and tested . . . all to meet the demands of a new world and the aspirations of a new generation of parents. By now, too, the newer universities have gained their own values and prestige . . . and their own special academic disciplines though for some the appeal of the older foundations remains. The staff, too, happily combine the old and the new traditions.

Every good school offers more than lessons: there is a leading to intellectual exploration and an exploitation of curiosity. There was, from the start, at Llandovery the luxury of an unusually fine library. When the new building opened in 1851 there was an extraordinary collection of books—Enfield's *Elocution* 1780, *Short Hand* by Gurney, 1789, *Handbook for Cricketers*, 1838 and a *Handbook for Swimmers*, a fine selection of literature—ancient and modern—history and antiquities, biography, law and medicine, European literature and Celtic literature among them. Although with the years many of such volumes disappeared, the 'Reading Room' was always an important corner of the school. Today the School Library is housed in what had been the 'Main Hall' and the two large stoves of earlier days are replaced by comfortable chairs and reading lamps. And a portrait of the Founder, book-collector extraordinary, presides over all.

There was indoor entertainment, too, when the exertions of lessons and games were done. The sing-songs of yesteryears, the repertoire of Gilbert and Sullivan, the Shakespeare play, the music recitals and the school orchestra all played their part as did the *Eisteddfodau*—poetry, prose, music, art, photography included. There were the early shows supplied by Magic Lantern, the illustrated lectures, Saturday evening films in the 'Gym', the offerings of the Arts Festivals and . . . television. Debates, chapel choir, business games, folk-dancing, ballroom-dancing all have had their part to play. And since 1968 girls have added new dimensions and quality to all aspects of life at Llandovery. By now they are part of the Combined Cadet Force and the Duke of Edinburgh Scheme with their notable achievements at Llandovery, their multifarious activities offering character training, rigorous self-discipline and experience. And outdoors, too, has been—over the decades—the challenge of Sport. Its distinctive part in the life of the College is described elsewhere in this book.

And what of the post-Llandoverian years when the 'dorms' and the exploits are part of the dreams of school years and the real challenges lie ahead? Not all left with academic honours. Why should they? The term 'liberal profession' of the Foundation Deed may well have been an all-embracing one, loosely interpreted by some Llandoverians! If they have become good citizens they have done Llandovery proud. But there were and are many Llandoverians whose contribution to the professions has been outstanding. They have served the Church, the Judiciary, the Civil Service, the Armed Forces, the academic world, the theatre, music, the arts and the world of high business with conspicuous success. Some are noted *en passant* in this book: others were listed in *Llandovery's Achievements* by C. P. Sharpe half a century ago. The extraordinary fact is the 'extent' of their contribution—Llandovery has supplied four of the Archbishops of Wales since its disestablishment in 1920—but it also gave Korea its first missionary and Washington U.S.A. a Bishop. It boasted a chairman of F. W. Woolworth & Co., a test pilot, an authority on radium and a chairman and managing director of the 'News of the World'. Its soldiers were brave and highly decorated. But it is not the past only that is the pride of Llandovery. Today it tells of recent appointments in all the major professions—university teachers and administrators, school-teachers, medical and legal men of note—a highly respected advocate in Hong Kong, a member of the Chambers of the Attorney General, one of the youngest generals in the British Army, the Director General of the Institute of Directors, the Director of the Welsh Centre for International Affairs, media producers and performers, opera directors, sportsmen and journalists—the list is the length of Tredegar. And it is anonymous because it would be invidious to select. But there will be one exception because he represents so many 'qualities' which might be regarded as Llandoverian and because his life was so closely connected with

Llandovery. Tom ap Rees, pupil from 1941 to 1949, Head Prefect, Captain of Rugby . . . Trustee of many years was killed in a road accident in Cambridge. In a moving tribute to him on 1 March 1997 in the College Chapel, the former Warden, R. Gerallt Jones paid this tribute: 'He was a most distinguished scientist, teacher of science, and science administrator at a national level. He was Professor of Botany and Head of the Department of Plant Sciences at the University of Cambridge. His role as Chairman of the relevant committee of the Biotechnology and Biological Research Council meant that he bore huge responsibilities and not inconsiderable influence in the matter of Science research funding for all the universities in the United Kingdom'. R. Gerallt Jones claims 'He was unquestionably one of the most distinguished products of this school by virtue of his academic eminence' but he also adds other measures of his distinction—*compassionate, gentle, concern, integrity, commitment, scrupulous fairness, meticulous care, stubborn independence*: he comments, '. . . he was to a degree formed by this school'. What a tribute it was to Professor T. ap Rees . . . and what a tribute to the school that helped to shape him!

*   *   *

On 24 July 1954 the chief guest at Speech Day was Sir Guildaume Myrddin-Evans KCMG CB, sometime Chairman of the International Labour Organisation at Geneva. From Llandovery he had proceeded to Christ Church Oxford where he took a first class honours in Mathematics: there followed a remarkable career in the Civil Service. He addressed the boys: '. . . Whatever your school days were, days mainly of happiness, or days mainly of frustration, or whether they were just one day after another, one thing is certain: they have created a bond between you and others which you may ignore but which can never be dissolved—a bond of remembrance, a bond of association, a bond of friendship, a bond of loyalty. And in the case of no society which I know, do I believe that the bond of loyalty is stronger or more enduring than in the case of the members of this old school of ours nestling in the Valley of the River Towy'.

That was almost fifty years ago, but the sentiments expressed remain true. Today, there is commitment, buoyancy and expectation. There are plans for a Performing Arts Centre and there are other ideas in the mind. The arms of the College, reminiscent of the emblem of the banner of the last of the independent princes of Wales flies high from the tower of that 1851 building. Thomas Phillips would have been pleased.

Section II

VOICES FROM WITHIN:
reminiscences 1848-1997

1848	Anon
1848	D. W. Herbert
1848-1852	Evan Jenkins
1849-1853	Watkin Watkins
1850s	Thos J. Greenfield
1854	Wm Scott
1858-1861	D. Edwardes
1861	D. J. Davies
1865-1868	Llywarch Reynolds
1868-1874	W. P. Whittington
1868	'To and from Llandovery'
1869-1909	'H.W.'
1872	David Samuel
1874	C. A. Buckmaster
1874-1885	A. G. Edwards
1876-1926	W. W. Poole-Hughes
1880	Cecil Owen
1885-1887	G. G. Coulton
1885-1889	John Owen
1890-1896	John Morgan
1892-1908 [Masters]	A. Pierce Jones
1893	Ernest Jones
1893-1901	K. F. McMurtrie
1898	The Townee
1899-1948	T. Walker Thomas
1901	A. Pierce Jones
1901-1905	Littleton Powys
1901-1907	A. G. Prys Jones
1902	A. F. Barnes
1903-1911	W. G. Curtis Morgan
1904-1908	Frank Stenton
1906	Hugh Spurrell
1907-1914	W. B. M.
1911-1916	D. H. Patey
1913-1956	H. J. Powell
1915-1928	Esther Poole-Hughes
1914	'Young Jennings'
1921-1930	V. G. J. Jenkins

1923-1927	T. S. Nevill
1930-1933	K. Imeson
1934-1936	J. R. Evans
1938-1941	Hugh Macdonald-Smith
1940-1947	D. R. T. Davies
1944-1949	P. M. Davies
1945	E. R. Davies
	[with the Revd J. L. R. Pastfield]
1956-1996	J. H. Thomas
1968-1970	Wendy Basey (née Thomas)
1986-1988	Elinor Wyn Reynolds
1989-1997	Cerith Rees

Vale Landubrium

Editorial Note

There follows a selection of reminiscences of the 'above-named' spanning one hundred and fifty years. I am deeply indebted to those who recorded such reminiscences and in particular to Sir Daniel Lleufer Thomas who one hundred years ago persuaded Old Llandoverians of the day to recall and to record. I am grateful, too, to those who have responded to my invitation. I thought long and hard about the selection of recent memories and decided to invite a few only to contribute. Those others who are moved to register their thoughts about the Llandovery of their day may wish to submit them to me in writing and I—following the example of Sir Daniel Lleufer Thomas—will deposit them in the National Library of Wales for editing in 2048! Memories, like good wine, are—in my book—the better for the keeping.

The order of entry might seem sometimes to be erratic. In general the 'article' is placed in the context of the years to which it refers . . . but occasionally e.g. in the case of Canon Poole-Hughes and Canon Walker Thomas there is a span of years and articles have then been placed at their earliest reference date.

I have included in most cases, at the end, reference to the source of the article and where possible some biographical detail which would seem to be of interest.

1848

Anon

I was sent to Llandovery School in 1848, when a lad of twelve years of age. The School was then held in a private house not far from Llandingat Church, afterwards known as 'Depository College', a bleak dismal-looking place when I first knew it. The headmaster was the Rev John Williams, M.A., afterwards archdeacon of Cardigan, and previously headmaster of the High School, Edinburgh [The Edinburgh Academy], where he had as pupils Archibald Tait, afterwards Archbishop of Canterbury, and the well known Rev F. W. Robertson, of Brighton, whose funeral sermon he was afterwards to preach . . . The second master was the Rev John Edmund Cheese, afterwards vicar of Bosbury, Herefordshire. Thomas Rowlands was pupil and Welsh teacher. He also taught the juniors. I know I was placed under him as a kind of private pupil for a time, repeating my lessons to him before going to school. I can recall no mathematical master when I first went there. A Mr Stewart, a Scotch graduate, who spoke with a broad Scotch accent, came there afterwards as teacher of mathematics. The whole of the ground floor was given up to the second master, and Mr Stewart. The headmaster had a room upstairs for his class, and adjoining it Thomas Rowlands—afterwards the Rev Thomas Rowlands, rector of Penant Melangell, and author of the well-known Welsh grammar, taught the juniors Latin and the seniors Welsh. What would the London School Board say if they saw the modest cottage in which the leading high school in Wales was started?

Llandingat

As regards the pupils—I was about to write boys—they were all ages, from eleven to five and twenty—the majority big fellows, some of them straight from the farm and the plough-toil, and none the worse men for that; they had worked hard at home and they worked hard at school and did well in after life. Of course, there were some ne'er-do-wells—lads who would do nothing at home and did nothing at school . . .

We had in our class a young man of five and twenty, a gentleman farmer's son from the confines of Pembrokeshire, a rider and shot, and very free and easy in his manner. He got up his Caesar manfully with a 'crib', he knew the English, but was doubtful about the Latin. One day we were up in class facing a window which looked out upon the main road leading to the town. A herd of black cattle passed. Springing up, he exclaimed, 'By George, there go some of our oxen!' The class exploded. The master failed to retain his countenance. He reprimanded the speaker, but he apologised most handsomely. 'I really beg your pardon, sir. I quite forgot where I was.' Then he said something about the oxen that caused another explosion. Ah well! he was not much of a hand at classics, but I have seen him bowl over many a rabbit and bring down a partridge, without even, I suspect, the aid of a licence from her Majesty's Excise. There was no cricket at Llandovery School in those days, and no football worth mentioning. The game of the school was hand-ball, or fives. There were some excellent players among the big fellows. One of the best was Edward Davies of Cefn Ceido, near Rhayader, afterwards rector of a parish in Essex. There were good players from Cardiganshire. Puritanism had not succeeded in putting an end to all manly games amongst the Welsh. Fives—and to some extent football—still survived . . .

The ball court was the pine end of the school-house, and was monopolised by the big fellows, who chevied the little fellows away whenever they ventured to occupy the court. We were driven to the necessity of exercising our skill against other parts of the school to the no little injury of the windows. These were broken, and it was a very difficult matter to find out who had broken them. One day I had the misfortune to break a window in the headmaster's room. This was serious. I was assured I should have to pay for it and all the other broken windows out of my pocket-money, be thoroughly caned by the headmaster, and then be ignominiously expelled. We all four (the set) went to the second master, who was our champion, and laid the matter before him, making the most of the fact that we were not allowed to play against the pine end of the building. He spoke to the headmaster, who issued a decree that no 'fives' was to be played against any portion of the building. This was a terrible blow to the big fellows, who almost broke into open mutiny, and threatened us with condign punishment. After hanging about the playground with their hands in their pockets, looking very disconsolate, they, too, formed a deputation to the second master, and asking his intercession and terms of peace. They were duly granted by the headmaster—the five courts to be open to small and great; the juniors not to be disturbed in their games by the seniors, but to be allowed to play the set out. How we little monkeys chuckled! The result was that out of school hours the court was continuously occupied by successive 'sets' during the summer months from eight a.m. till dark . . . I feel sure Llandovery at this time could have beaten any school in England or Wales at fives, as played there. This does not apply to Eton fives.

The headmaster had immense influence over his boys. To use a common expression, they swore by him—metaphorically, of course. He was an excellent classical scholar and a good all-round man—they believed him to be the best scholar in Great Britain. This influence he obtained by his sincere interest in the welfare of his pupils and his manifest desire to make men and scholars of them, but more especially from the fact that he was a Welshman, a Welsh scholar who was not ashamed of his nationality, and who used the Welsh language to awaken the intelligence of his pupils. He was not a 'Cymru Fyddite'. He was too well read and his sympathies were too wide to be confined to the aspirations of so narrow a school, had it existed then. Not Wales for the Welsh, but the 'World for the Welsh' was his motto. He was remarkably fond of philology. He would ask the English of a Greek word, then the Latin, then the Welsh, he would himself give the Gaelic. His residence in Edinburgh—the modern Athens—and his converse with the savants there had led him to study a language cognate to his own beloved Welsh. Then he would, perhaps, trace the word through the Latin-derived languages of Europe. All this expanded the boys' minds, and led them to see the close connection between the European languages. I remember distinctly the pride with which a Cardiganshire youth stated that he had answered a question that the whole class had failed to answer, and that was the Welsh word for the Latin 'insidias'—'am-bush'—he had given the word wanted, viz., 'cyn-llwyn'.

The headmaster not only interested his big boys—I think we called them his 'lambs'—in their lessons, but also in passing events—the making of history, and in the past history of their country and of the district in which they lived. A profound antiquarian and a piquant contributor to the 'Archaeologia Cambrensis', he told them—as no one else could—the account of the various places of interest in the district, and adjoining counties. Morever he instituted a monthly holiday—the first Monday in each month—when we were encouraged to visit these places.

Carreg Cennen

There were no railways in those days and the modern bicycle had not been invented. The only method of locomotion was by walking. What tramps we had 'o'er moss and fell', and what merry parties we formed! Five to eight was the usual number, embracing one or more of the headmaster's boys, who could tell us what he had told them. We visited the ruins of Cerrigcennin Castle, built on the top of a precipitous rock: the Van Peaks and pools, with their legend of a 'Lady of the Lake'. Our way hither was through Mothvey, and within sight of the former residence of Meddygon Mothvey, who were said to be descended from this mysterious lady. Here they compounded their marvellous, and . . . disgusting prescriptions . . . We made our way to the Trecastle Mountain to find traces of a Roman road . . . retracing our steps past 'Brutus's' house and the monument on the Llandovery road marking the scene of a coach accident. We explored Glanbran Park and house. We paid several visits over to the Roman lead mines at Conwil Caio. New boys had to be shown the curiosities of the district.

On one occasion I remember that after exploring the mines and getting ourselves in a very dirty state we wandered about and found a small stream. There was but little water in it at the time, but any amount of trout. The Welsh proverb says 'There are many ways of killing a dog besides choking him with butter', and there are many ways of capturing trout besides the alluring and deceptive fly. 'Groping' is one of these methods. And on the banks of a trout stream I had had experiences in many methods. Throwing off my jacket, I commenced work. A cousin, some years my senior—subsequently a highly respectable rural dean—followed my example. In an incredible short time we had caught a beautiful dish of fish, our companions depositing them in the fishing buckets in which luncheon had been carried. Working our way up stream we came in sight of a gentleman's seat at some distance, at the head of a broad expanse of meadow land. It was Dolaucothy, the residence of Judge Johns! Something seemed to tell us that we had better desist, and so, slipping on our jackets, we made our way to the village inn, and asked the landlady if she would cook some trout for us and furnish us with a dish of ham and eggs. She willingly consented, and took the fish from us. Presently she returned, looking very grave, and inquired where the fish had been caught. We replied 'In the neighbouring brook', whereupon she said that her husband would not allow her, under any circumstance, to cook the trout that had been caught in the Dolaucothy preserved waters, and we had been guilty of trespass and poaching! Here was a nice to-do. We stoutly denied the poaching; we had caught the fish fairly, in broad daylight (it requires more skill to tickle a trout than to catch him with worm or salmon paste). We knew nothing of the water being preserved. The landlord of the inn was obdurate. He was an old servant of the family's; he may have belonged to the Dolaucothy Estate, if I remember rightly. We stated that we were 'collegians', and would be answerable for any inquiries that might be made, and hold the landlord blameless! This had no effect, so we rode the high horse: we demanded our fish and said we would go elsewhere. Whether there was an opposition inn in the village I know not, but this threat produced the desired effect, and in due time a smoking dish of ham and eggs and another of trout were served up, forming a dinner fit for any king! And here I beg to offer a public apology to the Dolaucothy family, for having had a hand in capturing the trout but I think Judge Johns was to some extent to be blamed. Why did he put temptation in the way of thoughtless school boys by allowing his water to become overstocked? We did but attempt to preserve the balance of Nature!

But I have wandered sadly. On my return to school the second half year—there were no terms in those days—a wooden shed had been erected adjoining the pine end of the school cottage—for it was little more. This was to form the mathematical and modern side of the school . . . Here Mr Stewart endeavoured to instil a love of mathematics into the pupils, but with little effect. Llandovery was classical to the back-bone. The boys as a body despised that study in which the school has since excelled. Often I have overheard the mathematical master say 'Ye know nothing; ye don't know your own ignorance!' And he was perfectly right. I doubt whether half a dozen boys in the school knew what mathematics embraced, except that it meant arithmetic and vaguely something else. Mr Stewart resigned—it was said in disgust because the boys would not work at mathematics or possibly because he had obtained another post. But though Llandovery was strongly classical at this time, I am bound to confess that we juniors did not injure our health by hard work. The second master was somewhat lenient, and we took full advantage of this. One Monday morning—Black Monday—it was announced to us that we were to take our lesson to the headmaster. What blank dismay fell on the form! There were whispers, 'I don't half know it'. There were frantic inquiries for Latin dictionaries and beseeching entreaties for ''strues' from the big boys, who cruelly refused, and prophesied what a 'wigging' we little beggars would get! Upstairs to the headmaster's room we went, like so many convicts going to prison. Our forebodings were fully justified; we did not half know our lesson, and this the headmaster soon discovered. The head boy's Latin exercise was ignominiously hurled to the ground with the laconic word 'Next'; and 'Next', and 'Next', was heard in rapid succession as exercise after exercise strewed the floor. Then following such a 'wigging' I will say this for the then Warden of Llandovery Welsh Collegiate Institution, that I have never known a headmaster—and I have known a great many in my life-time, who could 'rate' a class of boys without losing his temper, and make them ashamed of themselves so successfully as the Rev John Williams M.A. What a lecture on idleness we had. The effect was magical. We worked with a will. A false report went out about once a week or oftener, that we were to be sent up to the headmaster the following morning. This had a most stimulating effect. The lecture was intended, I shrewdly suspect, to influence others besides our form. Anyhow, we were kept sharply up to our work after this, and additional burdens laid upon us, but no more than what we deserved amongst other things the repetition of so many lines of Latin poetry, a capital mental exercise . . . We learnt ever so many odes of Horace and lines of Virgil by heart. How well do I remember the dear old warden teaching us juniors how to repeat the Eighth Ode of the Third Book, keeping time, or rather marking accent, with his gold-headed cane . . .

I almost think the thing that struck us most in the headmaster was his power of hearing a class without looking at any textbooks. He would hear a lesson in Caesar, Virgil, Horace, or Homer, correct a bad translation, or supply a missing word without looking at any book. I presume it was years of constant teaching and his love of the classics that gave him this familiarity.

It was at the end of this or the following half-year that one of the head boys announced that our warden had been made archdeacon of Cardigan, and it was hinted that it might lead to a bishopric, so that in those early days the headmastership of Llandovery College was looked upon as a stepping-stone to the episcopal bench.

The succeeding half-year we were to meet in the new buildings . . .

(Western Mail, Tuesday 22 September, 1896)

1848

D. W. HERBERT

I was one of Archdeacon Williams' first pupils at Llandovery in 1848, and as far as I am aware there are only two still living out of the 12 or so composing the 1st Form to which the venerable old man paid special attention—The Rev T. Mortimer, Rector of Castle Bigh [Bythe], Pem.—and T. M. Hughes son of the late Bishop of St. Asaph and Professor of Geology in Cambridge. The Rev Edmund Cheese . . . had charge of the lower Form in the old square building near Llandingat Church, the Archdeacon occupying the upper room under the same roof.

. . . 4 of us matriculated at Jesus, Oxon, in 1850, and of the number William Hughes became scholar of the College, have obtained the Powis whilst in the School before entering the College.

The school discipline in my time was lax and not what it should be, and different I am pleased to find to what it is at present [1898].

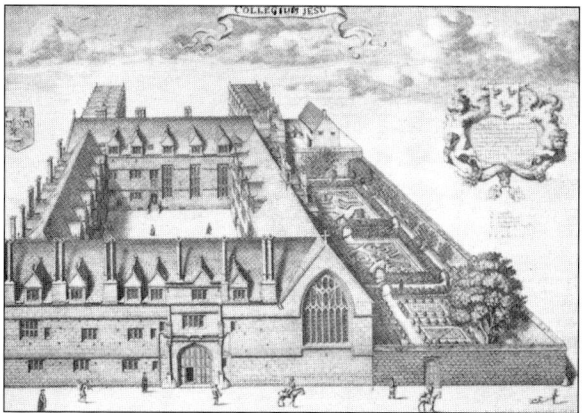

Jesus College Oxford

The School made a good start under the Archdeacon, but lost ground under Dr James who was not equal to the position. From Dean Phillips' time it has progressed satisfactorily and has attained, I should say, the highest position of all our Welsh Schools. My son, Dr Herbert of Denbigh, was a pupil under the Bishop of St. Asaph.

(N.L.W. Ms. C3/4/3. Letter to D. Lleufer Thomas 11 May 1898 from Tremain Vicarage, Cardigan. Crockford's of 1868 records Herbert as having graduated from St. Mary Hall Oxford as B.A., in 1853: he was made deacon in 1854 and priested in 1855).

1848-1852

EVAN JENKINS

. . . during the period that Archdeacon Williams was Warden, I was a pupil at the school at the time. The co-students whom I can especially remember were Thos McKenny Hughes son of the then Vicar, subsequently Bishop of St. Asaph; Watkins who afterwards became Warden; D. Thomas who became a distinguished Oxford Mathematician. There was also Basset Lewis, since head of the Carmarthenshire Police, Thos Wolsley Lewis afterwards of Cheltenham College . . . The 2nd Master was John Edmund Cheese . . . other masters were a Mr Morris—and a Mr Stewart. Welsh Master Rev Thos Rowlands author of Welsh Grammar . . .

. . . I remember well a Mr Morris, as undermaster at Llandovery. He was a man of small stature—a Cambridge Graduate—I think it possible that he was able to instruct a few of the more advanced mathematical scholars among whom I would include Thos McKenny Hughes; David Thomas now of Garsington; and Wm Watkins, afterwards Warden—but he was defective in ability to maintain discipline—and therefore the crowd of grown up lads of small attainments, and possibly boisterous manners made such little progress that the Archdeacon *took* the Euclid class—and I well remember, that I was selected to be the demonstrator —viz the one who drew the figures on the black board. The Archdeacon's intervention was attended with success—Mr Morris did not stay long . . . Mr Morris was followed by a Scotchman named Stewart—a *greater* but not a *complete* success. I do not know whether he was there when I left for Oxford in October 1852.

. . . There was also another master whose name I cannot recall. He also taught Mathematics. He looked like a man who had met with reverses—he had rooms at the College. He was married—I rather think that his wife was a foreigner and I can recall the children as presenting a half-foreign—not to say half-caste appearance. There lived at Llanfair-ar-y-bryn in those days a Madam Gibbert daughter of Col. Gwynne of Glanbran. She had living with her either a daughter or a friend whom Mr Morris was supposed to be somewhat sweet upon. The bigger lads were wont to taunt him with this—to his evident annoyance; this will partly explain his want of success in teaching Euclid.

. . . You are undoubtedly right in saying that the correct name was *Morris Thomas* . . . *I remember Mr Henry Knight*. He was a gentlemanly looking man of dark complexion—the other assistant—Mr Clint lived at the College. He was married—had children who looked rather '*Gipsy*' in appearance—and I imagine that the family had had a bad time previous to their arrival at Llandovery . . .

(N.L.W. Ms. 6241B. Letter to D. Lleufer Thomas August-September 1899 from Preston).

1849-1853

WATKIN WATKINS

... I was at the 'Welsh Educational Institution', Llandovery, as it was then called, from the year 1849 to 1853, and therefore chiefly under 'Old Archy' and after him for a short time during Dr James' Wardenship . . . The greater part of my time it [the School] was held at the old temporary makeshift building called the 'Depot'. But the Archdeacon whom we all adored for his mighty scholarship survived to occupy the New College for a while. Then came Dr James who made a great mistake in leaving the Pulpit and taking to the schoolmaster's desk for which he was not cut out and then head boys soon left. Of this lot I suppose I must have been one because I was one of the six Foundation Scholars appointed by examination, the other five being at that time to the best of my recollection Tom Hughes, son of the Vicar . . . John Morgan, Llwyn-close, Wm Walter Vaughan, a native of Radnorshire, Wm Watkins (a cousin of mine) afterwards Warden . . . D. Jones . . . also a relative of mine.

I am one of the few survivors of those happy days; I do not at this moment [1898] remember any one of conspicious brilliancy; but the impression I have carried with me to this rather advanced stage in my life is that we were a jolly healthy lot of boys who enjoyed their work as well as their play.

(N.L.W. Ms. 6241B Letter to D. Lleufer Thomas 13 May 1898 from Llanddewi Vicarage, Llanrwst. Watkins was Phillips and Senior Scholar at Lampeter. He was made deacon in 1857 and priested in 1858).

1850s

THOS J. GREENFIELD

Castle Hotel

The Llandovery of the early 1850s had not the railway advantages of a later date. Four mail coaches at the earlier period conveyed passengers, luggage and letters from outside districts to the town. The arrival and departure of these coaches naturally excited great interest and curiosity, and there was always a small assemblage of onlookers at the 'Castle' where they were horsed, to hear the news, and receive the burdens, which they discharged. These coaches started from Gloster and Carmarthen, respectively and the most interesting of the four was the morning arrival at 11, which met a train from London to Gloster at midnight, and performed its journey through Ross, Abergavenny, Crichowel and Brecon, in about 11 hours. On Sundays the letters, so conveyed, were sorted at the Post offices, and were ready for delivery for those who called for them, at the termination of the morning service at Llandingat. The 'Hereford Times' was the journal generally patronized at Llandovery, and it was the paper that gave the people there the first though tardy information—for it was a weekly—of the accident to and death of Sir Robert Peel, which created so strong a feeling of regret, if not of consternation in the country. The school . . . was at this date—1850+—in occupation of a white stucco sort of building, which had been, in the time of the French War, a Militia Barrack. There were rooms for 3 or 4 classes, and there was a small sweetstuff shop at one end, where old boys still alive will recollect as their benefactress, an old lady who sold tarts, eatable, if not exactly fresh, and fruit, if not exactly sound. The building stood at the Carmarthen road end of the town—and on pleasant summer afternoons games, such as 'fives' were played on a very accommodating side wall that faced the high road. The Masters of the School were at this early date in its history, the archdeacon of Cardigan, the Revd. John Williams, The Revd. E. Cheese for Classics, and Mr Thomas and Mr Rowlands for Mathematics and Welsh respectively. The Revd. John Williams—'Archy' as he was termed by irreverent schoolboys had left the Edinburgh Academy to take up the leading position at Llandovery. He was a massive figure, both physically and academically, but as he was somewhat short of stature, he had been heard to describe himself as a 'giant cut down'. As a double first Oxford man, and a renowned Greek scholar, his attainments were very high, and his hostility to a false quality was sometimes displayed by the discharge of the book he was holding at the falsifier's feet, and the abrupt break up of the class and lesson. He was the author of two books, very much spoken of at the time, a life of Alexander, and a book called *Claudia and Pudens* the latter strenuously supporting the antiquity of the old British and non Roman Church. At the time of the Papal Revival, he could not withhold his hostility to the Pope and wrote a piece . . .

The discipline at the School, as far as school hours were concerned was strict, but outside these hours, it cannot be said that there was any real discipline at all. Except in a few cases where scholars were placed in the Masters' houses, private lodgings were engaged, and as might be expected loose practices in ruinous forms and divers places followed. Public Houses were not unfrequently visited, smoking and card playing were freely indulged in, and prowess in some of these vagaries was considered more becoming than indulgences in less pleasant pursuits such as Grammars and Lexicons. There was at this time in the Market Street a watchmaker named Daniel James, whose place of recreation was always open to schoolboys, with a pack of cards ready at hand, and most interesting conversation always abounding—old boys will recollect the shop also its genial, if somewhat unsteady proprietor, and the many pleasant afternoon spent in its almost forbidden surroundings.

There was no bullying or fagging at the School, however dogs were kept and ferrets, and in one instance fighting cocks, and poaching, or perhaps we should say quasi poaching, was not unknown—but prosecutions never followed, although landowners and farmers were much annoyed, or pretended to be, at the sporting proclivities of the Llandovery youths. Excursions to orchards occurred at intervals, and bull terriers and bull dogs were not infrequently potted against each other, but gambling and betting were unknown, and the drinking, smoking, poaching dog training bell ringing &c. were more exhibitions of 'fast' life than inherent vices established or in embryo, in the constitutions of the Llandovery scholars of 1850+.

At the opening of the new schools in 1850 (1851?) a great display took place—Special Service in Church, general holiday, bands, fire balls, and everybody that could attend and were interested in the Establishment, including a nephew of the late Sir Benjamin and Lady Hall, did so. Of course the old stucco building was then given up and new classrooms, &c established and a most convenient change in all respects followed.

(N.L.W. Ms. D.LL.T. Papers C3/5).

1854

WM SCOTT

. . . I went there in August, 1854, at the same time as the late Dean E. O. Phillips, who had just been appointed Warden. The School was then at a very low ebb. We opened with 17 boys, not enough to fill the free scholarships. The number increased rapidly. I think 90 was our highest mark. The Staff at first consisted of the Warden, myself and R. Griffith Williams, Esq., who afterwards became an eminent Q.C. Dean Phillips in 1861 went to Aberystwyth. I continued under the new Warden, Rev W. Watkins. He was not a success. The School sunk to about 40. Altogether I was 13½ years at Llandovery, leaving at the end of 1867.

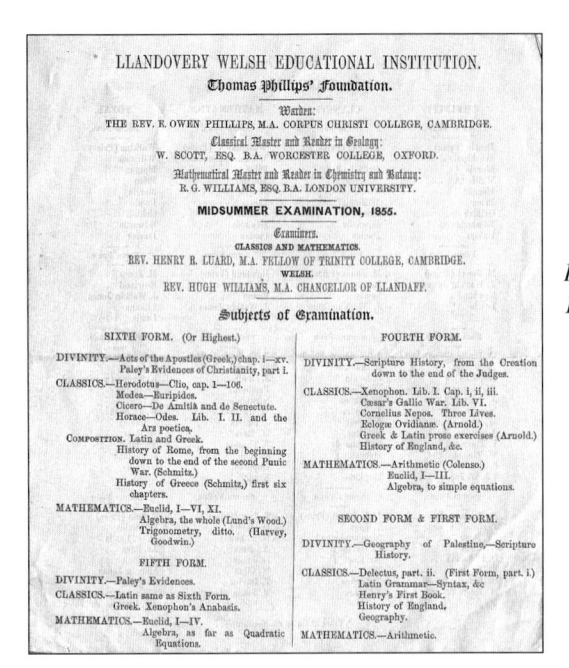

Front page of Midsummer Examination, 1855.

The list of masters I give is nearly complete, I believe. Rev Th. Thomas M.A. of Jes. Coll. Oxford; Rev Roger Williams, Welsh Master; J. Jones Esq.; Evan Evans Esq.; Rev Wolsley Lewis; Henry Edwards afterwards Dean of Bangor; Rev Trevor Owen; Rev Th. Llewelyn Thomas, Fellow and Tutor of Jes. Coll; Prebendary Morris, Jes. Oxford; Rich. Baddely, Esq. There were also French Masters. In those days about 20 boys lived with the Warden, 7 or 8 in my house, the rest boarded in the town. Some regularly disappeared on Saturday to fetch their weekly provisions from their homes, and might be seen on Monday, carrying small sacks. We generally had a preacher or two; once four. They always went on Saturday to keep their cyhoeddiad and came back on Monday afternoon. With one exception, none made much progress. More than once I caught a preacher studying his sermon in school. The boys were of all ages, small fellows and mature men. One was at least 30, a son of a Cardigansh. farmer. He hold me he had once headed a gang of labourers into England in the harvest season. One was bald, age doubtful, a splendid Welsh writer. We tried to exercise discipline over those lodgings in the town but it was very inefficient. They were too much for us. Occasionally something unpleasant occurred. I remember at one time the 4th form, with wh. I had a great deal to do, consisted of 18 big fellows, all about 18 or more. They were mostly very rough, and had to be kept in order by strong measures. Generally they were anxious to learn and would work well. Some were very deficient in English . . .

(N.L.W. Ms. 6241B. Letter to D. Lleufer Thomas 11 May 1898 from Haverfordwest. Scott was Master and Second Master at Llandovery. Scott graduated B.A. from Worcester College Oxford in 1855 and was ordained deacon by the Bishop of St. Davids in 1860).

1858-1861

D. EDWARDES

The Llandovery School, or as it was then called, 'The Welsh Collegiate Institution,' was now, under Phillips, coming into good repute. It was started in 1848 under John Williams, Archdeacon of Cardigan, a brilliant and a profound scholar, who had been bracketed in the First Class at Oxford with Dr Arnold, and as the head of the Academy at Edinburgh had turned out a remarkable group of scholars difficult to parallel in the history of education. Williams was probably not strong in discipline. At any rate, in that respect Llandovery had not a good name under him; but it must be taken into consideration that for the first three years the School was held in a most inconvenient house. And there is the additional fact that his name attracted from the North of England a batch of big, unruly set of fellows, some of whom probably had failed in other schools not from any fault of their masters. The School went into its permanent building in 1853, but Williams's health was now beginning to fail and he had to retire in 1854. He was succeeded by Evan Owen Phillips, afterwards Dean of St. David's. Phillips was a strong man but it took him some time to fix the discipline and eliminate the old traditions. Even when I joined the School in October 1858 the old larky spirit was not altogether extinct; but a wholesome fear of the Headmaster, or the Warden as he was called, kept it well down . . . As the last of the pupils of Warden Williams left the School the unhealthy tendency to frolic entirely disappeared. The tone of Llandovery became distinctly good, and the spirit of work which pervaded the School I have never known excelled. Phillips himself was an excellent teacher but he was not very fortunate in his Staff. His assistants were all good, nice fellows, but they were too shy and timid to do themselves justice with boys, or indeed to do the boys justice. They were conscientious enough, kind enough, good scholars, but all wooden in the extreme—Scott, Thomas, Evans, Sanders, all dead long ago.

When I went to Llandovery I had no idea whatever or even what I should like to do as the work of my life. I had read many lives of great men and saw that many of these had been at one time as modest about their ability as I felt myself. Indeed I had always found myself at all the schools where I had been a shade better than boys of my age and I felt certain amount of conceit which depressed me. I felt impatient to go to a good school where I should meet boys who would beat me. I think I was less anxious to discover what I could do than I was to find out what I could not do. This latter desire was soon satisfied at Llandovery where there were plenty of boys whose minds had been trained ever so much better than mine was . . . I thought it well to take a test subject and chose Mathematics, joining the Modern Side of the School but there called 'the Literary Form,' where one could choose one's subjects and was not obliged to do Latin. I began with Colenso's Algebra and worked out all the examples in it in five weeks. I think I was put down as a bit of a humbug and that nobody believed I had not been through it before. I spent the rest of the term over a more advanced book called Hall's Algebra.

I went back to School after Xmas and I began to attack Euclid. I had heard that Isaac Newton or somebody had learnt a book of Euclid every day. I exerted myself with all my might to do the same and I think I succeeded in writing out every Proposition that was set me for a test. But I broke down completely in Euclid at the Summer Examination. What had been learnt rapidly was very nearly all forgotten whilst I was doing my Trigonometry and Conic Sections, the subjects at which I employed myself for the rest of the half-year. At the Midsummer Examination I was very fortunate. I won a good number of prizes and amongst them Bishop Thirlwall's Welsh Prize of £5. Mr Phillips at the end of the Half sent for me and urged me to come back and begin Latin after Midsummer with a view of going up to Cambridge. My prizes also dazzled my people at home and the way to the University was made clear for me. The next term was the beginning of the School year. I went back and began my Henry's First Latin Book and began Greek also at the same time. This was the hardest work I have ever done and I got up to the top of the Third Form by Christmas.

At Midsummer this year I came out First in the Fourth Form and was taken up to the Sixth Form, missing the Fifth. To get up from the First Form to the

Sixth in a year was then a 'record' at Llandovery and I doubt that it has been broken ever since. I wrestled with the Latin and Greek of the Sixth Form and found myself badly grounded and quite out of my depth in Latin Composition. I had also now to begin High Algebra, High Trigonometry, Analytical Conics and Mechanics. I now hit upon a new friend, William Griffiths of Dryslwyn, an excellent Mathematician who helped me ungrudgingly. We became fast friends and remained so through School and College. He went out to India after taking his degree as a Wrangler at St. John's College, Cambridge, became the Principal of the Hoogley College, Calcutta, and came home to die sometime in the Nineties. I only saw him once after we parted at Cambridge. I owe much to the contact with him.

Of all years 1861 is the year I remember best, and the 9th of October in this year is almost the only date that has always been fixed indelibly in my memory, the day when I went up from Llandovery to Cambridge. I worked up to October with all my might and with considerable pleasure as the Classics were becoming easier. I also worked with enthusiasm at my Higher Mathematics, but it was ambition that frequently o'erleapt itself and too apt to fall on the other side. I was too eager to see what was ahead and satisfied with a very moderate amount of accuracy. This told against me all along even until I finished at Cambridge.

I forget where I came out on the list at Midsummer this year. The present Archdeacon of Cardigan was certainly first. I have a vague idea that I was second or that three of us were bracketed second. But as the Sixth Form that year was almost in a body going up to the Universities we did not pay much attention to the list. Phillips left now for Aberystwyth and was succeeded by Watkins. I believe Watkins was not supposed to be a great success as a Warden but the Staff he brought with him were as conspicuously brilliant as that of Phillips's were conspicuously wooden—Thomas, Edwards (afterwards Dean of Bangor), Lewis, Gent, all men of remarkable ability, zeal, and enthusiasm for their work. But in spite of this there is little doubt but that there was more work done, more life, more enthusiasm at Llandovery under Phillips than under Watkins. During the two months I was under Watkins I discovered no fault in him except that he was too shy, timid and self-conscious for a Headmaster.

In October this year Griffiths, Owen Jones and myself went up to Cambridge and stood for Mathematical Scholarships, Griffiths at St. John's, Jones at Sidney, and I at Jesus. We were all unsuccessful. I believe all three of us were complimented specially for our problems, but not one of us had learnt properly to write out bookwork, and I, certainly, had never grasped the importance of it.

Owing to an indifferent tutor who, at last, had been got rid of, Jesus College was at somewhat a low ebb as regards numbers. But this year 25 Freshmen entered the College, a number which I believe kept on increasing every October Term for some years. My University course was unique both in its beginning and its end. My Matriculation List was headed by Albert Edward, Prince of Wales (afterwards King Edward VII), and my Tripos List was headed by a Nobleman, the honourable John William Strutt (the present Lord Rayleigh), two men who, after their faces ceased to be familiar to me, did more to steady the world than anybody else I can remember on the spur of the moment. The King is gone but Lord Rayleigh the Senior Wrangler, now the Chancellor of Cambridge University, is still explaining to the present generation of men almost as fast as it can take it in, the mysteries of nature . . .

(The Reverend D. Edwardes was born in Cardiganshire on 1 July 1836. He had little schooling and went to Llandovery College at the age of 22 before proceeding to Cambridge. For 25 years he was Headmaster of Denstone College (where R. Gerallt Jones, Warden 1967-76, was later to be educated). The above excerpt is from his Reminiscences *published in Shrewsbury 1914.)*

1861

D. J. DAVIES

I was there only 2 years 9 months under Phillips and 15 under Watkins. The former was genial and popular and impressed himself in a remarkable degree on *some* of his pupils of whom his successor was one. The new Headmaster, or Warden as he was then called came with a great reputation. He had taken good honours at Cambridge—the first, I believe, from Llandovery that had ever done so, he had held a Mathematical Mastership at Eton and he was known to be, if not a protégé, a favourite of the departing Headmaster. His success seemed certain and during my stay there was no sign of declension either in the numbers or the distinctions of his pupils. In those days Welsh, Mathematics, Divinity and some Classics were always taught the Head Form by the Headmaster. Watkins was a conscientious and painstaking teacher. He never neglected even the Welsh lesson, and several English boys acquired a respectable knowledge of the language under his tuition. He was a good Welsh scholar himself and I have heard, brought out a book on the 'Pedwar Mesur ar Hugain'. After I left school I saw very little of him and I have not the least explanation to offer of his subsequent inability to attract scholars—throughout his Headmastership his pupils gained high honours at the Universities and possibly the highest ever obtained by a Llandovery boy were obtained in his time (G. J. Griffiths Christs 5th Wrangler Fellow T. D. Davies 2 Firsts Mathcs Oxford. Now Master in Clifton College). He was always kind to his pupils, but possibly he took less interest in them outside the school and after they left, than successful Headmasters usually do. Perhaps also he lacked 'push' and the art of 'bold advertisement'.

. . . the lodging house system . . . had faults and it had merits. Under it control was impossible and the formation of a good tone difficult. On the other hand, it enabled many poor boys to avail themselves of the advantages the School offered . . .

There were several old Llandovery boys at Cambridge in my time . . . Emmanuel . . . St. John's . . . Queens . . . Corpus Christi . . . D. Edwardes, Jesus, now Headmaster of Denstone College . . . Sidney . . . Magdalen . . . Pembroke . . . This shows that the influence of Llandovery on higher education at that time was very great. When we remember that the total nos. of boys at the school was only about 70 and that nearly if not quite 20 old boys were in residence at the same time at Cambridge . . . Welshmen had always gone to Oxford—but few until Llandovery opened the way for them had gone to Cambridge . . .

Whatever the shortcomings of early Wardens of Llandovery may have been, they effectually instilled into the minds of their scholars the desire to obtain the highest education possible . . . In my time and I believe for some years before and after the school numbered between 70 and 80, quite ½ of whom were sons of tradesmen in the town and farmers chiefly in Carmarthenshire and Cardiganshire—clergymen's sons formed another quarter and there was a sprinkling of squires', lawyers' and doctors' sons.

. . . The Welsh books in use in 1861-2 were Rowlands Grammar, Drych y Prif Oesoedd, and Bardd Cwsg.

(N.L.W. Ms. C3/4/13. Letter to D. Lleufer Thomas 25 June 1898 from North Benfleet Rectory).

1865-1868

LLYWARCH REYNOLDS

... I went to Llandovery in February 1865 and left after the Midsummer holidays 1868, and went to Oxford in October of that year. The Rev W. Watkins was Warden during my time and the Rev W. Scott 2nd Master for the first half and (the Rev.) W. P. Whittington for the latter part of my time.

... The Boarding Out system was in vogue in my time and I lodged at Collen House (in the Square) for the first term and afterwards at 'Belle Vue' (opposite the Clarence Inn) during the remainder of my terms. I had the 'Paltos' on one side of me and 'Sally Goch' and her husband 'Dai Fflach' on the other side. My fellow lodgers were our friend David Lewis, and John Davenport Mason of Tenby (son of Richard Mason, Publisher, Tenby), who entered the Ceylon Civil Service and ultimately became Chief Magistrate of Colombo . . .

I suppose a large percentage of my contemporaries donned the white choker of the Church of England—although in my time there were several grown-up men, some older than I, (and I was 23 when I went there) candidates for the Nonconformist ministry.

(N.L.W. Ms. 6241B. Letter to D. Lleufer Thomas 17 June 1898 from Old Church Place, Merthyr Tydfil. Llywarch Owain Reynolds 1843-1916 was the son of Jonathan Owain Reynolds, wheelwright, eisteddfodwr, *editor, translator of Shakespeare's tragedies into Welsh. Llywarch was a solicitor in Merthyr and clerk to Rhymney District Council. But he was an important Celtic scholar whose collection of books and manuscripts are now in the National Library of Wales. From Llandovery he proceeded to Jesus College Oxford).*

1868-1874

W. P. WHITTINGTON

The Warden, Rev W. Watkins, under whom I worked, was a man of decided ability, not merely Mathematical, but through a varied range of subjects—a good Welsh Scholar—well read in Greek and Roman history, a man who would take up a fresh subject like Botany and throw his heart into the study of it and then teach it well—and with the keenest interest. I used to admire the way in which he w^d identify himself with the subject in hand—and that very frequently a new one.

    The Warden was a great reader . . . Mrs Watkins, too, read a great deal and was so extremely kind and truly loveable in her disposition . . . both were devoted to gardening and I specially remember the lovely 'gladioli' which they used to grow . . . Their dinner parties were charming —they were such excellent hosts . . . I was often told by parents that they did not *like* to speak to him about their boys, as the Warden seemed to be so nervous and uncomfortable—this militated greatly against the school . . . he did not possess the 'business' aptitude of the schoolmaster . . . He conducted all matters connected with the School much as the Head of a College at Oxford or Cambridge w^d conduct the business of the College—in a dignified, quiet and gentlemanly way . . . Warden Watkins did not 'push' the School, as men do now [1898] . . . conscientious . . . always at his post . . . He did not advertise.

    . . . Classical side of which I had control . . . There was no odour of Classics about Llandovery: nothing was esteemed of any value except Mathematics, even Science was only just beginning to open its eyes, and to make some progress under Mr Bloxam. Few young boys entered in my time; the average age of entrance was 14-15. Young fellows, ill-prepared, but probably intended for the Church—very backward—too old to pick up Classics quickly and accurately [*exception*] Thomas Powell . . . a hard working fellow, who, I believe, won a scholarship or Exh. at Jesus Coll. Oxford.

... the greatest mischief was done by the parents and relatives, who invited boys into the public houses on market days ...

Athletics—Coming, as I did from Merchiston Castle School, Edinburgh, the best School in Scotland for Rugby Football, once finding that the boys at Llandovery played a *sort* of Association without definite rule—I *introduced* Rugby, and it throve wonderfully. The boys took to it, and rejoiced in it; and w^d never look at Association again.

There was no running, there were no recognised Athletic Sports—these I started—and a great success they proved . . . good prizes . . . the neighbourhood . . . is not wealthy . . . I often think how from that commencement Rugby Football has grown and flourished at the School.

The Masters of my time did all they could to foster a love of cricket and to create a good School XI, but Cricket did not thrive, like football . . . The Athletic Sports were very popular in the School, and amongst the gentry and townspeople; and the day was always deemed one of the most enjoyable in the year.

I always found Warden Watkins ready and willing to give me a free hand in all Athletic Matters, and he took the greatest interest in the Games, and very hospitable to all our neighbours on any of our gatherings.

. . . Mr Geo. W. Bloxam was an excellent Science Master, and did a good deal for the Laboratory himself, but boys did not take to Science much—although he used his best efforts to stimulate them. He used to take a great interest in Singing and train glee parties &c. and get up Concerts. As an active Volunteer Officer he was well known in the district and had an excellent Corps at Llandovery. In the Town: none of the Boys took part in the Volunteer Movement.

(N.L.W. Ms. C3/4/32. Letter to D. Lleufer Thomas 15 July 1898 from Ruthin School. Watkin Price Whittington M.A. was at Llandovery from 1868 to 1874. He was a graduate of Jesus College Oxford and prior to his coming to Llandovery —where he followed the Revd. Wm Scott as 'senior and classical master' on a salary of £200 p.a.—he had been senior classical master at Merchiston Castle School, Edinburgh. Later he was Headmaster of Ruthin School for 28 years. He was succeeded as Second Master by A. G. Edwards, later Warden).

1868

'To and from Llandovery'

There are two fast trains up in the day, starting from Swansea, and stopping only at the principal stations. The early train starting from Swansea at 6.30 a.m., picks up and puts down Llanelly passengers at Pontardulais Junction and, with another stoppage at Pantyffynon, reaches Llandeilo, where the first train from Carmarthen is met. At Llandeilo a number of men are now employed in constructing new points, laying fresh rails and new sidings to accommodate the extra traffic, and the traveller from Carmarthen, thoroughly aroused and pleased by the early morning ride through the Vale of Towy, is surprised to find the dull, forlorn station at Llandeilo looking quite gay and lively with business. An extraordinary civil [railway] guard, attired in the smart uniform of the London and North Western Company, is at great pains to find out where you are going, puts your luggage in the van and yourself in a through carriage, one of a train of eight or nine, and in two seconds you are off at a good speed. Everything seems fresh to one accustomed to the local lines. The carriages are strange, many of the officials new and obliging, the speed delightful considering that you are on the Vale of Towy [line], and despite glimpses of such familiar places as Glanbrydan and Taliaris, you can scarcely persuade yourself that you are not somewhere else, until you pull up at

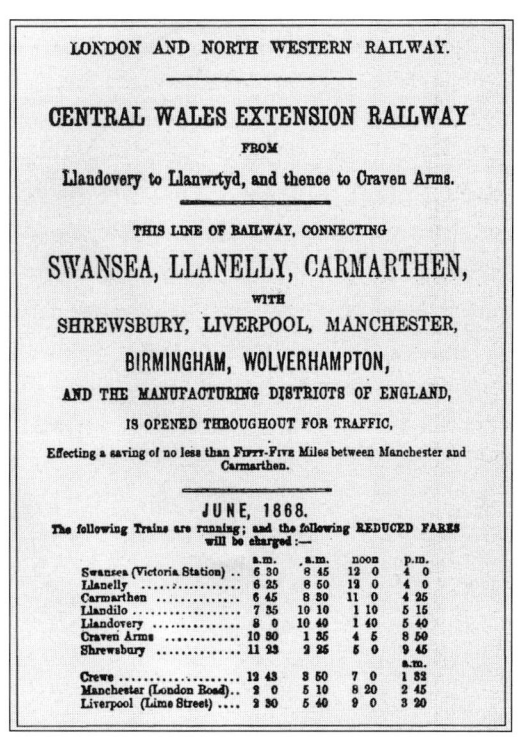

Llandovery, without any intermediate stoppage. Here a new platform and fresh works of various kinds are in course of procedure. Leaving Llandovery, we enter upon the twelve miles of railway recently opened, and which connects us with Llanwrtyd. The ride is short, but abounding in scenes of great beauty. The country on the right, face to the engine, is perhaps as finely diversified as any part of South Wales. Charming snatches of landscape, enticing valleys, and magnificent, thickly wooded hills flit past in rapid succession. So does the half-finished station at Cynghordy, about four miles from Llandovery, and in a few minutes we arrive at the splendid valley spanned by the wonderful viaduct. It is owing to the immense amount of work required on this fine structure that the opening of the line has been delayed. Some idea may be formed of the appearance it presents when we say that it is nearly 1,000 feet in length, and 109 feet high. The line of railway is carried over the chasm on a series of eighteen arches about thirty-six feet wide, and formed, not of ordinary stone, but of immense iron girders, placed on the top of a series of massive pillars built of stone from the Dunvant Quarry, near Swansea. This piece of work was commenced in March of last year. A good view of the viaduct may be obtained before reaching and after passing it, and while crossing it delightful views are to be seen up the valley, both ways. About three miles on we take a grand sweep round into a tunnel, nearly three quarters of a mile long. Then comes the fashionable watering-place, Llanwrtyd, which competes with Llandrindod for becoming the Cheltenham of the district.

(From 'The Welshman' 26 June 1868).

Viaduct

1869-1909

'H. W.'

The 4.55 (it was still the 4.55 forty years on) slowly drew into the station. A number of passengers descended from the train, among them a man of rather more than middle age, whose appearance betokened at least a fair degree of material prosperity. Eager though he was to alight, he stepped carefully down upon the platform, for forty years on we are not so active as once we were.

He stood on the platform in a reverie. The train whistled and left the station, and still he did not move. The Collector stepped up to him, and asked for his ticket. Mechanically, with his thoughts still far away, he gave it. His lips moved, but no sound issued between them. 'Forty years!' he was saying to himself, 'forty years!' Why haven't I returned before? Why haven't I?' Suddenly he roused himself, gave orders for his luggage to be sent to the 'Castle', and left the station.

Once in Station Road, he looked around him at the familiar landmarks, full of the very joy of recollection. The dingy station, the hotels round it, the stately trees which screened the College from his view, awoke within him a crowd of dormant memories. He stopped, and then, as he recalled the numerous precious moments he had lost through the closing of the gates across the road, let his eyes wander in their direction. A surprise was in store for him. The level crossing was gone! In their stead was a bridge over the road. The level of the latter had been lowered more than twenty years back, and the railway carried over it by a bridge. 'O sua si bona norint,' he murmured, as the tag leaped to his lips.

The visitor walked on slowly. On his right a new surprise met him. Facing the College, a noble pile of buildings rose, while further down the road, still on the right, was another. Stopping a boy who was crossing the road from the house to the College, he ascertained that these were two of the four new Houses erected since his time, and that in each house there were fifty boys.

He turned his eyes from the right of the road to the left, and a gasp of amazement broke from him. Between the boys' entrance to the College and

Garden Lane, where in his time had been nothing but a hay-field badly protected from the road by a low wall, a magnificent Chapel was to be seen. Standing in the midst of tastefully kept gardens and shrubberies, skirted by well-arranged paths, it seemed to him a worthy embodiment indeed of the spirit of progress, which had evidently since his time carried his old School on from triumph to triumph. He walked up to the porch, softly entered, and as, hand in hand, he gazed reverently around him, he saw that it was good.

Continuing his walk through the chapel grounds, he came out by the Gymnasium. It had been begun in his time, but he had left before its completion. At the time it had been thought a wonderful acquisition, but now it was the least of a series of new buildings. Further down New Road, he saw a fine airy two-storied building. Work was over for the day, and it was locked; but as he gazed inquiringly through its windows, he saw row after row of labelled bottles, and felt the aroma of unknown odours floating around him, and rightly guessed that he was in the vicinity of the new Science Buildings. On the wall he could descry, printed in large letters, the maxim 'Energy cannot be created or destroyed', and by its side was a long board containing a list of Science Honours won by old alumni. Close by stood a large rectangular building, the ground floor of which was obviously the new Library, while the upper storey, though he did not know this, was the Drawing School. A little to the right stood the two other new Houses, surrounded by trim lawns and flower beds, which gave evidence of care and love which was not bought with money.

He retraced his steps in the direction of the Tuck-shop and the Ball-courts. They were gone! New Ball-courts had been erected as part of the Gymnasium; while, where the Tuck-shop had been, he saw a pretty red-tiled bungalow, in which were numbers of small tables, at which boys were sitting indulging in ices and lemon squash.

All, all was new. He felt like one who passes from youth to age in a single night. A master appeared in sight. He did not know him. He passed another. A stranger too. An unreasonable feeling of disappointment came over him. He had come back after forty years to renew old memories of the school, and, lo! there was nothing save the memories that was old, and in the face of all these things that were new, the memories would not flood over him in the way for which he yearned. In the midst of his musing a ray of comfort came to him. Many things were new; but the old was not swept away. He would go and find some of the old familiar places. He entered, turned along the passage, and through the Hall to the old VB. Class-room, now the Middle Sixth. He entered with a strange feeling as of one who treads on holy ground. In the middle of the room he found a desk. Yes, it was the same at which he had sat through many an hour of old. Eagerly he scanned it, and O! joy of joys! found in the corner of the desk the small 'H.W.' which in his unregenerate days, despite threatened pains and penalties, he had carved upon it. Lovingly he fingered the clear-cut letters. A lump came into his throat. As he sat at that well-remembered desk, he became a child again; he was no longer forty years on; he almost persuaded himself that the map of his life had rolled years back. There let us leave him in the dim delightful dreamland of by-gone days.

Forty years on, he had been able to fly back on the wings of memory to those glad days, when forty years on seemed a thousand centuries away. So may it be with each one of us.

(School Journal, Midsummer 1909).

1872

DAVID SAMUEL

I was entered at Llandovery School early in 1872 . . . It was my misfortune . . . to be a fortnight too late for sitting the Entrance Scholarship for one of which had I been in time, I might have become a candidate. The School was then invariably known as the Welsh Collegiate Institution, a name which I regret has been superseded by the College . . . I remember with what boyish pride I wrote on my school text books 'W.C.I. Llandovery'.

My connection with Llandovery arose in this way. During the Christmas vac[n] 1871-72, it had become the great desire of my father (a small tradesman in Aberystwyth) to have me sent to one of the older English universities. It was thought that I had shown at the Aberystwyth Grammar School some aptitude for Mathematics. At that time I was much too young to be sent to Oxford or Cambridge. My father decided to consult Dean Phillips, then Vicar of Aberystwyth.

I was known to the Dean—he had seen me as a boy at the National Schools and had times without number examined me in Classics and Mathematics at the 'Gram' School. The Dean true to the old school over whose fortunes he had presided for many years as Headmaster and Warden, advised that I should be sent thither. Many lads from the neighbourhood owed their connection with Llandovery in the same way. Many said that the Dean had ulterior motives in thus sending boys, young nonconformists like myself to what was considered by many at that time (unfairly I honestly think) a thoroughgoing Church School; but I never could be brought to believe that the Dean had any motive beyond that of advising the best school in Wales to people of limited means, where a thorough liberal education could be given and the way paved for the universities of Oxford and Cambridge. About the end of January 1872 preparations were made for sending me to Llandovery. Llandovery was to a large extent to me at that time a *terra incognita*, and I found that there were great misgivings amongst many of the common people . . . As a good Calvinistic Methodist desiring of frequenting the Welsh Methodist chapel during my residence at Llandovery, it was necessary to get my ticket of membership—llythyr aelodaeth, before leaving home, and so I applied for it at the *Seiat* previous to my departure. At the close of the service, an old gentleman, pious but rather narrow-minded, came up just as the deacons were attaching their signature to my transfer, and said 'Pam mae rhieni'r bachgen bach yma yn ei anfon i Lanymddyfri? Pam na fuasen 'nhw yn ei anfon i Fangor?' meaning of course the Bangor Normal College and I remember the scathing reply of the leading deacon late Mr David Jones, Manager of the Nat. Prov. Bank, 'Beth 'dych chi'n siarad; y mae'r rhieni yn gwneud yn ardderchog iawn, y mae ysgol Llanymddyfri yn *good classical school*.' And so with this *envoi*, and accompanied by my father, I proceeded the next day for my new school.

Arrived at Llandovery we at once did what I suppose every parent and his lad does at his first convenience—we made for seeing the Warden—at that time the Rev William Watkins, an excellent man. We came upon him rather suddenly just issuing thro the gates leading from College Lawn down to the Station Road. He was proceeding evidently towards the town. An introduction was effected through the kind offices of my fellow-lodger and quondam fellow pupil at Aberystwyth Gramr School, Rich. Richards, who was at the time student at Llandovery. I shall never forget the first appearance I got of my old master. He appeared to me then as he always afterwards appeared a singularly handsome man. I remember the slightly springing gait. His fine and upright stature and his excellent complexion, ruddy and healthy. Being myself the

WELSH COLLEGIATE INSTITUTION, LLANDOVERY

THOMAS PHILLIPS' FOUNDATION.

WE, the Undersigned Trustees of the above Collegiate Institution do hereby appoint

to be a FREE SCHOLAR on the above Foundation, and to continue as such so long as he faithfully conforms to the Rules and Regulations of the Institution, regularly attends his Studies, and makes due proficiency therein, and his general behaviour and conduct is such as the Warden and Masters approve; in default of which this appointment is to cease and determine, and the Scholarship be declared vacant for the appointment of another Free Scholar in his stead.

Dated this   day of   187

shyest of lads, I could not but observe that my new master was one of the shyest of men, so very different from my boyish idea of a master of a great school. As soon as the Warden understood our purpose, he instantly returned, indeed he had been informed of our coming by letter from Dean Phillips. And we entered his study. Here the Warden directed his attention to me with whom he talked more confidently than he had done with my father. He plied me with questions as to my acquaintance with Latin and Greek, Algebra, Euclid, Trigon^y and Analytical Conics. I had at that time done a good deal of Math^s— my old master (Mr Edward Jones) at the gram^r school in my native town was an excellent mathematician, . . . My old master gave his pupils a thorough training in Latin Grammar . . . In Greek, at Aberystwyth School pupils did not do so well—Greek Gram^r was but indifferently taught . . . My Math^s the Warden considered very satisfactory and so he looked upon my acquaintance with Latin, but my Greek being somwhat defective, when he came to fix my place in School, he was somewhat puzzled what to do. He finally settled upon putting me in the Fourth Form. He did not err in fixing my class; for though my Math^s entitled me to a higher form, there were two boys at least in Form IV whose thoroughness in Classics, both Latin and Greek, were superior to my own, and there were others who were following close at their heels.

In 1872 there were four masters—the Warden, the Rev W. P. Whittington, Mr James Mortimer, and Mr G. W. Bloxam. There were occasional masters who out of school hours chiefly if not entirely I think, gave lessons in drawing and music. The Warden took a variety of subjects in his classes, as will be seen later on, but he might be looked upon as the senior Mathematical Master. Mr Whittington was styled the Second Master and Senior Classical Master. I do not know that in my day Mr Whitt^n took any subject but Classics. It was he that took Fourth and Upper Forms. Mr Mortimer, cousin of Mr T. M. Green Registrar U.C.W. Aberystwyth was assistant master, and took classics in elem^y classics (third form I believe and below) and Welsh from the lowest form to the Fourth (inclusive).

Mr Mortimer took a no. of Nonconformists—about 6 to his lodgings at Medical Hall in Stone Street on Sunday afternoons for Bible reading. I remember those lessons very well. We read *Ephesians* and my first real impressions of the profound problem of this Epistle date from those readings. I remember vividly how our teacher warmed over the subject as he spoke to us of coming 'unto a perfect man unto the measure of the stature of the fullness of Christ'—the amplitude of the sentence charmed my ear. I have often since regretted that Mr Mortimer did not turn these readings into Greek Test. lessons.

Mr Bloxam was our Science Master—during my first half year he took our Form and the higher in Chemistry and in the second half year, some boys in the *upper classes* destined for a more scientific career in life did *Geology* in addition. *Chemistry* was taught experimentally. The utensils and apparatus were brought to the master's classroom from the Labor. upstairs and we watched the experiment with very great deal of interest. Mr Bloxam took the elem^y classes in Math^s as well. It was he who took drill once a week viz. on Saturday morning from about 12 o'clock till near 1. Mr Bloxam was very *great* on drill, he had the appearance of a smart soldier—and he was captain of the Llandovery volunteers. In class he was a strict disciplinarian—a glance of his eye threw terror into us all. But he was kind withal, and in spite of all his seeming severity often cracked a joke. He was a Cambridge graduate and we often asked him very queer questions. I had then but very imperfect notions of Cambridge, its colleges, its students, triposes, and their curricula. A problem or a rider set at School often took me hours and hours to solve, and the longer the time spent over a problem, the harder I esteemed it to be. I remember asking Mr Bloxam in my simplicity how they did at Cambridge, how ever they could get thro' their work at the University with those hard problems of theirs, when my *simple* ones . . . took me such a long time to solve. Mr Bloxam's answer with a smile puzzled me greatly—'If a problem does not come out after half an hour's thinking, it had better be given up—students cannot afford to give more than that to a problem'—they would pass it over to a coach, 'time at the University is too precious.'

Each master had his own classroom—the Warden's room was the first on the right looking down the central Assembly Hall from the Apse, the next room was Mr Whittington's, then came Mr Mortimer's, the fourth was Mr Bloxam. The no. of boys in my day was rather smaller than it had been, and perhaps smaller than it soon afterwards came. I do not think that we numbered more than about 60 boys in 1872. In those days the School was divided into six forms—the highest being the 6th; but in 1872 when I entered, there were only five forms. The whole of the Sixth had left a little before the beginning of that year. When there had been a 6th Form the two highest in the 5th and 6th always worked together as one class.

The Warden had a few boarders at the School house and Mr Whittington had others (in my day, very big fellows) at his house—Prospect House, then as now the Second Master's house. But most of the boys who were not town boys— lived in licensed lodging houses—my own lodging was in High Street opposite the Wheatsheaf Inn and I had Richards as a fellow lodger. The boarding out system may have had disadvantages; but on the other hand it had enormous advantages. It was much cheaper to live in a licensed lodging house than according to the system now in vogue. There were boys at School in my day (and I must count myself among them) who could never afford the luxury of Llandovery training had they been constrained to live at the Master's house. We had greater freedom in those days than is possible under the present system and the discipline I apprehend was not less. The lodging houses were under the strictest supervision—printed rules were drawn up and schedules sent in to the Warden every weekend (I think) stating the hours observed by the pupils, and periodical visit by the masters enforced the rules which had been set up for the guidance of the lodging house keepers.

School began at 9 o'clock and continued till 12—lessons lasting an hour each. Afternoon school began at 2 and continued till 4 each lesson being of an hour's duration, as in the morning. Wednesday and Saturday afternoons were observed as half holidays. All the boys wore college caps, the 6th Form boys being distinguished by their wearing a black tassel to their mortar boards. The first Monday in the month was usually a whole holiday—some of us found neighbouring farmers particularly kind to us on these occasions—they invited us often to spend these days at their homes.

On opening morning and afternoon school, the 'roll' of pupils was called and in the morning prayers were read—this lasted only for a short time—both the Roll and prayers taken by the warden and very rarely was he absent from these duties. He was seated in his chair behind a desk in the apse of the Assembly Hall, having on his M.A. gown surrounded by the Masters also robed in their academic gowns. (No use made of Assembly Room except for roll call perhaps and at the time of written Exam[ns]. It was used of course then as now, at Prize Distributions). There must have been a system of giving marks to pupils on their work carried on by the masters—tho' I have quite forgotten what the system was. But of its existence there can be no doubt whatever, for the order of the names as read out at the Roll call differed every month, and the order of the names was regulated by the marks obtained by the pupils during the preceding month. When I first went to school, my name was the last amongst those called out of Form IV; in a couple of months, I had the pleasure of hearing my name fairly high up in the list, and in a month or so more, I remember being quite stunned to hear my name read first of my form. Each boy answered 'adsum' on his name being called. After roll-call the higher classes (perhaps also the lower) did Welsh during the first hour. I cannot recall what all the classes had for their curricula in 1872, but it may be interesting to state what my own class did. Take the work of the first hour—Welsh. We did *Drych y Prif Oesoedd* and Rowlands' *Welsh Grammar*. These we did while I was in Form IV with Mr Mortimer. It was my first introduction to a systematic study of Welsh. There were several of the lads who took a good deal of interest in Welsh. They turned out the Welsh words in the dictionary and thus got English equivalents . . . The systematic study of Welsh gramm[r] was a new book to me . . . I had never dreamed it possible to do for *bod* and *dysgu* what the Latin grammars had done for *sum* and *amo* . . .

In Greek, we did the *Iliad*, Books XX, XXI. The Greek lesson with Mr Whittington came in the afternoon. The gramm[r] used was Mood's Eton Greek Gram[r]—my copy has date Feb. 9, 1872, though I had used the book at Aberyst school.

In Latin, I cannot remember exactly what our textbook was from Feb to June 1872—I think it was 5th Book of Livy. For Latin prose we did T. Kerchever Arnold's longer book . . . For verse, which had to be ready on Monday morning, we did Walford's little book. Though I could scan Virgil's poetry well before going to Llandovery, I had never done Latin Verse . . . I recollect well that writing verses from Walford's book was my Saturday evening occupation and it was one that I was particularly fond of. For Repetition we had a couple of hundreds of lines of Arnold's *Eclogae Ovidinae*. My copy of the *Eclogue* is now before me and bears the date Feb. 15, 1872—it has, like all my books of that period, the name of the School under the old title 'Welsh Collegiate Institution'.

In Scripture, we did G. F. Maclear's 'Class book of O. T. History', though I have forgotten exactly what portions of the Book. In Math[s] the class was not taken collectively, but each boy worked separately, and each pupil started on the problem next to that he left off at on the preceding day. A boy who knew Trig. worked at that while his neighbours right and left might be at Arithmetic or Analytical Conics. The master seldom worked on the blackboard but sat at his desk, and the pupils, starting at the top of the class took up their work to him in turns. In Euclid, the class was taken rather more collectively, and they as nearly as possible did the same propositions. Todhunter's treatises were those generally in use . . . I noticed that while most of the pupils prepared their classical work in the evenings few, indeed only those who were likely to take up Math[s] for scholarships at Oxford or Cambridge, studied Mathem. Bookwork and tried problems and riders in the evenings as a part and parcel of their home work. The best scholars in my form were Cadwgan Powell Price (now vicar of Ffestiniog cum M) and James Jones Llwynjack (now of Harley St. London), the former was very keen on the Classics, and there was another lad, a native of Llandovery who was making great headway in Latin and Greek, J. W. Thomas (now vicar of Rhos.).

In Chemistry we did Barff's book—but the boys tho' they liked the experiments in class, took but little interest in the bookwork in their evening studies. As far as I can remember there were no Modern Lang^s taught at the School, nor was English gram^r and Literature taught except informally and incidentally. I do not think that English History had any place in the curriculum of the higher classes. Latin, Greek, Math^s and Science were the subjects to which boys bent their energies . . .

Before I had been long in school, I found that the extraordinary success of old boys in the school and college exam^s were cherished with my affection. Their wonderful sweeping of the school prizes often in most trying circumstances, was the topic of much talk amongst the boys, and the new pupils received the accounts of their prowess with gaping wonderment. I remember two names which Tradition had handed down as having accomplished wonders in carrying off prizes . . . one was Tom Powell (now Profess. at Cardiff) the other was T. D. Davies (now of Clifton and brother of another old boy, the Rev D. J. Davies who had graduated 13th wrangler and was soon to be elected as Fellow of his College Emmanuel). Powell had left school five or six years before I entered, but his name was handed down as having one year swept every prize in his form and done like things on another occasion. Davies had done similar things . . . G. J. Griffiths had only just gone up to Christs Cambridge when I went to W.C.I., and his name was largely spoken of as one who picked up the Classical and Mat^1 works with the utmost ease at school, and from whom much was expected in the Tripos. But hardly anyone expected that his name would be placed as 5th Wrangler in the Math Trip of Jany 1879.

. . . I met Griffiths first time at Llandovery in June 1872; he was particularly kind to me . . . On going to Cambridge, I read *Analytical Statistics* with him and remember his jubilation on his election as Fellow of Xt^s, in Michaelmas Term 1875 or Lent Term 1876.

The School divided the year into quarters as most schools did in those days and the mid summ^r vac^n was from the middle of June to about end first week in August. There were Prize distributions at end of Mids^r Term, the prizes being awarded on the results of the annual exam^n conducted by examiners not connected with the school. The Exam. was entirely I believe, by means of paper work. The Exam^r in June 1872 was Mr Chas Augustus Maude Farnell, Fellow of Jesus, Cambridge (9th Classic), a gentleman whom I saw often afterwards in the streets of Cambridge. The Prize day was a great function then as it is now, though perhaps not so largely attended a ceremonial. The Books given to the prize winners were handsomely bound with the dragon embossed on the cover, and in the inside the label indicated the character of the prize in words . . . 'Gwell dysg na golud—Welsh Collegiate Institution Llandovery. Midsummer Exam 1872. Form IV First Prize awarded to . . . W. Watkins MA Warden'. . . I remember some books that were given—Longfellows poems, Carpenter's Theoretical Philosophy, Gibbon's Decline and Fall. (3 vols), Herschel's Astronomy, Shakespeare's Poems, Stephens *Lit of the Cymry*. The prizes for Welsh were in money not in books.

The Dux of the School, as we invariably called the headboy was Eben Jones. There was much questioning at school with our 'Who will be Dux' as there is in the larger sphere of Cambridge—with 'who will be Senior Wrangler'.

On reopening after the mids[r] holidays, Form IV became Form V and what was Form V became Form VI, and the two classes hitherto working at different subjects in different classrooms now worked together—this had been the invariable custom at Llandovery I believe, the Fifth and Sixth always worked together. (All Boys throughout school wore college caps—the 5th alone privileged to wear black tassels to their mortar boards) . . .

. . . the work done by the higher classes in the year I was at School. Welsh, Latin, Greek and Math[s] were done every day. Roman history and divinity and science were done I think twice a week. That there were many and important gaps in the curriculum is clear at once—there were no modern languages taught and no English or Modern History, no English Literature except in a very irregular and spasmodic way. Even Science was limited, in my day to Chemistry and Geology. There was no Botany and no Physics, no Physiology, no Biology. In a small school such as Llandovery was then, with only about 60 boys it would be perhaps hardly possible to have a more extensive curriculum; but the work done in the subjects that formed the regular course of study was most excellent and thorough. The Warden often urged the more advanced pupils to go in for special prizes offered annually in Essay writing and Literature. I remember a prize offered for translation of one of Shakespeare's Henry's into Welsh verse, which some of the top Form Boys entered for at the Llandovery Eisteddfod (June 1872). The Warden who was one of the adjudicators urged some of the senior boys to compete for the English and Welsh Essays—I think 'Llandovery Castle' was a subject of essay which a prize was offered at that Eisteddfod.

With regard to athletics, the School did very well as regards Cricket. This game was much played and the boys were extremely fond of it. Some excellent batsmen and bowlers appear to have left before I entered School, but even with what was left in the Elevens (both 1st and second elevens) we did very commendably. The School played the Town and Lampeter College, and the rival school at Brecon. The match with Brecon was 'Eton and Harrow'. It was specially interesting to Llandovery boys whether the match was played on our own ground or the W.C.I. team drove in brakes to meet Brecon. The enthusiasm of our boys in the case of success was tremendous. As for Football, I do not remember a single match, nay more I can recall not even whether the School had a team at all! I am perfectly sure that if football (if there was a team at all) was not anything so popular a game then as Cricket—else it would have made a greater impression upon me. We had our annual Sports—and the day on which these were held was quite a red letter day in our Calendar. I remember some magnificent achievements of some of our athletic boys in the contests of 1872—especially the Long Jump and 100 yards of Tom Davies—a fellow pupil whom I afterwards met at Cambridge where he was undergrad. of Jesus Coll. (The sports were held in the School field close to the College — a field now no more used for these and similar purposes as it has been taken up by the railway authorities. The old field was admirably situated and singularly well-adapted for athletic purposes). The Boards in the Assembly Hall were not up in my day — the Boards containing the names of distinguished *alumni* were put up some years after I left. To my taste Llandovery has too many football boards and vastly too few Honors . . .

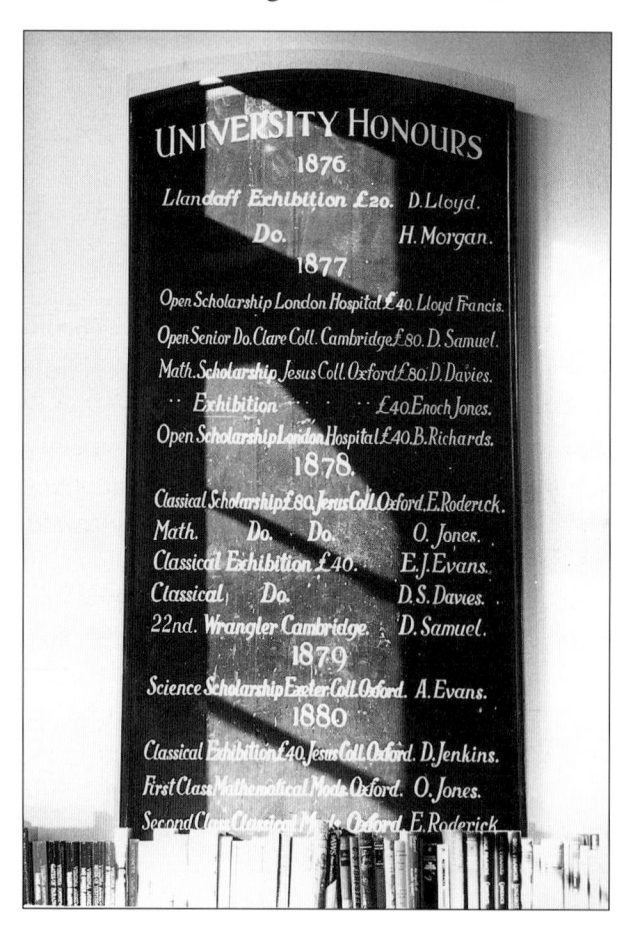

My second half year passed away as merrily and as happily as the first half—I liked the boys very much—they were always kind and cordial in their relationships with me. There were no cases of bullying the smaller boys by the bigger lads, nor making school life burdensome to them. I must say that the language and conduct of the older pupils were not always the most praiseworthy, though the morals of Llandovery would at that time compare with that of any other similar school in England and Wales. Many of the boys worked very hard all the year through. Some were, as in all schools very neglectful of their studies, but all worked with commendatory diligence as the time of the half yearly exam[ns] drew near . . . Papers were set in Latin, Greek, Math[s], Science, Welsh, Divinity, and I will be allowed to state here, with a pride which I trust is not unpardonable, that I had the extreme pleasure of finding myself, as a result of the Xmas Exam[n], Dux of the School.

I was for returning to Llandovery in Jan 1873 after the Xmas vac[n], but in Octob. 1872 the Aberystwyth College had been opened and my father thought it would be better (and financial considerations also weighed) to have me entered at the new college: this was done, and my connection with W.C.I. came to a rather sudden and very unexpected close (much against my will). The Warden wrote a very kind letter to my father in which he spoke of his boy in most complimentary terms. He had hoped, he said to see him proceed to the University, and he trusted that that idea would not be given up.

(N.L.W. Ms. 2841E. David Samuel was born 1 March 1856 at Aberystwyth; he was educated there, at Llandovery, the University College of Wales Aberystwyth and Clare College Cambridge. He graduated in January 1879 being placed twentieth wrangler. He taught at Appleby grammar school, Westmorland and Ashburn grammar school, Derbyshire. In 1887 he opened a private grammar school in Aberystwyth; in 1896 he was appointed Headmaster of the new Ardwyn County School there. He died in 1921.

He was a prolific writer, his bardic name was Dewi o Geredigion. He composed a short book in Welsh on Llandovery College—Ysgol Llanymddyfri which appeared in 1910).

1874

C. A. BUCKMASTER

Science at Llandovery never had a fair chance while I was there and that due entirely to lack of funds. No laboratory, no apparatus worth talking about, and only a dim realization on my own part of the absolute need of these things.

We did what we could. The Warden bought a certain amount of apparatus and chemicals and filled up a room with some sort of facilities for experimental work but every decent Higher Grade Board School is better equipped nowadays. To the best of my remembrance Geology had been the chief subject taught before I came. I continued this for a time but gradually dropped it substituting in various forms Physiology, Physics or Chemistry. Several old boys are as you know very successful as medical men and got their first taste of science—such as it was—at Llandovery. The four years I spent there were some of the happiest of my life. The school was growing rapidly in numbers and prestige and the Warden and my colleagues were most kind and helpful.

(N.L.W. Ms. C3/4/37. Letter to D. Lleufer Thomas 20 July 1895 from the Science and Art Department South Kensington. In the In Memoriam issue to W. W. Poole Hughes, September 1928 there is reference to Hughes '... entered ... the College at the age of ten. The present Archbishop of Wales (A. G. Edwards) was Warden; the Rev. G. W. Gent, afterwards Dean of Keble, and Principal of Lampeter, and Mr C. A. Buckmaster, at present at the Board of Education, were two of his colleagues.' A. G. Edwards was high in his praise of Buckmaster: 'With a most primitive laboratory, Mr C. A. Buckmaster achieved wonderful results at Llandovery').

1874-1885

A. G. Edwards

On the death of my father, I began under the tuition of a brother to read for Oxford, where, after a year's preparation, I matriculated at Jesus College with an exhibition. In this epoch of inflated prices it may be interesting to mention what seems strange to-day, that my total income at Oxford for my first year was £75, for my second £105, and for my two last years £140. The first year my battels slightly exceeded my income, but in the second year I was elected to a scholarship which ended my financial anxieties and indeed enabled me to save a little money. In June 1874, I took my degree and was appointed second master at Llandovery School, then, owing to a variety of causes, at the lowest ebb in its history.

The following year the head master resigned, and by his recommendation I applied for the post. The ruling spirit among the five appointing trustees was a lady. As soon as she heard of my candidature, the warden was requested to send me over to be inspected. Lady Llanover was devoted to Wales and the Welsh language. When I arrived at Llanover Park, her butler, with the name and the wisdom of Daniel, received me in the native language. Ushered into the deciding presence of the great lady, I got through the interview, and as I left I replied to her kind invitation to take some refreshment before starting on my homeward journey that the 'Pentrulliad' had already asked me to do so. I saw at once that she had failed to recognise the name given in the Welsh Bible to Pharoah's butler. A few days after my return, the warden told me that he had heard from Lady Llanover, who was greatly impressed with my knowledge of Welsh. My gratitude to Pentrulliad is sincere. I was appointed warden and head master in May 1875. There were only two other candidates.

Few cared to face the rather hopeless condition of the school. The boarding-out system had made discipline impossible. The masters were supposed to invigilate the boys in their lodgings. As second master my first experience of this task was instructive. Not a boy was in his lodgings. Much puzzled, I heard on my way back, in one of the streets, boisterous laughter from a long-room attached to one of the inns. I seemed to recognise voices, and climbed up the staircase to a room where I found the whole school seated at long tables and smoking, and presided over by the head boy, who, by the way, later on proved to be a tower of strength to the school and by this time occupies a position of much dignity. Here at any rate was one explanation of the low estate of the school. The condition of the buildings I first realised when I became warden. The whole place was ruinous and derelict. Only one dormitory was fit for boarders, the two other dormitories had never been plastered and were used for storing potatoes and geraniums. The rooms in the head master's own house were in a deplorable condition.

The salary of the head master was £135 a year and a house, and the tuition fees of £8 a year. Clearly the outdoor system must at once be severely limited if not entirely abolished. To this the trustees gave their consent. The school buildings, like the master's house, were in a wretched condition, but the rooms were large, and if put into repair might be made adequate and comfortable for a large number of boys. Then there was the solid fact of an endowment of £500 a year for assistant masters, and this was an invaluable nucleus. There were other grounds for optimism. Wales was athirst for education. But in spite of many favourable signs the outlook for Llandovery School was dubious enough to daunt the most ardent.

The first term was tremulous and anxious—only twenty-seven boys in the school, of whom three had soon to be sent away. Before the middle of the term drains made themselves known, and two out of the three boarders were down with diphtheria. An expert discovered that the drains emptied into an ancient and undisturbed cesspool under the floor of the entrance hall. The rest of the term was concentrated upon making the buildings sewage free. The cost of all this fell upon the warden. At this junction a dear old banker friend, who had known me all my life, lent me £300 without any security. This was the only money I ever borrowed in my life, and I adventurously spent it in offering higher salaries and thereby securing a highly qualified staff. Things prospered and numbers increased rapidly. Thus elated, I invited the Lord Lieutenant of the County to preside at a coming Prize-day. After several weeks an answer came from Cannes, 'Sir, I never presided at your institution, and never intend to do so.' I replied with 'humble apologies for my presumption, and with regrets that what I had intended as a compliment had been interpreted as an insult, but my excuse was that I thought the only first grade school in the county would not be without some interest to Her Majesty's representative.' A few months afterwards the Lord Lieutenant wrote me thus: 'I have founded two Golden Grove Scholarships in your school. Do you now believe that I take no interest in education?' From that day his kindness was unbounded. The Prize-days brought some distinguished visitors.

Dr Harper, Principal of Jesus College, Oxford, took the opportunity of a Prize-day to announce his scheme for throwing open scholarships and exhibitions at Jesus College, a scheme which probably saved the college from extinction. In 1883 the school had the honour of welcoming Dr Vaughan, Master of the Temple and Dean of Llandaff. That year the honours list included several open scholarships and exhibitions at Oxford and Cambridge—among them an open scholarship at Balliol—and ten higher certificates from the Oxford and Cambridge School Examination Board, in which the school gained, I believe, the highest number of distinctions in advanced mathematics obtained by any of the public schools in England . . .

The ten years (1875 to 1885) of my wardenship at Llandovery came at the very beginning of the great educational movement in Wales, and to those interested in Welsh education that decade of work at Llandovery yields a harvest of significant facts. When I gave evidence in 1880 before the Aberdare Committee there were 178 boys in Llandovery School, there were 111 boarders, 160 were born in Wales and 18 in England, 86 could speak Welsh fairly, 15 indifferently, and 77 only English. Of the 86 Welsh-speaking boys 37 came from Welsh-speaking homes, and 49 from English-speaking homes. The social status of the boys at the school was as follows: sons of tradesmen 27, tradesmen with private houses 24, tenant farmers 13, freehold farmers 13, clergymen 33, professional men 38, officers 6, private gentlemen 24. The poorest parents were among the tradesmen class. Classified denominationally, 125 belonged to the Church, and 53 were Nonconformists. The subjects of instruction were those usual in any first-grade school. All the boys learnt Latin, 172 learnt Greek, 62 French. In Latin and Greek composition in the more advanced stages the Welsh boys were distinctly slow in acquiring anything like taste and idiom.

It is noteworthy that up to that date the Hertford or Ireland Scholarship during the previous twenty-six years had never been gained by a Welshman, while out of the twenty-six Junior University Mathematical Scholarships awarded from 1854 to 1880, 15 per cent were gained by Welshmen, and of the twenty-six Senior Mathematical Scholarships for the same period 19 per cent were gained by Welshmen. Those figures seem to establish the fact that up to that date Welshmen excelled more in mathematics and science than in classics. Welsh boys showed great aptitude and intelligence in at any rate the elements of philology. In mathematics nothing but a favourable account can be given of the Welsh boy. Mathematics having no language at all, or rather a language of its own, enabled the Welsh boy to start fair in the race, and the lack of early preparation was less apparent. The rapidity with which the Welsh boys picked up mathematics was phenomenal. The same may be said of their progress in science. With a most primitive laboratory, Mr C. A. Buckmaster achieved wonderful results at Llandovery. Of the 178 boys then in school seventy-four intended, if circumstances permitted, to enter Oxford or Cambridge.

In the ten years 1875 to 1885 the number of boys under education at Llandovery was 512, and the subsequent history of those out of the 512 who had entered upon a career was as follows: 53 had gone to Oxford or Cambridge, 64 to business, 53 to the Church, 44 to the medical profession, 35 to the law, 23 to agriculture, 21 to banks, 13 to the colonies, 12 to the scholastic profession, 10 chemists, 7 sailors, 4 soldiers, and 4 engineers. During the ten years under review the following honours were gained by pupils of the school: seventeen scholarships at Oxford or Cambridge, and thirteen exhibitions in Mathematics or Classics or Science or History. In addition to these results, a number of minor honours were gained at other seats of learning . . . It is true that the boys who entered Llandovery School came with a very imperfect knowledge of English Literature. Mr Charles Williams, second master at Llandovery School, in his admirable evidence before the Aberdare Commission, gave the facts in detail. In his own class of thirty boys, 'their knowledge of the chief English poets is infinitesimal. The other classes tell the same tale. Many boys of fifteen when they entered the school had never read a line of Shakespeare, Milton, Tennyson, Byron, Longfellow, or Burns.' It may be that the man who knows something of two languages is better educated than the man who only knows one. But it remains a fact beyond dispute that an imperfect knowledge of English was a serious bar to a boy's progress at school, and at the university . . .

Boys at Llandovery up to 1875 were allowed to lodge out in the town. Fifteen years before that date, as a boy and subsequently as a master, I had seen the system at work. In my opinion it enabled a youth (generally *serus studiorum*) of small means to secure education at a very moderate cost, and I have known steady and hard-working youths of this type who did more work in their quiet lodgings than they might have been able to do in a large boarding house. On the other hand, they rarely met their schoolfellows except in the classroom, so that on the whole I incline to the view that what they gained by study in the isolation of lodgings was more than counterbalanced by the loss in social intercourse with their schoolfellows . . .

The rules of the school gave the pupils the fullest freedom and opportunity to attend the places of worship desired by their parents, who were invariably informed of the rule when they brought their boys to the school . . . I made it my business to see the minister of any denomination attended by boys in the school, and asked him to inform me as to the boys' attendance . . .

Before I quit Llandovery School, I give its record in the words of the Aberdare Committee: 'The school may be ranked among the most efficient in Wales, but, as will be seen from the return, the amount of accommodation is not really sufficient for the numbers now attending, and additional buildings must be provided if any further development of the school is to take place.' That result was achieved by a staff of distinguished scholars who shared the anxieties and kindled the enthusiasm of the place.

To Llandovery I owe my first experience in clerical work. I was accepted as a candidate for ordination by Bishop Thirlwall, ordained by Bishop Basil Jones, and licensed upon a title given by the Vicar of Llandovery in 1874. The vicar gave me a valued share during my diaconate in all the work of the parish. As head master of the school I was, by the vicar's kindness, permitted to hold in one of his two churches a service for the school, which the parishioners also attended, and I was privileged to do some visiting among the poor and to share in the management of the National school . . .

(This excerpt is from Memories by the Archbishop of Wales, published London 1927. A. G. Edwards (1848-1937) was son of the rector of Llan-ym-Mawddwy. He spent a year at Llandovery and then, after private tuition, entered Jesus College Oxford graduating in Classics in 1874. He was appointed Assistant Master at Llandovery, was ordained in 1875 in which year he also became Warden. In 1885 he was appointed Vicar of St. Peter's Carmarthen; in 1889 he was consecrated in Westminster Abbey as bishop of St. Asaph and was enthroned as first archbishop of Wales in 1920).

1876-1926

W. W. POOLE HUGHES

*Llandovery College Warden and Masters.
C. A. Buckmaster; C. P. Lewis; Rev A. G. Edwards (Warden);
Rev G. W. Gent; Henrich Wolfgang Just; Chas E. Williams.*

There were two other callings, and only two—other than schoolmastering—which I considered seriously at different periods of my life. The one was inevitable from my early environment. I spent rather more than ten years of my early life on the shores of Cardigan Bay. When I had done my lessons with my mother, and managed to escape her vigilance, I made for the harbour.

All young and self-respecting boys of Aberayron, who were strong and vigorous, were wild to go to sea. What wonder? For the sailors from those coast villages were second to none on the oceans of the world.

My prospects in that direction were abruptly extinguished by my mother returning to her native countryside—the Vale of Towy . . . I was entered for Llandovery College and was soon immersed in the life of the school, where, as it turned out, I was to spend eight whole years. The present Archbishop of Wales was Warden, the Rev G. W. Gent, afterwards Dean of Keble and Principal of Lampeter, and Mr C. A. Buckmaster, at present at the Board of Education, were two of his colleagues.

It was the long-drawn-out happiness of those days that made it impossible for me to think of any other career than that of a master in a public school. There were serious difficulties to be overcome, and it was on that account I had to consider the other career I referred to above. An opening, the main attraction of which was that business was carried on from 10 till 3 . . . was offered me. The matters were very seriously discussed, but we arranged that I should go up secretly to Oxford and enter for a scholarship examination.

In those days, after the examination, the candidates were called up to be interviewed. When my turn came, the examiners said that University College offered me a small scholarship. I remember how they laughed when I blurted out, 'Oh, I can't. The Warden doesn't know I am up here.' But that interview settled the question of my career.

Two years later I started my course at Oxford . . . One incident may be of some general interest, for it relates to the famous Master of my college, Benjamin Jowett. Soon after I went into residence, I received an invitation to take wine with the Master. My first instinct was to rush off into the darkness and finish with Oxford. However, in due course, I presented myself at his lodge. I shall never forget the scene I faced as the door was closed and I was left alone with the Master. The large wainscotted room, the gloom relieved only by the light of two candles, the small figure of the Master with his silver hair. A curt salutation and the pushing of his port decanter towards me were the only signs of recognition I received. We sat in silence for some minutes—or was it hours? Suddenly he jerked one word at me, 'Talk.' I had touched bottom. I have ever been thankful that my sense of humour came to my rescue. I said with a smile, 'It is the one thing I am incapable of doing, sir, at the present.' He was kindness itself to me from that moment. He did the talking and discoursed pleasant about many things. I remember he talked much about Tenby, which he had visited in his early years, and again of Archdeacon Williams, the first Warden of Llandovery . . .

Believe one, who after thirty seven years finds his pleasantest recreation in teaching when he asserts that no career offers greater happiness or better opportunities of doing helpful work in your generation. I have had the happiness of dealing with boys from nearly every kind of home and condition of life. At heart they are much the same . . .

May I add one word of tribute to my mother, whose strong and simple faith and self-denying devotion alone made it possible for me to realise the dream of my boyhood by becoming Warden of my old school? Her life was spared to help me for many years at Llandovery—to what extent I never realised till she passed away at the age of eighty years.

(This article, under the title 'My Career' was written by Canon Poole Hughes for the South Wales News *and appeared on 16 March, 1926. The article which follows by the newspaper's correspondent gives a biographical note—and brief assessment—of Canon Poole Hughes who held office at Llandovery longer than any other warden. He entered as a schoolboy aged 10 in 1876, was appointed Warden in 1900 and died in office in 1928.*

. . . No head of a public school in this country has a closer understanding of the psychology of boys than the Rev Canon W. Worthington Poole-Hughes M.A. It is an understanding based, primarily, upon a strong and abiding sympathy with young manhood, its recurring problems and difficulties, its doubts, and its aspirations.

The Rev Canon W. Worthington Poole-Hughes has held the wardenship of Llandovery College for a longer period than any of his predecessors, being appointed twenty-five years ago to succeed the Rev Owen Evans M.A., who had accepted the living of St. Peter's Carmarthen.

He is a mathematician of distinction. Entering Llandovery College at ten years of age as a new boy under the present Archbishop of Wales, he gained, in 1884, an open mathematical exhibition of Balliol, at Oxford, when he was 18, the celebrated Dr Jowett being then Master of Balliol. A year previously he had won the mathematical exhibition at University College, Oxford, and in 1885 he was awarded a mathematical scholarship of £80 a year at Balliol.

In 1887 he took first-class in Mathematical Moderations, and in 1889 a second-class in Mathematical Finals. While at Oxford he was a noted athlete, being chosen to play for the Oxford XV on many occasions; he figured prominently in the London Welsh and the Barbarians.

Electing to adopt the teaching profession, Canon Poole-Hughes was appointed assistant-master at Uppingham Lower School in 1889, and three years later became head of the Army side at Sherborne and school tutor.

On the first day of the present century, Canon Poole-Hughes became Warden of Llandovery. During his distinguished tenure a sum of over £17,500 has been expended on new buildings, the provision of modern laboratories, and a gymnasium, and very fine playing fields have been acquired for the school.

Under his control Llandovery has had a record of successes at Oxford and Cambridge not surpassed by any public school in the kingdom in proportion to its size.

(South Wales News March 16, 1926).

1880

CECIL OWEN

I myself am an old Llandovery Boy (of almost prehistoric time now). The late Archbishop Dr A. G. Edwards was Head Master and Mr C. P. Lewis was our chief exponent in Cricket, and Brecon either in Cricket or Football was our great rival. Mr Winter used then to look after our various musical attainments. Mr McIntosh used to take the Juniors in Greek in Ritchie's First Greek Method . . . and Valpy's Greek Delectus. Mr Judson used to take us Juniors in 'Maths' as they then were before Physics and Engineering became as fashionable as they seem to be today, and when we did fairly decent work in his Laboratory Class Room he would initiate us into the delights of coloured Giesler tubes and delightful shocks from the Wimshurst Machine. What a teacher Judson was and how humorous and just! Mr Williams was Second Master, and I fancy Mr Moffat had charge of the School Library, where among other delights was to be found Mrs Crowe's 'Night Side of Nature', 3 volumes, 1,000 pages, with a ghost on every page! Often have I hastened up the Tower Stairs fearing to sight any one of those thousand ghosts . . . Perhaps even in these much changed times Llandovery has a School Paper still. I hope (but I fear not) Greek still finds a place in the curriculum . . . Here in Kalgoorlie we live on gold but never see any thereof. I can only quote the Llandovery School Motto, which used to be 'Gwell Dysg na Golud.'

(School Journal, March 1951. Written by Cecil Owen of Kalgoorlie, Western Australia who was in School c.1880).

The School: 1883

LLANDOVERY SCHOOL,
CARMARTHENSHIRE.

THOMAS PHILLIPS' FOUNDATION.

TRUSTEES
Lady LLANOVER; The BISHOP of ST. ASAPH; Rev. CHANCELLOR PHILLIPS; JOHN JONES, Esq., Blaenôs; W. D. H. CAMPBELL-DAVYS, Esq., Neuadd Fawr.

VISITOR—THE BISHOP OF ST. DAVID'S.

WARDEN AND HEADMASTER
Rev. A. G. EDWARDS, M.A., late Scholar and Exhibitioner, Jesus College, Oxford; 2nd Class Classical Moderations Honours, 1872; 3rd Class Classical Honours, Finals, 1874.

SECOND MASTER
C. E. WILLIAMS, M.A., late Open Scholar, Queen's College, Cambridge; 26th Wrangler, 1874.

ASSISTANT MATHEMATICAL MASTER
A. MACINTOSH, M.A., Senior Moderator and Gold Medallist, Trinity College, Dublin; Fellow of Queen's College, Cambridge; 6th Wrangler, Cambridge Mathematical Tripos, 1880.

ASSISTANT CLASSICAL MASTER
Rev. E. J. McCLELLAN, B.A., Open Classical Hastings Exhibitioner, Queen's College, Oxford; 1st Class Classical Mods. Honours, 1867.

SIXTH FORM MASTER
H. MOFFAT, B.A., Scholar of St. Catherine's College, Cambridge; 9th in the Classical Tripos, 1882.

CLASSICAL MASTER
E. M. RODERICK, B.A., Classical Scholar, Jesus College, Oxford; 2nd Class Classical Mods., 1880; 3rd Class Classical Finals, 1882.

SCIENCE MASTER
T. H. JUDSON, B.A., Open Science Scholar, Merton College, Oxford; 1st Class Natural Science Honours, Oxford, 1879; Fellow of the Chemical Society.

MASTER OF THE JUNIOR SCHOOL
C. P. LEWIS, M.A., late Classical Exhibitioner, Jesus College, Oxford.

ASSISTANT MASTER
T. H. WINTER, B.A., late Open Mathematical Exhibitioner, St. John's College, Cambridge; 6th Junior Optime Cambridge Mathematical Tripos, 1882.

DRAWING
D. SAUNDERS THOMAS, Certificated Teacher of the Art and Science Department, South Kensington.

MUSIC MASTER
T. H. WINTER, B.A., 2nd in Music Cambridge Senior Locals, 1876.

DRILL
SERGEANT HOBAN.

EXAMINERS, 1883
OXFORD AND CAMBRIDGE SCHOOLS EXAMINATION BOARD.

1885-1887

G. G. Coulton

Work was a pressing question; and I was ready to take almost any teaching job rather than slide into unemployment. School-work is, or at least was then, a great lottery for those who had not definite Old Tie or similar connections. Paradoxically, much depends on being out of work at the right moment: once, for instance, I could have got work at Rugby if I had not recently taken a job at a less-known school . . . Here, in 1885, I was much disappointed by failure at Lampeter School, in spite of a very generous testimonial from Dean Vaughan. Two or three weeks later, however, I had an offer from a much better school. John Owen, who, as one of the Lampeter staff, had read my testimonials, was now appointed to the Headship of Llandovery, vacant through the promotion of A. G. Edwards to the See of St. Asaph. Owen afterwards became Bishop of St. David's, and might have been Archbishop if he had not studiously stood aside in deference to his old friend Edwards.

He had one quality which swallows up a host of minor deficiencies: deep, natural generosity. His father was of peasant and Nonconformist stock in North Wales . . . John Owen's speech, to the very last, was more natural in Welsh than in English. At Oxford, one of his cherished ideals was that he should never lose this . . . He was master of the 'hwyl', that cadence into which the true Cymric preacher falls—or rather soars . . .

Owen had not that narrow patriotism which is perhaps the greatest weakness of Wales, and which too often springs from an inferiority complex. He was no more in sympathy with the violent reaction at Llanelly, when an Englishman was appointed Chief Postmaster there, than the Birmingham newspapers would have been if a Welshman had been similarly imposed upon them. Therefore, much as he loved his native tongue, he favoured no violent efforts to revive it . . . Like others I have known he wrote English better than the average Englishman . . .

When he came to Llandovery, bringing two other new masters besides myself, I found immediate encouragement in work under this laborious and determined man. In those first days, he took practically no exercise, and paid nature for this by a bilious headache once a month; a whole day spent on the sofa, and then again *da capo*. Later, he played lawn tennis energetically, but remained a very hard worker until his death . . . We were five Assistant Masters then, increasing soon to seven; for Owen, wisely adventurous, made a point of over-staffing rather than under-staffing; with the result that the boys increased very rapidly in numbers, for his enthusiasm was contagious, and nothing succeeds like success . . . The main entrance bore a noble motto: GWELL DYSG NA GOLUD—*Better Learning than Gold* . . . The Library was specially significant. It was a capacious room, and the shelves were about half-full. But nearly all of the volumes had been bought, from time to time, in job lots at London auctions, and sent down at random to enrich this seat of learning. One very conspicuous item was the great Kehl edition of Voltaire's works, in seventy volumes. There were about eighty boarders in 1885; so the buildings were narrow for these boys and the necessary classrooms. Only one Master, Winter, had rooms in the place; the rest of us lodged in the town, on the market square. One fair-day a bullet went astray from the shooting-gallery, and drilled a hole through one of my colleagues' windows.

The want of a Common Room for the Masters was serious; for we had no refuge in the School House but Winter's room, where we had breakfast and tea; and this laid great stress upon general clubbability. Memory compels me to confess that I must have been the least clubbable, by the hard test of practical results; for to me alone, at any time, did Winter formally forbid his room. He was rather argumentative, and perhaps I was even more so . . .

As Class Master, I had the lowest but one, with French, English and History for the higher boys, until an Oxford man joined the staff, who had gone through the History mill. He was an enthusiastic and very successful teacher; his first success was with Frank Morgan, who finally became History Lecturer at Keble . . .

My junior, Walters of Keble, and his successor, F. E. Chapman of Sidney, taught with me in the Big Schoolroom. In winter, the draught which came down from the open ceiling went far to stultify the two stoves, even when we heated them red-hot. But irrespective of season, though we kept our little flocks as far apart as possible, each often found himself remonstrating with the other in Winter's room for aggressive loudness and emphasis of voice. A few years ago, I gave six talks on the wireless. Suddenly a postcard came from Chapman, whom I had not seen for a dozen years past: 'I switched on at random in the middle of something; and there was your voice forcing itself upon my ear just as it used to do almost half a century ago!'

These Welsh boys had, naturally, less general background than their opposite numbers in England. As Owen used frankly to confess: if you pick up a book of information in the Welsh tongue—history, geography, science—it is fifty years behind the latest English. But not more than twenty-five per cent, at most, came from homes where Welsh was the really predominant language. Frank Morgan's father, for instance, was editor of a Carmarthen newspaper: and we had a fair sprinkling from clergy of all denominations. And, for French, all started with an enormous advantage over the English schoolboy. They knew that there is more than one language in the world, and that it may be worth while to learn another language . . .

In many ways it is far better practice to teach a low form than a higher; and I have always been grateful for my two years at Llandovery. We did our work honestly, and yet found a little time for reading even in term time . . .

Here I tasted first the real pleasures of Rugby football. Having grown slowly, I was far more active and stronger at twenty-seven than at seventeen . . . The school always recruited from its staff for all matches except against their great rival, Brecon . . . The one drawback was, for out-matches, that I was in charge to stop smoking: and, during those two years at least, I was too new myself to wink at minor infringements. But the home journey, when not by train, was always worthy of musical Wales, and our wagonette could probably have been heard for a mile along the road . . .

Best of all, however—far beyond even the happiest of games—was the exhilaration of that Welsh countryside . . . Nearly always I took these walks alone; but once, to Towy source, I went with Aneurin Rees. His father, Rees of Ton, had bequeathed to him one of the finest existing libraries of Welsh manuscripts and rare books; but he himself was far more sportsman than scholar . . .

Llandovery had two ancient churches, Llandingat in the level land and Llanfair on the hill; both were united into a single vicarage. Service was in English at Llandingat in the morning, Llanfair in the evening. The vicar generally preached at this morning service. He was a rather grotesque person in every way; his wife was far cleverer, but somewhat eccentric . . . The boys were parked in a gallery at the west end, and the vicar never showed the least condescension towards them in his sermons . . .

Llandovery leads on naturally to Lampeter . . . in the eighties Lampeter had at least three young men who were already making their mark: T. F. Tout,

Hastings Rashdall, and E. H. Culley . . . It was a great pleasure to meet Tout and Culley when our team played at Lampeter; and Rashdall, to my abiding profit, came and examined at Llandovery from his newly won Tutorship at Durham University. His *Universities of Europe*, a few years later, became one of the books to which I have owed most.

The Jubilee year, 1887, began badly. Frosts and floods in the mountains wrought havoc among the flocks, and dead sheep drifted down past Llandovery to Carmarthen Bay. But with April and May came real summer; and men already began to speak of 'the Queen's weather': for Victoria, proverbially, had it almost always fine. June was sheer sunshine and good temper. A few neighbouring gentry had begun to recognize the rising value of the school, and we had charming picnics or excursions here and there; one, in especial, to the magnificent crag castle of Cerrig-Cennen, . . . For the Jubilee night itself, our college staff joined with a few friends in a drive to Llanddeusant and the Vans. It was deliciously warm, and we lay among the heather and fern on the upper slopes until it became time to climb the summit. From that we watched the beacons kindle one by one: fifty-seven we counted in all; one, over the sea, was evidently on Lundy Island. Then, after we had gazed our fill and sat down to supper, came the most picturesque sight of all. A party of miners had come up from Cwmamman; and now, in the small hours, they began to dribble down, taking each a burning brand to light his footsteps. We could thus watch the whole trail down into the distant valley.

Certainly that year was one of optimism and hearty enjoyment, especially when the daily sunshine had begun to give solid promise of 'Queen's weather'. The Towy valley is fairly rich in 'county families'; and all neighbours were beginning to take notice of the school's success under John Owen. Among the first were Sir James Hills-Johnes, who had been Lord Roberts' intimate friend and partner in India, and Lady Hills-Johnes, of the family of the well-known translator of Froissart and editor of much other valuable matter from his private mess at Hafod. She was learned herself, and the letters she received from Bishop Thirlwall of St. David's, who for learning had no rival on the bench if we except Stubbs at Oxford, are still worth reading. Besides their generous parties at Dolau Cothi, we had quite as many others in the Vale of Towy . . .

Next Term, when we all came back in mid-September, it was again a fine autumn. But before a week of Term had passed, I received a sudden passport to another world. A letter came from my old college chum H. v. E. Scott: would I accept a job at Heidelberg? A man was wanted to do chaplaining and scholastic work: but he must come immediately. The details Scott gave offered solid guarantees; and I put the matter at once before the Headmaster. He made the most generous allowances; and it was soon agreed that I should be free from the moment when he could find a successor. This took only a matter of days. Berryman came to fill the vacancy, and proved a most popular member of the staff.

On my last evening I climbed the hills above Llanwrda and watched a glorious sunset . . .

(This excerpt is from Fourscore Years, Cambridge, 1944. George Gordon Coulton (1858-1947) historian and controversialist particularly in the area of religious views. Educated at Felsted and St. Catharine's College, Cambridge. One of the outstanding scholars of studies of the Middle Ages, his publications include Five Centuries of Religion, 4 volumes 1923-1950 and Medieval Panorama, 1938).

The School Notes of the Journal, June 1886: 'Mr Edwards' successor the Rev. J. Owen, formerly Welsh professor and classical lecturer at St. David's College, Lampeter. The other new masters are Mr T. J. Richards, late postmaster of Merton College, Oxford; Mr G. Hartwell Jones, late scholar of Jesus College, Oxford; the Rev. G. G. Coulton, late scholar of St. Catharine's College, Cambridge; and Mr E. W. R. Walters of Keble College, Oxford . . . There are now 128 boys on the School books.' By December 1887 '. . . the number of boys has risen from 128 to 170'. It also reported '. . . Mr Coulton . . . left the beginning of this Term for a chaplaincy at Heidelberg . . . Mr Coulton will be long remembered as a splendid forward and an enthusiastic explorer of the hill scenery around Llandovery'.)

1885-1889

JOHN OWEN

Pan aethum i Lanymddyfri ym 1885 yr oedd yr Ysgol wedi cyrraedd safle uchel ym mysg ysgolion y deyrnas trwy allu ac ynni Archesgob Cymru yn ystod y deng mlynedd y bu yn Warden. Llwyddasai i ddwyn yno athrawon o'r radd flaenaf, ac enillodd yr Ysgol nifer fawr o ysgoloriaethau ym mhrif Golegau Rhydychen a Chaergrawnt. Peth anodd i'w gynhyrchu yw ysbryd iach Ysgol Gyhoeddus, ond llwyddodd yr Archesgob i wneuthur hynny, ac y mae effaith ei waith yn aros hyd heddyw. Cadw i fyny safon yr Ysgol oedd fy mhrif awydd pan ddilynais ef fel Warden. Bychan a feddyliwn yn 1885 na fyddwn ond pedair blynedd yn Llanymddyfri. Nid oedd yn amlwg yn 1885 beth a fyddai effaith sefydliad y ddau Goleg newydd yng Nghaerdydd a Bangor ar ragolygon yr Ysgol, ond argyhoeddwyd fi yn fuan fod i Ysgolion Lanymddyfri ac Aberhonddu le pwysig a pharhaus yn nyfodol addysg Cymru. Yr oedd cefnogaeth a chyfeillgarwch yr Archesgob yn fantais amhrisiadwy i mi, a bu dau o'i athrawon profiadol yn gymorth gwerthfawr i mi i gadw traddodiadau yr Ysgol. Llwyddais i gael athrawon newydd cymwys i gymryd lle yr athrawon a ymadawsant, ac ar ddiwedd y term cyntaf lleihaodd fy mhryder ynghylch dyfodol yr Ysgol. Hyfryd gennyf gofio am y gefnogaeth a gefais pan yn cychwyn yn Llanymddyfri gan yr efrydwyr a fuasent yng Ngholeg Llanbedr pan oeddwn yn Broffeswr Cymraeg, ac oeddynt yn offeiriaid, erbyn hyn, yn Esgobaethau Tyddewi a Llandaf. Gan nad oedd gwaddoliadau yr Ysgol yn ddigonol, dibynnai llwyddiant addysgol yr Ysgol ar gadw i fyny nifer y bechgyn. Fy unig obaith i wneud hynny oedd ymdrechu fy ngoreu i gadw i fyny safon addysg yr Ysgol. Yr oedd y cyfrifoldeb ariannol yn fawr, a llethasid fi gan bryder oni bai am yr hyfrydwch a gawn yn fy ngwaith. Yn Llanymddyfri y dysgais mai ofer pryderu ynghylch llwyddiant. Y cyfan a all neb wneud yw ymdrechu ei oreu gyda'r gwaith a fyddo ganddo, ac ymddiried yn Nuw am lwyddiant. Y mae hyfrydwch rhyfedd mewn gwynebu anawsterau pan ddysgant i ni werth ffydd. Cefais gipolwg ar hyn yn fy mhrofiad yn Llanymddyfri, a gresyn na ddysgaswn y wers yn well.

Arglwyddes Llanofer, yr Esgob Hughes o Lanelwy, y Deon Phillips, Mr Campbell Davy, a Mr John Jones, Blaenos, oeddynt ymddiriedolwyr yr Ysgol pan euthum yno. Yr oedd yr Arglwyddes a'r Esgob Hughes yn ymddiriedolwyr yr Ysgol o'r sefydliad cyntaf, a buasai y Deon Phillips yn Warden llwyddiannus yr Ysgol. Ni fu Mr Campbell Davy a Mr John Jones fyw yn hir a dilynwyd hwy gan Iarll Cawdor (Arglwydd Emlyn y pryd hynny) a'r Cadfridog Syr James Hills-Johnes. Ni fu yr Arglwyddes na'r Esgob Hughes yn yr Ysgol yn fy amser i. Cefais garedigrwydd mawr gan y ddau, ac ymwelwn â'r Arglwyddes unwaith bob term. Cymerai ddiddordeb dwfn yn yr Ysgol, a rhoddai bob blwyddyn wobrwyon haelionus ymhob dosbarth am wybodaeth o'r iaith Gymraeg. Cyfeiriais mewn ysgrifau blaenorol at ei gwladgarwch a'i thalent, ac at garedigrwydd yr Esgob Hughes a'r Deon Phillips. Braint fawr oedd dyfod i gysylltiad swyddogol ag Iarll Cawdor a Syr James Hills-Johnes, ac efallai y dylwn gymryd y cyfle hwn i gydnabod fy nyled ddofn i'r ddau hyd eu hangeu.

Yr Iarll a ddaeth yn Gadeirydd Ymddiriedolwyr yr Ysgol pan fethodd Arglwyddes Llanofer oherwydd henaint barhau yn y swydd. Ymwelai â'r Ysgol bob blwyddyn, ac yr oedd yn gysur mawr i mi gael y fraint o ymgynghori ag ef pan fyddai angen. Dyfnhaodd fy mharch iddo bob blwyddyn, ond pan ddeuthum yn Esgob yn 1897 yr adnabyddais fawredd ei gymeriad. Ysgrifennodd ataf y pryd hynny y gallwn ddibynnu yn wastad ar bob cymorth a allai ef roddi i mi, a chadwodd ei air yn ardderchog. Ni throais ato unwaith tra fu byw yn ofer am gyngor na chefnogaeth. Nid oedd dim anwadalwch yn perthyn iddo. Dyledswydd oedd cyweirnod ei gymeriad. Yr oedd yn weithiwr caled, er nad oedd ei iechyd yn gryf. Nid oedd dim yn ormod ganddo ei wneud dros les y wlad a'r eglwys . . .

Sir James Hills-Johnes, VC

Syr James Hills-Johnes oedd Trysorydd Ymddiriedolwyr Llanymddyfri. Nid oedd dim a werthfawrogwn yn fwy pan yn Llanymddyfri na'r gwahoddiadau mynych a gawn i gyfarfod Arglwydd Roberts a Chadfridogion enwog eraill a ymwelai ag ef yn ei gartref prydferth yn Dolau Cothi. Nid oedd gartref mwy gwladgarol a swynol yng Nghymru na Dolau Cothi. Yr oedd ei hoff Arglwyddes dalentog, sydd eto yn fyw, a'i chwaer yng nghyfraith, Mrs Johnes, yn ei galonogi i wasanaethu Cymru, yn enwedig yn achos Addysg, a mawr oedd gwerth ei wasanaeth i Brifysgol Cymru, a Choleg Aberystwyth, yn gystal ag Ysgol Llanymddyfri . . . Enillodd pan yn ieuanc y V.C., ac fel ei gyfaill mynwesol, Arglwydd Roberts, yr oedd yn Gadfridog enwog. Gwron oedd yn y fyddin, a gwron oedd hefyd yn ei ymroddiad i wasanaeth ei wlad a'i Eglwys hyd ei fedd. Braint fawr i mi pan yn Llanymddyfri oedd ei gyfeillgarwch...

Trefnwyd yng Nghyfansoddiad yr Ysgol fod addysg grefyddol o'r Beibl yn rhan hanfodol o addysg yr Ysgol. Yn fy amser i dysgid y Beibl yn Gymraeg i'r bechgyn a fedrent Gymraeg. Ni fwynhawn ddim yn fwy pan yn Warden na'r Ysgol Sul. Cymerwn dri dosbarth am hanner awr bob un, ar ôl ei gilydd, brynhawn Sul, yn yr Efengyl am y Sul; ac fel rheol pregethwn yn yr hwyr ddau Sul o bob tri yng ngwasanaeth yr Ysgol ar yr Efengyl a ddarllenwyd yn yr Ysgol Sul. Yr oedd cateceisio y bechgyn yn yr Ysgol Sul yn baratoad gwerthfawr at y bregeth. Yn Eglwys Llanfair ar y Bryn nos Sul y cynhelid gwasanaeth arbennig yr Ysgol. Yr offeiriaid oedd yn athrawon a gymerent y gwasanaeth, a Chôr yr Ysgol oedd Côr y gwasanaeth hwyrol. Yr oedd y canu yn odidog, a'r holl wasanaeth yn fywiog a chynnes. Nid oedd le i gynulleidfa fawr o'r plwyfolion yn yr Eglwys gan fod cynulleidfa yr Ysgol yn gref. Gwasanaeth Cymraeg a fyddai yn Eglwys Llandingat yn yr hwyr, a byddai raid i'r sawl o'r plwyfolion a ddymunent ddod i wasanaeth yr Ysgol yn Eglwys Llanfair ar y Bryn fod yn eu lle fel rheol agos i hanner awr cyn dechreu y gwasanaeth. Ar fore Sul elem fel ysgol i Eglwys Llandingat, yr hon oedd Eglwys y plwyf, ac eisteddai y bechgyn bob amser yn yr oriel, a minnau ac un arall o'r athrawon yn ei dro yno gyda mi. Byddai un o'r 'prefects' yn casglu yn yr oriel, ac elai gyda'r casglyddion eraill i'r Ganghell i gyflwyno yr offrwm. Yr ail flwyddyn o'm hamser yno y dechreuwyd casglu yn yr oriel, a chofiaf yn dda am y Prefect, sydd yn awr yn ŵr enwog, aeth y tro cyntaf a'r offrwm i'r Ganghell, a mawr oedd diddordeb y bechgyn yn sylwi arno yn myned. Yr oedd amryw o fechgyn Ymneillduol yn Boarders. Y rheol oedd iddynt fyned i'r lle o addoliad a ddymunai y rhieni. Cedwid rhestr o'r Boarders a elent i'r Eglwys ac i'r gwahanol gapeli, ac edrychwn dros y rhestrau hyn pan fyddai y bechgyn ar swper nos Sul, er mwyn cael eglurhad os byddai bachgen yn absennol o'r lle addoliad y dymunai ei rieni iddo fod ynddo. Bu y rheol yn foddhaol a dibrofedigaeth. Yr unig anhawster oedd gyda'r Ysgol Sul. Gan fod dosbarthiadau yr Ysgol Sul yn yr ysgol yn fywiog a byr, yr oedd tuedd yn rhai bechgyn Ymneilltuol i lithro iddi, ond ni chaniateid iddynt fod yn absennol o Ysgol Sul y Capel y perthynent iddo heb lythyr gan eu rhieni ataf yn gofyn caniatad iddynt ddyfod i ddosbarth Ysgol Sul yr Ysgol. Daeth dirprwyaeth ataf o un Capel yn cwyno oherwydd atdyniad dosbarthiadau Sul yr Ysgol. Cynghorais hwynt yn gyfeillgar i ofalu am athraw medrus i gymryd dosbarth bechgyn yr

Ysgol, a byrhau ychydig ar amser eu Hysgol, yr hon oedd oedd y pryd hwnnw, os wyf yn cofio yn iawn, yn awr a hanner. Cymerasant y cyngor, ac ni fu dim anhawster ar ôl hynny. Byddai gennyf ddosbarth Conffirmasiwn bob gwanwyn, a braint fawr a gyfrifwn baratoi y bechgyn at Gonffirmasiwn, ac nid oes dim mwy hyfryd yn fy mhrofiad fel Esgob na gwasanaeth blynyddol Conffirmasiwn bechgyn Ysgol Llanymddyfri. Yr wyf yn cofio yn dda mor falch oeddwn fy mlwyddyn olaf yn yr Ysgol pan ddaeth bachgen ieuanc Ymneilltuol ataf i ofyn i mi ei baratoi at Gonffirmasiwn yn ei Gapel. Yr oedd ei ddymuniad yn ddiddorol yn dangos fod ganddo hyder yn fy nhegwch ynglŷn ag Addysg Grefyddol. Cadarnhaodd fy mhrofiad yn Llanymddyfri fy argyhoeddiad mai addysg grefyddol yw sylfaen gwir addysg. Camgymeriad dwfn yw tybio mai y deall yn unig yw gwrthrych addysg. Y mae a fynno addysg a'r holl gyneddfau—yr ewyllys, y gydwybod, a'r serchiadau, yn ogystal â'r deall.

Gwaith hyfryd yw gwaith athro os bydd ganddo gymhwyster ato. Hanfod addysg yw datblygu cyneddfau bechgyn. Camgymeriad yw tybio mai cyfrannu gwybodaeth yw addysgu . . . fy mhrofiad yn Llanymddyfri oedd mai hyfrydwch gwaith athro yw datblygu cymeriad. Yr oedd llawer o ofalon yn gorffwys ar ysgwyddau Prifathro, a llawenydd oedd gennyf droi oddiwrthynt i addysgu dosbarth.

Pan ymadewais â Llanymddyfri yn 1889, yr oedd, os wyf yn cofio yn iawn, nifer y Boarders yn y pedwar tŷ oedd gennyf yn 118, heblaw oddeutu 20 yn nhŷ yr ail-athro. Y mae bywyd Boarders yn gyfle gwerthfawr, os iawn-ddefnyddir ef, i'w gwneud yn aelodau defnyddiol cymdeithas. Teimlwn yn ddwys y cyfrifoldeb oedd arnaf i roi iawn gyfeiriad i'r bechgyn hynny oedd ganddynt, oherwydd eu safle ym mywyd yr ysgol, ddylanwad arbennig ar fywyd cymdeithasol yr ysgol. Yng ngoleu fy mhrofiad fy hun, cymerais bob cyfle i graffu ar dôn ysgolion Llanymddyfri ac Aberhonddu y 33 mlynedd diweddaf, a da iawn gennyf ddweyd fy mod yn credu yn gadarn fod dylanwad y ddwy ysgol enwog hyn wedi bod o les mawr i Gymru. Y mae gan Gymru yn awr gyfundrefn addysg werthfawr, ond bydd lle arbennig o ddefnyddiol ynddi i Ysgolion Cyhoeddus fel Llanymddyfri ac Aberhonddu, lle y bydd Boarders o dan ddylanwad athrawon cydwybodol a doeth yn rhoddi i'w gilydd addysg gymdeithasol nas gellir ei gael i'r un gradd yn yr ysgolion dyddiol goreu.

Y mae i chwareuon le pwysig ym mywyd cymdeithasol Ysgol Gyhoeddus fel Llanymddyfri. Nid yn unig yr oeddynt yn fuddiol i iechyd corfforol y bechgyn, ond yr oeddynt hefyd, o'u hiawn arfer, yn llesol eu dylanwad er ffurfio cymeriad. Yr oedd Llanymddyfri, o'i maint yn ysgol enwog am chwarae Rugby Football. Bu tri o fechgyn oedd yno yn fy amser i yn Gadbeniaid Rugby

Football yr un flwyddyn ym Mhrifysgolion Rhydychen, Caergrawnt, ac Edinburgh. Byddai matches blynyddol mewn Football rhwng yr Ysgol a Choleg Llanbedr, ac Ysgol Aberhonddu, a chlybiau eraill. Prif ddiwrnod yr Ysgol oedd y Match ag Ysgol Aberhonddu bob blwyddyn, a chwareuid yn Llanymddyfri ac Aberhonddu bob yn ail flwyddyn. Llanymddyfri a enillodd dair o'r pedair blwyddyn y bum yno. Aberhonddu ar y llaw arall a enillodd mewn cricket dair gwaith yn y pedair blynedd. Yr wyf yn cofio yn dda i'r bechgyn ofyn i mi yn haf 1889, fy mlwyddyn olaf yno, pa dysteb a fyddai oreu gennyf gael wrth ymadael. Fy ateb oedd mai iddynt ennill y match flynyddol mewn cricket yn erbyn Aberhonddu, ac fe'i henillasant . . .

Yr Esgob Lloyd o Fangor ydoedd Athro Ysgol Aberhonddu pedair blynedd y bum yn Llanymddyfri. Yr oedd yn Brifathro rhagorol, ac y mae ei ysgolheigion heddyw yn wŷr enwog mewn gwlad ac Eglwys. Yr oedd yn Gymro cynnes ei galon a mawr ei allu. Yr oedd gennyf barch mawr iddo. Er fod Ysgolion Aberhonddu a Llanymddyfri yn cydymgeisio yn fywiog mewn chwareuon ac arholiadau, edrychwn arnynt y pryd hwnnw, fel yn awr, fel dwy Chwaer Ysgol Gyhoeddus o werth cynhyddol i gyfundrefn addysg genedlaethol Cymru . . .

Yn fy ail flwyddyn yn Llanymddyfri penderfynais benodi Athro mewn Hanes, a llwyddais i sicrhau gwasanaeth Mr Herbert Gregory o Goleg Magdalen, Rhydychen. Brodor o Manchester ydoedd, a chan ei fod wedi marw ers blynyddoedd, gallaf ddweyd nad oedd, fe gredaf, athro gwell ar y pryd yn ei bwnc mewn dim ysgol yn y Deyrnas. Gwnaeth les arbennig i'r bechgyn oedd yn y dosbarth uchaf, y Sixth Form. Yr oedd ganddo ddawn arbennig i ddysgu bechgyn i feddwl, ac i greu gwir ddiddordeb mewn Hanes ynddynt. Bu yn yr Ysgol yn ystod amser yr Archddiacon Owen Evans, ac am rai blynyddoedd ar ôl hynny. Enillodd amryw o'i ysgolheigion History Scholarships yn Rhydychen, a bu holl fechgyn y Sixth Form yn well dynion oherwydd bod o dan ei addysg. Y mae Hanes, yn llaw Athro cymwys, yn un o bynciau mwyaf gwerthfawr addysg yn ei ddylanwad ar gymeriad. Rhoddes Mr Gregory oreu ei oes i wasasnaethu Ysgol Llanymddyfri â'i holl galon, a gwn fod gan ei fechgyn fel y mae gennyf finnau gôf serchog a pharchus amdano.

Nid hawdd oedd ymadael â Llanymddyfri ddechreu Awst, 1889. Er mai ar ôl llawer o betruster yr elais yno Medi, 1885, yr oeddwn wedi dyfod i hoffi yr Ysgol yn fawr, ac yn llawn awydd ymdrechu cario allan y cynlluniau oeddwn wedi eu ffurfio er cynhyddu defnyddioldeb yr Ysgol i Addysg Cymru. Er hynny oll pan welodd Archesgob Cymru yn dda, ar ei benodiad yn Esgob Llanelwy, fy ngwahodd i ddilyn Dr James fel Deon Llanelwy, teimlais na ddylwn wrthod gwahoddiad caredig cyfaill a'm hadwaenai er pan elais gyntaf i

Rydychen. Ni fu Deon erioed a dderbyniodd fwy o garedigrwydd cyson gan ei Esgob nag a dderbyniais i yn ystod y tair blynedd y bum yn un o Ganoniaid Llanelwy pan yr euthum yn ôl i Lanbedr fel Principal. Cyn penderfynu derbyn y Ddeoniaeth yr oeddwn wedi llwyddo i berswadio fy nghyfaill Owen Evans i addaw ymgymeryd â chyfrifoldeb Wardeniaeth yr Ysgol os dewisid ef gan y Trustees. Swydd anodd ei llanw yw Wardeniaeth Llanymddyfri gan y gofynnir iddo fod yn offeiriad hyddysg yn y Gymraeg. Nis gellid . . . cael gwell Warden, a'r gwasanaeth pennaf a wneuthum i'r Ysgol oedd ei berswadio ef i gymryd y swydd yn fy lle.

Llandovery College had a long and chequered history. The outgoing Warden was the Rev A. G. Edwards (afterwards Archbishop of Wales), who had been Warden for ten years. He had done much to improve the school. He had restored the buildings, had abolished the old system of boarding out the pupils at various houses in the town, and had also cut down the time (an hour a day) which had previously been given to the study of Welsh, for, by the terms of the Trust, the College existed to promote the study of the Welsh language. As a consequence, the boys had more time for their Classics and Mathematics, and their improved standard had been seen in the winning of scholarships at the University, and in the Oxford and Cambridge Joint Board Examination lists.

But at the time John Owen took over the school, the numbers had dropped to eighty, and the staff consisted of the Warden and only three Assistant Masters. It may fairly be said that it ranked very much on a par with a good class Grammar School, always remembering that it catered mainly for boarders, and in this lay future danger. It was almost a certainty that there would be within a few years a Welsh Intermediate School Bill. Would Llandovery be in a position to survive the rivalry of so many new Secondary Schools, and would it be able to retain its distinctive Church character and its status as a public school, or would it be submerged and sink to the level of the new Intermediate Schools?

Such were the considerations which Archdeacon Edmondes had pressed upon the Welsh Professor, and they had decided him. He had made his application accordingly to the Trustees, and was appointed Warden. The leading spirit among the Trustees was old Lady Llanofer, a great Welsh patriot, and a fervid lover of the Welsh language. She was an enthusiastic supporter of one who had proved at Lampeter that he loved and valued the Welsh language as keenly as she did. She had heartily disapproved of the new policy at Llandovery, and hoped that Professor Owen would see that the Welsh teaching was given a prominent place. It is pleasant to find that her last letters to him were as cordial as her first. True, the new Warden was far too wise to revert to the old system, but he taught much of the Welsh himself, had Welsh prizes, and a yearly Welsh examination, and always had a Welsh Report read at the Annual Prize Day.

Meantime, in that August, 1885, the new Warden gave himself up to much hard thinking. If Llandovery taught him not to fear responsibility, it also brought out his latent business sense and capacities for organization. He saw that if Llandovery was to be raised to the level of a first grade public school, it must win its position by merit. His first object must be to find boys with a good brain power, and educate them in such a way that they would be an ornament to the English Universities, the school, and the community. He saw at once that would not be done unless he could get together a brilliant staff of Assistant Masters.

That very August he had to fill up a vacancy in the staff. Instead of appointing one man, he appointed two, and secured a third to come at Christmas. These included Mr Hartwell Jones, afterwards Doctor of Divinity, who had had an excellent record at the University, and Mr G. G. Coulton, later a Lecturer on Medieval History at Cambridge, and a well known Historian. These appointments were a distinct venture of faith, as they were more than the actual number of boys in the school warranted, but they had their reward in public confidence. The number rose steadily: by June 1886 he had 128 boys on the books; in December 1887 he had 170. When he left, the numbers were close on two hundred, and he had increased the number of the staff correspondingly year by year.

When he came to take stock of the school, he found the need for strengthening the athletic side—especially in cricket, and in order to increase the prowess of the school he appointed masters such as Mr Chapman (the father of the Test cricketer) and Mr Kitto, fine athletes both. Mr Chapman, who came as a Junior Master, was made especially responsible for helping in the school playing fields. He found a Warden to work under who was not only singularly appreciative of any efforts he made, but ready to spend money on improvements. He allowed the engagement of a professional, and had a large additional part of the cricket-ground levelled and laid by a Nottingham firm. More than that, the Warden by his personal keenness, interest and enthusiasm put heart into his teams with such purpose that Llandovery once more beat Christ's College, Brecon, at football and in 1889 at Cricket also, while his Old Boys became University Blues, and indeed Captains of their Universities in football. In one eventful year the captains of the Oxford, Cambridge and Edinburgh Rugby teams were all old Llandovery boys, and pupils of John Owen.

'Who that knew him then,' wrote one Old Boy, 'can ever forget his violent partisanship—the expression sounds harsh, but is literally correct—during those Olympic contests between Llandovery and Christ's College, Brecon, at football and cricket, Rugby football in particular. He used to race up and down the touchline with the ardour of a boy, shouting the school's battle cry.' Few things endeared him to his scholars more than these displays of partisanship.

And how his will to success inspired them—'Nicholl,' he said to his captain before the great football match, 'what are you going to do against Brecon today?' 'We hope to win,' was the optimistic but non-committal reply. 'Hope, my boy, hope! You've *got* to win,' was the retort.

In yet a third way he laid deep the foundations for a successful school. He attracted to it boys of real ability from all classes of society—if they had brains. He went out of his way to look for them and never allowed financial gain to enter his calculations. If the school fees were too much for individual parents he always reduced them, regardless of pecuniary loss; ('I'll not make my fortune here,' he wrote to a friend in 1886), and once he found them, he spared no pains with them, watched over their careers individually, showed them how much he believed in them, and what great things he expected of them, until they began to try very hard to get nearer to his estimate.

Then successes came. Scholarship after scholarship was taken at Oxford and Cambridge, 1888 being a record year, with nine such successes, and in 1887 Llandovery stood third on the list of 22 first-grade public schools for successes in the Oxford and Cambridge Certificate Examination, with one Llandovery boy first in all England, and another third. 'At last Llandovery has done the trick,' he wrote to one old boy with whom he kept in touch: and with what wholehearted joy the Warden with his school gave themselves over to rejoicing! A holiday was instantly granted, for the headmaster was then in spirit a Llandovery boy, and the most ardent of them all, for he was first and foremost a Welshman, and his love for his school and his boys was not cold and formal, but eager, warmhearted and devoted.

'I am keen on boys again,' he wrote to Mr Roberts in 1886, and went on to tell how he hoped to keep up the Church tradition of the school. 'I have started a Sunday School here with a Bible Class but more is to follow—Catechism and Prayerbook Classes among them. There shall be no mistake about our colours, though Dissenters shall be as free as air. I like my work thoroughly, but it takes up time. There is always some lame lamb to get over a stile.' His influence on his pupils was certainly deep and abiding. He knew all his boys individually—all their family circumstances and past history, and never forgot a single detail about any of them. He encouraged confidence in school and out of school, and all loved him. They loved him all the more for his humour, and many is the tale which has been passed down through the years wherever his old boys met together—how that one day the Warden solemnly announced to the lowest form IIB 'that two boys would be moved up to IIA not for any signal progress or marked ability, but for long service.' It was only in later years that his old boys could see that all the while he was always instilling pluck and determination into them, and that it was the Warden's infectious enthusiasm which had inflamed the will to win in many a boy's mind. Archbishop Prosser and Mr Frank Morgan, first Secretary of the Representative Body [of the Church in Wales], were started by him on their careers.

As with boys, so with his staff. The Warden never showed any trace of the weakness of concentrating almost entirely on the boys and leaving the staff to look after themselves, 'It was a delight to work under him,' wrote one of his old masters, 'for he kept a sharp eye on all that was going on, was ready always with a word of commendation and encouragement for any extra effort made by masters and boys, and if ever there was occasion for blame he spoke with a gentleness and tact which never hurt. Consequently we all loved him and did our work *con amore*.' 'He was very generous to us all,' wrote another, 'and a real friend.' He always saw to their comfort and took a sympathetic interest in all their doings, and these were many and varied. Llandovery College, in those days, was the centre of the social life of the town and neighbourhhood, so there was always plenty of hospitality offered to the masters. Moreover the countryside is very attractive, for Llandovery is situated on the upper reaches of the river Towy, and is surrounded by hills. It affords great scope to the botanist and bird lover, and those who enjoy country walks and cycle rides. In the winter there would be busy preparations for the annual performance of a Gilbert and Sullivan opera. Here Mr Winter, the school housemaster, and a distinct personality, came into his own. He was more than an ordinary musician, and he liked nothing better than to act as musical director, and to be coaching the soloists and chorus. But summer and winter alike, they noticed that the Warden took little or no relaxation (though later he took to playing tennis). They marvelled at his power of hourly concentration on his particular job, and recognised that concentration would carry him through. And the Warden for his part backed them up loyally, and tried to screw them up to educational enthusiasm, which was not natural perhaps to any of them.

They were nearly all English, and not given to enthusiasm. They were inclined at first to think that the Warden took his masters' meetings too seriously, and held them too frequently: they even scoffed sometimes at his ardour and at his belief in the boys. An account of one of the masters' meetings in 1886-87 has been left on record. It was held in his study, which reeked of tobacco. He would be seated on the sofa to begin with, but presently he got excited and walked about the room, copious and vehement in speech even to the verge of unintelligible haste, in proportion as he found himself confronted by the cynical incredulity of X who took music and lower Mathematics, and Y (whose main qualification was that he had once very nearly bowled for Oxford), or by the more Olympian hesitation of his sixth form master, Mr McClellan, or Mac, as he was known to generations of boys.

There were always schemes to discuss—a new gymnasium built in 1886, new classrooms (in 1888), improvements to the reading room, and always the different possibilities of this boy and that.

The Warden's great days would come at the Annual Speech Day. His speech chiefly consisted of an enumeration of the year's successes which were really exceptional, increased numbers, increased staff, increased classrooms, new houses taken for boarders, and scholarship successes, with Llandovery placed third of all the schools in the United Kingdom, in the Certificate Examination. Sir James Hills-Johnes would voice the opinion of all when he said, 'All this is due to the good judgement, energy, powers of organization and liberality of the Warden.'

If sometimes the Warden felt the pressure of his work for the school, and desired more leisure, it was not to spend it on recreation, but, reading the newspapers as he did, diligently, and looking out of Llandovery windows at the outside world of Wales, watching the signs of the times—he longed to be up and doing, and at work for the Church . . .

When the Warden left in 1889 he passed on to his successor, his great friend, the Rev Owen Evans, a school, which in numbers, efficiency and tone, could compete with some of the best public schools—a school which, as the sequel showed, could ride out any storm.

The Rev A. G. Edwards of St. Peter's Church, Carmarthen, the late Warden, became known during these years as a great Church defender . . . He compiled facts and figures of the Welsh Church for the Church Congress at Truro, and the Warden proved a great help to him at this time. John Owen delighted in statistics, and found great joy in helping to sharpen his friend's weapons for active warfare, though he himself had to stay quietly by the school. Still later in the year, his friend, Mr Jayne, the Vicar of Leeds, became Bishop of Chester. Then the bishopric of St. Asaph fell vacant, and Mr Edwards himself was chosen to fill the vacancy.

Great was the enthusiasm at Llandovery when the new Bishop arrived early in 1889 to see the Warden. How the boys cheered him, giving him a rousing reception, which culminated in the granting of a whole holiday. They little guessed that in the study the new Bishop was pressing the Warden to come with him to North Wales as Dean of St. Asaph and his lieutenant: but so it was. Early in the summer the news was publicly announced, and the pride of the school was great when the Warden first donned his gaiters and apron. One young wag spread the mythical story round that he had gone to see the Warden, and had been met by the words, 'Go away little boy. I am a Dean now.' The words were true: his work as a schoolmaster was finished, but his work as a great Church leader was just beginning. Much later he was to come back to Llandovery as a Trustee, and to act in the same capacity for the rival school at Brecon. His loyalty would always be great and his recollection tender. At no official meeting at Christ's College, Brecon, whether Speech Day or more private occasion, would he omit to mention (even if it were in a loud aside), his connection with and his affection for Llandovery.

(The Welsh excerpt appeared in 'Y Llan' in 1922: it was reprinted in the School Journal, Summer 1978. The English account is form The Early Life of Bishop Owen by Eluned M. Owen M.A. (Oxon) 1958 reprinted here by kind permission of the publishers, Gomer Press.

John Owen (1854-1926) was born in Caernarfonshire, educated at Botwnnog grammar school and Jesus College Oxford having read Classics and Mathematics. He taught at Appleby grammar school, then in 1879 was appointed professor of Welsh at Lampeter. He was priested in 1880. He succeeded A. G. Edwards as Warden of Llandovery in 1885 and became Dean of St. Asaph in 1889: he returned to Lampeter as Principal in 1892 and was appointed Bishop of St. Davids in 1897. He retained, always, a lively interest in the School).

1890-1896

JOHN MORGAN

Petaswn i am wneud i'm gwrandawyr ieuainc oll wylltio, mi ddechreuwn drwy ddweud wrthynt fy mod i'n mynd i sôn am amser gorau eu bywyd! Ni bydd y bachgen cyffredin yn coelio peth fel yna: mae ganddo ormod o ddiddordeb yn y byd tuallan, y caiff gipolwg arno yn ystod ei wyliau. Ond bydd y rheini ohonom sy'n hŷn yn tueddu i edrych yn ôl ar ein dyddiau ysgol â math arbennig o hiraeth. Y pryd hwnnw yr oedd bywyd yn llai cymhleth o lawer, ac yn sicrach: y tu cefn i bawb yr oedd dau beth a ymddangosai mor gadarn â'r graig, sef y cartref a'r ysgol. Nid oedd fawr o newid ar y naill na'r llall. Yr oedd y ddau beth yno bob amser. Felly 'rwy'n siwr y maddeuwch imi os dywedaf ychydig wrthych am y blynyddoedd a dreuliais yng Ngholeg Llanymddyfri.

Cefais fy rhoi yn fy lle yn iawn pan ymwelais gyntaf â'r ysgol ac yr oedd hynny'n beth iachus iawn imi. Yr oeddwn wedi cynnig am ysgoloriaeth mewn mathemateg, ac, fel y lleill, cymerais yr holl bapurau a osodwyd. Nid oeddwn yn rhyw anfodlon iawn ar fy ngwaith: yn bur fuan dangosodd y Warden, Canon Owen Evans, yn eglur imi 'i bod hi'n annhebyg iawn y deuwn byth yn fathemategydd. ''Does dim synnwyr yn y peth,' medde fo'n blwmp ac yn blaen, ''Does gennych chi'r un *sum* yn gywir yn y papur Arithmetic; a 'does gennych ddim crap ar nac Algebra nac Euclid, ond mi gawsoch yr ysgoloriaeth arall, ac felly rhaid i chi gymryd honno neu fynd adref.' Cymerais hi: nid oeddwn am fynd adre'n waglaw a di-anrhydedd, ac felly o'r flwyddyn mil naw cant hyd mil naw cant a chwech bûm yn aelod o'r ysgol. Yr oedd rhai ohonom yn byw yn yr ysgol ei hun, rhai yn Llandingat House, rhai yn Prospect House, a rhai yn College House, ond i bwrpas gwaith a chwarae yr oeddem yn un gymdeithas. Am resymau amlwg, 'fedra'i ddim dweud llawer am y rhai a oedd yn fechgyn pan oeddwn innau'n fachgen. Mae'r rhan fwyaf ohonynt erbyn hyn—wel, yn 'hen a pharchus' ac ni chawn ddiolch ar eu llaw pe soniwn am eu triciau diniwed. Ond gallaf sôn am y wardeniaid a'r athrawon, mae hynny'n eitha' teg, ac ni allant hwy ddial arnaf yn yr hen ffordd arferol. 'Rwy'n cofio un tro ar y cae hoci i ben caled hogyn bach cydnerth daro yn erbyn gên athro chwe throedfedd o daldra a'i thorri hi: ni hoffwn ddweud ein bod ni'n gofidio oherwydd hynny. Gyda llaw, nid myfi oedd yn gyfrifol. Ond yr oedd gennym y parch mwyaf i ddynion fel Billy Richards a fedrai gynhyrchu'r peraroglau pereiddiaf a rhyfeddaf yn y *laboratory*, ac i Henry Knight a wnaeth ei orau i bwnio peth mathemateg i'n pennau. Un o'r pethau a fyddai'n rhoi difyrrwch parhaus inni oedd gorffen y brawddegau a adawsai Herbert Gregory, yn ddiffael, yn anorffenedig, a thrwy hynny byddem yn rhoi yn ei enau bethau na fyddai fo wedi breuddwydio am eu dweud. 'Fedra'i ddim gweld y Mikado heddiw heb feddwl am MacClellan a'i olew berwedig. Am y Wardeniaid, rhyw ffigurau olympaidd oeddyn' nhw: byddem yn gwneud ein gorau glas i'w hosgoi, ond heb lawer o lwyddiant. Yn fy amser i daeth y Canon Poole Hughes yno yn olynydd i Owen Evans, a chariwyd ei waith ymlaen wedyn gan y Canon Thomas ac yn awr gan y Warden presennol, Canon G. O. Williams. 'Rwy'n siwr mai gwaith di-ddiolch oedd ein dysgu, ac erbyn hyn, ar funud edifeiriol, mi hoffwn yn aml fod yn hogyn unwaith eto a mynd at bob un ohonynt a dweud 'Diolch i chi, Syr.'

(Broadcast in Children's Hour 9 December 1949 in the series 'Pan oeddwn fachgen'—'When I was a boy'. It was reprinted in the School Journal, Easter 1950.

John Morgan, 1886-1957, was the son of the Revd. John Morgan then Rector of Llandudno who had been Master of the National School at Llandovery before proceeding to Cambridge to read Mathematics and then returning to the priesthood in Wales, later to be appointed Archdeacon of Bangor. The younger John possessed a fine voice and became a scholar of Llandaff Cathedral School from where he entered Llandovery—hoping for a Mathematical scholarship but being awarded a Classical one! He proceeded to Hertford College Oxford, then to Cuddesdon. After ordination and Truro and an army chaplaincy he returned to Wales. In 1934 he was elected Bishop of Swansea and Brecon, translating to Llandaff in 1939. In 1949 he was enthroned 4th Archbishop of Wales).

1892-1908
[MASTERS]

A. Pierce Jones

The success of Llandovery on the academic side during the years 1892-1908 was largely due to a group of masters who served the school for many years. It was A. G. Edwards, afterwards Archbishop of Wales, who initiated the policy of securing the ablest possible men for the staff, and making it possible for those who were a success to remain. John Owen, his successor, afterward Bishop of St. David's, continued the policy, as did Owen Evans after him.

REV. E. J. McCLELLAN
In 1900 the second master was one of Edwards' appointments, the Rev E. J. McClellan. He was an old boy of St. Peter's, York, and like so many Northerners, had been to Queen's, Oxford, where he took a First in Classical Mods. and a Third in Greats. He taught at King Edward's, Birmingham, whence he came to Llandovery and stayed for 25 years. He taught Latin, Greek, and Scripture to the Lower Fifth, and Latin and Scripture to the Upper Fifth. He also worked in some English Literature in the Lower Fifth, and Latin Literature and some antiquities in the Upper Fifth . . .

As a master 'Mac' was a Holy Terror. A slightly built man, his discipline was iron. Burly school forwards shivered before him. His teaching was inspiring, and his humour in imparting knowledge removed from the work any sense of drudgery. He brought to the birth in many the love of the classics. It was his sound grounding that gained for Llandovery the reputation it had at Oxford, that while it was deficient in the finer points of scholarship, its more elementary work was exceptionally sound. Old Mac would have his Syntax learnt. He retired from teaching 1904. A photograph was taken of Mac's last Lower Fifth, in which appear T. W. Thomas, afterwards Warden, Seager Thomas, who achieved fame in forensic medicine, A. G. Prys-Jones, Inspector of Schools, L. V. D. Owen, a Professor of History, W. E. Rhydderch, now a Knight, with lesser lights including myself.

Warden and Masters 1903.
From the left.—First Row: Mr F. J. Newton, M.A.; Mr R. B. Calcott, B.A.; Mr Brabant, M.A.; Rev D. E. Roberts, B.A.; Mr F. Exton, M.A. Second Row: Mr H. H. Knight, M.A.; Rev E. J. MacLellan, M.A.; Rev W. W. Poole Hughes M.A. (Warden); Mr T. J. Richards, M.A.; Mr H. H. Gregory, M.A. Bottom Row: Mr Wilde, B.A. ; Mr J. H. Winter, B.A.

J. H. WINTER

A master who served the school for at least twenty years was John H. Winter. A Yorkshireman, and proud of it, he had been to St. John's College, Cambridge, and taken Honours in Mathematics; he had also studied music, singing bass in its famous choir. Only the boys at St. John's are on the foundation, the men's voices being supplied by undergraduates. What he had done before coming to Llandovery I do not know, nor do I know his age. We all looked upon him as old, and I note that Powys refers to him as the old music master. He taught maths. and various junior subjects for a full teaching week, only having, as other masters did, two free periods out of 28, when the junior school assembled for drill and drawing. In addition to this, he was for many years the College Housemaster. As music master, he taught the more advanced piano pupils, and trained the choir, playing the organ at Llanfair Church, where the school was responsible for Sunday Evensong during term. He also had to organise and work up the concerts, all this out of teaching hours. It will be seen then that he worked hard. His teaching of arithmetic was exceptionally good. His Yorkshire origin showed itself in his speech and his organ style and love of Handel. He did no voice training with the choir, but was thorough in his preparation of the Sunday's work. Under Owen Evans, who loved music and sang well, he was encouraged to have anthems, and we did three or four every term. Winter was a friendly man, he would help and advise anybody, and loved to discuss music with anybody who was interested. Winter was known as 'Johnny Book' (pronounced long, as such words as cook, look, etc. are pronounced in the North of England). For this reason he never used the word, always saying 'Shut your histories'; 'Open your grammars'; 'Watch your copies'; etc. He would drop into Yorkshire in condemning stupidity 'You Gowk' (Cuckoo), 'You silly galoot,' etc.

A. F. BARNES

Winter was succeeded by A. F. Barnes . . . A former Organ Scholar of Keble, he was a master of voice production. The choir was better under him than it ever was before. Owing to the function of the Opening of the New Buildings, there was no concert that year. He only remained three terms. He enjoyed teaching Maths. and English, but his real interest was in developing the musical side and using the undoubted talent there was. He was a humorist, and reasonably good cricketer.

J. S. HEAP

Barnes was succeeded by John Sebastian Heap (called 'Uriah' by his colleagues, but not by the boys). He was the son of a distinguished organist and had been Organ Scholar of Exeter College. He was a fine musician and often played his own compositions and improvisations. The occasion when he came out was the concert in 1904. The programme was admirably chosen, well within our capacity, and well rendered. From the moment he took the baton, Heap revealed himself as complete master. He departed the following Easter, I think to take over his father's work at Liverpool.

F. H. SMITH

F. H. Smith was not a university man but an ex-pupil of Ouseley at St. Michael's, Tenbury. He had also studied in Germany. He remained for several years. He was not an outstanding performer at any instrument, but he had a wide knowledge of music and considerable experience as a teacher. He taught excellently the organ, the piano, the violin, and solo singing.

T. J. RICHARDS

The science master, T. J. Richards, was a remarkable and mysterious man. He was like Melchizedek, in that he had, so far as anybody knew, no ancestry, and certainly no descendants. He merely appeared to do his work and disappeared behind his veil of mystery. He had been Postmaster of Merton and had taken three First Classes in Schools. He never conversed with anybody, and in his dealings with his pupils was a master of incisive speech. A spare, dry man, he always wore the same clothes, black jacket and striped trousers. His jacket and gown were more green than black. He had the reputation of being an authority on chess, botany, Shakespeare, and music. Undoubtedly a brilliant man, he sought no publicity, but lived in his own temple of the mind. With poor equipment, he produced scientists. He would seem to have been the Warden's staff officer; coping with the time-tables, lists of masters' duties, etc. In spite of his name, he was not Welsh; I am inclined to think, from the tones of his voice, he might have been Cornish. He had the reputation of being an agnostic, but I never heard that he ever discussed religion. Perhaps his religion was that of a sensible man, which, we are told, the sensible man keeps to himself. Was he entirely an intellectual machine? One fact about him shows he was not. He was in politics an incorrigible and prejudiced Conservative. Nothing that any other party could do was right, in his eyes. One is grateful for the touch of humanity there. He retired in 1908, and lived in Wilmington, Sussex, where he died . . .

H. H. KNIGHT

The senior mathematical master was H. H. Knight. A cousin of Knight of the Algebra, he had a brilliant Cambridge career by a Fellowship of Clare. A shy man, he would spot any boy with an aptitude for maths., and could pump maths. into him. The list of successes in that subject was impressive. He was, as Powys has written, a great botanist, specialising in mosses and brambles. It can never be known how many lives were saved by the results of his researches into mosses, some of which stop bleeding. He was one of the unknown great. He used to play football in his earliest years at Llandovery, and always helped up those whom he tackled, hoping they were not hurt. He once collided with a goal post, and humbly apologised to it. He still played cricket, always opening the innings for the masters. Once he was their top scorer. He could not play slow bowling. He helped Powys with his Field Society, and I think thoroughly enjoyed the tramps over the mountains with its senior members.

As Latin for night is Nox, by analogy the Latin for Knight must be Knox, and by that name he was known. Many a new boy innocently spoke of Mr

Knox. Once an entertainment was given in the town to raise funds for the restoration of Llandingat Church. The programme included the farce 'Box and Cox.' It ends with a message being received that the dispute between Box and Cox fell away, because 'she had married Knox.' *Both*: 'Three cheers for Knox.' The school rose and gave three rousing cheers for the old bachelor, to the bewilderment of the players, the unconcealed amusement of the staff, and the hardly successful unconcern of Mr Knight. He resigned in 1907 and lived in Cheltenham long enough to become an octogenarian.

HERBERT GREGORY

The remaining master of the group who served Llandovery for a score of years and over was H. Gregory. A little, highly-strung man, who walked rapidly with a staff jerky gait, he had gone from Manchester Grammar School to Magdalen, Oxford, where he took a second class in three Final Schools. No great disciplinarian, he retained the attention of his forms by making the work supremely interesting. Having heard the lesson set, he would then discourse on some historical or literary subject directly or indirectly arising out of it, which was of great educational value. He was easy money for mimics, but the mimicry of him impressed his sayings on the memory. His discourses seemed devoid of punctuation, sounding something like this. 'Edward did not wish merely to tyrannise over the Welsh he wanted them to stop fighting—Jones—and turn to something more profitable—Evans—so he encouraged them to use their mountains as pasture for sheep and as I see Parry is consulting his book he must write the lesson out three times, and he established markets for their wool etc.' Unlike his colleagues Knight and Richards he was talkative. He remained a Manchester Liberal, reading the Manchester Guardian all through every day, and sometimes contributing letters seasoned with Attic (or Oxford) salt. While he had his strong opinions, he would argue on any side of any subject. His moods varied between those of an Oxford man who had come from Manchester, and a Manchester man who had been to Oxford. He could soon spot a boy of promise. One morning in the Lower Vth a new boy arrived some time after the beginning of term. During that lesson Gregory put a question to test the intelligence of the form. It went round, and the boy gave a good answer. 'What's your name? You've got some brains.' That boy was L. V. D. Owen, whose brilliant career was recently recorded at his early death. Gregory occasionally took a term off, for his health, and he left in the middle of the Michaelmas term 1904 and did not return.

F. M. STENTON

F. M. Stenton was a brilliant historian, who had been near a Fellowship of All Souls, and was sent by the late Frank Morgan (O.Ll.), Tutor of Keble. He is happily still alive as Sir Frank Stenton, and is engaged on the history of the Parliaments. I will only say that I owe more to him than to any man under whom I have sat. His brilliance, his patience, his kindness and practical wisdom brought to birth and nurtured anything there is in me, and it is my sorrow that I have not more to show for it. When I think of those tranquil afternoons in the Library, as he criticised our essays and expounded political, social, and literary themes, I regard them as typical of the peaceful days before 1914 when the world blew up, since when nothing else seems to have gone right. He was a brilliant pianist, a composer in his spare time, and played the organ, though he had not gone far in this. His home was at Southwell, where he may have been chorister. He carried on the choir for a term, after Heap's departure, with John Morgan (the present Archbishop of Wales) as organist. He left, with Exton, at Easter, 1908.

THE BARON

A formidable master for nearly twenty years was R. Berkeley Calcott. He taught French from the 3rd Form upwards, and German to any who learnt it. He also taught Latin to those working for the London Matric. and history and geography to one of the junior forms. He had charge of Breakfast, and his formula at Grace was a standing joke. 'Those who were late this morning will write 100 lines from the reign of Henry VIII (or any monarch that occurred to him). For what we have received may the Lord make us truly thankful.' He was a good cricketer, and had charge of the cricket until the arrival of L. C. Powys to take over. Powys describes him as aristocratic, which indeed he was, in the best sense of the word. He was the kind of man who has made the name of England great all over the world. Strict, impartial, never unintentionally rude, furious at anything underhand, and somewhat unimaginative, he ran true to form as a well-born Englishman. The description of Dr Frederick Temple by a Rugby boy could be applied to him. 'A beast, but a just beast.' Out of school he was friendly, dignified, and a model of courtesy. Most of us valued, respected, and liked him. He was a man of the world. If he intended to sit on you, he gave you fair warning. If he threatened, he fulfilled his threat. On one occasion he found he had been unintentionally unjust, so he apologised to the boy in the presence of the form. He was for years housemaster at Llandingat House, where peace and order were maintained, and trespassers were hardly dealt with. He left during the First World War, having been for some years second master. He taught then at Blundell's and at Harrow, where he was so much liked that he was invited to join the permanent staff. How long he remained there I do not know. He was in 1935 living at Bath, and was an octogenarian.

There were several noteworthy masters who stayed for shorter periods. The Rev Thomas Nicklin was Sixth Form Classical Master for four years. First of all a priest. He became a distinguished theologian, and articles from his pen appeared in many of the theological journals. He became Warden of a Theological College at Manchester, and he died at over 80 years old, having been totally blind for years.

He was succeeded by G. F. Exton, about whom nothing need be added to what Powys has written about him. He was a brilliant and conscientious master, who interested himself in all that went on. Many successes were gained by his pupils, who remained his friends. In addition to his neatness, his not unkindly sarcasm, and his fine scholarship, he had perfect facial control, an invaluable gift of teaching. He left in 1908 for Cheltenham, where he died last year.

H. S. Brabant did much in various ways. He taught Maths. and other subjects in the middle and junior forms, and was a helpful teacher. He did much for the athletic sports, and would always give his time to organising informal hockey or Gym. when there was nothing arranged otherwise. He sang tenor in the choir, on which he was very keen. He left at Christmas 1901 for Wellington, where he remained until he retired.

A. J. Fenn was a good all-round man who was at Llandovery for about four years. He had distinct literary gifts, and contributed to the Journal.

L. C. Powys has written interestingly and adequately about himself in his book 'The Joy of It.' He threw himself whole-heartedly into his work. He encouraged the appreciation of good literature, and by his Field Society got many to share his love of Nature. An absolutely first-class cricketer, he did much here, but he did not remain long enough to see the fruits of his work. A succession of wet summers hampered the cricket.

He was succeeded by S. M. Toyne, who inherited the best XI I remember. But that summer was exceptionally wet. He only stayed a year, leaving to take a post at his old school Haileybury and later became Headmaster of St. Peter's, York. A fine man who only remained for one term was 'Dollie' Chambers. He took the chance of a post at his old school, Beford, but unhappily did not live very long.

Lastly, let me not forget Ifor Jones (O.Ll.). No intellectual giant, he was a thoroughly good sort, if ever there was one. He was everybody's friend. He played football long past the customary retiring age for that game, and never tired of expounding it. He coached the juniors at cricket, and organised the O.Ll. Society. He left in 1914 for a small parish near Brecon, and during the war began to teach at Christ College, where he continued for many years. He died about two years ago.

G. K. Chesterton wrote: *'We may not remember what we were taught at school, but we never forget those who taught us.'*

(School Journal May 1957. On A. Pierce-Jones see infra.)

1893

ERNEST JONES

When I entered Llandovery College sixty-one years ago, in January, 1893, there had recently been a change in the Wardenship. The previous Warden, the famous John Owen, who later became Bishop of St. Davids, had recently left, but many tales of him lingered. Because of his apparent predilection for 'the poor little man from Joppa' he was always called Joppa himself. His successor was of a different type and a good deal less popular. Being a Canon of the Church he was naturally christened 'Pistol'. He did not seem to find it easy to gain our confidence and with boys, as well as with men, this is an all-important matter. The new Warden, Owen Evans, was the only Welshman on the large staff and his influence was used strongly in favour of Anglicising the school and bringing it into line with the great English public schools. In his time Llandovery was well in the front rank in the numbers of passing the School

Certificate, but this prowess was achieved by getting the same boys to take the examination over and over again, a practice not followed by our English rivals.

The senior master, the Rev E. J. McClellan, was an excellent teacher of Latin, for which I have had cause to be grateful. Another good teacher was T. J. Richards, the science master. I can remember his announcing to us the news of Lord Rayleigh's discovery of argon in the atmosphere, one which had unexpected consequence later. He was not strict, but so serious that there was always perfect discipline when he took Prep . . . I have often wondered why. Another master, less successful in that respect, was Andrews, a Senior Wrangler, who was kind but humourless. When he called out: 'Cachinnation must cease in the north-east corner of the hall' the scene that ensued was the reverse of what he hoped for. Then there were the two brothers Chapman who ascribed all our shortcomings to our nationality. If only we would try to get over being Welsh and behave properly as all English boys did all would be well. I need hardly say that no Welsh was taught in the school, although one patriotic boy used to go to the town to take lessons from the local curate. It was a deficiency for which I have never ceased to blame my old school, and I am glad to hear it has long since been remedied. There was one other reproach I have subsequently thought of: that we were never told anything about the extraordinarily interesting part of Llandovery played in both Roman and Norman times; I am sure it would have heightened our local patriotism, for Brecon was far behind in those respects. And what about Twm Shôn Catti?

In my time the prizes were always distributed by Sir James Hills-Johnes of Dolaucothi . . . Sir James had won the V.C. in the Crimean War, a hundred years ago now, and that gave him a special claim to our respect.

What I most enjoyed in my school days were the unusually beautiful surroundings of Llandovery, in which it is blessed above any other school I know. It is a feature which, with a certain type of boy, parents may well bear in mind when choosing a school. Then there was the river itself with its delicious bathing, masters and boys entirely naked, and the terrific swimming tests upstream to the bridge. Much could be done with that river. In one hot summer I resolved single-handed to dam it and make it into a reservoir. I got as far as the last two feet, but never managed to close the final gap. There were two exceptionally cold winters in my time, and I doubt if the feat of skating on the river from Llandovery to Llangadog has been repeated since. I did not think then that half a century later I should write the standard work on Figure Skating, the impetus to which must have dated from those days.

Llandovery was then the nursery of International Rugbyians. They usually graduated via Oxford. I wonder if the name of the great Conway Rees is still remembered in the annals of Rugby. What stays in my mind as a personal reminiscence is an occasion when I tackled his younger brother who defended himself by thrusting a finger in my eye, which brought me two days as a hero in the sanatorium.

Of the schoolfellows in my form, several of whom have subsequently had distinguished careers, I have a vivid memory but I will mention here only two of them. One was a remarkable youth, H. R. V. Ball (how well one remembers initials). At our entrance examination for scholarships he came first, winning one for £25 a year; I got the second one for £15. Six months later we passed the equivalent of the School Certificate examination when he obtained the then unprecedented number of eight distinctions. We were friends and used to go for walks together. He always seemed to be in the clouds and I remember coming to the conclusion that he must always be thinking of his mother; I knew he had no father. He later had a very distinguished educational career and I met him not many years ago at a Llandoverian dinner, shortly before his death. To my astonishment he could not recollect my existence nor that of any boys in our form. Then he said casually that the first thirty years of his life seemed to have been passed in a dream and that he had only vague memories of them. He added: 'It was only then, when my mother died and I got married, that I seemed to wake up.' The story is meant to reflect on my acumen on psychology, which has been my life's work.

The other friend, with which I am still in contact, was Arthur Davies, who attained a high position in the Treasury. I had spent a year doing nothing but mathematics in the hope of winning a scholarship to Cambridge, but my patience gave out and I changed over to the University of London where one could begin one's medical studies at the age of sixteen instead of eighteen. So we worked together for a year studying for the London Matriculation. Arthur came out sixth in Honours in the whole Kingdom, while I had to be content with a mere first class. He also repeated Ball's performance of two years earlier in the School Certificate.

I often pass through Llandovery on my way from England to my little home in Gower, but I have only visited the College once since leaving it. I was interested in the enormous improvements and additions that had been made in the fifty years since I left, but I was sad to see that the studies in the Tower were considered no longer safe to be used. One could descend from them along a rope and gather mushrooms in the dawn, which were then cooked over a fish-jet gas flame. Climbing up again was of course arduous.

I will end again on the note of how lucky Llandovery boys are to be educated in such wonderful surroundings. In later days I have explored many of them by car and think I was the first to make the perilous journey in that fashion (frequently aided by planks) from Cilycwm to Abergwesyn where the inhabitants refused to believe my story. Perhaps now they had a road where there was once hardly a track.

(School Journal March 1954: Dr Ernest Jones who died in 1958 aged 79 was the leading British psycho-analyst of his day; he enjoyed an international reputation. He was born in Loughor. After Llandovery at the age of 21 he qualified as a doctor in London, winning a gold medal for both his M.B. and later M.D. degrees. He was a life-long friend of Sigmund Freud and one of his staunchest defenders. Ernest Jones had been Professor of Psychiatry at Toronto 1908-1913: he returned to Britain to devote his time to the study at practice of psycho-analysis. His first wife whom he married in 1917 was the distinguished Welsh composer, singer and pianist Morfydd Llwyn Owen 1891-1918. In a tribute to Ernest Jones in 1958 Dr Gwent Jones remarked '. . . he was never without his Old Llandoverian tie of which he was immensely proud. Nor would he ever miss the opportunity "to talk Llandovery", ancient and modern, for he regarded his entry to Llandovery College as the turning-point of his early life.')

1893-1901

K. F. McMurtrie

I was at Llandovery from 1893 till 1901 and was head prefect 1900-1901. First I was in the Tower dormitory and one of the other boys with me there was Ken Oliver Carter (known as Kenobler) who is now a Catholic Missionary in India and still corresponds with me. Later I was in Emlyn House and then Llandingat House and later still back in the College. In Form 5 my bugbear subject was

History in which I always did badly though I did make an attempt to succeed. One day when I had done particularly badly the History Master—Mr Gregory (known as 'Gracchi')—told me that at the end of the hour I must accompany him to the Warden's study. Mr Gregory stated his case against me to the Warden (Canon Owen Evans) and retired. Of course I expected the Warden to pitch into me, but to my delighted amazement he said, 'Well, McMurtrie, I see that you have no taste for History and I also know that you have a real aptitude for Science. I shall therefore arrange that for the future when the other boys attend the History hour, you will work in the Chemistry Laboratory on your own.'

I could hardly believe my ears on hearing this good news, and my respect for the Warden, which had never been small, was enormously increased. In my first years at Edinburgh University I gained a medal for Chemistry without doing a stroke of work at that subject—the grounding I had been given at Llandovery by Mr Richards ('Billy Dick'), the science master, had been so excellent. My chief and happiest recollections are of the time after I had become head prefect and had charge of the Gwent dormitory with its twenty-two boys. I took a very fatherly interest in that fine set of boys, an interest which showed itself partly in the presentation of a very large cake occasionally, also in giving readings after the boys were in bed and before putting out the light. I remember that one book I read to the boys in this way was 'Dr Jekyll and Mr Hyde.' Another memory of the Gwent dormitory is of how I woke in the middle of one night to hear the sound of water dripping from the ceiling. A water pipe had burst above the ceiling. I went off to the bedroom of the house master, Mr Winter ("Johnny Buke") who slept in a distant room above the Reading Room of those days. Mr Winter was—as often—somewhat *hors de combat* and welcomed my suggestion that he need not disturb himself if he would give me leave to go down to College House and get hold of the manservant Daniel who alone knew how to turn off the water supply to the leaking pipe. At College House I could arouse no one with my rappings on doors and windows, but happily I found one window which was not keyed and I was able to open the top part of that window and climb inside. After a search I found Daniel who returned with me and did the necessary hydraulic performance. Even if I had not found on the following day, that my action had won some kudos for myself, I should have been quite satisfied with the enjoyment of the adventure.

I was still presiding in the Gwent Dormitory when—at the time of the Boer War—the news of the relief of Makeking reached us one night after we were all in bed. The intense joy among masters and boys was so unlimited that the masters made no attempt to control the actions of the boys and we all trooped off, in our night attire, and paraded the streets of Llandovery singing and shouting. The Warden (Canon Owen Evans) was extremely patriotic and was determined to hear all war news as early as possible. There was no 'wireless' in those days, but all who were prepared to pay a reasonable sum to the Post Office could receive copies of all press telegrams of war news as they arrived. The Warden suggested that the School Reading Room should finance the scheme of procuring these telegrams for the school and they were posted up regularly near the School Hall. I remember once how the Warden asked me to tell him what was the consensus of opinion of the boys as to the implication of a certain telegram which arrived. I managed to give some fairly satisfactory answer, but I felt that the boys were more concerned about forming a consensus of opinion about the prospects in next Saturday's Rugby match than about the latest war news!

I was head prefect when Canon Owen Evans resigned and the Revd. Poole Hughes became the new Warden. I had a tremendous admiration for the new Warden who had come from being a Senior Master at Sherborne. My admiration was not quite shared by all my fellow prefects, some expressed forcibly their opinion that Sherborne ideas and methods should not be introduced at Llandovery. One of my fellow prefects was particularly hostile towards some of the ideas of the new Warden, and in consequence he and I became decidedly hostile towards each other. I remember how when I left school that particular prefect told me that if he ran across me again in later life he would manage to get his revenge on me. We have never met again, and even if we should do so now I imagine that in 50 years his ire would have had time to cool down.

One of my most vivid recollections is about my attempt to enforce a certain amount of discipline in my capacity as head prefect. Occasionally in the absence of a master I took charge of the boys during evening Preparation and at meal times. At supper time the boys at the junior tables often became rather noisy and disorderly and it was my duty to get up from the head prefect's chair and walk up to the noisy area and pick out one or two victims to come to the prefects' room after supper. It was an unheard of thing for a prefect to have to deal with boys at the senior tables. But one day at supper a senior boy did become (not for the first time) decidedly rowdy. I walked up to him and requested him to come to the prefects' room after supper. In the silence that followed this unprecedented step one could have heard a pin drop. After supper the whole school stood still watching the rowdy boy and myself proceed up the staircase and to the prefects' room. Apparently they thought I would deal with the senior boy as if he were a junior. I have always been a slow thinker, but the right thought did come quickly into my head on this occasion. It was a cold wintry night and there was a lovely fire in the prefects' room. I picked out the most comfortable chair set in on one side of the fireplace and asked the boy to sit there. I took a chair on the other side of the fireplace and we had a little friendly chat about a prefect's difficult job to keep order if boys did not co-operate with him. I quite won his heart, and we became good friends. He not only gave me no further trouble but he was one of my great supporters in maintaining discipline from that day forwards.

I was always very poor at athletics. Once, and once only, I was picked to play for the second XV in a Rugby match, more on account of my *avoirdupois* in the scrum than for any skill in my play. I well remember how I had to apply to Mr Richards in the Chemistry Lab. for permission to go out of school early to get ready for the match. He was a very silent man but his raised eyebrows and amused smile spoke volumes. I did once win a prize (2nd) in the mile and a 3rd prize in a cross-country run. But I did some good long walks on whole holidays (usually St. David's Day). Once I walked with two masters to the top of the Van Mountain. I remember the walk very well but I am ashamed to say that I remember even more vividly the simply marvellous supper which I enjoyed with the masters on our return to College House. But my record walk was to Lampeter College and back (42 miles if my memory is not at fault) on one St. David's Day. My companion was H. S. Vinning, who was a talented organist, and, I believe, became a master at Eton later on. I loved to act as organ-blower for Vinning when he practised on the fine organ at Llandingat Church.

Such are some of my happy memories of life at Llandovery.

(School Journal May 1957. Dr Kenneth McMurtrie was born in 1881. From Llandovery he proceeded to Edinburgh University and qualified M.B., Ch.B. In 1908 he was the first medical missionary to be sent out by the College of St. Luke and worked with the Society of St. John the Evangelist in Griqualand East. He remained in Africa until his death—noted in the Journal of 1975. He had kept contact with the Revd. A. Pierce Jones of Cape Town, a contemporary of his at Llandovery.

On 27 October, 1900 he had read a paper on 'Modern Theory about Ghosts' to the School Literary and Debating Society).

1898

THE TOWNEE

Dear Mr Editor,

They call me a 'Townee' but I don't mind; I'm as good as any of them. I was at the school myself once—for two terms. My father took me away because they would teach me Latin Prose. He said there was no money in Latin Prose. He's a clever man—my father. So he put me into business in the town. No, I'm not going to say what the business is—but it don't disturb my digestion like Latin Prose did. The boys at the school now are a poor lot. There's only a few of them that shave. In my time all the Sixth had razors and one of them waxed his moustache, but the only chap now who could wax his moustache is not in the Sixth. Yes, they're a poor lot; so haughty and exclusive, you know. There's a boy they call 'The Robin' or some name like that—well since they made him a prefect, he's too proud to be seen walking down Buck Street with me—if I'm smoking a clay pipe. So I got a briar, but even now he walks on ahead if he sees a master coming. Beastly side I call it. Sometimes of a Sunday evening I go and sit on the window sill of that house in the corner, and listen to the conversation inside. What rot those chaps do talk. Once I tried to join in the conversation, but they were very rude to me. A chap named Twm actually told me that if he'd a face like mine he'd send it out to the heathen, and then there was a great roar of laughter. There was a fellow there called Handel Jones—with a laugh like a drunken hyena. I'd have given him a licking, only they told me he comes from the Rhondda. But it's all beastly exclusiveness. Why, I've a lot better time than they have. I can stand all day in front of the 'Queen's Arms' with my hands in my pockets if I like. Even a chap in the Modern Vth couldn't do that. I can go down to the cricket matches and smoke on the pitch, which even a prefect daren't do. I never take any notice of a master when I meet him, to show my independence. When I go to Llanfair Church in the evening I talk as loud as I like; while if poor old what's-his-name—that boy in the football team—tries to do it they shove him in detention. O lor, yes, I've a much better time than they, and just wait and see how I'll come out at the Jubilee. I've got a new tie and a new waistcoat and a new pipe and I'll be there.

Look out for me.

I am, Mr Editor,
Yours very truly,
THE TOWNEE

(From The Llandovery School Tatler No. 2 Vol 1. July 1898 reprinted in School Journal November 1969. However much "Townee" felt that 'The boys at the school now are a poor lot', the London Daily News of Wednesday, July 20, 1898, notes its distinguished academic results—bracketed with Winchester: in the editor's words 'the striking success of Llandovery, a School of only 160 boys').

High Street, Llandovery 1903

1899-1948

T. WALKER THOMAS

In 1899 on the advice of Watcyn Morgan, later Dean of St. Davids, my parents decided to send me to Llandovery. My first impression was not favourable because all the windows carried heavy iron bars. However I settled down and played for the School for three years in rugby and cricket. In 1907 I applied for entry to Corpus Christi College, Oxford, where I read for Honour Moderations and Classical Finals. I spent a fifth year at Oxford reading Theology, before going to Pembroke Dock as junior curate to the late Bishop Prosser. In my second year in the parish, Canon Poole Hughes and his brother called to see if I would like to join the staff at Llandovery in the place of Ivor Jones who had been appointed to the living of Llyswen. In March 1914 after an interview at Camarthen I was appointed by General Sir James Hills Johnes V.C., Chairman of Trustees and the Warden to a post on the Phillips Trust.

In my first term as a master at Llandovery the School was served by a very fine staff: Berkely Calcott who taught French and German, a disciplinarian, who after twenty years at Llandovery went on to Blundells and Harrow, Atkins, Senior Maths Prizeman at Oxford, A. P. Williams later Headmaster of Cowbridge Grammar School. Hewlett, Tilly, Lockyer and Matheson are some of those I can still recall.

The School at this time had about 135 boarders and a dozen or more day boys. The rugby and cricket teams were good and there were promising boys in the Sixth Form. Everything seemed to be running smoothly . . . and then, during the Summer holidays, the 1914 War broke out. Three masters promptly enlisted and I was summoned by telegram to be told where my duty lay. Conditions deteriorated and replacements could not be found and so the Warden engaged two Sixth Form boys, D. R. Williams and T. H. W. Hill to help with the teaching. In the following years they were the mainstay of the School.

In the meantime I tried to get my release from the Chairman of Trustees and was told to do what the Warden required. Some time later Bishop Owen summoned me to the Palace and at the end of a long interview told me that 'one man could not save the Empire but that one man could save the School'. However, I decided to go my own way and enlisted in the Honourable Artillery Company. After the war I could have returned to Llandovery but I felt that the wiser course would be to seek experience in English schools. In 1919 Greek was made an optional subject for entry to Oxford and so I decided to go to the University in Paris to work on French and Phonetics. I was then appointed to a post at Cranleigh School in 1921.

In July 1928 Canon Poole Hughes died after a long illness. He had been Warden for twenty-seven years and during that time he had instilled discipline and pride in the School. The New Buildings were opened in 1902, the Gymnasium was built and the Laboratory was given by his friend Mr Benjamin Evans. This period was critical for the School. Properties like the cricket ground, Bank House, Cerrig Cottage and Llandingat House, vital to the development of the School were being put on the market. Miss Thomas, Llwynmadoc, granted a mortgage but unfortunately died soon afterwards and the executors called in the money. The other Trustees were not interested but allowed £500 given by Mr James, Llwynjack, to be used for the cricket ground. Fortunately the Warden was in a position to buy the properties with the intention of selling them to the School at cost price, plus legal expenses.

When I entered the School in 1899 the buildings were quite inadequate. To increase classroom space Bishop Owen had been allowed to use the capital of the Blaenos Scholarship to build the block which contained the Reading Room and three small classrooms. Buildings ended at the Reading Room and at the Masters' Common Room facing New Road. Chemistry was taught in the Classroom Changing Room. By 1907 the School had a new gymnasium and a laboratory, but they were devoid of equipment. Boarders were housed in the School, Llandingat, College House, Emlyn House and with the Second Master, the Reverend E. J. Maclellan in Prospect House (now Lloyd's Bank).

When Canon Poole Hughes died in 1928 the Trustees owned the School buildings and half the football field together with a debt of about £700 on their fund. The only other assets were a War Memorial Fund of £900 in the National Provincial Bank dating from the 1914 War, and an income from endowments of £700 for repairs. The new Warden would have to buy all the contents and equipment necessary for the working of the School and pay a rental of 5% on the playing fields and other property belonging to Mrs Poole Hughes. The Clerk was instructed, but he never drew up his agreement, and died soon afterwards.

The list of applicants for the wardenship was reduced to three and with some difficulty Bishop Prosser got the Trustees to meet on August 19. The other two candidates would not consider the appointment when they heard the conditions: one described it as a gamble. I had been chosen as their candidate by the Old Boys at a meeting in Cardiff and relying on their support I decided to accept. Owing to the delay in appointing a new warden and the fact that Llandingat was not ready until September 1st for Mrs Poole Hughes to move in, there was very little time to prepare for the opening of the School on September 14. The difficulties were greater because there was an increase in the number of boarders.

On arriving in Llandovery my first task was to re-furnish the Senior dormitory and to commence work on the sanitary arrangements. The existing system could have been condemned at any time. This work was completed during my first term. The lighting was also very poor. The pipes in the Old Buildings were badly corroded and leaking and the fittings were all out of date. These were taken out and replaced. A few years later electricity was brought to Llandovery and all the School buildings were provided with electric lights.

It was also found necessary to take out *all* the windows on the front of the Old Buildings and the Tower because the wood had perished. They were replaced with Criltal steel frames, lead flashings were put on the School Hall in place of zinc and the lead valley above Classroom dormitory was also renewed. In the same year the School Hall, Gwent Classroom and part of Tower dormitory were re-floored. A few years later new desks were placed in nearly all classrooms.

The bathing arrangements were also very unsatisfactory. Baths were scattered in different parts of the buildings. Owing to the length of piping most of the heat was lost. If boys were drawing hot water in the New Buildings, the Old Buildings could not get any. I got the approval of the Trustees to convert the old dining hall into a bathroom with fifteen showers and eight baths with the boiler house next door. This was working well when I left in 1948.

In the meantime difficulties of a different nature had arisen. A week after I had paid for the furniture and equipment Professor W. J. Gruffydd of the university in Cardiff made a vicious attack on the School and the Western Mail gave it full coverage on the front page under the heading: 'Immoral use of endowments at Llandovery College'. Questions were asked in Parliament and the Ministry of Education arranged for the Chief Inspector to check annually on the teaching of Welsh. Thomas Phillips, the founder, had been a prime mover in establishing St. David's College, Lampeter, to provide bilingual clergy for the Church in Wales. After a disagreement he decided to found a school to carry out this work and also to provide an education which would fit pupils for other walks in life. Welsh was made compulsory for one hour a day. The revenue of the Trust was allocated to masters as follows: Classics £200, Maths £150, Science £140, Writing £8.8.0, the Warden £135 and a house with the profits from pupils' fees with £5 for repairs. The scheme was not a success from the outset. Parents were sending their sons to English schools. In 1875 when Archbishop Edwards was appointed warden there were three boarders and twenty-seven boys in lodgings in the town. Ten years later by concentrating on subjects required for university scholarships, he had raised the numbers to one hundred and eighty seven. This policy was followed by the wardens in later years. I was sent to Llandovery because it was a Welsh school, and relatives had gone there since 1848. I considered that parents, who paid fees, had a right to decide, but I made provision for those who wished to learn Welsh by appointing a master who had specialized in Welsh at the university in Aberystwyth and had taken his M.A. degree. The Chief Inspector was satisfied and I gathered that Professor Gruffydd felt that I had done more than he had expected.

At the outset of my career I realised that, if we were to keep the teaching staff, it was necessary to institute a *salary scale*. My experience at the end of my first year was evidence of this. More than half the staff were planning to move on. Their contract had ended with the death of the Warden and the delay in making a new appointment to September 1st had left them in suspense. Moreover, owing to the fact that we were not entitled to take part in the Government Pension scheme, the scale had to be better than that laid down by the Burnham Committee.

In my second year the Great Depression hit the School. The entry dropped and so many parents had a financial interest in the coal trade that in one term more than forty parents gave notice that they would have to remove their sons. About twenty of them asked if I would take a provisional notice: if they did not lose their post, the boys would return. The number of boarders dropped to less than one hundred in 1933 and then picked up steadily.

I accepted the post of Warden in the belief that I could get the support of Old Llandoverians. I had spent eight years at Llandovery as a boy and three as a master. To stimulate their interest in Llandovery and restore their confidence in the future I suggested to the Trustees than an *Old Llandoverian Trust* should be formed to control the playing fields and other properties which were being bought by the subscription of Old Llandoverians from Mrs Poole Hughes. For my part, I undertook to put Cerrig Cottage and Bank House in a good state of repair with modern conveniences and to pay £150 a year in lieu of rent.

When I arrived in 1928 the sole adornment of the school consisted of portraits of Thomas Phillips (Founder) and John Jones (Cefnfaes) in the Dining Room . . . and rugby and cricket photographs. I was able to buy some original paintings and many Medici reproductions of good paintings. The result was that friends of the school gave some good pictures—Sir Charles Venables Llewelyn, Lady Peel of Danyrallt, Captain Crawshay, Mrs Poole Hughes, Mrs Thomas, Cilgwyn . . . and the Old Llandoverians.

In these early years, the laboratory was equipped to enable boys to take the Higher Certificate or First M.B. in Chemistry, Physics and Biology. Two pairs of oak doors for the Tower Entrance, an oak staircase and panelling in place of the old which had become dangerous, an archway leading to the cap room were some of the improvements. Central heating was also installed in the New Buildings.

In 1932-3 Bishop Prosser (Old Llandoverian), who had already given £2,000 to endow scholarships, generously provided the money for building a School Chapel and placing a reredos behind the altar. Other Old Llandoverians readily responded to the appeal for money for the furniture which cost about £1,500. I was responsible for the central heating and I was able to secure a good organ for the chapel. It was built under the direction of Colonel Dickson of St. Bees, consultant to Westminster Abbey when the new organ was installed there. Before the dedication, two of my friends, Dr J. Lloyd Davies and Dr T. W. David offered to join me in providing new Entrance Gates. Judge Frank Davies found the gates for us.

In 1933-4 the Tower Studies were re-floored with new joists and boards, the tower was re-pointed and repaired by a Cardiff firm and the rest of the front re-pointed by a local mason. The stone was porous, but by treating it with a waterproofing liquid every three years it was possible to retain the natural colour of the stone. Unfortunately the War intervened.

At the time of my appointment in 1928 Mr F. W. Gilbertson prepared a report for the Trustees on the 'Playing Fields'. In his view 'the ground beyond the boundary of the Old Cricket Ground was of little value for agriculture and of no value for schoolwork'. In 1937-9 two men with a truck and rails filled two river beds and doubled the size of the cricket ground. The next step was to build a new pavilion. Major J. R. Jacob gave £50 and Mrs Jacob presented the clock. A few Old Llandoverians sent subscriptions, but they were left in the Old Llandoverian Trust Account in case of emergency.

In 1936 I appointed a P.T. instructor and set up a miniature shooting range in the Gymnasium. The necessary equipment for gymnastics and boxing was provided. A year later, thanks to the help given by Brigadier Evans, we were able to start the O.T.C. The Officer Commanding Brecon Barracks sent the R.S.M. and several instructors to get the contingent into shape. A. Pryse Davies was the first O.C. and when he rejoined the Army, the Sergeant Instructor had been recalled as a reservist, D. W. Pye took over the command and carried out the work of commanding and instructing all through the war with very good results.

In 1936 the stone flags were removed from the corridor in the private house and replaced by oaks boards.

When I had been Warden for ten years the Trustees, in 1938, invited the Ministry of Education to make a full inspection of the School. Their report was very favourable. The School had a good staff and we had survived the Depression. Our numbers were steadily increasing.

In 1937-8 nearly all the classrooms were furnished with new desks and the Old Llandoverian Society had bought the land and trees on the far side of the river. Most of the material needs of the School had been met, but to secure a stable teaching staff it was necessary to have a pension scheme. The Trustees approved of the suggestion of an Insurance Policy providing £200 a year at the age of sixty.

When I had been ten years at Llandovery the Inspector of Taxes informed the Accountant that he was going to tax improvements made during that time. A barrister was employed to take up the matter with the Treasury. The verdict was that 'they were penalising a man for trying to do his work properly' and that I could spend on the School without being taxed.

Then came the 1939 War. The School was put on the list of Emergency Hospitals and we were liable to be turned out on very short notice. Many of the masters were called up for military service, the domestic staff disappeared and we had to depend on married women and boys who volunteered to help at meals. It was almost impossible to buy books and rationing caused extra work and anxiety. Owing to the 'black-out' epidemics broke out in 1939 and I had to send the boys home at half-term and re-pay the fees.

In my early years I had appealed to Old Llandoverians for £5,000 to form a Reserve Fund and if they did this I would hand over to the Phillips Trustees all the furniture and equipment of the School. The response was disappointing. During the Depression well disposed Old Llandoverians were short of ready money and unsure of the future. There were others. The Reverend A. Pierce Jones appointed himself spokesman and informed Old Llandoverians at a Whitsun meeting that he and his friends were afraid that they would be putting money in the pocket of the Warden, if they contributed. It was an interesting point of view seeing that he had spent nine years at Llandovery at a cost of ten shillings a week to his widowed mother and, in the last three had practically individual attention, in the History VIth, from Stenton, later Professor of History at Reading.

During the war it was almost impossible to get materials or skilled labour and so I had to give up all idea of further improvements. I set aside the money to build a fund to meet any emergency and make it easier for my successor to take over the School. Such an emergency arose after the war when Mrs Poole Hughes decided to sell Llandingat House. On the evidence of her solicitor, A. W. Andrews (Old Llandoverian) she agreed to sell it to the School at cost price plus legal expenses. With the help of a legacy of £90 from Gower Griffiths (O.Ll) I bought Llandingat and invested it in the Phillips Trust. Urgent repairs were carried out and furniture provided so that it could take a master and about twenty-five boarders.

In my last year the Trustees decided to accept six 'bursars' a year from the County Council and left it to me to draw up an agreement on the conditions with H. Wyn Jones (O.Ll), Director of Education. We chose the first six bursars and I believe that the scheme has been a success. In this year it was found necessary to raise the fees from £81 to £90 a year to meet the rising costs in wages and salaries. This was the first increase since the 1914 War.

As I planned to retire in 1948 I transferred to the Phillips Trust (various accounts) and the furniture and equipment of the School.

I wish to convey my sincere thanks to all the masters who served the School loyally during these difficult years in and out of School hours, and especially to T. H. W. Hill, T. P. Williams, R. N. Dore and in my last years C. Bell.

(These notes were written by Canon Walker Thomas in June 1971: they were 'in response to a suggestion made by the late Archdeacon Tree and recently by Mr D. Joshua Evans J.P., that I should write an account of the years I spent at Llandovery and especially of the years 1928-1948 when I was Warden . . . The Old Llandoverian leaflets and the School magazine have recorded the achievements of boys' in school work and games and in their careers after leaving School, but there was no record of the changes and developments which took place in the buildings and properties of the School. Dates and minor details have grown dim with the passing years, but I can claim that, on the whole, it is an accurate account'.

T. W. Thomas was educated at Llandovery College, Corpus Christi College Oxford and the Sorbonne in Paris. He was ordained deacon in 1912 and priested in 1913. He was Curate of Pembroke Dock 1912-1914, Assistant Master Llandovery 1914-1919, Assistant Master St. John's Leatherhead 1919-1920, St. Peter's Radley 1920-1921, Cranleigh School 1921-1928 and Warden of Llandovery College 1928-1948. He was made Canon of St. Davids Cathedral in 1940. His widow, the late Mrs Marjorie Walker Thomas left a substantial bequest to the College).

Canon and Mrs Walker Thomas

1901

A. PIERCE JONES

It was a cold grey January day when a group of us arrived from North Wales at 5 p.m. wondering very much what we should find in the person and doings of a new Warden. As we came to the foot of the stairs we met him, and saw the strongly built figure and napoleonic head of W. W. Poole Hughes for the first time. He spoke to us, shaking hands with our senior Hugh Morris (killed at Trones Wood, 1915) and saw that there was tea for us. The group included John Morgan, now Archbishop of Wales. At 8.30 the new Warden came in for prayers, and was received with a long round of hand-clapping as a welcome. One change was evident at once. We stood in silence for prayers. The previous Warden, Archdeacon Owen Evans, when he took evening prayers, used to intone versicles and collects to which we responded in like manner, and led us in singing the Nunc Dimittis.

As we were preparing for bed in the dormitory, we heard the Llandingat bell begin to toll for the death of the aged Queen Victoria, and felt that a new era had begun indeed, not for the school only, but for the world.

There had been much sadness at the departure of the old Warden. He was a capable but unassuming man, with rather a stern face and a strong voice, which concealed the kindest of kind hearts. He was not the orthodox headmaster, keeping as he did somewhat in the background. But he knew everything that went on. His policy seemed to be to give masters and prefects their head, trusting them to do their best. My impression is that his trust was generally justified. The masters were an able set of men, some of whom had been there for many years, two in fact having been on the staff when the new Warden was still a boy at the school. The management of games was left to the School Committee, under the chairmanship of the second master. The domestic side was under the management of the Warden's sister, Miss May Evans, affectionately known (behind her back) as Auntie May. She had become engaged to be married to Lincoln Lewis (O.Ll.), and the prospect of carrying on without her was a problem to the Warden which was solved by the Bishop of St. David's, his predecessor, appointing him Vicar of St. Peter's, Carmarthen, and Archdeacon. The news was known before the Warden announced it at prayers, and the vocal expression of sorrow at the announcement and the Warden's reasons for regretfully laying down his burden made a scene which remains in my memory. The relationship of the Warden and the boys was patriarchal. Towards the end of the term we were entertained to tea, when presentations were made to the Warden and his sister, and a sincere and eloquent tribute was paid to them by the Head Prefect, K. McMurtie (now a doctor practising in Zululand).

The new Warden lost no time in establishing himself. If he had any inward doubts of his ability to govern, he showed none. There was an instant tightening up all round. Undoubtedly there was need for this in many respects. The old Warden had broken down during his last term, under the strain of the problems to which I alluded, and was laid low with severe lumbago. He was absent from duty for some weeks, and was probably not fully restored afterwards. There were one or two curious features in the school life, and my impression, for what a small boy's impressions were worth, was that in some respects things were better managed at Friars School under Glyn Williams than at Llandovery.

The immediate changes were—everybody went to bed earlier, the juniors immediately after supper, and others correspondingly earlier; the tolerance of lateness at breakfast once a week ceased, every such offence being punished; all the masters now attended morning prayers, and went at once to their classrooms. Before, the masters went to their classrooms after not attending prayers, and their punctuality depended largely upon their personal habits. Tea now preceded afternoon school during the winter months, so that football was played every afternoon. Previously, junior games were played from 12.15 till dinner at 1.15. Morning school was now from 9.15 instead of 9, and break lasted 15 minutes instead of 10. Attendance at tea and supper was now compulsory. Lastly, Wednesday afternoon detention was abolished. The Warden took charge of all discipline, and offenders' names were written in a book which was taken round during last morning period with the absentee book, by the prefect on duty.

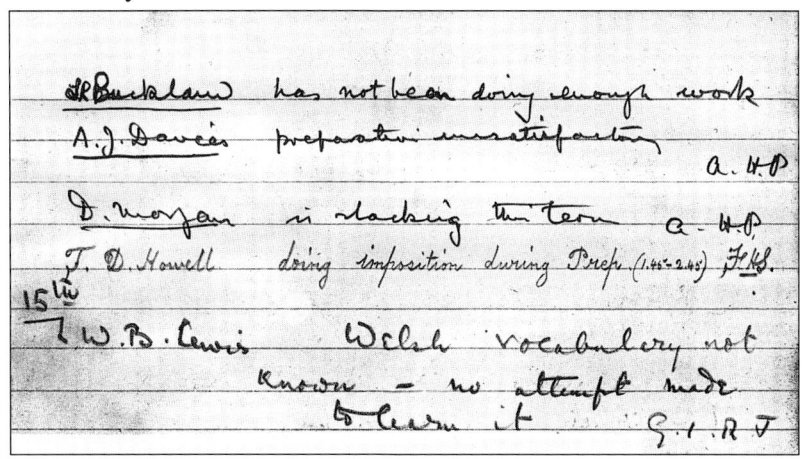

A new arrival that term was G. F. Exton as 6th form master, whose name should be remembered with those of McLellan, Richards, Knight, Gregory, and Calcott, as one of the really great masters who have served Llandovery. A temporary master was one Hill, a musician, whose fine playing at the Memorial service to Queen Victoria I still recall. The organ at Llandingat had fine points, but it was only occasionally that they were heard. One was at the service of thanksgiving for the new buildings, when the train bringing many of the visitors was late, and Mr A. F. Barnes (now Doctor) gave an impromptu recital, mostly of French music. A new time-table came into operation in a fortnight or so, of which the only feature I remember was the disappearance of geography from the curriculum of some forms. It was the work of Richards, who possessed the chess-problem mind necessary to keep all masters employed, and available classrooms occupied, and all subjects taught for the requisite number of periods.

It was soon after this that I had to leave for home owing to the unexpected death of my father. I caught the same illness and was not back for some weeks.

The breaking of this news was the first painful duty Poole Hughes had to perform, and I think that neither he nor I ever forgot it. The event, and the consequent leaving of our beautiful country home with its grounds and gardens made its additional impression upon me at the beginning of the new century.

On my return, I was told, 'Everything is different now. The masters will report you for anything.' Poole Hughes had got every string into his hands. Masters had little or no discretion about punishment. Every breach of discipline had to be reported, likewise every bit of bad work. That was the system that prevailed for the next 27 years, while Poole Hughes reigned longer than any of his predecessors until his death. The powers of the School Committee were severely pruned; no team could be published without the Warden's approval; colours could not be awarded without his approval. It seemed that every detail, however trivial, had to be referred to him.

There can be few left who remember clearly this transition, and it may be of interest to have it on record.

(School Journal March 1956. The Revd. A. Pierce Jones joined Llandovery College in 1901 from Caernarfonshire, where his father was rector of Aber. He proceeded to Keble College Oxford and was ordained in 1913. Between 1913 and 1921 he served in parishes in Kettering and Brighton. From 1921 he worked in South Africa . . . Railway Mission Chaplain, East Transvaal . . . Chaplain of Holy Cross Homes, Irene . . . Vicar of St. Martin's-in-the-Veld, Irene, Transvaal . . . Rector of St. John Capetown. He was President of the Cape Cambrian Society.

The "new Warden", Poole Hughes came with the warm commendation of the Headmaster of Sherborne: 'His zeal is unremitting, his interest in boys very deep, his tact unfailing, his disciplinary powers of the highest order . . . I have never come across a more able teacher of mathematics, or a man in whom his pupils have a larger confidence'.)

1901-1905

LITTLETON POWYS

I was an assistant master at King's School, Bruton, when in October, 1901 I received a letter from the Warden, W. Poole Hughes, asking me to go to Llandovery for an interview as he wanted a House Tutor and a Fourth Form Master. Off I went, very pleased, because I had just become engaged to be married and I wanted work in a larger sphere.

Littleton Powys and Mrs B Poole Hughes on a later visit

Well do I remember the journey along the South Wales coast, and changing at Landor, with its smouldering slag heaps. Of course, I knew Poole Hughes well, as he had been a master at Sherborne from the time that I was a boy there. I remember his talking about his old school, Llandovery, and being very pleased when the great C. B. Nicholl, captain of the Cambridge rugger side, came to stay with him.

He gave me a warm welcome and told me what my duties would be and took me round the buildings and class rooms and introduced me to some senior boys; C. A. Lidbury, Grif. and Perry Owen, and Mostyn Davies come to mind. Then he took me into a room where the music master, an old fellow called Winter, was having a choir practice of the younger boys; they were singing an Ancient and Modern hymn '*Far Down the Ages Now*,' I did not know it and was delighted with the vigour with which the little fellows sang, and felt straight away I should be very happy with boys like that. In the evening I was taken round the dormitories, the chief of which was called 'Gwent', and had a talk with the little chaps in their nightshirts, when they are always most confidential. And I went to bed feeling very happy.

When I told my father that there was a possibility of my going to Llandovery, he was very excited. He counted himself of Welsh descent, and much liked the idea of his second son working in Wales. He produced his map and together we examined Llandovery and its surrounding country. When he saw the mountains and rivers everywhere, he rubbed his hands together and said, 'Littleton, my boy, I wish I were going with you, you will have to explore all those hills and you will come across most interesting birds and flowers.' And so, when I came down next morning, I was all for seeing something of the countryside. In the course of the morning the Warden took me for a walk round the grounds and then along the river bank to Dolau Hirion Bridge. It was then there occurred what I counted a good omen. I saw a butterfly with brilliant Trifiliary colouring, and when it settled and I saw its ragged wings, I knew it to be a Comma, a butterfly I had never seen before alive. Now they are common enough in Dorset. That incident gave me great pleasure. We went on to Dolau Hirion Bridge with that glorious salmon pool and the school bathing pool too. I looked up-stream to Monk's Head and Forest Hill, to Cilycwm and the high hills above it, and I was well satisfied: and I hoped that Poole Hughes was too. In the afternoon he wanted me to play football; I had no clothes nor boots; but they were forthcoming, the boots belonging to a Mr Roberts whom I was to succeed, so I was literally stepping into his shoes. I greatly enjoyed the game and was impressed by the boys' play, especially in the open. I believe a burly forward called A. W. Davies was the Captain.

Dolau Bridge

At tea, after the game, the offer was made to me and accepted at once, and during the rest of the day I was introduced to my future colleagues, who were very kind to me. On the next day I returned to Bruton. It was in January, 1902 that I found myself a member of the staff of Llandovery College.

No one could have been kinder to me than the Warden, and often staying with him was his mother, the most picturesque old Welsh lady imaginable, and so very good and kind. The second master was the Revd. E. J. McClellan. He had been at Llandovery for a very long time and was the senior classical master. I was much impressed by the obvious ability of the senior members of the staff, who seemed quite content to remain at Llandovery all their teaching years. There was a very able scientist T. J. Richards, H. H. Knight who had been 7th wrangler at Cambridge, H. Gregory a gifted and very popular history master, R. B. Calcott a somewhat aristocratic teacher of French, afterwards at Harrow, G. F. Exton a first class Classic and a first class teacher, afterwards at Cheltenham, H. F. Newton of Oxford a mathematician and a fine footballer, old Winter the music master, succeeded by a man named Barnes, a good musician, Ifor Jones who took one of the lower forms, a very enthusiastic Llandoverian; he was ordained and subsequently given a parish near Brecon, becoming a member of the staff of our rivals, Christ College, Brecon; N. L. James just down from Oxford, a vigorous, happy fellow, afterwards ordained and finding his life's work in Swansea. We were very happy together. The senior men had never had much to do with the boys out of school; but the younger generation, headed by Exton, were as active in the boys' welfare out of school as in it.

My fourth form, which contained as fourth forms usually do some of the most promising boys of the school, gave me much interesting work. With my inward eye I can see many of those boys, none more clearly than A. G. Prys Jones, who was all ears and eyes as during the last few minutes of some period I read some poetry to them. They enjoyed this little recreation, and I can see their eager attentive faces now. Then I used to take a number of able boys who had discarded the Classics for other subjects, and found they needed them again to pass Smalls at Oxford and the Little Go at Cambridge. We used to read together as best we could, not a few of the works of Latin and Greek authors, and together we struggled with grammar and a weekly Latin prose. Grif. Owen was one of these, and also Stanley Evans who afterwards distinguished himself in the law. They were usually successful in their exams.

Such was my actual work in school. But I also had supervision duties, being responsible for the boys' tea and supper. I also had a number of private pupils. Out of school the cricket was in my hands; and in the winter term Newton asked me to train the forwards, an employment after my own heart. In 1903 we introduced hockey in the Lent term and although the change was not very popular, the game had quite a good following. I always felt that the less robust boys, who were somewhat frail for Rugby football, otherwise good with bat and ball, should have the chance of full enjoyment of one of the winter terms, and we had quite successful seasons.

Managing the cricket was no light task. The boys did not take to it naturally as boys do in England, and there was not the same keenness as with football. I always fancied it was because most of the boys came from homes among the hills, where there were few grounds suitable for the game. But we had many good games, and in 1904 defeated Brecon, thanks to some very fine bowling by Allan Davies. I worked very hard to try and improve things; not only did we use the nets for the eleven, but also as special nets as we called them, for the more promising of my boys. Their nets were taken between school and lunch.

I loved the cricket ground, so flat and firm, giving us excellent wickets, and so beautifully situated, with the glorious river Towy flowing on one side and beyond it the trees down beside its waters . . .

The Football was of altogether a higher standard than the cricket, and our XV was usually good. How well I remember my satisfaction when at Cardiff we defeated my old school Sherborne; I sat in the pavilion, watching it with my old friend, G. M. Carey, and felt so proud of my side and of its captain, and out half, Hughie Morris. The rugger sevens of the present day show how good the School Rugger still is.

I used to have my own cricket too, playing for the Town; we had quite a good side, captained by that giant amongst athletes C. P. Lewis, and there were the good cricketers Milne Jones of Velindre and Douglas Jones, a lawyer, who lived down the river. We were strong enough to hold our own against most sides, and I remember once defeating Swansea, in which match I got 100 and N. L. James 89 not out; but their best bowler, Criber, was not playing.

But when I look back at those 3½ years, it was nature that gave me personally the greatest pleasure. I loved the hills and the rivers, I loved the flowers, many of which I was not familiar with. To enjoy it to the full was made easy for me by the Warden himself, who, after I had been there for a month called me into his study, and said, 'I think, Powys, you are doing more work than most of us; in future I shall excuse you from all Sunday work and you can get away to your hills.' How thankful I felt to him, and soon I found out that H. H. Knight had similar tastes. He used to ask me to have breakfast with him, providing sometimes a pheasant or a woodcock: and then off we would go, taking our lunch with us, for tramps amongst the hills.

It was a wonderful experience for me, for I could not have had a better and kinder tutor in botany. He introduced me to many flowers I did not know, and ferns and mosses. He wanted to make me keen on microscopic work, but that was beyond me. Together we went to the tops of the Vans quite a number of times, together we explored the Sawdde valley, we went upstream to Craig y Rhayader and the great moorland above it; more than once did we go to Twm Shôn Catti's cave, and Rhandirmwyn; I rejoiced in his companionship.

I have always felt that Field Natural History was one of the most important of school subjects. And to help in making boys interested I have started Field Societies wherever I have been, at Bruton and then again at Llandovery. At my own school at Sherborne there was a Natural History Society.

The opening of the new buildings in November, 1903, was a great affair. It was carried out admirably by the Headmaster of Sherborne, Canon F. B. Westcott, much to my joy.

In August, 1904, my wedding took place, and for two terms my wife and I lived in the last house but one of the New Road, from which we could step out onto the hills. She loved the mountains as I did, and so did our visitors.

I had been invited to go back to Sherborne and take over the Preparatory School. No offer could have pleased me more. So in April, 1905, we said 'Goodbye' to Llandovery, my heart full of thankfulness, for all the place had meant to me, and for the kindness I had received from one and all, masters and boys alike.

(School Journal November 1955. Littleton Charles Powys was born in 1874, the son of the Revd. C. F. Powys who claimed noble Welsh ancestry. Littleton's mother numbered the poets Cowper and Donne as ancestors. He was one of eleven children, three of whom became notable writers—John Cowper Powys, T. F. Powys and Llywelyn Powys.

Littleton Powys' autobiography, including a charming chapter on 'Llandovery' appeared under the title of The Joy of it, *published by Chapman & Hall, 1937.*

He died at West Pennard, Glastonbury, Somerset, on 27 September 1955. After leaving Llandovery he was Headmaster of the Preparatory School at Sherborne from 1905 to 1923).

1901-1907

A. G. Prys Jones

I came to Llandovery in the first year of the present century as a boy of under 11 to join some 140 others. I doubt whether the total number of pupils during my seven years at the School ever exceeded 150. The great majority were boarders, with about 15 to 20 day-boys at most.

The Houses then were 'The School', Llandingad, College House, Emlyn House (which accommodated only a few boys and was afterwards occupied by assistant masters) and Prospect House. The last was conducted independently by the Senior Master, the Rev McLellan, who had taught the Warden of my period, Canon W. W. Poole-Hughes, at the School. Rivalry in sports ran very high between the Houses. I have played a fair amount of Rugby football in my time, but have rarely taken part in tougher or more exciting games than those full-pelt, all-out House matches of my school days.

My reference to the Senior Master, known as 'Old Mac' brings back some tremulous memories. He was an excellent teacher in many ways, but his manner was crisp and sometimes harsh, and he could be a terror with his tongue. One of his unfortunate habits was to drop heavily and regularly upon two or three pupils in his Latin Form against whom, for some obscure reason, he appeared to nourish a grudge. I happened to be one of them. Another was a friend who is now a very prosperous South American farmer. During one term Mac's sarcastic invective proved too much for my fellow-victim, who absconded home on foot to Lampeter. When a thrilled class broke the portentous news to Mac the following morning in the hope of seeing him rend his gown in sorrow, he showed not the slightest sign of contrition. We were ploughing heavily through 'conditional clauses' at the time: and Mac, wagging a minatory finger at me, said in his best mock-bland tones: 'Ah, Prys-Jones, I perceive that you are still with us. Kindly translate into the Latin tongue, "If little Isaac had not run away from his teacher, he would undoubtedly be here among us now".' That got me to the bottom of the Form again.

At that time a sinister-looking volume called 'The Black Book' was brought to every class-room during the last period of each morning by the prefect on duty. It was then returned to the Warden's study duly inscribed with the names of those deemed guilty of indolence, inattention, impudence, unruliness or other misdemeanours. After the Warden had scanned the list of delinquents and their offences, they were summoned individually into the presence, and promptly dealt with. One entry in 'The Black Book' was bad enough, but three successive entries amounted to a heinous degree of criminality. Mac had written my name down on three mornings running! And the astounding miracle was that, even late on the third day, no dire summons had reached me. This stay of execution became so unbearable that I decided to get things over. I would appeal, in person, unto Caesar, before my case came up. The charges laid against me were that I had grossly neglected to prepare my Latin Grammar.

So, with a speech of defence on my lips and my Grammar book in my hand, I sought audience of the Warden after his dinner. Almost out of breath I explained that Mr McLellan invariably gave me the works and the jitters, thereby confusing and flustering me into a condition approaching panic. Hence my failure to answer questions intelligently, and the unpleasant entries in 'The Black Book'. Further, would the Warden kindly consent to test me himself in the work wherein I was found wanting: and 'here's the book and the exact pages. And if I can't answer correctly, I'll take my tanning.'

The Warden was in a genial mood, and I well remember the broad smile which came over his face as he took my Grammar book and asked me a few perfunctory questions. As my replies happily coincided with those in the book, he patted me on the head and said: 'You're rather a silly little fellow. Don't you know yet that Mr McLellan's bark is much worse than his bite? He used to be a bit hard on me, too, when I was a boy here, but he's really very kind at heart. Now off you go, and remember never to irritate him. He's getting on in years.' After that interview my relationship with Mac, though never very cordial, was at least reasonably friendly. I strongly suspect that the Warden had passed on a gentle rebuke to him.

Probably, I imagine, as a result of inheriting a somewhat ill-disciplined and high-spirited crowd of boys on his succession to the Wardenship, Canon Poole-Hughes was a firm believer in the doctrine of original sin, and in certain direct methods of keeping the manifestations of this primal curse well down to their minimum.

He was a headmaster of the traditional Public School type who combined kindliness, generosity, urbane wit and physical prowess with a literal firmness of hand which became proverbial. A former Balliol scholar, he was a fine mathematician and an excellent raconteur. He had taught at Uppingham and Sherborne, and had played Rugby for the Barbarians. He detested cant and humbug: and two of his major gifts were an uncanny skill in spotting slackers, frauds and delinquents, and a remarkable ability for selecting good, enthusiastic assistant masters. He was devoted to the School, for which he did so much in securing its 'New Buildings', and in maintaining its reputation for scholarship and games. He was also devoted to his mother, one of the most charming and handsome old ladies I have ever met.

No civil authority in Britain today possesses the power of summary jurisdiction which he exercised over us. He united within himself, with fair justice and with dignity (he had the lineaments of a Roman Emperor), the functions of judge, prosecutor, defence counsel, jury and jailor, without, as far as I remember, every slipping up on a case.

The reasons for this were based upon sound premises in natural logic. No boy, he used humorously to say, could possibly go through a single term without deserving at least a mild hiding for one thing or other. If anyone performed this feat, then either there was something wrong with him physically, in which case the services of the school doctor were urgently required, or he had just happened to get away with it. In the latter case, a hiding was merely overdue.

The Warden maintained, in some ceremonial state, two major instruments of justice. One was a birch-rod of sound local growth which was duly renewed as occasion demanded. Some of us christened this 'The Greater Celandine'. The other, a more foreign importation, was a supple cane, generally known as 'Little Benjamin'. The birch was used upon the more hardened cases, and the cane upon lesser offenders. Both induced complete cures over specific periods, usually a couple of terms in the first instances: and both were applied to that part of the anatomy which was popularly regarded in those days as having been at least partially provided by a wise Providence for this particular purpose.

As time went on, however, the necessity for this draconian treatment appeared to diminish appreciably. I received the attentions of 'The Greater Celandine' on one occasion only. My crime, for which no ingenuity could frame a valid defence, consisted, in the Warden's own indictment of 'having conspired and taken part in an organized depredation' upon the ample remains of a sumptuous evening feast provided for a visiting team of Old Llandoverians in the new dining hall. The removal of these appetising left-overs to the kitchen had been delayed until the next morning. Somehow the news came through 'on the grapevine' that there was much corn left in Egypt: and a small commando raid was hurriedly arranged. Unhappily, owing to the amount of plunder available, greed prevailed over discretion, and retreat was not sounded quickly enough. The whole party was surprised, *flagrante delicto*, and frozen into instant immobility, with full mouths and bulging pockets, by the Warden, who appeared, like the angel of doom, suddenly at the side door. Retribution came, inevitably, on the following day. I encountered 'Little Benjamin' twice, in expiation of two broadly identical offences. The first was for removing (or 'borrowing', as I vainly attempted to describe the act) three glass fairy-lights from the trees in the drive after some festive illuminations were over, and adapting these for common use in our dormitory after lights-out. Owing to inept carelessness they were discovered by the Matron who quite rightly deduced that they might have set some of the beds on fire, and reported the matter.

The second was for kicking a football, with felonious intent, into the Warden's orchard. Unfortunately I emerged through the hedge not only with the ball but also with a number of apples secreted in my clothing. My two fellow-conspirators had wisely and silently melted away during my absence under cover, and had been replaced, surprisingly enough, by the Warden, who said, 'Well, well, I think that even you will admit that this is what you would describe as a fair cop.' This business of 'even you' had reference to the fact that I had tried his patience rather severely on two or three occasions by putting forward arguments which had been successful in saving me from the worst penalties. Once, after a hard verbal tussle, he had informed me that if I went on like this I would end up as a shyster lawyer, a political agitator, or even on the gallows. Happily none of these gloomy prognostications have materialised. I must have taken his solemn warning to heart.

When I arrived at Llandovery there was a notable trio of masters who had become almost permanent parts of the School, Gregory, Knight and Richards. These gifted teachers, aided by the solid foundations insisted upon a Vth Form level by the meticulous McLellan, were largely responsible for the remarkable number of 58 Scholarships and Exhibitions won by their pupils at Oxford and Cambridge between 1889 and 1901. As these masters retired they were succeeded by others who did much excellent work for the School in various directions. They included G. F. Exton, who later went to Cheltenham; R. Berkeley Calcott, who left for Harrow; S. G. Dunn, who became Professor of English at Allahabad University, India; F. M. Stenton, later Sir Frank Stenton, Professor of History at Reading University and President of the Royal Historical Society; and Littleton C. Powys, one of the famous Dorset family of literary brothers, who afterwards became Headmaster of the Junior School at Sherborne. It was in his study at Emlyn House that Sir Frank Stenton completed his first major historical work, 'William the Conqueror', published in the 'Heroes of the Nations' series by Fisher Unwin. Then there was the Rev T. W. Lumb, whose scholarly handbook for Sixth Formers on 'General Knowledge' deserved to become a minor classic of its kind. Among other masters of my period were those keen Rugby enthusiasts, W. Newton (an Oxford blue), the Revs. G. I. R. Jones and N. L. James; H. C. B. Lloyd, and the cricketer S. M. Toyne, who later became Headmaster of St. Peter's School, York. A part-time master who taught Welsh at this time was the Rev Gruffydd Evans, later Vicar of Kidwelly. He made substantial contributions as an antiquary and folklorist to the Transactions of the Honourable Society of Cymmrodorion. His book on *The Ancient Churches of Llandovery* was published by the Society. Littleton Powys, a keen nature enthusiast as well as a fine cricketer and a delightful reader of poetry, founded the Field Society and initiated many of us into the lively and varied natural interests of a rich and beautiful countryside. S.G. Dunn and H.C.B.Lloyd founded a Play-reading Society, and later a Shakespearean Society. The only genuine 'eccentric' among the staff was the very able organist, choirmaster, and producer of Gilbert and Sullivan operas, H. Winter. He was, in my time, a man of uncertain habits, and achieved some degree of immortality by bursting forth upon the organ at Llanfair Church into the then highly popular tune of 'Yip-i-addy' as an additional voluntary at the close of one evening service.

To all these masters I shall always feel that I owe a great debt, especially to Sir Frank Stenton, Littleton Powys and S. G. Dunn. I had the privilege of corresponding fairly regularly with Littleton Powys up to the time of his death.

Two other School 'faithfuls' were Tom Soar, the old Hampshire cricketer who became our professional during my days; and Miss Smit, who was the College secretary for most of her long life, and the kindly friend and confidante of so many of us as small boys.

* * *

If the measure of a school's success in equipping its pupils for life can be gauged by the varied and often outstanding positions attained by former scholars (and I can think of no better criterion) then I was privileged to have been at Llandovery in what must be one of its rare vintage periods. I am happy to place this on record.

When it is realised that at no time during these years did the average enrolment exceed 150 pupils, (something less) these achievements are, to say the least, remarkable. I am relying upon my memory in giving the following details. So it may be likely that some names which should have been included have escaped my net, and that in some cases my memory has erred. But all who are mentioned were, at one time or another, my contemporaries at School.

THE CHURCH

Pride of place must be given to Dr John Morgan who became Bishop of Llandaff and Archbishop of Wales. He was the third Old Llandoverian to attain the latter high dignity. Next should come Canon T. Walker Thomas whose dedicated period as Warden of his old School entitle him to be described as its 'Second Founder'. Others who took Holy Orders include Keble Williams, William Davies, Joseph Rosser, Ebenezer Jones, John Jones-Davies, Alban Davies (International Rugby forward, Wales), Gordon Williams, William Rees and Goronwy Jones (Oxford Blue). Rees became a Senior Chaplain in the Air Force and Goronwy Jones was an Army Chaplain. He was also one of the School's generous benefactors.

LAW

The legal profession attracted a highly successful group. Three became Judges, T. W. Langman, Ernest Evans (also for a time Liberal M.P. for Cardiganshire) and Frank Davies. Another three were appointed Stipendiary Magistrates, Stanley Evans (Pontypridd and the Rhondda), Hubert Llewelyn Williams (Swansea) and Joshua Davies (Aberdare and Mountain Ash). Hubert Ll. Williams, a former School Trustee, unsuccessfully contested the Carmarthenshire constituency as a Liberal candidate. This was a seat once occupied by his O.Ll. uncle, the historian and writer, W. Llewelyn Williams, KC, a radical Liberal. A first cousin of Hubert Ll. Williams, D. Morgan Evans, was for some years a senior barrister on the Wales and Chester Circuit, Chairman of the Cardiff Rent Tribunal and Deputy Chairman of Cardiff Quarter Sessions. Among those who became solicitors were two who took degrees at Oxford before qualifying: Arnold Davies who had an extensive legal practice in Lampeter, and Griffith Owen (son of a former Warden, and Bishop of St. Davids) who was Diocesan Registrar at Carmarthen. D. J. Parry served for many years as Clerk to the Glamorgan County Council, at that time the largest regional Authority in Wales.

The oldest surviving O.Ll. and Welsh International Rugby player, also a former School Trustee, Ewan Davies has long been prominent in Cardiff civic and business circles. Others who followed the same profession were Teddy Evans (Aberdare), Harry Noyes (Aberystwyth) a brother of the once highly popular poet Alfred Noyes; Henry Enoch (Swansea), Edward Kelly (Rhyl),

Parry Jones and Cecil Owen (Denbigh), and R. Wilfred Rees (Cardiff), Raymond Barker, who may have qualified in Law, was Clerk of the then North Wales Mental Hospital, Denbigh.

MEDICINE

Despite the meagre provision in my time for the teaching of the Sciences, a number of my contemporaries became doctors. J. Lloyd Davies, F.R.C.S., established a wide reputation as a gynaecologist and general surgeon in Swansea and West Wales, and Barry Collins, F.R.C.S., practised similarly in Cardiff. W. R. Spurrell, F.R.C.S., a member of the well-known Carmarthen publishing and antiquarian family, became a distinguished Professor of Physiology at Guy's Hospital, London. Two Havard brothers (sons of a Newport, Dyfed, doctor) practised in the same area. Hughie Morris, a most popular and lively personality at School and at Oxford where he only just missed a Blue for Rugby, was killed early in the first war, typically enough while attempting to rescue a badly wounded soldier—under fire.

Two other brothers, Dan and Edgar Llewelyn from Ogmore Vale became doctors. The latter who practised in Cardiff was Senior Medical Officer of the Order of St. John of Jerusalem with its Welsh Headquarters at Cardiff. T. W. David was the Senior Medical Officer for the Neath Division of the South Wales Coalfield. G. W. Parry was a popular general practitioner at Abergavenny. Both qualified from Guy's Hospital, London. I well remember visiting them there when they played a somewhat gruesome practical joke upon me in the dissecting room! Dannie Evans, if I remember rightly, succeeded his father in practice at Llanelli. A younger pupil, Col. Alex Dixon-Smith, also worked in the same town. G. R. Seager Thomas, a Cambridge graduate, was a surgeon at the Westminster Hospital during the first war. A class friend of mine, I sought shelter in his quarters on several occasions when air raids happened to catch me in central London. His brilliant prospects were grievously curtailed by early ill-health: but he recovered sufficiently to become Police Surgeon at Southampton.

Leo H. Davies (younger brother of Judge Frank Davies) another of my friends, took a degree at Oxford before qualifying. He became Medical Officer of Health for the former Cardiganshire and later for Devonshire. In company with Goronwy Jones (with whom I maintained a life-long friendship) we three embarked on a punting trip from Oxford to Reading at the end of a fine summer term. Sleeping rough, but amply provisioned we enjoyed a happy, leisurely and hilarious experience. Sunburnt and blistered after four and a half days, we abandoned ship at Reading after arranging for the punt to be collected, and returned by train!

The Home Civil Service rewarded three contemporaries with Knighthoods: Sir David J. Lidbury, D.S.O., K.C.M.G. (Director of the London Postal Region); Sir William E. Rhydderch (Customs and Excise), and Sir Myrddin Evans (Ministry of Supply). Two others entered the Indian Civil Service; F.L. Brigstocke (of the well-known Carmarthen family whose older brother had secured a Home Civil Service post before my time), and Dudley G. Davies who was unfortunately invalided out after 14 years and took Holy Orders later. An excellent poet who has contributed to leading literary periodicals, he is among the very few O.Ll.s. whose poems have been published in volume form. Now long retired and living in London, we often exchange visits, and regularly shout for Wales when watching International Rugby matches on Television. A sixth O.Ll., D. T. Lloyd, became an H.M. Inspector of Taxes. Another, A. W. M. Griffiths, a Boxing Half-Blue, was appointed by the Colonial Office to an administrative post in the former Tanganyike Territory. Among his charges were the Highland African People renowned for their prowess as warriors, the Masai. He became deeply attached to them, describing them more than once to me as 'my children'. He died young, after returning to duty in Africa.

EDUCATION
Quite naturally a number of O.Ll.s. of my time entered the educational field. Canon T. Walker Thomas taught at Cranleigh before becoming Warden. Two others who were Undergraduates with him at Corpus Christi, Oxford, had secured Scholarships in Classics at the College. The senior, D. Gwyn Williams, who had taught at Bradford Grammar School, was for many years Headmaster of the Crypt Grammar School, Gloucester. A man of rare gifts as a classical scholar and existential philosopher, he was also a poet of quality. Some of his poems were included in my early anthology of Anglo-Welsh verse published in 1917. The other classical scholar, W. Shaw Rowlands, was something of a junior prodigy for he had been awarded a scholarship to Oxford as a result of his performance in the Central Welsh Board's examinations at the age of 15, before he came to Llandovery. He too, taught at Bradford Grammar School, and became Principal of Juddlepore University College, India, where he was highly successful and much regarded. I spent an evening with him at the Regents Palace Hotel, London some time before his death: and had the privilege of writing an obituary tribute to him for the Western Mail, Cardiff. A lively and popular personality with a keen sense of humour.

L. V. D. Owen, who won a History Scholarship at Keble College, Oxford, was my fellow-pupil in the 'Historical Sixth', with the outstanding historian, Sir Frank Stenton, as our tutor. Owen was awarded the University Stanhope prize for his thesis on the 'Wool Trade with Flanders', and became Professor of History at Nottingham University. Possessor of a remarkable memory he could draw historical maps and diagrams with astonishing ease and accuracy.

Another contemporary in the same Sixth Form was the Rev Arnold Pierce Jones with whom I shared the Tower study. He became Principal of the Diocesan Training College, Cape Town, South Africa. An inveterate punster, he often roused the ire of our third study inmate, Simon Andrews, a born naturalist and fisherman whose talents, alas, found little encouragement at School. But his contributions of Tywi trout were welcome additions to study suppers. I never heard what he did in later life. Pierce Jones visited me some 10 years ago: and together we attended an O.Ll. Branch meeting in London but without meeting any contemporaries there. Among Headmasters were Jacob Morgan and A. B. Mayne. Jacob Morgan, William Davies and myself won our Scholarships to Jesus College, Oxford, at the same grouped examinations. These were gained respectively in Mathematics, Classics and History. We also played for the College Rugby team, again respectively, as three-quarter, forward and full-back. Jacob Morgan and A. B. Mayne, who became brothers-in-law, were first-class mathematicians. They collaborated in producing some school text-books. William Davies became a Vicar in North Wales. D. T. Evans, Headmaster of a large Primary School in Carmarthenshire, was a prominent member of the County Branch of the N.U.T.

Levi Evans ran a successful Preparatory School on the South Coast, transferring to Cardiganshire during the second World War. I had the pleasure of visiting his School in an official capacity, and found it a happy and efficient little community. W. G. Curtis Morgan now a Llandovery resident, conducted a successful coaching establishment for foreign and other students, after serving in the carnage of the Somme battle, and later in the Indian Army. He is also a playwright and a pungent political commentator.

Among assistant masters were Reginald Lloyd who taught at Bradford Grammar School, and secured a Blue at Oxford for Rugby football; W. W. Humphreys at Wigan Grammar School and Alec Smith at Llanelli Grammar School. Smith became well-known as a leading Welsh golfer.

JOURNALISM AND THE STAGE

T. E. Elias, a senior in the 'Historical Smith' and a graduate (of Keble College,

Oxford), was Deputy Editor of the Economist; and D. Percy Davies who qualified as a Barrister, became Editor and later managing director of the News of the World. Roddy Hughes, a popular comedy actor, often appeared in London plays.

BUSINESS, FARMING AND THE ARMY

Colin Mason, a generous benefactor of the School and a former Trustee, became a successful Swansea stockbroker; and Peredur Owen (son of a former Warden, and Bishop of St. Davids) was a partner in a London stockbroker firm. Two Seymour brothers whose family were Carmarthenshire coal-owners, followed into the business.

Brian Rhys (son of the poet and litterateur, Ernest Rhys, who launched the famous 'Everyman' series of classics for J. M. Dent) became the firm's representative in Paris. He, too, wrote poetry, and some of his work appeared together with poems of his father's in my 1917 anthology of Anglo-Welsh Verse. W. W. Humphreys, after teaching Mathematics at Wigan became a director of a Cardiff Shipping Firm. He graduated from Jesus College, Oxford, where he was a scholar.

C. P. Sharpe, one of the most ardent workers for his old school, and who did so much to make the London Society of O.Ll.s. a success, was a senior executive in a furniture firm. Sir John Owen, Bart, held a similar position in a Cinematic Film Distribution firm. Charles Lidbury (younger brother of Sir David Lidbury) was general manager of a chain of dry-cleaning shops. He had also devised with some measure of success, a method of extracting oil from coal.

Isaac Davies (younger brother of Arnold Davies O.Ll., the Lampeter solicitor) became a prosperous farmer . . .

[Another contemporary was the distinguished soldier D. D. Pole-Evans who was awarded three military crosses. Later he volunteered for service with the 'British Military Division' in Southern Russia] . . . By a strange coincidence he was saved from capture by the Bolsheviks and tended as a very sick man by one of my two doctor brothers who was the medical officer attached to a small group of Air Force officers and men sent into the Ukraine to assist General Denikin and his Tsarist troops after the Russian Revolution . . . At a remote station a Russian girl besought them to take charge of a sick young, English officer . . . My brother and an armed party found him gravely ill . . . he was given medical treatment and nursed by the Russian girl who insisted on coming with the group to Sevastapol. Here the patient was put into hospital, and my brother became heavily occupied with an epidemic of typhus for several days. When conditions eased off, he went to visit the young officer, found him much improved in health and able to converse. The latter's first request was for my brother's name in order to thank him and the group for their timely services. When the name had been given, the patient asked whether a relative had been a pupil at Llandovery. When this had been duly established, he said, 'Tell your brother when you see him next that you saved the life of D. D. Pole-Evans, the chap who beat him almost at the tape in the Junior School Steeplechase'. Of course I remembered the occasion well, a most exciting finish, with Pole-Evans as fresh as a daisy dashing past me 10 yards from the finishing post . . . [Pole-Evans] married his Russian girl-friend . . .

The only contemporary I can remember who found a permanent career in the Army was Col. Graham Prichard (son of an O.Ll. Cardiff doctor) who became a Staff Officer at the War Office and an expert in fortifications. An O.Ll. who rose to the rank of Colonel with a D.S.O. during the first war, was I. T. Evans.

* * *

Like a number of other boys during my time, I came of a Nonconformist-Liberal family. But as Welsh Calvinistic Methodists some of my close relatives considered that we were only reluctant absentees from an Established Church which had treated us rather shabbily. In any case, my father, a wise and tolerant man, prominent in his denomination, had no qualms at all in sending me to a Church School. He believed that youngsters should be given the opportunity of experiencing other forms of worship in addition to their own, and maintained that staunch Nonconformists and Liberals like Sir Lleufer Thomas and W. Llewelyn Williams, K.C., M.P. had suffered no loss of religious or political principles by being educated at Llandovery.

So I was allowed, with other boys, to practice an interesting religious dichotomy, with a foot in both camps, or betting the best of both worlds! On Sunday mornings I attended the Williams Pantycelyn Memorial Chapel, and the parish Church of Llanfair-ar-y-bryn for the School evening service. This habit of divided worship had its merits. Sunday mornings encouraged us occasionally to access the sermon under the three traditional heads, or if it was long and dull, to catch up with a bit of homework under the cover of the gallery balcony. The evenings taught us to appreciate the attractive liturgy and music of the Church, to use the English Book of Common Prayer without fumblings, and, indeed, to those of us whose mother tongue was Welsh, with considerable benefit to our English speech-rhythms. Some of us owe more than we realise, I'm sure, to those simple, dignified and often moving evening services in the ancient, dim-lit Church of Llanfair-ar-y-bryn, built within the site of a Roman auxiliary fort which also, no doubt, had known the worship of Mithras, the god of the Legions . . .

Here then was woven the first strong stand of my love for Carmarthenshire, and this itself is intertuned with my profound sense of gratitude and affection for my old School to which I owe so much. This included the privilege of spending one's formative years among a lively, goodly company of boys and masters in what now seems a halcyon period before the dark clouds of perils and disasters had come to menace continents and seas.

(Compiled from contributions to the School Journal, December 1959 and Summer 1978. A. G. Prys Jones 1888-1987 was born in Denbigh, educated at Llandovery College and Jesus College, Oxford. In 1919 he was appointed Staff Inspector of Secondary Education in Wales. He published six volumes of poetry and is regarded as being a significant figure in the development of Welsh consciousness in the twentieth century. His first published poem appeared in the School Journal of Christmas 1903 . . . and they continued to appear over the years. He was the author of a much acclaimed two volumed History of Carmarthenshire.

Littleton C. Powys was to record his own memory of Prys Jones: Powys remembered to the end of his days 'those same brown eyes that used to look so earnestly at me in the IVth Form room at Llandovery'. (The Powys Review, 22).

A major study is to be found in A. G. Prys Jones, 1992 by Don Dale-Jones published by the University of Wales Press in the series 'Writers of Wales' edited by Meic Stephens and R. Brinley Jones.

'The sinister-looking volume' was to be the subject of an ode written in 1914:

> *O Hateful book, O record of my crimes,*
> *Wherein are writ the evils of the times;*
> *Before mine eyes I see thy form appear,*
> *Which makes me tremble, shake and fear.*
>
> *Of old within the study thou didst stand,*
> *Of him whose iron rule lay in his hand,*
> *Of him who oft the wand and branch did sway,*
> *And on his knees the lazy scholar lay.*

Ystwyth.

1902

A. F. BARNES

It is difficult to cast one's mind back 55 years, but I can still remember the Rev Poole Hughes, Newton, Powys, Richard and Knight, both of whom lived at Bank House with me and also Gregory. I remember too the zealous contests on the rugger field against Brecon, but the thing I remember most vividly was a Saturday upon the afternoon of which Wales had been beating England and I was taking Preparation that evening; a bewildered novice trying to maintain some semblance of order in a seething mass of excited sons of 'The Land of my Father'.

But most dearly do I remember the lovely scenery, the river and the hills behind. I have never forgotten these.

Music at Llandovery was my first job on leaving Oxford . . . So the College provided me with my first experience in unsheltered existence and it taught me much. Besides Music, I had to teach elementary English and Mathematics . . .

(School Journal May 1957. Written by A. F. Barnes M.C. D.Mus. (Oxon) FRCO from Paignton in Devon. Reference is found to Barnes in 1892-1908 [Masters] by A. Pierce Jones).

1903-1911

W. G. Curtis Morgan

I was sent to Llandovery on May 6th, 1903. We were five new boys, making the number at the school about one hundred and sixty. Levi Evans, one of these, very many years later had a Prep. School on the South Coast which in World War Two he was forced to transfer to the safety of Abermad, near Aberystwyth. Another, two years old than the rest of us, Andrew Goronwy Jones went into Form Three. My father, an O.Ll., then vicar of Pontarddulais and Gorseinon, had persuaded Goronwy's father to send him along with me. Goronwy became an Anglican chaplain in the Forces and later inherited the wealth of a bachelor uncle who had a linen factory in Belfast. Much of this he left to Llandovery College.

We were placed in a new dormitory on the top floor west of the tower. It had large windows overlooking the lawn. Next to it were the rooms of Miss Smit, veritably the Mr Chips of Llandovery, who was secretary to wardens over forty years. Most boys returned to school with pocket money of five to ten shillings. This was handed in to Miss Smit, our banker, and drawn on at specified periods till it was exhausted. Most received weekly pocket money of sixpence to a shilling in letters with stamps, then currency. We all had tuck-boxes replenished by two or three parcels per term sent by train and when parents visited us.

Miss Smit   Miss Lewis   Warden   Mrs B. Poole Hughes

These were locked in a room with access only after lunch. We were allowed our own sardines, jams and fish pastes at tea. The main tuck shop was at what became the Belle-Vue Dairy. A few years later the College opened its own tuck-shop.

The food was plain and unappetizing, though food was then wholesome and cheap. The bread and butter was cut in half-inch slabs. For breakfast it seemed to have been cut the night before from the very large loaves baked every five days. At breakfast in the winter terms porridge was available as an extra; eggs likewise in summer. The midday meal consisted of roast meat with two vegetables and somewhat anaemic gravy, followed by rice pudding, apple tart in season, French pancakes or 'spotted dick'—suet pudding with currants. Supper was the deadly meal—bread and butter occasionally with cheese and cocoa.

The main hall was heated by two large stoves, the classrooms by fires in the grates. Heating began on the arrival of the first ice or snow. Heating in bedrooms was unknown nor was there hot water in the wash-rooms attached to the dormitories, but we did have modern hot baths in the new building, which is more than they had in most Oxford colleges at the time.

No one left the school throughout the term in normal circumstances.

We were allowed in New Road and as far as the Printing House in Broad Street, where the text books were sold, also into the country as far as the third milestone. Passes into the town on half-holidays were available from Miss Smit. There was also a matron and small sick-room and any number of young girl servants.

In the summer term we had a period from 7.15-8 a.m., breakfast being at eight. In summer we were allowed our own bicycles, useful for riding to Dolauhirion where those who had passed the test were allowed to swim under the eye of a master. In 1904-5 this master was Tommy Pearson, a long-distance running blue from Cambridge. In alternate years bicycles enabled us to go to Brecon for the cricket match.

WORK AND DISCIPLINE

We certainly did not work anywhere near as hard as the young do today for the simple reason that any Llandoverian was later assured of gainful and often pleasant employment. Most took Holy Orders, or went into the medical or legal professions; some into higher education.

Thus discipline was paramountly concerned with slacking. In the period before lunch a prefect took the report book to each class-room and any master who so wished would enter the name of any boy in need of punishment. Those reported were spanked on the bare bottom after lunch. For more serious offences the cane was used, for cribbing, for example. The birch was not used in my time. If it had been it would have been instead of expulsion. Boys were caned for smoking. Two were expelled for inebriety.

We had nothing to do with girls; perhaps because the boy was expected always to pay for entertaining any girl and we hadn't the money.

Conditions in Llandovery were nowhere near so Spartan as in English Public Schools. There was no bullying, little fighting and no fag system. Nor were prefects allowed to use the gym shoe. Masters, of course, often gave lines instead of reporting.

The cleverest boys usually worked hardest. At that time some of these went into the Home or Indian Civil Service. The Egyptian and African Services were open to Blues with modest academic qualifications. Those serving on the West African gold coast were superannuated after seven years, but thanks to yellow or blackwater fever few lived to receive their pensions. Two of my contemporaries, D. J. Lidbury of Cardiff, head prefect in 1903 and Myrddin Evans, my age, went into the Home Civil Service and ended as Knights. A third, Dudley Davies went into the Indian Civil Service in Bengal but was invalided out and became a clergyman and has had his poetry published in quality magazines and in a book. He is now living in London as is also A. G. Prys-Jones, another poet who became an Inspector of Schools and in retirement wrote a two-volume history of Carmarthenshire.

A contemporary of Sir D. J. Lidbury was John Morgan, later Archbishop of Wales. In my early years in Llandovery the four bishoprics in Wales were held by O.Lls. or former wardens. Dr Pritchard Hughes of Llandaff was not only an O.Ll. but was born in Llandovery vicarage, then situated in its own grounds, below Llanfair Church. The two sons of Bishop Owen of St. David's, former Warden, were at the school at this time, Griffith becoming a Diocesan Registrar and Perry a stockbroker.

To revert to work, everyone from the bottom form upwards was instructed in Greek, Latin, French, Maths and the usual school subjects. At the end of each term the whole school sat for an examination in Latin grammar. There were one hundred questions, most of them demanding a one-word answer. The result was read out after prayers, the youngest boys scoring a few marks, those in the classical sixth over ninety-five.

Most boys did not go to universities except to promote specific careers. I can remember no one in my time going to any university other than Oxford, though in my father's time, 1876-82, several went to Lampeter, the oldest college in

England and Wales outside Oxbridge. My father won an exhibition in Hebrew at Lampeter, which one assumes, he had learned in Llandovery, the clergy then being expected to be able to read the Bible in their original languages.

Few potential solicitors went to a university; medical students went to hospitals, but two of my friends went to Oxford and read Physiology in finals, though this added two years to their period of qualification. One, L. M. Davies, brother of Judge Frank Davies, also an O.Ll., went to Lincoln, the other, D. Ogmore Williams, to Jesus. Ever since the last war Dr Ogmore spent a week in June and November in Llandovery and in his last years was a Trustee. As full-back for St. Thomas' he once converted sixteen tries in a match against the Royal Military Academy, Woolwich.

One period a week was allotted to Welsh, the master being the Rev Gruffydd Evans, the local curate. Many years later, Gruffydd Evans wrote the first history of Llandovery town. Farmers and others from the rural areas did not send their sons to Llandovery to learn Welsh.

MASTERS AND HOUSES

In 1903 there were twelve masters, all but two, celibate as was then customary. Three were in Holy Orders, the Warden, the Rev W. W. Poole Hughes and the Revs. E. J. MacLellan and Ifor Jones both married.

MacLellan was a housemaster of the kind common in English Public Schools. He lived in Prospect House, now Lloyd's Bank, and with Mrs McClennan was responsible for boarding and feeding some eleven boys. Both Poole Hughes and my father had been pupils under McClennan now approaching the day when he would retire to a country vicarage in Breconshire.

The other married master was Ifor Jones. He had been rugger captain at Keble, and though not an oustanding forward was a great leader of the pack. Ifor Jones' best friend at Llandovery as a boy was T. Odwyn Jones also of Keble. T. Odwyn played at full-back for Oxford . . . and died in his one hundred and first year. Another contemporary of both had been D. Vaughan Thomas M.A., Mus.Doc. (Oxon.), composer of *Llynafan* and other musical works and father of Wynford. Dr Vaughan Thomas had won an open scholarship in Maths at Exeter, Oxford. Ifor's elder brother, also an O.Ll. was Dr Arnallt Jones of Port Talbot. He closely resembled in physical appearance King Edward VII, and once on a visit to a London theatre, when entering a box overlooking the stage, the audience below rose from their seats. Ifor Jones left Llandovery for a rural benefice near Brecon and for many years was a master at Christ's College.

The young G. F. Exton, a Bell prizeman in classics at Cambridge, under whom I spent my first year in the classical Sixth, was in charge of Emlyn House with some ten boys: these had their meals in the college. Emlyn House now faces the War Memorial.

A large number of boys lived in College (now Clarence) House under Billy Newton, another Oxford full-back. Newton oddly enough, was a graduate of Queen's, to which I was destined to go eight years later and later still T. 'Pope' Williams, the outstanding rugger coach and master. In College House Mr Smith, the music master, had rooms. During his stay the ballad *The Norman Baron* (Longfellow) was performed by the school choir on a wintry afternoon in December. Hulley's orchestra had arrived in mid-morning from Swansea for rehearsal, returning after the concert and tea for duty at the Grand Theatre. In those days the G. W. and L. & N.W. Railways provided an excellent service. The overture by the orchestra was the *Little Michus* (Meesho) which many of us had mispronounced . . . Mr Smith left Llandovery for Rossall.

The most striking member of the staff throughout my time was R. Berkeley Calcott called 'the Baron'. He was in charge in Llandingat. Tall, impeccably dressed, with the carriage of a Colonel in the Guards, he exuded an aura of *gravitas*. Needless to say, he was able to exact discipline without ever writing names in the report book. Daily he received a copy of *Le Matin* from Paris and one morning read us the account of what may well have been Wales' first visit to France. To our amusement the correspondent had referred to the Welsh as *les disables rouges*.

Other masters were John Knox (Maths) and W. Richards (Chemistry called 'Stinks'). Both had been at the School for twenty years or more. Younger masters were L. Powys (John Po) and A. C. B. Lloyd, son of the Squire of Waunifor. Both of these were later to take over Prep. Schools in S.S. England. John Po's famous brother, John Cowper Powys, once visited us to give a lecture. I still remember his fulminating in impassioned tones against 'the dirty creeping Saxons'. Masters who came and went were Sammy Toyne and Bathurst, both Blues and Hampshire cricketers, Toyne later representing England in Racquets.

In 1907 Bailey Davies joined the staff: like the Rev Strand Jones many years before, he had played rugger for Lampeter, Llanelly, Oxford and Wales. He left us for Merchant Taylors and took Holy Orders. F. M. Stenton, who many years later was knighted as Vice-Chancellor of Reading University, was for a time history master. Stenton was a short man with a prominent nose and a strong voice. Occasionally declaiming on the purple patches of history, he once said of some hapless figure: 'They probably cut off his arms and legs and boiled him in oil.' Faint voice from the rear: 'Did he die, sir?' Answer: 'He died all right.' Another master, N. L. James, played centre for Llanelly while at the school. An O.Ll. he later became the vicar of a parish in Swansea.

Weeks and I went to Oxford for the first time in December 1910 for scholarship examinations at Jesus College. Neither of us was successful. The classical master at Llandovery then was a Jesus man, T. Wallace Lumb, a first in Greats. On enquiry, he was told that I had come out top in Latin prose but had done very poorly in Unseens . . . We stayed for a week at a guest house . . . After dinner on our first night we were cheered by a visit from Goronwy Jones of Pontarddulais . . . The Maths master at Llandovery, Pullinger advised Weeks to go to his old college, Queen's, which he did and I accompanied him . . . On a night in the first week of December 1914 I dined in Queen's for the last time as an undergraduate . . . I was commissioned on February 23rd 1915 and posted to the 9th South Wales Borderers, Pembroke Dock . . .

PRIZE GIVINGS
In my day at Llandovery an Oxford don used to invigilate at the summer examinations. One of these was Prof. E. C. Merchant (Lincoln), an authority on Thucydides. In his brief report recalling a previous visit and commenting on the progress made since, he stated that on the former occasion 'the examination was held in an upper room in the King's Head from which we could hear the jovial sounds of the rustics enjoying the good things provided below.' A guest

speaker was also present. One of these was William Brace, a Labour M.P. from a Monmouthshire constituency, whose son was at the school.

Invariably present was a Trustee—Lieut.-General Sir James Hill-Johnes, V.C., C.B. of Dolaucothi. Sir James Hill had married the rich Miss Johnes and in accordance with the custom of the time had added his wife's surname to his own. His friends, Field-Marshals Lord Roberts (Chief Imp. Gen. Staff) V.C. and Lord Methuen, household names throughout the Empire during the Boer war, were frequent visitors at Dolaucothi, Field-Marshal Lord Methuen later residing in the mansion overlooking the road to Lampeter just beyond Pumpsaint. Roberts and Hill had won the highest honour for bravery as junior officers on the North West Frontier of India. Physically neither was an imposing figure being of much the same stature as Lloyd George.

RELIGION

The school attended morning service in Llandingat. On Saturday evenings, the clergy on the staff and the school choir conducted the service in Llanfair, the townspeople occupying the pews south of the aisle.

Those were the days of bitterness between Nonconformists and Welsh Anglicans. Lloyd George was one of the protagonists campaigning for the disestablishment and disendowment of the Church of Wales. From a public platform he once referred to A. G. Edwards, Bishop of St. Asaph and a former Warden as 'a first-rate agitator, a second-rate scholar and an irate priest' . . .

There were some twenty boys in the school who attended the various Nonconformist chapels in the town. This bad feeling throughout Wales certainly in no wise extended to the school. One of my best friends was a Nonconformist—Hubert Llewelyn Williams, nephew of the sitting Member for the Carmarthen Division, an O.Ll., Hubert went to Lincoln, became a barrister and eventually Stipendiary Magistrate in Swansea. He was also a Trustee.

GAMES

Rugger was played in the Christmas term; hockey in the Easter and cricket in the Summer terms. The last two weeks of the Easter term were devoted to training for the annual steeplechase and athletic events. Fives were played in an indoor court and two outdoor courts. There was no tennis.

The only schools we played in rugger were Brecon and Sherborne. The teams from Llandovery and Sherborne, at which the warden had been second master, took the train to play at Cardiff. We played Brecon at cricket. In my time Llandovery usually won at rugger; Brecon at cricket. Occasionally the cricket ground was the venue for the Carmarthenshire team in the Minor Counties' Competition. Tommy Soar, late of Hampshire, the school professional and some of the masters played for Carmarthenshire.

The rugger field used for matches was called the Union, because it was parallel with the Union or Workhouse, now the Hospital, the present row or Council houses not then existing.

Harry Watkins, an O.Ll. and the owner of a brewery behind Stone Street and at the time playing for Llanelly and Wales, used to play sometimes for practice with the boys in the first game. On one occasion a team from Cardiff came to play the school. It contained four current internationals—Dr Timms from Ireland and Harding, Gwyn Nichols and Percy Bush from Wales . . .

Games were compulsory as was attendance at matches.

Two of my contemporaries played for Wales—Ewan Davies and the Rev Alban Davies, who while a curate in Swansea, played for many seasons in what then was called: 'The terrible Eight'.

Goronwy Jones had a devastating swerve as a wing and just missed his Blue but represented Oxford in athletics in the high or long jump, I forget which.

ACHIEVEMENT IN THE COMMERCIAL WORLD

C. P. Sharpe, who contributed so much to the success of the London Society of O.Lls., was a top executive with Cavendish's, the furniture firm.

S. V. Swash, a Maths open scholar at Oxford, became managing-director of Woolworth's, Great Britain.

Sir John Owen, Bart., from Pembrokeshire became a top executive in the Cinematic Film Distribution Business.

D. Percy-Davies, Barrister-at-law and the son of an Editor of the *Swansea Post*, became managing director of *The News of the World*.

The three Morgan brothers, the sons of the owner of a small coal-mine, discovered and commercially developed the now famous Danyrogof Caves near Craig-y-nos, once the seat of the fabulous Madame Adelina Patti.

All the above-mentioned were at the school during my eight years.

IN MEMORIAM

The most popular boy in the school during my time was Hughie Morris, a North Walian. He had much more pocket money than most of us but was modest and generous. He possessed that inborn quality, rare in the young, of being what the Italians called *simpatico*. Captain of rugger, he went to University

College, Oxford, a college which—with Trinity—in those days dominated the Oxford rugby scene. He was equally popular at the 'Varsity and also just missed a Blue. He was one of the first O.Lls. to be killed in the War.

Friends of my age, give a year or so, and all some four or five years younger than Hughie Morris, who lost their lives were: Sinnett Jones (Mountain Ash), Oswald Williams (Risca, Open Maths Sch.) both of St. John's; L. G. Cooper (Abergavenny, Open Cl. Sch. Jesus) and E. de Q. Mears (Open Cl. Sch. Worcester). Mears was the son of an Essex vicar and a descendant of de Quincey. My fellow-Queensman, Herbert Weeks of Ninian Road, Cardiff, was killed as Adjutant of the First Battalion, South Wales Borderers along with his Commanding Officer when a shell chanced to hit their Headquarters dug-out well behind the front line.

In March 1916 I was posted to the Sixth S.W. Borderers (25th Division, 17th Corps). On arrival, by one of those coincidences that seem to happen in War, I found an O.Ll. as platoon commander in 'C' Company, in which I had now been given a platoon. He was Nicholas Griffiths of Splott, Cardiff. After thirty-five days in the battle of the Somme I contracted trench fever and was sent home. Nicholas was not so lucky and was later killed.

Among O.Lls. there must have been many others, known and unknown to me, who made the supreme sacrifice. I left for the Indian Army in 1918 and did not visit Llandovery again for fifteen years.

(These reminiscences are compiled from a contribution to the School Journal of Summer 1977 and his autobiography My Life Through Six Reigns *published by the Starling Press, 1983*

W. G. Curtis Morgan was a familiar figure in the Llandovery of my warden-ship. Born in 1892 at Talybont near Aberystwyth where his father (an Old Llandoverian) was curate-in-charge. The family moved to Llandeilo Talybont in 1897, a parish embracing Pontarddulais, Gorseinon, Pontlliw and Grovesend. It was from here that Curtis Morgan proceeded to Llandovery College, then to the Queen's College Oxford. He served in the Army, the Indian Army and, in the Second World War, in the Royal Air Force. He travelled widely, undertook teaching at private establishments, wrote novels and scripts and was a frequent correspondent to the Press. He was a talented tennis player. In the Journal (XXI) of 1931, the Old Llandoverian Notes record, 'W. G. Curtis Morgan represented Wales in the International Lawn Tennis Match v. England at Newport.'

In 1978, in his 86th year he derived great pleasure in being guest of honour on high table at Llandovery College and at the Queen's College Oxford).

1904-1908

FRANK STENTON

Llandovery College played an important part in Frank Stenton's life although he was there for less than four years . . . He never tired talking about it. It was . . . a Welsh school for Welsh boys and it was fortunate that patriotism was as strong in Wales then as now, so that many sons of families known as 'plas people' as well as boys and farming and trading families came and mingled in the same school instead of being sent as many still were to English public schools. In the nineteenth century, while many little boys as young as 12 were sent there, pupils in their twenties were still being entered at Llandovery. Even in Frank's time he had vivid memories of the bearded young man kept on to defeat Brecon at football, who at early prep. (7.15-8) sat round the stove cracking nuts.

The years he spent at Llandovery made him a lifelong lover of Wales and its people. In the library he rejoiced to find a Monasticon and other books he needed for his own work. In Wales and the Marches he found castles which delighted him and were responsible for the Historical Association tract, *The Development of the Castle in England and Wales*, first printed in 1910 . . . By a stream of picture postcards of Welsh castles, rivers, mountains, roads, and little country towns he tried to keep his mother in touch with his activities and show her something of the charm of the Principality. Among the tough boys at Llandovery College he gained great respect by his conquest of mountain tracks in the long bicycle rides he took at weekends and whenever time allowed; by his work on William the Conqueror and Domesday Book which was going on all the time; and by his music of which the school made full use. His altogether unjustified reputation for toughness meant that he never had any difficulty in dealing with even the bearded footballers. Many scholars of Frank's and earlier generations found their first posts in Wales. G. G. Coulton was at Llandovery for a year or two and left behind him the reputation of a difficult eccentric. If he could not open a window he took it out. T. F. Tout was at Lampeter and became mayor of the town. A. G. Little was at Cardiff. All agreed in one thing, that they found friendship and inspiration in the Principality. Frank remembered the Llandovery masters of his day as very good teachers whose best pupils won Oxford scholarships. Knight, who taught Mathematics at Llandovery for twenty years, and Richards, who taught Science there for twenty-three, were both friends of Frank's and stayed in the holidays at South Hill. L.V.D. Owen, who was in the History VIth and won the open scholarship at Oxford, which Childs and Frank had won in their day, was a lifelong friend. His father sent Frank a pound of tobacco when he won his scholarship. His neat handwriting, very like Frank's own, enabled him to help copy out *William the Conqueror* while at school and help in later plans when he was Professor of History at Nottingham. It gave Frank enormous pleasure when an old pupil appeared here one summer afternoon in the guise of the Archbishop of Wales, having brought a cricket team from his diocese to Reading by bus to play a local team in the playing field behind Whitley Park Farm.

The four years at Llandovery proved that Frank would never be deflected from his destiny as a historian. He was working hard all the time as a schoolmaster, writing and publishing . . .

By the modest standards of the early years of this century Frank regarded the financial rewards of Llandovery as good. He was paid £70 a term, resident . . . The future was opening out, but there was no possibility that success would be achieved without very hard work and it made no promise of riches. Every day he tried to write a page or two of *William the Conqueror*. He was lucky enough to buy a fine copy of *Orderic* for eleven shillings on 12 February, 1906. On 22 January he noted, 'Begin to see how to treat the Confessor's reign.' This was the day he rode to Llanwrtyd and back and saw the Sugar Loaf. On the 4 February he noted that he had written twenty-six pages this term. Then a bad cold came on and he had to knock off for a time. When his head was not clear enough to write sentences he wrote out lists of places where Anglo-Saxon kings went to die or made notes about coins or place-names. One Sunday afternoon he spent checking figures relating to sokemen tenements and another day 'amused myself with Anglo-Saxon genealogies'. But it was a hard term, in which he had two bad colds. On 19 March he rode to Llangammarch and to the top of the Eppynts. His tea and dinner cost five shillings and sixpence. Before the end of the term he had drafted the Domesday chapter under fourteen headings and the chapter remains today to show how carefully the headings were drafted and how exactly the draft was followed . . .

In the summer term 1906 Frank noted a number of exhilarating rides, sometimes with two masters who were his closest friends at Llandovery,

Richards and Knight. With them he went to Llanwrtyd on 15 May, perhaps to celebrate the fact that on 13 May he 'killed the Conqueror'. His birthday he celebrated by going to Llangammarch. Often a ride is followed a few days later by a bad cold, as it was after his ride 'to Brecon and Crickhowell with Tretower castle on the way back, got in at 11.30'. He did not give it time to get better, but 'rode to the British camp', with the result that he noted 'cold very bad on chest' the next day, and the following day 'cold utterly incapacitating'. Towards the end of the term he spent some days 'copying *William*'. He 'took Ivor's prep for him', for he could copy *William* while superintending the boys . . .

The diary for 1907 shows that Frank wanted very much to get away from Llandovery. He was not tired of Wales, but he was tired of schoolmastering. He took to writing music more seriously again and took even more rides than before. Even Domesday Book seems to have become a burden. He wanted to move on to something else. During the spring term he finished Leicestershire and began on Rutland. He engaged himself to do Lincolnshire and Oxfordshire. In May he sent off the second 'Utwara' letter which was soon in print. In June to took his M.A. and on Friday, 19 July he 'resigned 2.10-2.20'. To celebrate his resignation he took a tremendous ride, starting by 'training to Llanwrtyd at 10.30, cycling to Abergwesyn and seeing Strata Florida by the head-waters of the Towy and then by Pontrhydfendigaid and Ystrad Meurig, (castle) Train to Lampeter and bicycle from there to Llandovery 10.15'. Now the Welsh Mountain Road makes these parts more accessible, as we found going much the same way by car in May 1960. The manuscript of *William* went off to Putnams in mid October, and Frank was anxiously looking for another post. The possibility of lectureships at Oxford excited him, but nothing came his way . . . As the term and year drew to an end the Warden raised the question of Frank's return to Llandovery in 1908 for a little longer, and, after consulting his mother, he agreed to do so.

As this third year in Wales drew on Frank began to feel that he must move or he would find himself at 70 pensionless, still teaching there. Moreover, he found that the climate of Llandovery had given him asthma, and that he suffered from continual incapacitating colds. Nor did he like the food supplied to the masters in Bank House, where they lived. His mother sent him from home hams, bacon, and pork-pies as well as asparagus and other foods from the garden. He also established friendly relations with a number of country inns—Llanwrtyd, Llangammarch, the Ivy Bush at Carmarthen, Senny Bridge are often mentioned. If ordered betimes an excellent meal of roast duck or the like could be obtained, washed down by a modest bottle, and followed by a pot of good brown Welsh tea before a hospitable fire as the turning-point of a ride. The inns were simple, but the beds not uncomfortable and the meals and the rides were remembered over the years. Long afterwards, as we drove over the Welsh roads improved out of recognition from the rough surfaces which lived in his memory, Frank talked of the days of his youth, the pleasures of companionable rides with other young masters who, like himself, had books on the stocks and looked ahead to the pleasures and pains of a scholar's life. For Frank it meant looking back to Reading where Childs was trying to raise a modest sum sufficient for him to invite Frank back there as a Research Fellow in Local History.

The spring term of 1908 was Frank's last term at Llandovery. He was beginning to feel like his predecessor and with no certainty of another post he left the school at the end of that term. He had undertaken a substantial programme of *Victoria County History* work. As well as the Domesday articles he had in hand, he had already agreed to write the articles on the social and economic history of Worcestershire and the city of Worcester. He noted on 9 March that he had 'sent Page the Rutland Introduction' and on 3 April he left Llandovery for good . . .

(Taken from Frank Merry Stenton 1880-1967 by Doris M. Stenton, from The Proceedings of the British Academy, Volume LIV.

Sir Frank Stenton, the distinguished historian, was professor of Modern History at Reading University 1912-46: he was Vice-Chancellor 1946-50. Stenton was the author of a number of seminal studies including Anglo-Saxon England (1943). He was President of the Royal Historical Society 1937-45. Of him one of his Llandovery pupils, A. Pierce-Jones recalled '. . . I owe more to him than to any man under whom I have sat.'

The author of the above excerpt, Lady Stenton, was also a historian of distinction).

1906

Hugh Spurrell

The College
Llandovery.
May 3 1906

Dear Mother,

The Warden has just examined me and he was surprised to find that I had done any Algebra. In Mathematics he told me to go to Mr Fenn's form, IIIB. In Classics I am in IIIA, Mr Joyne's form, 2 forms above Courteney. I like the place very much especially the Tower dorm.

Hugh

Mrs W. Spurrell
37 King St
Carmarthen

*   *   *

The College
Llandovery
Sep. 9. 1908

Dear Mr Spurrell,

I enclose Hugh's Certificate and I congratulate him on his marked success.

I may also say that he won the French prize by 1 mark. At present I haven't a Prize Book in hand, but he shall receive it next term.

With kind regards,
Yours sincerely,
W. W. Poole Hughes

(NLW Ms. Spurrell 26).

1907-1914

W. B. M.

Seven years ago—how the time has flown—I came here as a youth of twelve. That term there were about thirty five of us who started on our academical career, all hoping that very shortly we would be head prefects, captain of Footer etc., but now, when I look round, I can see but one of the thirty five left still struggling with the mysteries which pertain to a scholastic career. Many are now at Oxford, yet there are still a few trying hard to get there. When I look round on the faces of the masters I can see but two who welcomed me here an unruly child. How everything has changed, even the School itself. Outside the Dining Hall, where two solitary apple trees grew amongst the potato beds we find the noble Science Schools, and facing them we find our beautiful new Gymnasium, where now we hold all our school 'sing-songs' lectures, concerts, etc. Of former years all these pleasures used to be held in our School Hall.

How we used to bless the walk back from the Union Footer field after a strenuous game, but now all that is done away with; we have a fine footer field adjoining the School, for which we will ever be indebted to the late Lord Tredegar.

There is just one alteration which we all grieved over, but it was one which no one could prevent. Two years ago the School lost its greatest friend, one who found a place in the heart of every boy in the School. I remember well my first day, it was a lovely September afternoon in 1907, being welcomed here by one who, until she was called from us, was as a mother to us all, especially the Junior members of the School.

But at last the time has come for me to depart. Many a time I have longed to leave; longed to call myself an Old Llandoverian, but believe me, now that the time has come, I find that it is a lot harder than I thought it would be. To leave the boys, the games, my fellow prefects, the masters, and all the glorious walks, it is harder than one would think.

LLANDOVERY COLLEGE.

Third Term.

1907.

Warden and Head Master

The Rev. W. W. POOLE HUGHES, M.A.

Assistant Masters

H. H. KNIGHT, Esq., M.A.

T. J. RICHARDS, Esq., M.A.

R. BERKELEY-CALCOTT, Esq., B.A.

G. F. EXTON, Esq., M.A.

The Rev. G. I. R. JONES, M.A.

S. G. DUNN, Esq., M.A.

F. M. STENTON, Esq., M.A.

A. J. FENN, Esq., B.A.

A. C. B. LLOYD, Esq., M.A.

F. H. SMITH, Esq.

W. W. H. NASH, Esq, B.A.

Music.

F. H. SMITH, Esq.

I cannot tell what I owe to my School, but I sincerely hope that, as time goes on, I shall, upon returning as an Old Boy—how strange it sounds—see the School in a more flourishing condition than it is at present, if such a thing is possible.

Who knows how soon we might see our new Chapel built on the ground at the top of the Gymnasium and Science Schools. How sorry we all were to leave the beautiful Llanfair Church. Oh! that we could still have it for our own. But it was not for us to decide, or if it had been, we should still be there.

How strange it seems, after seven years, to have to say good-bye to every thing which I hold dear. But all these things must one day come to an end, so, with a cheerful face, which betrays anything but a cheerful heart, I say 'good-bye' to my old School, and as a word of advice to its younger members I can but say, 'Remain Llandoverians as long as you can.' To be an Old Llandoverian is something hateful compared with it.

(School Journal 1914).

1911-1916

D. H. PATEY

I went to Llandovery at the beginning of the summer term of 1911 and left at the end of the summer term of 1916 at the age of 16¾, in order to get a year in at a London medical school before routine call-up for the army at the age of 18. I have no records personal or official to consult, and what I write is necessarily impressionistic and subject to the vagaries of memory of someone who has just entered his seventy eighth year.

My parents like most other parents of boys at the school sent me to Llandovery for two main reasons; it had an excellent academic reputation, when most of the state secondary schools, then termed 'Intermediate Schools', had an indifferent reputation, and the fees were low. We could be divided into two main groups, the Anglo-Welsh and the Welsh. The Anglo-Welsh, of whom I was one, consisted mainly of boys whose parents had settled in South Wales for at most a few generations, being attracted by the opportunities afforded by industrialization. Most of us did not know or speak any Welsh with the exception of the Welsh National Anthem, which we sang with fervour, and a number of swear words. Under the influence partly of geography, partly of rugby, however, we without question regarded ourselves as Welsh. Though Welsh was taught, it was an optional extra, and few even of the Welsh-speaking boys took it. The latter came mainly from the rural areas of Central and North Wales. Because of the relative densities of population in the areas from which we came, the Anglo-Welsh probably outnumbered the Welsh-speaking Welsh. One thing we had in common was that our parents, though not really poor, were far from well-to-do, and we were conscious of the sacrifices they were making on our behalf and anxious to justify them. There were a few English boys, and in one form we had a Turk. As regards social class, a big group came from the class perhaps best described by the French terms 'petits commercants' or 'petits bourgeois' and in the case of the South Walians mostly from the industrial valleys rather than the big towns, presumably because in the latter there were better educational opportunities. Of the professions, sons of clergymen overwhelmingly predominated, though there was a sprinkling of sons of doctors and lawyers. The aristocracy was only a name to us, though we had one baronet, generally and affectionately called by everyone John Bart. I don't think that during my time was ever in the school a boy from 'the working class', partly because the parents could not have afforded the fees, partly because of the tradition that on finishing primary school the boy went out to work and began to earn.

The school was much smaller then than it is now; at a guess I would say there were about 150 of us. Because of the smallness of the two out-houses, Llandingat and College House, and the absence of clear architectural divisions into houses in the main school block, there was only a rudimentary house system. Though there were house masters and house prefects, there was little in the way of house loyalties or inter-house games or competitions. Instead, for example, there were junior and senior league matches in which attempts were made to pick evenly balanced sides which played each other for the championship. Though artificial creations, these matches aroused intense rivalry and enthusiasm in the junior league.

Defining culture in the limited sense of a knowledge and appreciation of literature, drama and the arts, we were in general a pretty uncultured lot. No one would have dreamed of trying to compose poetry, such as feature of the Journal in recent years. There was only one debate that I can remember, and there was no dramatic society. There was a small reading room with a borrowing library, largely consisting of books of adventure. An exception to this generalization is that we had nearly all of us been soaked in the literature and theology of the Bible in Church or Chapel, Sunday School or Church School.

A boy never addressed another boy by his Christian name, nor a master a boy. Most boys had nicknames, and for the few who did not, one used surnames. This curious sense of modesty about Christian names was typical of the time and not peculiar to Llandovery, and it prevailed also during my years as a medical student in London. One feature of conversation among the boys was the frequency of swear words. I don't know whether this was a general characteristic of public schools at the time or whether it has persisted, but it would have been difficult to count, for example, the number of 'bloody's' in a conversation of any length. As I have already mentioned, we also added a number of Welsh words to our repertoire.

Among the many new buildings which have gone up since my time is the School Chapel. When I first went, the school held its Sunday evening services in a little church in a village two miles or so to the north of Llandovery, the name of which I have forgotten. We enjoyed these services, which had the intimate atmosphere of being in our own school chapel and were conducted by our own clergymen masters. But after my first term and for reasons of which we were unaware, to our regret this arrangement ceased. For the rest of my time we used the parish church at Llandingat for all services, the school clergymen masters taking the morning services and the parish clergy the evening. The boys with the other masters occupied one of the aisles and the townspeople the rest of the church, and the atmosphere was naturally less intimate. The Warden, who in those days was by tradition a clergyman, gave most of the sermons. I can't remember any, but I vividly remember how often in 1915 and particularly in 1916 they were preceded by obituaries of old boys and old masters killed in the war. Llandovery was a Church of England school and naturally most boys were members, though there were a few nonconformists who attended their own services in the town. This was a time when the disestablishment and disendowment of the Church of England in Wales aroused angry political controversy, which we became aware of particularly since our bishop, Bishop Owen of St. David's was a leading and exceedingly vocal opponent of the measure. This is perhaps the place to mention briefly our religious attitude. We were all of us I think unquestioning Christian believers, completely unaware of the attempts at the reformulation of traditional Christian beliefs in light of modern knowledge taking place within the Church, or of the agnostic and atheistic attacks increasingly assailing it from outside. We

Warden's Sunday School Class 1916

unashamedly knelt down to pray by our dormitory beds before going to sleep, and we firmly believed in the efficacy of petitionary prayer. Our prayers were particularly fervent on the eve of the Brecon matches. They were usually favourably answered for the rugby matches, but much less often for cricket.

In my time at Llandovery as in most other public schools classics occupied the central predominant position in education. In the lower forms we concentrated on Latin grammar; in the intermediate and higher forms we added Greek and the history and literature of Greece and Rome. Llandovery had an excellent record for university classical scholarships, Oxford being the principal goal and very few boys trying for Cambridge. The school also had a good record for mathematical scholarships, and I remember one famous year in which we won both a Balliol and Christ Church major scholarship in this subject. There was a historical sixth, but this subject was regarded as a soft option, though one boy did win an exhibition to a Cambridge college. French was the only foreign language taught but, as was usual at that time, largely as a grammatical exercise than as a living language. The life was also taken out of English Language by the attempt, general at that time, to treat it in a similar manner to a rigid Latin grammar from which it had managed to free itself. Science was substantially non-existent, and the school did not possess a single science laboratory. Though we had the good fortune to be surrounded by a varied and attractive countryside which contrasted with the scarred industrial valleys from which many of us came, we took little interest in natural history, chiefly I think because of the absence of the stimulus of a science department. I can describe very simply the preparation for medicine at Llandovery in my time, as for all other careers, since it can be summed up in one word—classics. In this, Llandovery was not exceptional but typical . . . For Llandovery, science virtually did not exist. There were no laboratories, no biology, no physics, and chemistry consisted only of a few didactic lectures to a few boys taking London matric . . . The literary language was regarded as the main vehicle of education, and the cultivation of observation and experiment largely ignored.

An important event in the school year was the Latin grammar test, which all the school took at the end of the summer term. The test consisted of one hundred questions and aroused tremendous excitement in the junior forms, though the seniors tended to be rather blasé about it. The Warden read out the results at school assembly, starting with the lowest scores. Two such occasions still stand out in my memory. At end end of my first term I felt myself a miserable object when I was one of three boys who 'failed to score' and filled with envy of those superior beings from among my classmates who scored a few marks. The other was in form 3b, the master of which was the Rev Ifor Jones, known for obvious reasons as 'Long 'Un'. He used to give every boy in his class a target mark, which if achieved won a tea in tuck. Great was my pride and joy when I just managed to bring it off.

I expect all of us have special memories of certain masters and I would like to mention three, Long 'Un, Mr Lockyer and Mr Wiseman. Long 'Un's Latin classes in form 3b consisted of a preliminary relaxed period in which we discussed the latest school matches, or the good or bad marks earned by individuals in our junior games. The second part consisted of sudden-death questions on the Latin grammar we had prepared for the lesson. The number of misses allowed was greater for a group of weaker brethren who sat at the back of the class and enjoyed the epithet of 'the royal standbacks'. At the end of the lesson Long 'Un used to send the boys on the defaulters' list out to the Warden for tanning. There was one older and bigger boy among the royal standbacks who nearly always was one of those sent out, and he used to be put in charge of the group. His technique was to knock at the Warden's door and say: 'Please, Sir, Mr Jones asked me to bring along these boys to be tanned', staying outside himself during the process. As far as I know he was never found out. Mr Lockyer was the master in charge of the junior dormitories in my early years, and one night caught me out of bed playing the fool after lights out. He said he would come along the next night to tan me, explaining that he made it a rule not to act under the influence of anger. I have tried, often unsuccessfully, to live up to this useful rule. Mr Wiseman had the biggest influence on me. He was master of the 4th form when I reached it. At the end of the first term he sent for me and said that, though I was doing all right in my form subjects, I was dreadfully ignorant generally. He prescribed for me a list of books to read, and thus started me off on a love of reading and the acquisition of knowledge. I was fortunate in that he was transferred to 5b at the end of the year, and thus became my form master during the important year when we sat for the Junior School Certificate, roughly equivalent to the modern 'O' Level. Mr Wiseman did not return to the school for the Christmas term of 1914, having joined Kitchener's Army at the beginning of the war. With so many thousands of others he was killed on the Somme in 1916, and this added to the aura surrounding him for me.

Discipline was enforced in two chief ways, by tanning and by keeping us fully occupied during our waking hours. Tanning by the Warden, the housemasters and the prefects was frequent, the one relief being that there was no tanning on Sundays. We were kept occupied for most of the time that we were not doing our school work by compulsory organized games. If the weather was too bad for these, the authorities fell back on compulsory cross country runs. One Easter term the theory broke down because everywhere was frozen up, and day after day we were left to our own devices. A group of boys out of boredom started a competition in throwing stones at the china insulators on the top of telegraph posts, and soon they had to walk long distances to find any unbroken ones. Nemesis came one February day when we saw a police man accompanied by an important looking man in civilian clothes arrive at the school.

Food could be described at the best as simple and limited. The official breakfast consisted of a mug of hot tea and rationed unappetising slabs of bread and scrape, on which we spread our own marmalade, jam or golden syrup. Even porridge was an extra as was bacon and egg, but only a few boys of better-off parents took the latter. Dinner was a reasonable meal from the point of view of bulk—meat with potatoes and a vegetable followed by puddings, of which the most popular were the occasional heavy boiled puddings because of the lovely full feeling they gave. At tea we again had the slabs of bread and scrape, and what we had for supper I can't remember but it was certainly simple and limited. I don't remember ever having soup, and cake was rare and exceptional. Friday's dinner was an excellent example of the absence of 'feed back', or if it existed it is ignored. Big dishes containing fish stew was placed in front of the masters sitting at the end of each table. They took some, but during my whole time at school all boys systematically refused it and took only potatoes and vegetables, there being a stupid tradition that the fish were bad. The fish dishes were then returned to the kitchen substantially untouched: we never knew what happened to them. With this spartan fare we naturally brought back to school as much food as we could in our tuck boxes, and appreciated very much food parcels from home. When we were asked out to tea by married masters it was the custom for our hosts to withdraw at the end of the meal, this being the signal for us to fill up our pockets with any transportable items that were left to give our friends. In spite of our spartan fare we remained in general a very healthy lot of boys.

Finally a word about hygiene and sanitation. The indoor arrangements were satisfactory, the wash room and bathroom facilities being adequate. We washed in cold water and could have a cold bath every day if we wished. We had a routine hot bath once a week. There were jerries under all dormitory beds. The outdoors toilet arrangements were primitive in the extreme. The 'bogs' was a hut like building adjacent to Tredegar Close, the receptacles of which were emptied only at half term and during the holidays. There was no attempt even at what is euphemistically called 'chemical sanitation', and understandably the building declared its existence from afar.

Summing up, for most of us I think our time at Llandovery was neither 'the happiest days of one's life' of the cliché, nor the 'hell on earth' response to public schools of the time of the memoirs of so many liberal intellectuals, but an undoubtedly tough but on the whole reasonably happy experience which provided for many of us an avenue to higher education which we might not otherwise have found.

(School Journal, Summer 1977 annotated with an extract from 'Some Personal Reflections on Forty-five Years of Medicine', Journal, June 1961.

David Patey M.S., F.R.C.S., was born in Monmouth in October 1899: he was 12 when he entered Llandovery College. From there he proceeded to the University of London and was awarded the 'Gold Medal' in his M.B. examination. He pursued postgraduate studies with conspicuous success winning the Jacksonian Prize of the Royal College of Surgeons of England; he had become a Fellow in 1924. He was twice Hunterian Professor of the Royal College of Surgeons and was founder and first President of the Surgical Research Society. He gained a very considerable reputation for his operation for the treatment of early breast cancer.

Patey distinguished himself not only as a general surgeon in the London hospitals but also as an outstanding teacher. He retired to Hythe where he gained great pleasure from birdwatching).

1913-1956

H. J. POWELL

Hadn't I been captain of rugger? But this bravado only increased the nightmarish uncertainty underlying my excitement at returning to Llandovery for the first time since leaving in 1913. Term hadn't started. I liked the dignified new entrance gates at once. Then, just as the stucco work of the new Chapel caught my eye, Mr D. J. Evans made himself known and I explained myself. In his sympathetic hands much of my lost feeling went. He told me that stucco had to be to protect the porous stone.

The Chapel inside is simple and pleasing: may its light never be dimmed by dull stained glass. The oak reredos is lovely. I thought it a pity its live figures have, medieval fashion, been painted. Then I found, what I so much wanted to see, the names of those killed in World War I. I couldn't find my young brother's name quickly enough. He was recommended for the V.C. at Looswill the 9th Welch; I have the Colonel's letter at home. He scored against Brecon from, he afterwards boasted, a solo dribble from our line but actually 'fell on' in a forwards' rush from our 25, or was it theirs? So many were of my time, their names sounded like roll. My thoughts stayed longer on some: L. G. Cooper, scholar at Oxford; a light Ivor Morgan, had three shots at Responsions Maths and three at me with his slipper my first night. When we were in the team he explained he had just been made a prefect, and, having to make a beginning, had hit on me, so hurting my feelings; C. B. Davies played for Cardiff in the hols, would have played centre to his brother in the Welsh team; leg-pulling Carl Davies played second row too with me in a Sandhurst War team; short-sighted Mears, exhibitioner at Oxford, began Welsh as a joke and became useful at it according to Appy. And so down the list, most of them recalling some memory. Jumbo Weeks, cheekiest, cheeriest, of cadgers: Pa his brother who invited me, a lone new boy to walk to Church with him and Nick Griffiths. Nick was Captain of Cardiff University and about the first death in my battalion; Ivor Williams the soundest of all centres in whom we forwards had every trust; brilliant Oswald Williams, scholar at Oxford, in all the teams and I think Ladies Prize winner: while in the Maths VI won—it sounds incredible now—Classical VI Latin prize and Historical VI prize. He was degraded for the rest of the term for poaching salmon with laughable simplicity and keeping them fresh in Juniors' bath.

Sympathetically Mr Evans kept up a flow of small talk when I rejoined him, and there, welcome as a familiar face in a strange place, were the old Fives Courts with the same old pot holes. These were real: no thrown slippers would wake me to the dorm. 'Look,' I pointed, 'The Classroom dorm. I was prefect there. Hide-a-way of the wide boys of my time—those frightful fifteenagers, terror of the toughest pref. half of them shaving long before, the rest long after, they should, pimples, scurf and all.' Mr Evans was happy to inform me it still is and is.

The school inside is painted in cheerful colours with colourful paintings and reproductions everywhere. I peeped into the Reading Room where, as a rustic new boy from an Oxfordshire village school, I had read to pass the time with a cautious eye and ear to that strange land of my fathers. It is now the Masters' Common Room and was being cleaned out. By extraordinary chance—ask Mr Evans—of the hundreds of groups taken over the years, the only one showing was the fifteen in 1911 with me on it. Thus Llandovery quietly reminded me I still belonged.

The 'Big Hall' in 1919

On to the Big Hall: was this delightful hall with its oil paintings and striking floor the bare old white washed barn of my time with its hissing gas jets and fuming stove? The heavily initialled tops of those massive oak tables, how grand they are, have been reversed or I could have gone straight to my initials. I looked for the Honours board covering my period; young Whosit, his Eton suit a sight too tight for his plump rump, now a big surgeon; 'Young Spug,' Professor of Physiology, gold medal and that; 'Old Spug,' exhibitioner at Cambridge, not the bishop I prophesised, but M.C. and Colonel in the Somersets; that reluctant washer a Sheriff; earnest G.M., Scholar and Maths Scholar at Oxford, a knight; Young Stan, Scholar at Oxford, M.C., barrister and Head of Woolworths; Comical H.S. not a Leslie Hensh but a parson still young in heart and producer of Blues at Magdalen College School; his brother—Mervyn Johns; and so on. The whole set up all hay wire. Yet was it? Of most one could say 'I told you so.' Of the death of Oswald Williams and those others? If one could have foretold the War, yes, the Oswald Williams's would be killed.

A step into VB classroom, cheerful like the rest, where the grand master The Baron was wont to propound basso profundo '"Me le, me la, me les, tu le, tu la, tu les BUT le lui, la lui, les lui' OR I shall give you such a clonk".' Sitting at my old desk, like a medium, I began reciting, 'With imperare and obey studere, nudere, nocere to these add envy, trust, forgive, resist dida dida dida.' What case they take I haven't the foggiest. Let 'X' = the unknown: it does. 'The Prefects' Room?' I asked, and there I got my biggest shock—it hasn't changed one iota: the same dull paint, the same comfortable old desk chairs and shabby inked cloth; the same lexicon and books chucked on to the window sill: yes, I swear, even Rolly Bumps' old No. 10s cricket boots in the corner left over from last term. Cave! That's Pooley's slow measured tread clanking upon the iron treads of the stairs. Mr Evans said it has become a prefects' tradition that this study remains untouched. What would Dr Ernest Jones make of this?

No wonder Mr Evans is so proud of his fine laboratories—the science block of course is after my time. I gave them a close once-over and they compare very favourably with those of the medical school of my hospital in London, but the school I imagine needs more than this. In the vestibule an old photograph of Ben Evans, that early benefactor, welcomed me and connected this fine department to my Llandovery but where used that photograph to hang?

Next Mr Evans took me to the latest addition to the school, the magnificent Lawrence Jones Santorium. This too being up my street just left me gasping—goodness gracious me Lawrence bach!

And so at last, my throat now really painful from the long strain of trying to suppress my emotions, I came to—the Tredegar Close: as moving to me as those names in the Chapel and part of them. This pitch is real, real even to the still faint ridge across the centre where formerly was a hedge; no need to pinch myself now; quite overcome and to blazes with being grown up—I salute it—and its ghosts. Listen. That's the Rev G. I. R. Longun's ghost rampaging 'Feet! You ass! Feet! Hundred lines for picking up' and he fetches the ghost of my youth, a one which I am proud to see is returned with respect and interest. A fleeting grin, a bellow 'get in your sluggard! Kick him off! Heel! Blast you; Wake up!' Right O, Long-un—sorry-Sir, I wake up all right—to my senile wheezing, to my sixteen stone all in the wrong places, yes wake up to—how come?—1956.

(School Journal November 1956. The reminiscences are signed 'DAD P'— Dr H. J. Powell who was Captain of Football in 1912).

1915-1928

ESTHER POOLE-HUGHES

John and Esther

In childhood our lives—John and mine—were bound up in the life of the College. The School buildings provided a never-ending source of exploration particularly, of course, in the school holidays when we were much freer to go where we wished.

In those days the Warden's residence was entered by what is still called 'The Warden's Entrance'. I remember the Servants' Hall—the first door one came to after leaving the 'private' side of the house—the long tables and benches and, in particular, the large slatted high backed chair for cook—who always wore a hat. There was a 'townie' who laid the tables and brought in the food etc. John, who was addicted to cards from an early age, enjoyed himself playing with anyone who happened to be in the room.

I remember the kitchen with its large coal ranges and the scullery beyond. All the cooking for the School and private house—including the nursery—was done here. I remember the dairy beyond the kitchen and the great pans of milk (from the cows which my father kept) and seeing butter made. Then there was the boys' dining hall supervised by the maid-in-charge who was not all keen on us riding our tricycles in the vicinity.

One of my favourite visits was to go out through the back door (behind the kitchen) into the yard and thence to the laundry. There was the large boiler (I have one of the scoops used there to this day), the duckboards and of course steam everywhere. And all who worked there were so cheerful. I remember, too, the small room next door with a coke-store and the flat irons heating all around it. Maggie Richards was in charge and she, it was, who milked the cows daily.

Beyond the laundry yard there was an open area and we would follow a path alongside the Gym (given to the School, I believe, by my mother's uncle Ben Evans) into a small farm area. A cowshed with two cows and sometimes a calf; a pigsty (my father used to tell us he paid for our annual holiday in Borth from the pigs!) and a marvellous haystack . . . not to mention a selection of hens.

We loved the summer holidays when the maids had less to do. It became a tradition that we persuaded some of them to dress up with us from the acting costume trunks kept in the Gym. My mother would take our photographs. I was very fond of sport of all kinds and we organised maids' cricket matches on the side lawn by the back gate. These events, unfortunately, were brought to an end when one of the maids on the 'Private Side' sprained her ankle!

The maids in fancy dress . . . with Esther and John

The 'Private Side' was ruled over by Lizzie, 'Lizzie College' as she was known in the town. As a young widow she had come to look after our grandmother when my father came to Llandovery early in the century. When our grandmother died and my father married, Lizzie stayed on. There were usually two maids under her. She was talented in many ways and we enjoyed being with her in the Pantry when, later on, the governess had her afternoon off. (She came with us when we moved to Llandingat House and was an important part of our early lives).

We were, of course, keenly interested in 'The Boys', particularly, their prowess on the games field—chiefly in their rugby and to a lesser degree in their cricket. I shall never forget—standing on Tredegar Close—the agony of anticipation as everyone turned to watch—first, the visiting side who were greeted by polite clapping and, then, the members of the 1st XV emerging in their white shirts and blue shorts from behind the Fives Court and the shrill chorus of 'School' which greeted them. The Brecon Match was, of course, the climax of the Rugby Season: when it was played at Brecon, John and I really did feel we were on 'enemy territory' . . . and our parents did their very best to make us see sense!

The Old Boys' Cricket Match, too, was one of the highlights of our year: many of them had been at School long before our time but we got to know them as they returned year by year. I remember one match in particular when V. G. J. Jenkins playing for the School XI for the first time (aged 14) made 50 runs thereby winning 10/- promised by the manager of the local National Provincial Bank (Mr Jones). I remember my father saying: 'But he's good at his lessons too!' . . . no doubt hoping I would take note.

I remember going to sing-songs in the School Hall. Concerts and social events were always held in the Gym. We always joined in the two minutes' silence on November 11th: I can see my father's face now, grey and solemn; he must have had memories of boys leaving to go out to France.

We saw practically nothing of my father in term-time but when the mornings were light he would take us up New Road at 7 a.m.—with me, usually, throwing our small-sized rugby ball between the three of us—and then back again. There was no traffic to worry about in those days!

I remember joining in the School Dancing Class one year and John and I were members of the School's Sketching Class for two years or more and enjoyed it immensely.

In the holidays we often went for trips in my father's 1907 Rover car (adapted to suit his girth!) He used to take us up to castle ruins in the Towy Valley, to visit churches and all kinds of interesting places. I remember going with him to Dolaucothi to visit Lady Hills-Johnes (widow of Lt. General Sir James Hills-Johnes who had been a Trustee of the College from 1886 to 1918). She was bedridden and I was sent to play in the garden and watch the peacocks.

Esther with her father, 1925

I remember now how appalling was the condition of the road to Lampeter—totally untarmacked.

Although quite young I was aware that my father's priesthood meant much to him: how much he would have loved to have had a School Chapel! He so much enjoyed going to Sunday Evensong in Llanfair Church which, of course, he had known well in boyhood. Now he lies buried in Llandingat churchyard; in the church is a memorial tablet to him: 'He was not only a scholar but a great teacher, loving his pupils, generous to those in need. And devoted to Llandovery College and Town.' It was such a privilege—and so much fun—for me, and John, to have been part of his years at Llandovery.

(Miss Esther Poole Hughes is the daughter and elder child of the late Canon and Mrs Poole Hughes; her brother John was Bishop of South West Tanganyika and later Bishop of Llandaff. Miss Poole Hughes resides in Hereford.

Her uncle was Benjamin Evans: the Journal of Easter 1913 noted 'Through the splendid generosity of Mr Benjamin Evans, one of the Trustees, a beautiful block of buildings is to be added to the School. It will contain Chemical and Physical Laboratories and Classrooms. It is a noble gift, and of its kind unparalleled in the history of the School.' He was to die shortly after that tribute was written).

1914

'YOUNG JENNINGS'

> Mapperley,
> Nottingham,
> NG3 5JL
> Tel. (0602)
>
> June 23rd 82
>
> Dear Sir,
> In 1913 my brother, Hayward Jennings, was a pupil at Llandovery College. He played goal for the school football team. I have in my possession his team blazer and cap. They are in good condition, and I am wondering if they would be of any use to you. Have you a school museum? It seems a pity to throw them away.
>
> My brother was one of the senior boys, and he left school to join up during the first world war. He did not come back.
>
> The headmaster at that time was Mr. Poole-Hughes.
>
> Yours very truly,
> (Miss) M.L. Jennings.

G. Hayward Jennings was the son of the Rev. Richard Jennings. He was born at Glynceiriog on Jan: 5th 1897. He was a pupil at Llandovery College, and played goal for the School football team. In Dec: 1914

Hayward left school and on his eighteenth birthday, Jan: 5th 1915, when he could say he was in his nineteenth year, he enlisted as a private in Kitchener's Army. Later he obtained a Commission in the 21st Batt. Royal Welch Fusiliers, and was sent to France. The 21st Batt. had been up to the front line

and were back at base when word came that the 13th Batt. had been badly cut up and were short of officers, would any officers of the 21st Batt. volunteer to go up? Hayward was one who volunteered. He was killed in action a few days later.

(The name of G. H. Jennings appears on the Great War Memorial Plaque in the College chapel.

A commemoration of him—and the others lost—is to be found in the Book of Remembrance 1914-1918 by Harold W. Evans and Patricia J. Evans.

Those lost in the Second World War and the Korean War are commemorated in a similar volume by John R. Evans.

Both volumes were dedicated by Bishop Ivor Rees at a special service held at the College chapel on Saturday 8 November 1997).

1921-1930

V. G. J. Jenkins

*V. G. J. Jenkins
1929*

'Spartan' is the first adjective that comes to mind in trying to describe life at Llandovery in my time. I seem to recall that in the ancient Greek city it was the custom to expose newly-born babes on the mountainside and if they survived, well and good; if not, it was just too bad! Things were not as tough as that with us, but there was an element of the survival of the fittest about it all, and those that came through were well-fitted for most things in later life.

When I first arrived there the food was frugal, to put it mildly, and without our tuck-boxes, and parcels from home, some of us would have been in poor shape. It was not long after the first World War, and the aftermath was still being felt. Also the fees our parents had to pay were only £80 a year—'cheaper than keeping them at home' I remember one of them saying—and there was quite a fuss when they went up to £90 a year. Even allowing for present-day inflation, it was remarkably little to pay, and I sometimes wonder how they were able to feed us at all. The big treat, I remember, was to have an egg, usually hard-boiled, on Sunday mornings—the only one we had during the week! Physically, too, we were put through our paces. In the winter it was a case of Rugby practically every day of the week, in all kinds of weather, and the drying facilities were none too good. Wet jerseys, from the day before, are something I recall vividly. Yet we were a very happy crowd, on the whole, and the boys I grew up with at school have always been my best friends since.

It was in September, 1921, at the age of 9, that I first set out for the school—in a railway carriage from Port Talbot with two other boys who seemed enormous to me at the time. Their names were Rice Williams—from Barry—and Emmanuel, and I can see them as vividly now as I did at the time. I was apprehensive, too—what 'new boy' is not?—especially of Emmanuel, who must have been at least 12 and looked a giant in my eyes. Both he and Rice Williams had been at the school before, and were sporting their school caps, whereas I had none, pending my arrival at Llandovery. The psychological effect of those caps was considerable, and it was a subdued 9 year-old, in my case, who eventually arrived at Llandovery. Once there, and installed in 'Cawdor', with a crop of other new boys, the initial 'scares' gradually wore off; but I doubt if anyone, whatever befalls him later, ever forgets the trauma of his first few days at school.

Boys on the Cricket Field: waiting to watch the game 1925

I was to spend nearly nine years there—I left at the end of the Easter term in 1930—and perhaps that was too long. It might have been better to have spent a few years at a 'prep. school' first, but there was no 'Junior House' in those days, or different individual Houses, as now. We were all lumped in together in the main school, except for half-a-dozen or so boys at 'Coll. House'—on the corner opposite Llandingat as you turn into the town. Llandingat, at that time, was a private residence, and Tŷ Ddewi had not been built. We were only 120 boys or so, all told, and at one time, in the 'slump', I believe the number went down to only 87 . . . It was like growing up in one large family, and it certainly made for a strong community spirit, which remains to this day.

Yet it is people, not food or surroundings, that really make a school, and in that we were well blessed. There were certainly some 'characters' at Llandovery in my time, not least the Warden when I first arrived there. His full name was the Rev Canon William Worthington Poole-Hughes, but to us he was known, no doubt irreverently, as 'Pud' (as in 'm'lud,'!). Short, thick-set and rotund, he had been a very good rugby forward, we were told, in the days when 'mauls in goal' were said to have lasted five minutes or so. He was certainly rugby-minded, and if he caught us playing soccer, even with a tennis ball, he used to set about us with his walking stick, to make us mend our ways.

Warden Poole-Hughes and his car 1927

Corporal punishment was still very much the vogue in those days, and 'Pud', who had been a housemaster at Sherborne before coming to Llandovery (where he himself was educated), was very much one of the 'old school'. He wielded his 'Benjy' (swishy cane) and the birch with telling effect on those who offended against school rules, and there was no question of padding one's trousers. Instead one had to take them down, bend over, and lift the tail of one's shirt. Many a 'martyr' proudly displayed his 'war-wounds' afterwards and felt quite a hero. I shudder to think what the Press would have made of it in these days, but at least it taught us to grit our teeth and take what was coming to us. The psychiatrists would no doubt say it did us lasting harm, but perhaps it did us a lot of good, too.

There were other sides to 'Pud,' though. He had been an outstanding academic in his day—a scholar of Balliol at both classics and mathematics, I believe—and had collected some fine teachers around him. My own in the Classical VIth, Donald Pye, a scholar of Winchester and New College, Oxford, was one of them, and there is no man, still, whom I respect more. He laboured mightily on our behalf, and threw himself with zest into all the activities of the school—even rugger, which he had never played before arriving there. Tom Hill, later also to become a Reverend, was in charge of maths, and was an outstanding teacher, who wrote several text-books on his subject. Then there was D. R. Williams—elder brother of the one and only 'T.P.', and just as good a rugger coach in his way, though with the emphasis on forwards rather than backs. 'D.R.' ran not only the rugger, but practically everything else in the school, or so it seemed to us. Later, when 'Pud' died and the Rev Walker Thomas took over as Warden, 'D.R.' moved on to Cheltenham. There he became a housemaster and made himself an even bigger reputation. 'T.P.' joined us later, towards the end of my time at school, and there is no need for me to elaborate on all that he did for the school for many years afterwards. Chris Bell, too, endeared himself to many of us who came down for Old Boys' cricket matches after leaving.

Among the boys there in my time my first hero was D. R. Hughes, the head pref. when I arrived at school. He held the school record for the 100 yards, and went on to win a half-Blue at Oxford for long-jumping. He then entered the Royal Navy and ended up, I believe, a Lieutenant Commander. Rugger players we produced in plenty. Dudley Bartlett and Arthur Jones (wings), Graham Jones (centre), Cliff Jones (fly-half), Arfon Roberts (scrum-half) and Arthur Rees (wing-forward) all played for Wales later on, and W. D. B. Hopkins and T. R. Thomas, both scrum-halves, won Blues at Cambridge and Oxford respectively. This at a time when there could have been only 30 or so boys in the school over the age of 16. It was rather a remarkable record, but we owed a lot to 'D.R.' and 'T.P.' They certainly knew their rugby!

At cricket the school pro was one Tom Soar, who had played for Hampshire as a fast bowler before the turn of the century. We used to admire his old county cap, hanging up in the pavilion, and he helped to produce some wonderful pitches for us, on the same ground as now; but he was well on in years by this time, and died not long after I left school. His methods were a bit out-dated, I suppose, of the old 'forward school' variety, and I remember him best as an 'encourager'. What schoolboy batsman does not need one?

We played hockey in the Easter term for my last two years—largely because we had on the staff F. C. Stocks, a member of the famous England hockey family of that name. It was said that the Stocks family could put out a team to play the rest of England!

Academically I would describe the school at that time as 'good average', without reaching the heights. There were so few of us and the sixth forms were so small. In the Classical VIth, I know, there were only two of us in my first two years, and never more than three. Out-of-school activities, other than games, were very limited, I fear, and nothing like as well organised as they are to-day.

I remember being in the choir, first as a treble than as a bass, and taking part in endless rehearsals for 'Hiawatha's Wedding Feast' with the school operatic society; but for some reason—our own limitations, probably!—it never reached the stage of a public performance. The debating society, too, was a very haphazard affair. 'Sing-songs' were about as high as we reached in the matter of musical culture! The School Magazine had to be produced three times a year, and most of its contents, I am afraid, seemed to be connected with Rugby, or cricket. I was one of the two deputy-editors for a year or two before I left, which perhaps accounts for my future life-style!

From what I see and hear of the school at the present time, it seems a better place than it was in my day, with more variety and a much wider spread of interests. That is as it should be, with the passing of time, but I and my contemporaries still feel we owe a great deal to the school. Whatever we are, Llandovery shaped us—and of one thing I am sure of the school's successes, whether it be in beating the old rivals, Brecon, at Rugby, or in more exalted spheres. Floreat Llandubriense, now and always!

(School Journal Summer 1977. Vivian Jenkins the distinguished sports journalist was born in 1911: his connection with the College remains and he is a familiar—and revered—figure at Speech Days. His career at the College was remarkable . . . Head Prefect, Sub-editor of the Journal and where he achieved great distinction in Hockey, Rugby and Cricket. From Llandovery he was awarded a Meyrick Exhibition in Classics at Jesus College Oxford. At Oxford he gained three rugby 'blues': he was capped 14 times for Wales. He was Sunday Times rugby correspondent for a quarter of a century—his column marked always by astute observation and an engaging style).

1923-1927

T. S. NEVILL

I don't suppose any new boy arriving at Llandovery Station at the beginning of his first term ever felt more lost and lonely than I did on a September evening in 1923 when, after practically the whole day in a series of trains from London I reached that quiet little town in the Towy valley which for the next four years was to be my second home: I am quite sure that no young schoolmaster ever had a happier or more interesting four years in his first teaching post.

The 'new-boy' feeling quickly wore off in the genuinely friendly atmosphere of the Llandovery of those days and just to share a study, as I did for my whole first year with 'D.R.', the finest all-round schoolmaster I have ever met, was an education for a young man starting the job and began for me a friendship which has lasted ever since.

In the early twenties there were many personalities at Llandovery both in the School and in the town. Supreme above them all was the Warden whom I think we all feared a little, but for whom it was impossible not to feel affection. I have vivid memories of him, standing watch in hand, outside the Hall at 7.15 of a summer's morning checking the punctuality of staff and the boys at Early School and woe betide you, boy or master, if you were late!—and equally vivid memories of a day when he suddenly told me to make arrangements for my classes and whisked me off in his car to St. Davids, where he had a meeting, bringing me home through Fishguard and Cardigan. He spent much of his time in the Inner Study—the Outer Study was little more than a place of execution!—with the door firmly locked and to penetrate to it unbidden was something of an ordeal. You knocked and a voice—a rather heavy voice which matched his build growled: 'Who's there?' When you answered—I remember I once replied, 'The Warden, Nevill,' but he didn't seem to mind—you were formally admitted and then, if you had a real problem or difficulty, nobody could have been kinder or given wiser advice.

Then on the Staff, too, there were Freddy Stocks, English Hockey International and Oxford Cricket Blue, at Llandingat, Tom Hill at College House, and, later, Donald Pye, Edwin Hickox and Tom Charles Edwards, a descendant of the famous Dr Thomas Charles, of Bala, who brought the Bible to Wales.

In the town, to mention only a few, I recall William Williams the Cabs and his brother David, builders—they built the Gym. between them, I believe, for about £800—carpenters and above all craftsmen, Jones the Bank, 'Scribbler Bill,' Dr Tom Morgan, brother of the famous Dr Teddy, the Misses Lewis' and the Williamses of Llanfair Grange. And then the boys—what floods of names

LLANDOVERY COLLEGE.

Second Term.

1927.

Warden and Head Master.

The Rev. Canon W. W. Poole Hughes, M.A.

Assistant Masters.

T. H. W. Hill, Esq., M.A.
D. R. Williams, Esq., B.A.
T. S. Nevill, Esq., M.A.
A. H. Rodgers, Esq., B.A.
D. W. Pye, Esq., M.A.
E. H. C. Hickox, Esq., M.A.
T. Charles Edwards, Esq., B.A.
L. W. G. Spooner, Esq.

come back to me and all of them personalities in one way or another—'An Bible,' 'Pulpeet,' John Zammitt, whose mother was, of all unexpected occupations, a steeple-jack , Dai John Rees, always known as 'Hands' who, if he hadn't smashed his leg in a holiday game one September, might have been a greater fly-half than his contemporary Windsor Lewis, 'Chicken' Jones, Arthur Jones, Vivian Jenkins, who, like Arthur Jones, started life as a scrum-half, A. M. Rees, Odo Saunders, Jack Stephens, J. D. Bartlett, M. H. Evans, W. D. B. Hopkins, our only Cambridge Blue during my time, and his brother, Hector, who I can remember stopping me once in a 1st game on Tredegar when I was going all out for the line, though he was only thirteen. His arms weren't long enough for him to get a grip on both my legs, so he froze on to one and brought me to a stop. I thought I knew something about Rugger when I came to Llandovery, but those afternoons on Tredegar taught me more about the game than I had known before or have ever learnt since.

A favourite winter recreation was cross-country running either alone or with one or two of my colleagues or the occasional boy. But perhaps the most delightful memories belong to fine summer afternoons with hours of cricket by the river, bathing up the valley and sometimes tennis parties at the Warden's always followed by wonderful teas.

Prefects 1926: Stephens, Rees, Bartlett, Beith, Evans, Reed

The accommodation in those days was very primitive and when, after the great flood, which I think was in the spring of 1927, there was no main water in the town for nearly three weeks, things became even more primitive. I seem to remember that our only hot washes for some time were in the laundry, where coppers full of well-water were kept constantly on the boil. There was no electricity anywhere and gas only in the main buildings: in College House,

Llandingat and Bank House, occupied then by various bachelor masters, nothing but lamps and candles were in use.

Other unforgettable memories concern great walks on various Dai's Days; an incredible 'away' Cricket match against Brecon when, with forty minutes to go, our ninth wicket fell and two bowlers, who had scarcely scored a run during the season, confidently played out time, put on nearly fifty runs and came within twenty or so of the Brecon total; choir outings to Llanwrtyd Wells—it was singing in the College Choir that first gave me a love for Choral singing—and a very good choir it was, too, trained by a Mathematician while a Scientist played the Organ; the unmerciful ragging of a member of the staff, by, I regret to say, one of his colleagues; journey to Neath to watch the XV playing the famous Neath Ex-Schoolboys, and, later the same evening, Albert Freethy telling most dramatically the story of how he sent the New Zealander, Brownlee, off the field at Twickenham when the All Blacks were playing England; 'I saw a great mass of flesh and bone come tearing down the field with teeth bared and fist clenched'; Tommy Vile, quiet, collected and supremely competent, refereeing the Brecon match on Tredegar.

Llandovery may have been small in those days, but it was a happy place and I constantly give thanks that it was there and not somewhere else that I started my teaching career.

(School Journal November 1953. Nevill was then Headmaster of Wellingborough School. In the Journal Notes of Easter 1930 is recorded 'T. S. Nevill played for Wales v. Scotland at Hockey').

1930-1933

K. IMESON

In earlier times first the Romans, then the Normans and later the English barons left their homes and crossed the Marches into Wales to subdue the unruly Celts. More recently, in 1930 to be exact, I joined a small band of colleagues in a descent on Llandovery with similar intent. The local chieftains, Ward Hill and T. P. Williams, appeared to welcome this regular invasion by the English three times a year, possibly for the civilising influence they were supposed to bring or more likely to strengthen their hands when the peasantry got out of hand.

So, on a bright autumnal afternoon I arrived at Llandovery on the through train from Paddington via Shrewsbury (it always seemed to me an odd way round) intent on my new task of dispensing mathematics instead of absorbing it as I had been doing for almost twenty years.

After unpacking my bags in Bank House where I was to live for the next three years during term time, I was introduced to my colleagues who included four other foreigners like myself as well as the two natives who obviously ran the place, Ward Hill, the Second Master and chief organiser, and T. P. Williams, whose multifarious duties it would be difficult to define. I found that I was down to teach, not only mathematics, but English (which to a few boys from remote parts was a foreign language), Geography and Science, none of which I was, in a formal sense, qualified to teach. Although I possessed an honours degree in Mathematics, I had not taken the course for the Diploma of Education, and so was expected to teach by the light of nature. I like to think that my methods compensated by their originality for their lack of expertise.

On the first day I also made the acquaintance of the Warden who had appointed me several months before by telegram, without an interview, relying on those who were kind enough to vouch for me. I often wondered if he were possessed of second sight because nearly all the men who went to Llandovery not only served the College well but made a success of their careers afterwards.

During the time that I was on the staff, the Revd. T. Walker Thomas was Warden. To a young, unfledged schoolmaster straight from the University, and not long separated from his own schooldays, he presented a stern and somewhat forbidding appearance. It was like replacing one headmaster by another. In retrospect, I believe the impression he gave was due to an innate shyness which made it difficult for him to express his true feelings publicly, for he had a keen sense of humour and, when a master (or a boy) needed help in solving a personal problem, he could show great understanding and kindness.

I did not know then, as I do now, what a difficult task the Warden had to face in the early 1930's. Those were the days of industrial depression when all the public schools, especially the smaller ones, were having difficulty in filling their places and some were in desperate straits. The numbers at Llandovery had fallen to about 120, as far as I can remember, simply because many prospective parents could not afford the fees in those difficult times. Strict economy had to be exercised in the running of the school, and naturally there were some who grumbled. It is a great tribute to the faith and wisdom of the Warden and Governors of that time that the school survived, and those who are still alive must be very proud to see the developments which have taken place since then, based on the secure foundations they laid. The Warden also had to contend with a mainly young and untrained staff, most of whom had no experience of teaching or of boarding school life when they came. Yet we all respected his wisdom and his dignity in often trying circumstances, and we came to share his intense pride in the school which persisted after we had left, as I know from meeting in later years a number of men who had taught at Llandovery.

On the day following my arrival we assembled for the first staff meeting . . . After this my troubles began. Faced with my first class, I found that at least three-quarters of them shared five surnames—Evans, Jones, Rees, Thomas, Williams. This caused a certain amount of confusion at the start because, if you called on a boy by his surname, four or five would shout the answer to your question. I was being tried in the fire.

As I have said, the 1930's were times of difficulty for the Public Schools during a time of economic depression, few middle class parents could afford the fees. One result was that entrance standards were lowered and some boys entering the School from Welsh-speaking homes at 8 years of age hardly knew any English. One boy in the first form, asked to read a passage of French from a book with the English translation on the opposite page, asked: 'Sir, which is the French?'

Classrooms in those days were not centrally heated, as I suppose they are now, and in morning classes we were greeted with roaring coal fires which gradually died down without replenishment during the day. By the time afternoon school came round, the rooms were so cold that we had to wear our overcoats. By then the gas lamps had been lit, and after supper the boys sat in the hall, as near as they could get to the huge iron stoves, for supervised prep while those masters not on duty retired to their rooms to do their marking and preparation by the kindly light of paraffin oil lamps.

After my first few days' teaching I was exhausted, and I welcomed the respite to be given by the half-holiday on Wednesday. At lunch time I happened to glance at the games notice board and found that I had been put down for a practice game of rugger which I had never played before in my life. I went to inform T.P. of this fact and that I was a soccer man. 'Not at Llandovery, you aren't,' he replied, and, as it was obviously no use arguing with T.P. at this stage, I meekly submitted and pitted my ineffectual efforts against the cream of schoolboy rugger players.

These practice games were unique and I doubt whether their pattern has ever been repeated. Usually, the 1st XV were pitted against a scratch side consisting of five or six masters augmented or diluted—whichever way you like to put it—by members of the 2nd XV. T.P. captained the scratch side, although it was sometimes difficult to determine which side he was on. Not only was he short-sighted but his sympathies were often with the opposing side, and his tactical moves were somewhat unorthodox. I remember once when he threw out a pass to his fly-half and then proceeded to tackle him. On another occasion he led a foot rush which penetrated the opposing defence, but, before his forwards could score, he fell on the ball. In one of my earliest games, roused at last by T.P.'s repeated cries of 'Fall on it!' I did so, only to wish I hadn't when I saw, out of the corner of my eye, the doughty Arthur Rees bearing down upon me. However, it was too late to withdraw, or to give the impression that I hadn't meant any harm, so I waited for the crunch as Arthur's boot gave me a firm and far from friendly kick in the stomach as if to say 'That's for the detention you gave me last week!'

Not only did T.P. play indiscriminately for both sides, but he often refereed as well. I usually played on the wing, and it was diconcerting when one received the ball and sprinted for the line only to be whistled up so that T.P. could give a lecture to some unfortunate boy who had failed to tackle me. Under T.P.'s tuition and with the experience of playing against experts my rugger improved, and when I left Llandovery I even managed to play for a minor club side with some success. My proudest moment, of which I still boast, was when I once tackled Cliff Jones who said to me: 'Well tackled, sir!' but I am convinced that he allowed me this privilege as a reward for the number of abortive attempts I had make to tackle him in the past. You can imagine with what pride I told this story to my friends later when we were watching a Varsity match or an international in which Cliff was, as usual, distinguishing himself. Other players of that era whose names I remember were H. O. Edwards, W. H. B. Hopkins, J. E. and H. M. B. Talbot, Bowen Jones, D. T. P. Lewis—names that come back more clearly to me in my dotage than those of other much more recent pupils. Some of these were good cricketers, too, but cricket was not a religion to them as rugger was, and they treated it in a much more light-hearted manner, except the Brecon match. In the season before I arrived, Brecon had thrashed us. We had been dismissed before lunch and a chap named Jones had piled on the runs against us, getting a century in the process. 'Dicky' Dore, with help from Hodges and myself, may have contributed something to the avenging of that defeat the following year. Possibly my appointment had something to do with my being a keen cricketer, and this may have outweighed the fact that I was a 'soccer' man who even had the temerity to play in cup ties for Llandovery Town on Saturdays when there was no home rugger match which had to be watched.

Some of my happiest memories of Llandovery were those of the games field. There was intense rivalry between masters and boys which gave rise to a healthy respect for one another. The boys were undoubtedly better than us at rugger, but I think we had the edge on them at cricket and hockey, while we were about evenly balanced in the cross-country and steeplechase.

In those days one's school duties and obligations filled most of one's time for seven days a week, and even on Sundays there was a service at Llandingat Church in the morning, a Bible class to be taken in the afternoon, and another service in the evening, followed by society meetings. All but the two senior masters had to take a Bible class and try to answer the wide variety of theological questions fired at them, such as, 'What is a concubine?' or 'What happened to the fishes in the Flood?' Some masters were more inventive than others in making the biblical stories more diverting than they usually are. 'Louis the Loup,' the French master of the School just before I came, once gave an exciting and detailed account of one of Joshua's battles. The History master, R. N. Dore, overheard some of the boys in his House discussing it afterwards and was so puzzled that he asked 'The Loup' where he had got his information. 'Napoleon at Austerlitz, of course,' was the reply; 'it does them good, you know.'

But there were three Sundays a term when we were free between morning and evening service and most boys were taken out by their parents. On these days the five or six unmarried masters (we couldn't afford to get married early then) used to take a car to some remote spot and climb the surrounding mountains, bathing in the clear, cold lakes and streams we came across on the way. At other free times we paid visits to the nearest cinema at Brecon, or to an international match at Swansea, and sometimes in the evening we would visit one of the lonely country inns at a discreet distance from Llandovery, to join the locals in singing their national songs.

Having been brought up in the great metropolis, London, I found these contacts with the outside world insufficient. Moreover, I suppose I was something of a rebel, and might have continued to be had I not been made a headmaster. Not only did I play for the local team at soccer and tennis, but I attended Hunt Balls, consorted with the County School staff, and generally mixed with 'The Town,' something which I do not remember any of my contemporaries doing. No doubt the situation has changed now and the College has closer links with the local community, but the public schools in those days tended to keep to themselves and ignore the outside world. *Autre temps, autre moeurs.*

So far I have dwelt more on incidents than personalities, but it was the personalities who really counted in a place like Llandovery, as they do, I suppose, in any school. I have already mentioned the Warden and after him, in order of seniority, came Ward Hill and Pye, whose wisdom, experience and married status provided a steadying influence on the more youthful members of the staff. Both were gifted teachers who were always ready to help their less experienced colleagues with their classroom problems. As a mathematician, I came under the influence of Hill, who had already written two books on the teaching of mathematics which proved to be a great help to me, and was later to gain a national reputation for his pioneering books for Secondary Modern Schools. Pye was a distinguished classical scholar with a dry wit who succeeded Hill as second master. Many bachelor members of the staff will remember the gracious hospitality offered to them by Mrs Hill and Mrs Pye in their homes. One also remembers tea with the Warden after a game of golf. He tried to teach me this game which was new to me, but had to give up, and I was reduced to playing with T.P. Our average score on that mountainous nine-hole course was six lost balls and two lost tempers.

My next recollection is of Hickox, in age somewhere between the 'elder statesmen' and the younger element. He was an eccentric of the 'old school' who taught science, but was also a gifted musician and a self-confessed rebel with a puckish sense of humour. Not content with playing the piano and organ, at which he was expert, he was teaching himself the 'cello, and as I happened to occupy the room next to his at Bank House, I suffered the agonies of his early efforts. I confess to being a greater lover of music, but Hickox killed any liking I might otherwise have acquired for unaccompanied 'cello compositions. He was also renowned for his water-throwing exploits, and woe betide anyone returning late to Bank House and disturbing the rest, as his window was directly over the doorway. He was the first of us to own a car—an open, bull-nosed Morris—and, not being a games player, he spent his free afternoons or evenings exploring the local countryside until he knew every road and cart-track for miles around. It was a privilege—and an adventure—to be taken by him on one of his expeditions which usually ended by traversing a ploughed field or fording a swollen stream because he said it kept the underside of his car clean. At the time I knew him, he must have been in his middle thirties. As a young man he had been drafted into the Army during the First World War and, being the rebel he was, had devised various means to flout the authority which he felt had been imposed upon him. When asked what his religion was, he told them he was a Buddhist. No-one could prove he wasn't, so he was excused church parades. On another occasion, when he asked to be excused a particular parade for what he regarded as a good reason, he forged the colonel's signature to get a pass.

The most senior of the younger generation by a year or two (apart from T.P. who was ageless) was R. N. (Dicky) Dore, a dapper little man who taught history and was a fine hockey player and cricketer. He was also a great lover of music and to him I owe a lifelong devotion to the music of Sibelius to which he introduced me on his gramophone. He would be surprised to know how far that influence spread. Three times in the past year I have met or heard from former pupils whom I taught at another school over thirty years ago, reminding me of a talk I gave at intervals to the school Music Society on Sibelius. It is surprising how often, in the course of a schoolmaster's career, he finds that he is remembered, not for the work he was appointed to do, for which he might claim to have some expertise, but for the casual and apparently unimportant contacts he had with his pupils in fields outside his normal province.

Another of my contemporaries at Llandovery was G. H. Hodges, a tough little man from Cambridge who taught Classics in the same way as he led the forwards at rugger (although, like me, he had been a soccer player before coming to Llandovery) with sharp, barking noises, and woe betide the boy who hadn't done his prep or who didn't push his weight in the scrum. He was fanatically imbued with the competitive spirit and all the boys were after his blood. Yet he commanded their respect and indeed admiration, as so often happens with masters who are tough with their pupils but essentially fair. He was also a good runner, and I remember one incident which illustrates his competitiveness in this field. Just as I had been roped in to play rugger in my first term, so I found myself running in a cross-country race after Christmas for the first time in my life. Hodges had briefed me beforehand, but being inexperienced I ignored his advice and led off at a cracking pace. As the race progressed I began to feel very pleased with myself, as I was still leading with about half-a-mile to go. No-one seemed to be challenging seriously, and although Hodges was creeping up on me he was still 100 yards behind. I managed to sprint down the hill to the bridge over the Towy, and collapsed exhausted having beaten them all—as I thought! Seconds later, Hodges ran by shouting: 'It's not *this* bridge, it's the next one down the river: Come on!' I replied, like Good King Wenceslas's page boy, that I could go no further, but one could not for long resist Hodges' goading challenge: 'Come on! You can't let the boys beat you,' so I trailed along with him for another mile. All the time, the leading boys were catching up, but Hodges stayed with me and, encouraged by his constant exhortations, I managed to finish abreast of him, just a yard ahead of Arthur Rees, who had left his final sprint a fraction too late. The next time I went out with them I finished well down the field as I am sure I should have done the first time had it not been for Hodges.

Another man in the Hodges mould was Fisher, who taught Modern Languages, a tall, heavy, tough forward, who usually came into the showers covered with blood, and when one commiserated with him about his injuries it became clear that he hadn't even noticed them.

Lastly there was Gwilym Davies from Cardiganshire, who came to teach Welsh to the boys and the ways of the Welsh to the staff. He had a fine voice, and used to sing his beloved Welsh hymns and songs to us on winter evenings.

Having recorded my impressions of my colleagues, I cannot forget those in the background who contributed to the Llandovery scene: firstly, Matron, who not only managed to feed us well in those difficult times (although we often grumbled) but, together with her assistants, supplied that feminine touch which every predominantly male establishment should have (I had four *mistresses* on my teaching staff at Nottingham). There was also Miss Smit who lived in Castle House. I came to know her well through a common interest in music, and it was she who introduced me to chamber music to which we used to listen on her radio. She was devoted to the College, to which she had been attached for many years, although I never discovered how she got there. She was a quiet soul but had great force of character. One winter when the town was flooded she was marooned in Castle House and cut off from the College where she used to have her meals. Ward Hill gallantly offered to take them to her, and the sight of this portly gentleman, dressed in oil skins and Wellington boots, carrying a hot meal on a tray, like a waiter, was one which astonished the eyes of us all. After wading through the floods to Castle House he presented his offering to Miss Smit, whose only remark was: 'Where's the salt?' Hill never got over it.

It may seem odd that I have not so far mentioned much about the boys at the College for, without them, we should have been out of a job. Llandovery was, as I have said, a very small school at that time, and the staff knew most of the boys but, at a distance of forty years, I have forgotten all but a few of their names. They were a mixed bunch, as they are at most schools, some clever, some in those days pretty dim (although I expect that has changed now!) but they all had something to contribute to the school and no-one was 'written off.' The boy who was dim in class (I can think of several, but I will not embarrass them by quoting their names) might be in the 1st XV or excel in some other direction. Each had his part to play and gained in self-confidence and self-respect by coming to recognise this. The other principle which operated at Llandovery was that of justice. The rules were hard and if a boy was caught breaking them he was punished. If he thought he was being treated unfairly he could appeal to the Warden and know that his case would be heard, but he also knew that he would get short shrift if his appeal were proved to be groundless.

So I come to the end of my reminiscences of Llandovery. I had no true 'call' to teaching, for I came down from Cambridge during the Great Depression when one was lucky to find a job at all, and teaching was the natural outlet for graduates at a time when Industry had little use for them. Fortunately I enjoyed teaching from the first, and have never regretted entering the profession. Whatever success I have achieved in it I owe in some measure to the experience I gained at Llandovery. I learned how to handle boys by living with them (and there is no better way); I learned how to work with my colleagues as a member of a team, each of whom had something distinctive to contribute to the life of the school.

I look back with affection to the few years I spent at Llandovery and to the people—staff, boys and others—whom I met there. As I said at the beginning, I came to Llandovery as a foreigner. When I left, I had been assimilated, and there will always be a part of me which belongs to Wales. In the words of Julius Caesar (slightly amended): *Veni, vidi, victus sum.*

(Compiled from contributions made to the Journal in 1970 and 1978. Kenneth R. Imeson was Headmaster of Nottingham High School for many years, retiring in 1970. Occasionally he would re-visit Llandovery: the last occasion, I remember, was with his wife, the distinguished Cambridge Italian scholar, Dr Barbara Reynolds).

1934-1936

J. R. EVANS

I am a hoarder of unconsidered trifles and so, when Dr Brinley Jones invited me to set down my recollections of my own school-days in Llandovery, during the 1930s, I was able to dig out the College Prospectus of those distant years. It first tells me the cost of attending the School:

'Inclusive Fees—£27 0s 0d a Term. Entrance Fee—£1 1s 0d.'

I entered Llandovery at a time of great financial stringency in the aftermath of the great financial crash of 1929. The number of pupils had dropped below 130 and the annual income of the School was less than £10,500. This was reflected in the austerity of life at the School during the early 1930s.

'The original buildings have been altered and modernised.'

The overwhelming impression that I still retain is of a drab and grey school, of grey stone walls, stone stairs and flagstones, of long rows of iron-framed beds in 'Claggers,' of the enamel chamber-pot beneath each bed—a very necessary utensil when I realised that the only lavatory provision stood a hundred yards distant, down those stone stairs, along those stone-flagged corridors, then out into the open and across the grey stone quadrangle. There was no hot water supply, only cold water for morning and evening ablutions. Once a week each dormitory had a communal bath-night when we bathed in pairs. Central heating had not yet reached Llandovery and we kept warm only by courtesy of two immense cast-iron stoves in the School Hall around which we huddled and roasted our daily harvest of chestnuts.

The austerity was epitomised in our daily garb which consisted of a black jacket and pin-striped trousers. We still wore a black tie to commemorate the death of Queen Victoria at the turn of the century! On Sundays the school prefects wore mortar boards and, in the summer sunshine, we all wore Harrow-style straw hats, or 'bashers' as we called them, which became 'frisbies' before their time and frequently ended up floating down the river Towy.

Whereas most of the school did their evening 'prep' in the School Hall we sixth-formers, and some fifth-formers, were privileged to share, in groups of five, some minute studies in which we prepared for our examinations and cooked some clandestine evening meals.

'The College is surrounded by some of the finest scenery in Wales.'

We had a limited view only, as our perambulations were strictly restricted to a two-mile radius of the School, and in no circumstances were we permitted to enter the township of Llandovery itself, which was held out to us as the Sodom and Gomorrah of the Towy Valley, full of iniquitous ale-houses and other unmentionable establishments not at all suitable for the young gentlemen of the College. The road to Rhandirmwyn, however, was particularly popular and on half-term Sunday only we were allowed to take the Brecon Road, through the Town, as far as the Stage-Coach monument, provided, of course, that we looked straight in front of us and did not stop on the way!

'All Boarders have their meals in the College. The matter of a plentiful supply of good wholesome food and proper cooking receives the most constant attention.'

This bears little semblance to reality! It is true that the midday meal of a roast followed by a pudding might be considered adequate, but otherwise the austerity in which we lived extended also into the Dining Hall, where breakfast, tea and supper consisted solely of small bowls of tea accompanied by half-inch thick slices of bread with a scraping of butter. Should we require jams or marmalade then we provided these ourselves out of our own 'tuck-boxes'. Two or three times a week our meagre breakfast diet might be supplemented by a small sausage roll or, perhaps, a boiled egg. Small pieces of bacon could be obtained three times a week at a cost of a further guinea a term.

On summer evenings there might be a jug of lemonade on the table and, during the winter months, a jug of milk which those of us who had studies immediately poured into jam jars which we carried upstairs and boiled it in a communal saucepan on our minute coal fires and added 'Camp Coffee' essence. We toasted the bread and embellished it with such tinned butter, beans, fish or pastes as we could still find in our 'tuck-boxes' and ate these delights on tin plates held under our table in anticipation of the nightly visit by T.P., heralded by his warning cry of 'Who's cooking?'

Without our 'tuck-boxes' we would certainly have starved. We brought them back at the beginning of each term, full of an assortment of preserves, tinned meats and fish of all descriptions, tinned beans, other vegetables, cake, biscuits, regularly replenished by our parents on their infrequent visits or by post. Sometimes we acquired eggs from the local hedgerows during our country walks and regularly replenished our meagre coal supply by surreptitious visits to the local Great Western Railway coalyard! We jealously guarded our tuck-boxes, kept in a special 'tuck-box room' to which we had access twice a day. Our only other source of sustenance was T.P.'s School tuck-shop out of the immense profits from which we were convinced that he ran his MG motor-car!

'Boys are prepared for Scholarships and Exhibitions at the Universities in Classics, Mathematics, Modern History and Natural Science. Boys who are intended for the Medical profession are specially prepared for Oxford, Cambridge and the London Hospitals.'

The quality of our life was austere but was balanced by the high standard of education that was offered throughout the School, especially in the Sixth Form. We were taught by a small group of inspired and dedicated teachers who were mostly Oxbridge graduates, well equipped to communicate their knowledge to us.

R.N. (Dicky) Dore taught English and History with equal facility; D.W. (Billy) Pye was a brilliant Classicist who had previously taught at Winchester; T. H. Ward Hill ('Tom Bom' to us all) had written erudite books on Mathematics; Beynon Davies and Mr Fisher were accomplished linguists in Welsh and French; Messrs Hodges and Hickox knowledgable scientists. Then there was, of course, the quite unique T. P. ('Pope') Williams, a graduate of Natural Science, who taught a bit of everything to everybody in the Lower and Middle Schools. Above all stood the remote and somewhat intimidating figure of Canon T. Walker Thomas, the Warden, who exercised the ultimate sanction over us all but was a generous man who, we felt, had the interests of us all at heart.

We pupils were, indeed, a mixed collection, ranging, as we did, from the intellectually brilliant to the academically mediocre, from the industrious to the outright lazy. Some left School at an early age to enter the world of banking, industry or commerce. The majority went on, after taking their Higher Schools Certificates, to enter University, generally to Oxford or Cambridge to pursue their studies of the Classics, the Arts or the Sciences. In 1934 no fewer than 14 former pupils were undergraduates at those two Universities. A great many studied Theology and entered the Church, such as Hilton and Graham who eventually became worthy Canons of St. David's and Llandaff Cathedral respectively, Ernest Evans who became Archdeacon of Monmouth and his brother Johnny who achieved the more glamorous title of Archdeacon of the Western (or was it the Eastern) Mediterranean.

Many others, after taking their First M.B. at School, entered the London Hospitals and had distinguished careers in Medicine and Dentistry. Three of my contemporaries became leading Consultant Surgeons or Physicians. Dill Jones became one of the world's leading jazz pianists!

Dill Jones

We were, indeed, cruel in the nicknames that we bestowed on some of our fellow pupils, often because of some alleged (although generally untrue), physical characteristic. There were 'Chimp', 'Monkey', 'Mouse', 'Pussy', 'Skinny', 'Dai Thos' and, more kindly, 'Smiler'. Then, there was, of course, 'Pope', the name by which our esteemed rugby Master became known throughout the rugby-playing world.

'There are various School and House Societies where papers and plays are read. Every boy is encouraged to take an active part'.

We were kept occupied ex-curricularly in a variety of ways. There were a number of popular Societies, organised enthusiastically by members of the Academic Staff, in which plays or stories were read and music played. Beynon Davies ran a Welsh Society with the customary energy he displayed on First Game. The most successful and ambitious Society was, undoubtedly, the Senior Dramatic Society, always well-attended by members of the Sixth Form and run with great keenness and enthusiasm by its President, Dicky Dore, in whose rooms meetings were held.

At each meeting members were given parts to read in some classical or popular modern play. I recall readings of such contrasting works as Shaw's 'St. Joan', 'Journey's End' and 'Night Must Fall' by Emlyn Williams, the dramatist flavour of the month! Sometimes Dicky spoke to us of his love of mountaineering in the Coulins of Skye or Billy Pye regaled us with readings. Each meeting concluded with a musical item played by Dicky on his somewhat battered portable gramaphone—Gustav Holsts's 'Planets' was particularly well received.

Each Christmas the Society presented an appreciative audience with a dramatic production in the School Gymnasium, transformed by the Science Masters into a passable 'Old Vic'. These plays, skilfully produced by Dicky, with the invaluable assistance of the Matron, Miss White, as Mistress of the Robes, and her assistant, Miss Roberts, in charge of make-up, invariably discovered some new dramatic talent. I recall John Davies' splendid portrayal of Richard Dudgeon in Shaw's 'Devil's Disciple' and his personal triumph in the title role in 'Clive of India' in which I struggled to remember my own lines as the Governor of the East India Company!

The female roles were invariably taken, in true Shakespearean fashion, by boys, as yet unshaven, whose 'down' still lay fair on their cheeks and who, generally, had to be cajoled into their parts. Pere was always a voluptuous and convincing woman and little Larry Rees was a skittish and romantic 'Raina' in 'Arms and the Man'. Sadly, only four short years later, he was to take his 'last curtain call' when he failed to bring back home his crippled Whitley bomber aircraft from a night raid on Hanover, Germany.

'Religious instruction is given throughout the School. Boys attend the place of worship selected by their parents.'

The newly constructed and dedicated College Chapel, the gift of an anonymous Old Llandoverian, was first used for worship in the year when I entered the Sixth Form. Many years later, as the Chairman of the College Trustees, it gave me considerable pleasure to arrange that it should be dedicated to the memory of the actual donor, Bishop David L. Prosser, the later former Archbishop of Wales. Many of the Chapel furnishings were the gifts of, or were given in memory of, other former Llandoverians and the Chapel pews were subscribed for by pupils then at the School whose initials are carved on the ends. The Chapel played a prominent part in our lives. We Anglicans attended Morning and Evening Services there each Sunday, conducted by the Warden or by the newly-ordained Reverend T. H. Ward Hill. Each weekday also commenced with a short service at which the whole School were present. In consequence of a musical upbringing I found myself press-ganged into the role of Chapel organist. The organ was not electrified and so the necessary wind-power was provided by a hand-pump operated by a daily rota of stalwart forwards taken from First Game. They were not always reliable and, when only a weak sound emanated from the organ, it was a sure sign that one or other of them had dozed off. (It was a very special pleasure for me when, 50 years later, my eldest grandson was to become the Chapel organist).

Nonconformist boys were permitted to attend their own peculiar places of worship in the town, to which they were marched on Sunday mornings. They were regarded with some envy by the rest of us as it gave them licence to enter the town and see, but never to speak to, girls, an opportunity which was denied to us Anglicans on pain of instant summons to the Warden's study, with inevitable painful consequences.

I particularly remember the occasion, one Sunday morning when the newly-elevated Bishop John Morgan, 'John Cop' as he had been known during his days at School, preached his first sermon in the Chapel following his installation to the See of Swansea and Brecon.

On Sunday afternoon we attended Bible Classes conducted by the Warden and Form Masters. Our spiritual welfare was, indeed well-catered for and left little remaining time on Sundays to write our compulsory letter home!

'Rugby Football and Hockey are played in the Christmas and Easter Terms. T. Soar, late of the Hampshire Cricket XI is resident cricket coach to the School.'

Sport generally, and Rugby Football in particular, had immense importance in the life of the School. We basked in the current achievements on the international scene of Vivian, Arthur, Chick and Cliff, who had but recently been our fellow pupils and avidly followed their deeds in the daily newspapers. On one occasion 'Tom Bom' invited us to sit on the floor of his Cerrig Cottage to listen to the wireless commentary from Twickenham on the 1934 Varsity Match in which Vivian, Arthur and Cliff were all taking part.

Our own daily round seemed to revolve around First Game in which the leading two dozen players in the School played, augmented by half-a-dozen of the Masters, necessary due to the low number of pupils able to take part at that level. This certainly gave the boys (and the Masters too) an opportunity to redress their mutual grievances. I remember Dickie Dore suffering in succession a broken nose and a dislocated shoulder, whilst even 'Pope' himself suffered a broken collar-bone. 'Pope' was totally committed to First Game, in which he played scrum-half, refereed and coached both teams all at the same time. 'Pope' also coached us individually and Horace reminded me the other day of how he had us running around him in ever-widening circles whilst he sprayed us with passes from all angles—and woe betide us should we drop one!

There were many, in my time, who added to the traditions of the School.

Horace Edwards and Rees Stephens later played in the Welsh senior side, half-a-dozen won Schoolboy 'Caps' and Bob Parry, Rufus Thomas and Hugh Rees were awarded Rugby Football 'Blues' at either Oxford or Cambridge. 'Chimp' even won a Heavyweight Boxing 'Blue' and Herbert Arnold an Association Football 'Blue' at Cambridge, only two years before he was to die leading his infantry Platoon against the German Gothic Line, North of Florence, Italy.

Our tradition of defeating Christ College, Brecon at rugby continued unbroken. The 1934 game was memorable when, after himself scoring three brilliant tries, our captain, Horace Edwards, was seen to be stretched senseless on the field of play. With the game going on around him, as Horace himself reminded me recently, 'My mother ran on to the field, cradled me in her arms and applied eau-de-cologne to my forehead. I eventually came to but was then a passenger.' It was a sight which those of us who witnessed it will never forget long after the memory of his three glorious tries has faded away!

We were never so successful at cricket, despite many a fine innings played by Horace or 'Smiler' and 'Dai Thos' leg breaks, which were almost as huge as his side-steps on Tredegar Close. I remember the Warden demonstrating cover drives with his walking stick and Tom Soar rolling the pitch with the aid of the College Horse and bemoaning his failure ever to take a hundred wickets in a season for Hampshire! We bathed in the River Towy near Black Bridge and were allowed to use the Deep Pools should we succeed in swimming across the river. On now looking back to my years at the School I feel convinced that Llandovery was the first truly 'comprehensive' school, where the academically poor mixed on equal terms with the intellectually rich, and where all of us were given equal opportunity to develop our individual talents and establish our own relationships. The friends which I made there have been with me all my days. Undoubtedly the austerity, discipline and toughness that we experienced there built up our characters and equipped us for entry into the world outside, and certainly, as Malcolm Cooke reminds us, trained us well to survive in many theatres of war.

During our years at School we had little contact with the outside world and many traumatic events passed us by. The death of the King, the Abdication crisis, the advent of Adolf Hitler, Abyssinia and the increasing menace of Fascism then had little meaning for us. Little did we then appreciate that, as we stood together in the College Chapel and sang together 'Jerusalem' and the customary school hymn, 'Lord dismiss us with Thy blessing' on that last morning of the summer term in 1936, in a little over three years time we would be wearing a different kind of uniform and would march to a different tune! We did not realise that a score of us there present would soon give our lives for the cause of freedom, including Bill Davies, Tom Roberts and 'Barber' Thomas who would first play together in yet another winning side against Brecon; that Charley Price would win his DFC before his aircraft went down into the North Sea off Holland, that Tucker Jones would die on the beaches of Normandy and that George Stead would lie beneath the desert sand at El Alamein, or that 'Smiler' and 'Chimp' would each win their Military Cross in the hills of Tuscany.

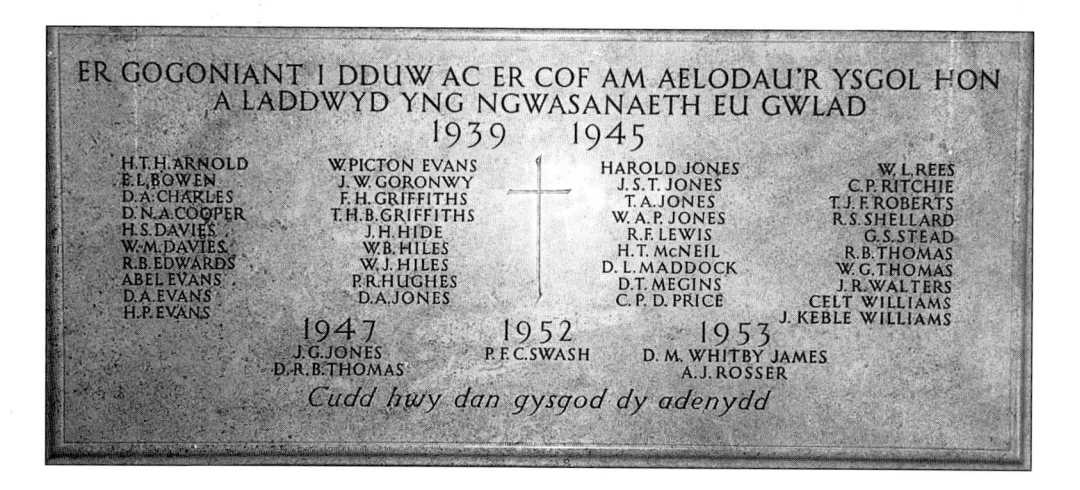

ER GOGONIANT I DDUW AC ER COF AM AELODAU'R YSGOL HON
A LADDWYD YNG NGWASANAETH EU GWLAD
1939   1945

H.T.H. ARNOLD	W. PICTON EVANS	HAROLD JONES	W. L. REES
E. L. BOWEN	J. W. GORONWY	J. S. T. JONES	C. P. RITCHIE
D. A. CHARLES	F. H. GRIFFITHS	T. A. JONES	T. J. F. ROBERTS
D. N. A. COOPER	T. H. B. GRIFFITHS	W. A. P. JONES	R. S. SHELLARD
H. S. DAVIES	J. H. HIDE	R. F. LEWIS	G. S. STEAD
W. M. DAVIES	W. B. HILES	H. T. McNEIL	R. B. THOMAS
R. B. EDWARDS	W. J. HILES	D. L. MADDOCK	W. G. THOMAS
ABEL EVANS	P. R. HUGHES	D. T. MEGINS	J. R. WALTERS
D. A. EVANS	D. A. JONES	C. P. D. PRICE	CELT WILLIAMS
H. P. EVANS			J. KEBLE WILLIAMS

1947   1952   1953
J. G. JONES   P. F. C. SWASH   D. M. WHITBY JAMES
D. R. B. THOMAS   A. J. ROSSER

Cudd hwy dan gysgod dy adenydd

Bill Perkins and I would next meet when we played alongside each other for an Army team in the Isle of Man late in 1942 and I next saw Pere at an Artillery School on the shores of the Arabian Sea, not long before the end of the Japanese War. We talked long of Llandovery! As Horace says, 'Whenever I hear "Jerusalem" the memories come flooding back.' I am sure that that remains true for all my generation of Llandoverians.

(John R. Evans was born in Pontypridd, educated at Llandovery and Exeter University where he read History. For three years he was on the staff of the National Library of Wales, then he turned to Law and practised as a solicitor in Cardiff. He was President of the Cardiff and District Law Society 1981-82. During the Second World War he served in the Royal Artillery as a commissioned officer. As a Lieutenant-Colonel he later commanded the 6th (Glamorgan) Battalion The Welch Regiment (T.A.). He was appointed a Thomas Phillips

Foundation Trustee in 1973 and Chairman of the College Trustees 1981-92, a period of very considerable redevelopment and refurbishment of the College).

Lt. Col. J. R. Evans (Chairman of Trustees), Dr R Brinley Jones (Warden), H.R.H. The Prince of Wales, in the background Mr A. M. Rees (Trustee) and Miss Llinos Lloyd (Head Girl) 1985.

1938-1941

Hugh Macdonald-Smith

My sojourn at Llandovery College was a relatively short one and covers three years only—and all in the 6th Form so that my experiences are perhaps untypical. However, they were three very eventful years both for me and the nation since they covered the period 1938-41 and hence the outbreak of the Second World War and the 'Finest Hours' of 1940 . . .

I could perhaps summarise my years at Llandovery as providing me with a foundation of academic learning, of Christian and moral teaching, of experience and interest in team sports—and a relatively spartan existence. Standards of living, however, change and what seemed spartan to me at the time was not so categorised by my father, who was also an Old Llandoverian, having been at school at the turn of the century as a contemporary of the Warden of my time—Canon Walker Thomas. Canon Thomas was a stern disciplinarian and a Classics scholar who admitted to a blind spot in mathematics and science. Science and mathematics were my subjects, and so, perhaps fortunately for me, we had no common subject on which I could readily be interrogated. Llandovery also provided me with my first taste of what eventually became my profession; that of soldiering. The school OTC at that time was in its infancy; it was compulsory for senior boys and, at a time of national re-armament in the late '30s was much encouraged by those concerned with it.

However to revert to our spartan life; my recollections are of cold and wet winters with only two large pot-bellied stoves in the main hall by which to warm oneself, unless one managed to dodge authority and sneak into the boiler room. Cold water only (and cold showers for the hardy) was available for the morning wash and certainly there were a few occasions when the ice had to be broken beforehand. Maybe, however, I exaggerate and anyway, the summers were warmer and balmier in the delightful countryside around and in winter one warmed up on the rugger field almost every afternoon, with the reward of a hot bath before tea.

Another popular activity was 'Society', organised by the Masters on Sunday evenings throughout the winter and spring terms and involving cultural evening play readings and listening to classical music on a clockwork driven 'needle' gramophone. The 6th form, in particular, welcomed the break after early supper on Sundays when they proceeded to Bank House for 'Society'. This had several advantages: it took one out of school for a short period, the music and play reading were always popular and there was always a glowing coal fire to sit around in Bank House.

Two episodes concerned with Bank House 'Society' come to mind, both in the 'blackout' and therefore probably sometime in the Winter of 1939-40.

The draw of the Bank House fire was such that competition was extremely keen to 'bag' a place close to it and soak in enough warmth to last the ensuing week. Since it was a case of 'first come, first served', and since we were released *en masse* after supper, the move from the College to Bank House was very much a race. One evening, in the pitch blackness of the blackout, the stampede proceeded towards the town, and the leader mistook his whereabouts, anticipated his left turn into the front door of Bank House and charged instead into a similar private house a few doors nearer to the College. The pack like sheep followed, racing through the front door and up the stairs to be confronted by the occupant half-dressed on the landing and only then realising the mistake. It was then a case of 'those behind cry forward and those in front cry back' and the ensuing chaos can be imagined. Since the retreat was almost immediate and no word was spoken what were the reactions of the owner I find it hard to imagine. However, he must have been very understanding since I do not recall any sequel!

The other event did have a sequel and changed the course of the Sunday evening steeplechase. This was in progress some time later than the first incident I have described but as the pack stormed through the pitch darkness they ran into the Warden—literally that is to say—and henceforth when he had picked himself up and after disciplinary measures had been taken, the move to Bank House was pursued for ever after as a 'crocodile' under the charge of a prefect who also had the unenviable task of allotting the fireside seats.

The most noticeable change when school re-assembled in September 1939 —just after the declaration of war was the blackout and this, as can be imagined, was a major task in all the rooms of the College. The prevailing feeling amongst everyone, however, was that any chink of light was an open invitation to the enemy immediately to drop a bomb—even in a rather remote area of Wales some very considerable distance from the German bases. Air raid precautions were nevertheless strictly enforced and 'trench shelters' were constructed on Tredegar sports field and air raid practices held periodically. Since these shelters rapidly became waterlogged during the first wet winter of 1939 it is just as well that we were not called upon to occupy them. In the event there was only one 'live' incident which occurred during the blitz on Cardiff and Swansea. Very shortly after an aid raid alert sounded in Llandovery a stick of small bombs were dropped by a, no doubt lost, German aircraft. It was about 11 p.m. on a Sunday evening, when most boys were in bed. I still recall the whistling descent of the bombs and the all too slow realisation that this was the real thing. Fortuitously the bombs landed on the far side of the river playing fields and although some slight damage was caused to the railway line there were no casualties other than a few frayed Llandovery nerves.

The War produced another innovation in that a school wireless set was permitted (they had previously been strict contraband). The set was installed in the Dining Hall and we were permitted to listen to major broadcasts and to the morning and evening news bulletins. Thus were we privileged to listen to many of Winston Churchill's famous broadcasts of 1940-41.

June 1940 was, however, the time when invasion fever was as its height; senior boys were permitted to enrol in the 'Local Defence Volunteers' or the 'Home Guard' as it eventually became. Those of us in the OTC had the advantage of some elementary military training and also of possessing uniforms and some rifles (though most of those had been reclaimed by the Army to relieve the critical national shortage and replaced by wooden 'mock-ups'). By contrast, the local volunteers from the town initially had nothing except LDV armlets and a few shotguns.

The first task given to the College contingent after the fall of France was to assist in the construction of local defences and for several afternoons during the hot summer of 1940 we were taken in an old contractor's truck to dig 1914-18 War-style trenches along the line of the Brân streams beyond Llandingat church. The trenches were enormous earthworks complete with firestep, parapet and parados and even a small 'dugout' command post. It was all an exciting venture at the start but hard work with pick and shovel soon brought out the blisters and the realisation that this was serious.

Apart from training, the next main Home Guard event was the patrolling of 'Vulnerable Points' and the one allotted to the College was Cynghordy Viaduct, which we were required to take our turn at guarding through the night. The whole school turned out to see the first section of heroes leave for war complete with full kit, rifles and live amunition, rations and blankets. Transport was provided by the OC contingent's car and no war volunteers ever received a greater send-off. Again, the novelty soon wore off and a long night on sentry-go at such a remote and exposed place was enough to dampen the ardour of even those keenest to defend their country. A well practised challenge of 'Who goes there?' was seldom employed, although it was all in earnest, with a full magazine and finger on the trigger. How a few stray sheep or the odd farmer and even our comrades were not shot I really do not know but fortunately as winter 1940 advanced we were relieved of this task and put instead to guard an emergency food store in—of all places—Llandovery Town Hall, requisitioned for the purpose. Whether we were guarding against the rationed citizens of Llandovery or the Germans I never discovered but this particular task lasted much longer and two hours on and two hours off from 7 p.m. to 7 a.m. was the lot of many of us throughout the cold winter nights of 1940 and 1941. The reward was the feeling of doing something for the war effort, an added respect from the juniors—and a hot bath, a special breakfast and a two-hour lie-in on return to school.

Another wartime change was the increasing number of old boys, many only recently school-boys, who visited the school in their Naval, Army or RAF uniforms. Masters and college domestic staff were also 'called-up' and progressively more and more of the 'chores' ranging from maintenance of the ground to indoor domestic duties had to be undertaken by the boys.

Then came the casualties. Sadly, most of those who gave their lives in the Second World War and who are commemorated on the plaque in the College chapel were my contemporaries and I remember them mostly on the sports field or as carefree school-boys:

> 'They shall not grow old as we that are left grow old
> Age shall not weary them nor the years condemn
> At the going down of the sun and in the morning
> We will remember them'.

(School Journal Summer 1977).

1940-1947

D. R. T. Davies

My parents were keen for me to go to College as a day-boy and so a few months after the Second World War began, my father took me to see the Warden. It was a very informal interview; I remember being asked, 'If you were a bomber-pilot in the R.A.F., which German cities would you expect to be ordered to bomb?' I suppose that a year earlier the question may have been posed in slightly different terms—'Which are the chief cities in Germany?'

I started in College in September 1940, dressed in a dark striped trousers, black jacket, black shoes, white shirt with a starched collar and a black tie. I would not have been out of place attending a funeral! Ken (J.K.L.) Hughes, son of the manager of the Gas Works, called on his way to collect me. Within minutes of entering the College buildings I was confronted by an enormous figure—and he was only a member of the Sixth Form—one by the name of Rees Stephens.

T. P. (Pope) Williams seemed to be in charge of most things which affected me in the early days. He equipped pupils with second-hand books, exercise books, ran the Tuck-Shop, put up team lists for the junior rugby games (Bank games) which took place every day except when the XV had a match, and *then* we had to line the touch-lines and cheer. This was nothing new to me since I had watched the College teams in many rugby and cricket matches since I was about seven years old. Besides all this T.P. taught us French 'La plume de ma tante, le père est dans le jardin . . .' English, Geography, 'Draw a map of . . .' and even Science.

I remember last lesson on Saturday mornings in my first year was Geography and when the XV were playing that afternoon, T.P. would sail in through the door, give back last week's work and then, 'Get out your atlases, draw a map of Italy, etc. etc.'. His mind was elsewhere as he paraded back and fore across the room, giving his trousers, supported by an old College tie, a hitch up every so often. It wasn't difficult to work out even after only a few weeks at school that there appeared to be a strong correlation between one's performances in rugby on Bank Game and marks given for map-drawing.

Life was hard and discipline was strict. On Thursday afternoons, when the Seniors were on parade in the J.T.C., Pope would come to watch us on Bank Game, looking for talent. Often he would take out the corner flag and use it for purposes other than for what it was intended. This improved our tackling no end.

Every day at noon the duty prefect would take round the Report Book in which masters entered the name of any boy guilty of such misdeeds as 'incessant talking . . . no prep . . . lost his book . . .' Then periodically the Warden would call out the names at morning roll-call with the instruction to parade outside his study at 12.20 (end of morning school) for suitable punishment. I never recalled anyone whose name was in the book being allowed to get away without three, if not six, of the best. Waiting in the queue outside the study and hearing the swish and thwack coming from the other side of the door, followed by the unfortunate boy emerging holding the seat of his pants, doing his utmost to hold back the tears, was often far worse than the actual cane.

I remember the end of term when most boys went home by train. Not many people owned cars then and those who did were subjected to petrol rationing. Elvet Williams who was in charge of Grounds would take all the trunks and tuck-boxes to the station ready for dispatch and, yes, it was that man again T.P. who would arrange for all the tickets to be purchased in advance. As the G.W.R. train with its tank engine left the station at 8.45 am, with long blasts on the whistle, boys would be waving and shouting at the windows and as they passed the engine-sheds the detonators placed on the track by railway staff would add to the noisy and happy send-off after another long term.

Every morning after breakfast there was an assembly in the school hall (now the Library) and the duty prefect would call the Roll and back would come the reply 'Ad'. Then we went over to the Chapel for morning service; at this time the organ-blower had to be operated manually and there was a rota of Fourth Formers who performed this most important task. Very occasionally things went awry and the Revd. Ward-Hill would be ready to play the first verse of the daily hymn only to discover that there was no-one on the pump!

Members of the Sixth Forms were allowed to do their prep in their studies but others had to sit at the long tables in the school hall or in the adjoining classrooms. If we were involved in anything in the evening, or perhaps returning from an away cricket match, we were still expected to do our prep for the following day—even if it meant getting up an hour earlier next morning. Heating in the Hall and the classrooms was by coal or wood fires. There were two large cast iron stoves in the Hall and if one dropped the flap at the top it was possible to toast a slice of bread impaled on a 12-inch wooden ruler. Needless to say, quite a few pieces of toast were lost and most rulers were incapable of measuring more than nine inches due to the burnt end.

One of my greatest regrets in life has always been that I was never taught music in my schooldays. There were no lessons but later on my appetite was whetted when we had various recitals given by visiting artistes—violin, cello and most memorable of all, an oboe recital by the great man himself Leon Goossens. Sgt. Shellard, who assisted with the J.T.C. and was in charge of P.E. was soon called to the colours and we were told a year or so later that he had been killed in battle in Crete. So—no music and no P.E. When the Old Gym was wired for electricity we were able to form a film club and some of the first films we saw were Charlie Chaplin in *The Rink*, Harold Lloyd in *Haunted Spooks* and Laurel and Hardy in *Smithy*.

Tredegar Close was dug up for growing potatoes in 1942 and matches were transferred to the cricket field. Flower borders were also transformed into vegetable plots tended by members of a newly-formed Gardening Club. Food was strictly rationed and the staple diet consisted mainly of potatoes and bread. When one reads nowadays of the special diets which are said to be required by members of rugby squads, it seems amazing that we were strong enough to lace up our boots let alone play a hard game!

In the very severe snowfall of March 1947 I recall going for a walk up Heol Rhos and the snow was so deep that we were actually walking on top of the hedgerows. When we returned we immediately made a special roll-call to check that we had not lost one of the juniors in a snow-drift. The river Towy was frozen over and it seemed odd that we were skating where a few months previously we had been bathing. There were still Italian prisoners-of-war in the area and they helped to clear the snow-drifts in the town and the senior boys used to help out our coal supplies by sawing wood. Twenty minutes at a time soon brought a glow to one's cheeks.

During the war years we had Double British Summer Time which meant that the clocks were two hours ahead of G.M.T. and it was light until past 11.00 p.m. from mid-June to the end of the term. One punishment used was rolling the cricket square with the heavy roller and weeding; members of the cricket XI often went down to the cricket field after supper, equipped with old kitchen knives to dig out the plantains growing on the square and anything else which did not look like grass. In the Spring term the seniors played hockey though the weather in 1947 severely curtailed the season.

Terms were long compared to today's. For example the summer term often ran from 1st May to about the 25th July, and winter terms from about the 8th September to the 16th December, with no half-terms or exeats, and at the end one felt in need of a rest, boys as much as masters. In the summer holidays we were sometimes given a holiday task, usually a novel to read, and on our return we would be tested. One novel I remember being set was *The Bridge of San Luis Rey*. Very often one ordered a copy of the book at the start of the holidays and only got it a few days before term began so that time was limited to say the least.

I remember a trip to Neath with T.P. at Christmastide 1946 in his two-seater sports car. We left Llandovery on a cold morning and journeyed over the Black Mountain, through Pontardawe and down to Neath. Included in their team that day were three Old Llandoverians, Rees Stephens, J.W.D. (John) Jenkins and H.O. (Horace) Edwards. I don't remember much about the game—I think it was against Combined Services—or who won, but I can still recall quite vividly the journey home. It was dark by the time we left the Gnoll and it was raining. What with a malfunction of the windscreen wipers, the car's poor headlights and the poor eyesight of the driver, it was miraculous that we reached Llandovery in one piece!

On the eve of my first Brecon match T.P. gave us our final pep-talk. 'I don't mind if Brecon win tomorrow—it's high time that they did. *But* when you come back as an Old Boy I should hate to remember you as a member of the first side that lost to Brecon after all these years.' That was enough to give us a win by two tries—scored by our wings—to nil.

Pope often complained about the lack of commitment by some of the XVs in the early forties. 'I must emphasise that the main duty of the members of the first game is to tackle and go down on the ball and provide tenacious opposition to the 1st XV in practices.' But by 1947 he was able to report that the XV had returned to its pre-war standard of dash and determination. On the cricket field I well remember the match against Brecon in 1944. I am pleased to say that I was not a member of the side having bowled out Brecon for a paltry 52, found itself being skittled out for 11. No wonder Mr Huntley, in charge of the XI, described it as 'a matter for tears' and announced that no colours would be awarded.

The town and all shops were out of bounds and day-boys were often asked to make small purchases by the boarder. School uniform was far more relaxed by 1943 when everyone received clothing coupons. Grey flannels and sports jackets were the order of the day as they could also be worn in holiday time.

Straw boaters usually worn in the summer disappeared but the school cap remained—an easy way of identifying a boy as being a member of the school. Recently I met a lady who was evacuated to Llandovery at the age of 14 with other girls from her Notre Dame Convent School during the years of the Blitz on London. Only those whose parents who wanted their daughters evacuated came, together with a few teachers and when they arrived at Llandovery station the first thing they saw was a crowd of College boys standing on the bridge over the railway crossing (removed about thirty years ago) cheering like mad as the young ladies alighted. Strange to say that we never saw much of them in their three year stay in the town but then I was only eleven when they arrived. They had their lessons in the Church Hall and were billeted with families in the town.

There was a well organised Junior Cadet Corps in the war years under the command of Captain D. W. Pye. Cadets took a Cert A—I cannot quite remember what the 'A' stood for—and practised foot-drill, map reading, 0.22 shooting on the indoor range in the Old Gym. Our parade ground was in front of the fives-court and we marched down the drive as far as the main gates, up and down, back and fore. Today this would not be possible with the large number of cars and mini-buses parked in that area. We had Field Days each year and towards the end of the war we attended summer camps. In my last year a number of us went on a camp to join O.C.T.U. at Eaton Hall, Chester, where we were told that we were to regard ourselves as soldiers. Our section approached me to see if we could have the same privileges as the Officer Cadets, the most important being a ration of duty-free cigarettes. It must have been hard for Mr Pye to approve of this but he did and he went up in the estimation of his Corps. We had one shooting match with, I think, Brecon which we lost rather badly, each team shooting at its own base and posting the results to each other. Also in about 1946 the old Italian rifles we were using (did we call them Garribaldis?), were replaced with more modern equipment.

I have made much mention of T.P. but there were other masters who made a big impact on our lives. The Revd. T. H. Ward-Hill's (Tom Bom) subject was Mathematics but he did not teach me until my School Certificate year in the Fifth Form. He was an excellent teacher, the author of many text-books, and it followed as night the day that when I went into the Sixth Form my main subject was Mathematics. Our set was a very small and select one and included John Staff who was later in life to marry Kathie, better known perhaps as Norah Batty in *The Last of the Summer Wine*. Mr Ward-Hill often used to ask to see our exercise books at the end of the day so that he could sign them to indicate where we had finished our day's work and, then, next day he would be able to see how much we had added in our prep. Having jumped a year lower down the school I had taken my Higher School Certificate Exams with still another year to go and I was going to spend this last year preparing for the Higher Mathematics papers. Just after Christmas the Warden sent for me and told me that Mr Ward-Hill had been taken ill and that it was obvious that he would be away for some time. He had advised the Warden to ask me to look after his forms as best as I could, even some of the Higher work. So each day I would visit him at home at Cerrig Cottage

Cerrig Cottage

and he would tell me what to do next. This probably decided my future for on leaving I read Mathematics at Swansea, followed by a P.G.C.E., two years National Service and a life-time of teaching Mathematics at a Boys' Grammar School.

One of my supporting subjects at Higher School Certificate was Physics taught by another reverend gentleman, the Revd. J. L. R. Pastfield who had been in the Battle of Jutland. He was known as 'Allelulia Joe' and was a wonderful character. I remember going into a Physics lesson to find him with his pipe fixed in a vice, hacksawing off part of the bowl. He explained that the Budget announced that afternoon had increased the price of tobacco and since he always liked a pipeful when he lit up, the only way he could afford it in the future would be to reduce the size of the bowl!

Mr D. W. Pye (Billy) taught me Latin in the Fifth Form and although I had not found it an easy subject earlier probably due to my jumping a year, I suddenly found that I was beginning to enjoy the subject; he made it all look so easy. If it had been possible to take it in the Sixth Form no doubt I would have chosen it. I also had much contact with him through the J.T.C. and later in life I came across him again. My professional union, The Assistant Masters' Association, published a monthly magazine which usually included a very advanced Mathematics problem. In the very short list of correct entries published each month there often appeared the name of D. W. Pye and on two occasions he actually set the problem. This knowledge of his mathematical ability was never revealed to us at school and perhaps even Mr Ward-Hill didn't know it existed.

I remember Mr T. B. D. Drought who taught Mathematics lower down the school, took us on Bank Game on the rugger field and called nearly everyone a 'perisher'. Two more reverend gentlemen whom we held in high esteem were the Revd. Emlyn Davies, vicar of Myddfai, who taught part-time in the junior forms and the Revd. J. N. Hughes (Dinky). He often joined in First Game practices together with Mr W. Beynon Davies, who taught Latin and Welsh in the Lower School. He was a big man and his strength and bulk gave the XV pack something to scrum against. Dinky on the other hand was of very slight physique and ran like a whippet on the wing and his tackling for a small man was outstanding and an example to us all.

Mr Charlie Bell arrived when the war was over and in addition to his classroom duties took charge of the XI. Mr Emrys Davies, senior professional with Glamorgan C.C. was instrumental in our having the opportunity of playing against some of the Glamorgan cricket ground staff; his son, P. M. Davies was one of the junior members of our XI. P.M. went on to excel in both rugby and cricket and was certainly the most talented batsman I came across in my time at school and afterwards. I wish I had been at school longer under Mr Bell's wing for I am sure that my cricket would have improved considerably. In my last year we had the opportunity to learn some German with a young and beautiful lady called Beryl Evans who subsequently married another master. Our lessons were arranged for the gap between the end of morning school at 12.20 and lunch at 1.00 and there was always a full attendance in her lessons— she even had us singing 'Der Tannenbaum'.

When we returned at the start of the summer term in 1947, without any previous warning, the whole school was given, on the second day of term, a Religious Knowledge test on the Gospels and the Acts: it is no surprise remembering the number of reverend gentlemen on the staff! All forms had the same questions but fortunately I and two others were away on a course for the first few days of the term and escaped it. Or so we thought until at the end of our first day back the Revd. Ward-Hill informed us that we would take the test on the following morning!

The Warden, Canon T. Walker Thomas known to us as 'Studge' or 'Tom Bola', was a big man and a strong disciplinarian. The regime of the school was so geared that it allowed boys to have very little leisure time. Lessons and sport dominated and if one did not excel at sport, life was very much harder to bear.

Although I was a day-boy, life at home was still quite spartan during the war years and afterwards—food was rationed until 1953. As I have mentioned there was quite a liberal use of the cane and even the handful of prefects, who wielded so much power, were allowed to tan with a slipper. I often recall the Warden standing outside the cricket nets behind the batsmen, illustrating with his walking-stick how to play the appropriate stroke. Perhaps he was at his best demonstrating the pull-shot with a full follow-through. We were never to know whether this had been perfected through use of the cane in his study or vice-versa.

My third subject at higher School Certificate was French, not I may add through choice but because the Warden took the group and if one had shown any aptitude for the subject in the Fifth Form then one could not escape.

During my years, austerity was the order of the day. Even the masters had their share of it: their working hours and their terms were long. But austerity or not, being at that place at that time gave one perspective and values. I owe so much to the experience of those years.

(Roland Davies, who was Captain of the XV in 1946, left Llandovery for the University College of Swansea. After a period of National Service he was appointed to Lawrence Sheriff's Boys' Grammar School, Rugby, later to become Head of Mathematics and Deputy Headmaster there. On his retirement he returned to Llandovery).

1944-1949

P. M. DAVIES

I began my time at Llandovery in 1944. The word 'austerity' comes immediately to mind. It was a word that governed life generally in that time during and after the war. It applied to school as to everything else. Looking back now over fifty years, I sense that what I then did and said and thought must have been much influenced by a few people in particular, and in each case that word 'austerity' applies in one way or another. Walker Thomas was Warden. Running a school at that time must have been nightmarish. He had considerable restrictions at all levels—food, travel, teaching staff, fuel, not to mention money. He must have operated on a shoestring, simply because there was no other option. And he must also have used up most of his own resources to do so. With austerity comes discipline. Walker Thomas was a disciplinarian, not only in what he expected from pupils, but in his teaching style. I learnt my French grammar and verbs in a way never to be forgotten—not exciting but indelible.

Every headmaster needs a strong second master. Throughout my time, T.P. fulfilled that role. Another austere man, and another disciplinarian. The content of some of Pope's teaching programme was so austere as to be non-existent, or so it seems now. The way he chose to teach subjects as diverse as science and scripture did suggest he had other and weightier things on his mind—which, of course, we all know is true. He is, rightly, a beloved rugby legend, but his success depended utterly on austerity and discipline. To T.P. the game was essentially very straightforward. If we did the few basic things right, and did them better and more often than the opposition, we were bound to win—and we usually did. No pandering to flamboyance or flair. Keep it simple. And so training, going over move after move, for hour after hour, in warm relentless Welsh rain, produced a very basic approach, but also a remarkable teamwork. None of us was outstanding. We all relied on each other. That is what T.P. set out to do. And that is how, year after year, he managed to fashion such a competent XV from so few available pupils in a school of our size. In a wild and totally uncharacteristic moment, I once dropped a goal against Monmouth. It was towards the end of the game, we were in no danger of losing, and it was worth four points in those days. Pope's reaction was swift and typical. I had 200 lines—'I must not drop goals with a centre and wing outside me'. I am sure he had a twinkle in his eye, but it was necessary to be seen to exert discipline.

Tap Rees and 'Pope'

Isn't it odd how a rigorous, even draconian, style can yet bring forth devotion in the recipients? I suppose it depends on motivation. When T.P. was dissatisfied, he used to say so in no uncertain language, and then add, 'It doesn't worry me if you want to play badly. But I wouldn't like to be in the first team to lose to Brecon for 25 years'. That was always more than enough. We were then, once again, willing to lose an arm and a leg for him, and often did.

A Warden needs not only strength in his second master, but also, and just as important, reliability in his head prefect. The character of any organisation depends on the calibre of those at the top. Their ability, or lack of it, sooner or later cascades down to the lower levels. School prefects have a far bigger influence than they probably realise at the time. In my years at Llandovery, Tom ap Rees was an outstanding head prefect. Totally committed to the rules of the day, but completely fair in their application, he was the right hand of each of the two Wardens he served. It was a strict regime, but we still lived well and contentedly because we knew exactly where we stood.

A change of Warden must always add to the interest of school life. And so it did when G. O. Williams succeeded Walker Thomas. In one sense, the years of austerity were still there, even though the war was over. Food and fuel were still scarce. Parcels of tuck were prized like nothing else, and it paid well to befriend those whose mothers were renowned cake-makers. It was, however, a two-way process. Large sums of money were wagered on the Brecon match by Llandovery's poacher community and their Brecon counterparts, and the mothers of our winning team used to go home at the end of that day with parcels of eggs and butter and half a sewin. But in another sense, G.O.'s arrival gave Llandovery a welcome relaxation. He allowed people to develop their own personalities. His own teaching style in English classes was a new experience to all of us, as was the sharpness of his own mind. It was unnerving to have a conversation with someone who knew what point you were going to be making in five minutes' time. His sermons in chapel, with their careful, tidy logic, were also something novel and helpful.

Every school needs a change of approach from time to time. G.O. was good for Llandovery after the years of stringency. The danger is that such a change brings with it so much relaxation as to get out of hand. G.O. was a kindly and gentle man, a good Christian pastor and a very able teacher. But his wardenship was a success, not only because of himself, but because he had alongside him the likes of T.P. and Tom ap Rees to maintain the rules. It was a good combination that served Llandovery well.

G.O. was to have someone else who became a staunch support. At about the same time as he arrived, so did Chris Bell. From Army service in the North African and Italian campaigns, he brought with him not just a whiff but a gale of fresh air. Heavy smoking, debonair, some earthy language, a love of history and a genuine wish to teach it to others, and perhaps above all a reverential zest for the game of cricket, he brought an optimism and an exhilaration quite new to Llandovery. My earliest recollection is of him playing very stylishly in a practice match at the start of his first term. He was made to run a fourth run, and collapsed exhausted. When he came to, he was asked, 'Do you want any help, sir?' 'Yes, a large Scotch would be rather gratifying.' The impression on young minds was irresistible. Like T.P., Chris Bell was to give the whole of his teaching life to one school. T.P.'s case is perhaps more understandable; he came back to the place he knew as a pupil. Chris was entirely different. As English as they come, he gave himself to this small Welsh school in the back of beyond, as Llandovery must at first have seemed to him. And over time, we saw his love, of the school, of the town, and indeed of most things Welsh, grow and become deep-rooted. More than anyone I remember, he became the Mr Chips of Llandovery. Among the boys who knew him well, he inspired a devotion of a kind we are privileged to have experienced.

This is one of Llandovery's best attributes. Particular friendships I made there, with boys and masters, have had a lasting quality beyond anything in other parts of my life. I am not sure I can explain it, but the place, its ethos and its size have led to loyalties of a very enduring and special kind.

Other snippets of memory. The weather. It was forever raining. (When I eventually went to Cambridge and a different climate, I found great difficulty, to begin with, in catching and kicking a dry ball). And it seemed particularly wet in the cricket term. There was always mist or worse coming up the Towy from the west. The cold winter of 1947 stands out. The river was frozen hard for many weeks. We had ice hockey, with Chain Bridge as one goal and Dolau Bridge the other. Blizzards had piled up the snow in the front of the school to the height of the Tower balcony.

Speaking of balconies, I remember two of us shinning up the wooden columns in the hall. There was a working radio there. We went up before breakfast on December mornings to hear the crackling commentary of test matches from Australia. At close of play one morning, Bradman and Barnes were batting. When we switched on the following morning, they were still batting. They each scored 234.

School walks were special too, those permitted and those not. The rolling gentleness of north Carmarthenshire has become imprinted on my mind, with the kite and the buzzard scavenging like sheep.

In days of austerity, cultural activities were not easily come by. We had the occasional visit by a notable musician, but I don't now recall them. What I do remember is the 'Society' that Steven Huntly ran upstairs in Bank House on Sunday evenings, when some of us listened to classical music from his 78 rpm records, on a gramophone that wheezed as much as did Steve himself. He was another master with a heart of gold. Further up the road, we met once or twice in Donald Pye's house, where I listened to records of Shakespearean actors reading English with a style and a meaning I had never heard before. That man had a genius as a classics teacher for those who would listen. As we struggled to keep up with him in Latin, he was also giving us a first-class grounding in English grammar. I only realised it years later, and am still profoundly grateful.

Feeding a school of 200 plus in those days must have been one of the biggest headaches of all. I have little memory of the food itself, probably because most of it was unmemorable. No wonder tuck-boxes were prized. Hungry children will eat most things in the end, and we did. And visits from home were anticipated, not only to see parents, but to be taken for ham and eggs, cooked by Mrs Davies at the Bear.

End of term was relished, therefore, for the improvement of food to come. Such were the thoughts, as we sang, more lustily than any other hymn, 'Lord, dismiss us with thy blessing', and climbed into the Coffee Pot, en route to Llanwrda, Llangadog, Llandeilo and all stations to Llanelli.

God is good. As time goes by, he gives us very subjective memories. What I now write about 1944-49 is undoubtedly selective. There must have been bad days and sad, and many of them. But the memory slate has been wiped clean of most of those. There abides only the people and the events one wants to remember. I suppose we were sent to Llandovery in order to learn, but long after we have forgotten all we ever learnt, the people and the place live on.

(Peter M. Davies was educated at Llandovery and Trinity Hall Cambridge where he graduated M.A., Ll.B. He gained three rugby blues—1952, 3, 4 and never lost to Oxford! He qualified as a solicitor and later became Secretary and Director of Imperial Tobacco Group. In 1992 he became a Reader in the Church of England and since 1990 has been Chairman of The Garden Tomb (Jerusalem) Association. He was Trustee of Llandovery College 1976-1993).

1945

[The Revd. J. L. R. Pastfield]
E. R. Davies

Sometime Scholar of Keble College Oxford, the Revd. J. L. R. Pastfield M.A., read Chemistry before taking Holy Orders. I know little of his early career but learned from him that he had done missionary work in Japan at some stage. His wife was Norwegian which probably explains how he came to be a proficient skier. He even skied to school one snowy winter. He was well established in Llandovery when I came to the Science VIth in January 1945 and he taught me most days for the next eight terms.

He had an imposing presence—dressed in clerical black and wearing a torn gown . . . and taller than most, except perhaps E. S. Huntley. His head was bald and deeply suntanned, his face bespectacled and clean shaven and rubicund. His jutting jaw was purposeful and accompanied by long rapid strides that brought him up from Bank House like a ship under full sail. Occasionally, on Sunday, he would preach in the School Chapel, giving a characteristically unequivocal exposition of his views.

Mr Pastfield had a habit of referring to us by the title 'Mr' followed by initials, thus 'Mr E.R.' or 'Mr W.J.C.' . . . or when he was irritated or forgetful 'Mr Thing'. In return we referred to him affectionately as 'Mr Joe'.

Among his extracurricular interests was Naval History and when I left school he gave me a signed copy of his published monograph on *The Battle of Jutland* during the Great War of 1914-18.

My only strict contemporary in the Science VIth was W. J. C. Thomas who sadly died in a climbing accident a few years ago. Each of us was committed to a career in Medicine and we were studying together for the 1st M.B. examination of London University. Alas, Bill Thomas found he was too young to be admitted to the examination and soon after that he left to go to Dulwich College where his father was teaching. Thus I enjoyed individual attention from Mr Pastfield and from B. L. Morgan who taught Biology—and who sent me home one summer holiday with a small bottle of chloroform so that I could catch and anaesthetise frogs in order to revise my dissection skills!

The London 1st M.B. gave me exemption from Parts 1, 2 and 3 of the Cambridge 1st M.B., and when I returned to school in September 1946 I wanted to prepare for the Entrance Examination to Clare and for the 4th part of the Cambridge 1st M.B., in Organic Chemistry. 'Mr Joe' was keen to help me and said that although he had never taught Organic Chemistry to anyone, there was no reason why he shouldn't, provided he read the books first and then passed them on to me! And so it was. Following his advice the School set up a bench of Organic Chemistry reagents at the back of the upstairs Science Lab, for my sole use. There I toiled enjoyably and successfully under 'Mr Joe's' watchful eye, and with his enthusiastic encouragement. We worked through the syllabus quite quickly and thereafter I sat as many old examination papers as we could get hold of, under exam conditions. My enthusiasm for Organic Chemistry was so fired by this experience that I continued to read it for a further year at Clare.

One of life's amusing episodes was enacted and re-enacted on Saturday mornings during the winter terms. All the VIth Form Chemists were in the upstairs lab of the Science Building. Some of us were in the 1st XV. The room across the landing was occupied by a lower school class who were having their general education improved by Mr T. P. Williams. Later in the morning, when he judged that we had more or less finished our experiments, T.P. would come in silently via the connecting door between classroom and laboratory, holding his hands characteristically with fingers locked and palms facing downwards, and ask innocently, 'Is Mr Pastfield here?' If the answer was, 'Yes, Mr T.P.', he would ask, 'Have you got the right time, please?' and on being told the time he would retreat to consult the large clock that he tended to carry around with him. Usually, however, the answer was, 'No' as we had been left to our own devices at that stage. T.P. would then drop all pretence that he was really interested in the time, unlock his fingers, gather the 1st XV members and launch into a 'pep-talk' for the afternoon's match.

I cherish my memories of the times I spent with Mr Joe and with T.P. for I am deeply indebted to both of them.

(Eurfil Rhys Davies CBE was educated at the Rhondda Grammar School at Porth, Llandovery College, Clare College Cambridge and St. Mary's Hospital in London. His twin brother—D. Eifion Davies, also an Old Llandoverian, was Classics Master and Second Master at Llandovery; their father Dan Haydn

Davies was a notable radio drama producer. The 'Cambridge Letter' in the *Journal of Midsummer 1948* reports '. . . E.R. . . . is at Clare. His room is adorned by the inevitable skeleton of every medical student. He lives underneath the Senior Proctor's suite and his staircase is the highway for the bright sparks who climb in over the wall in the early hours of the morning'! The staircase, however, was to lead to a distinguished academic career: E. R. Davies is the author of many scholarly works; he was Professor of Clinical Radiology at Bristol 1981-1993.

'Old Llandoverian News' recorded in the Journal of March 1953 the death of the 'Revd. J. L. R. Pastfield M.A. (Oxon) aged 64. Senior Science Master 1941-50. Vicar of Norton, Radnorshire since 1950').

1956-1996

J. HUGH THOMAS

Little did I think on that afternoon in September 1956 when I became a pupil at the College that I would spend all but three of my next forty years there. My immediate thoughts were to wonder why my parents had abandoned me in this strange place, surrounded by people, all bigger and older than me, whom I did not know.

The first couple of years were very hard, particularly as I was a year younger and less mature than my form mates. My parents were always caring and wanted the best for me, but they could have had no idea of what boarding school was like. Still, it was virtually a necessity to send me away to school, as they would be travelling abroad in the near future, my father having joined the Air Ministry; the piecemeal education in many different schools which I would have received had I moved with them would not have given me the opportunities which I subsequently received. What made it harder, too, in the first couple of years before their move to Germany, was that they lived 150 miles away, in

Abingdon, near Oxford, and petrol was rationed due to the Suez crisis. New boys were always asked 'Where do you come from?', and so I became known as 'Abingdon'. One of my closest friends, and a rival when it came to playing the chapel organ, was Rhuddian Davies from Caerphilly, and it was he, in one of our 'goonish' conversations, who named me 'Schnabingdon', from which my nickname of forty years derives. At last the mystery is revealed!

I had never played rugby before Llandovery, and I did not look forward to practices. I was younger and weedier than most of my year, and being put to play as hooker did little to fire any enthusiasm for the game. However, I enjoyed watching the 1st XV, most of whose fixtures were played against invitation sides, and many Welsh internationals would turn out on Tredegar Close, a tradition which happily continues to this day. The first 'big' match I ever saw was the Brecon match of 1956, when a certain D .I. Gealy scored five tries in a 31-5 win, a record unlikely ever to be broken. It has been a great joy to get to know and to work with Dai, who has been a valued friend for over 30 years.

The condition of the school was spartan in the extreme in the early years: one locker, a chair and a bed in a dormitory lacking any privacy, baths once a week when two or sometimes three of us would be pushed into one bath rather like sheep into a sheep dip, communal toilets without doors, and gloomy corridors, some of which survived until very recently with the advent of the development known as the 'concourse'. Gradually, things improved with the advent of the house system in 1961. Hot water became available for washing, a television set replaced the old 'wireless' on the balcony which was the only contact with the outside world, and newspapers were provided.

Opportunities to see one's parents were rare: a 'leave-out' consisted of five hours on a Saturday afternoon, usually with a rugby match to watch, or from midday to 6 p.m. on a Sunday (but not both!). Half-term was a special treat: we were excused our letter-writing prep on the Sunday morning, so the half-term stretched from eleven in the morning until six at night. How things have changed! We slept in school from the first night of term to the last, as did the house staff, and visits to town were forbidden.

Many memories remain vivid to this day. On the day I started in September 1956, two young members of staff also began their careers at Llandovery. Timothy Lewis was my Maths teacher from Form One up to A and S level, and he was inspirational in channelling my precocity, and some natural talent, into the skills which were to take me to Oxford to read Maths. He was eccentric to say the least, and his driving of fast sports cars can only be described as mad.

Timothy lived in Bank House, and he would walk briskly up the College drive each morning reading *The Times*, as if steered by automatic pilot. His routine was once described as getting up five minutes late, and spending the rest of the day trying to catch up with himself. He moved to Charterhouse, where he remains to this day, in a senior position.

Carwyn James also started at the same time. He taught both Welsh and English to Form One, who were divided at that time into Welsh speakers and non Welsh speakers, rather than by the more usual alphabetical divide. We all benefited from his enthusiasm and skill; he was a natural communicator, whose happiest days were spent at Llandovery. We admired his natural ability at sport, and we were immensely proud when Carwyn made his debut for Wales in 1958. I was fortunate that Carwyn was still on the staff during my first two years' teaching at the College, when I really got to know him well. There are many happy memories, and so much has been said and written about him. Suffice it for me to say that he was the kindest man I ever met.

The first Warden I remember was the Revd. G. O. Williams, later to become Archbishop of Wales. I was there for his last two terms, but I got to know him better subsequently, as he was a Trustee of the College when I started teaching. Here was an incredible mind at work, and a phenomenal memory. He could remember things about me in the first form which I could barely recall myself. The last time I saw G.O. was when he preached at the Rededication Service of the College Chapel in 1990. The mind was as sharp as ever, the construction of the address meticulous, the delivery so focused.

G.O. was succeeded in 1957 by Canon Ronald Tree, who was Warden for the rest of my student days at the College. I found him to be a kind, sympathetic man, although it was often said that he was better suited to a parish rather than a boarding school. He became Archdeacon of St. Davids, and he and his wife kindly provided a superb tea when the College Choir went to sing evensong at the cathedral one summer evening. One evening Canon Tree was watching the dress rehearsal of one of Chris Bell's Shakespeare productions, when he decided that the front of stage footlights interfered with the sightlines. The audience could not see the actors' feet! Tree enjoyed carpentry and practical hobbies, and decided to lower the footlights that evening when everyone had gone. For the first performance, the front half of the stage was in Stygian gloom: the lights were below stage level! Bell's remarks are unprintable.

When I started in College, many of the teaching staff had been there for a great many years. Donald Pye, an erudite classicist whose fine collection of texts were bequeathed to the College Library, was also a fine mathematician. After his retirement he would often set the Mathematical Problem in our teachers' union magazine, and on the rare occasions when I could solve it and submit an answer, he would reply with a fascinating analysis of alternative approaches. In Mr Pye's time there would be some 9 or 10 sixth-formers in each year following a full classics course, Greek, Latin and Ancient History. *Tempora mutantur, nos et mutamur in illis!* I was in his last 'O' Level class, and we were not particularly talented. He was reputed to have said to his Upper Sixth during the following lesson: 'I've taught the Fifth for the last time. Good riddance! I expect that they're saying the same about me'.

'Dick' Drought taught a little of everything, but he taught me Geography. He ran 'Second Game' for the non-specialist rugby players, and his interpretation of the laws was unusual, to say the least. Each game would start with the pronouncement 'Blues this side, Whites that side, Blues kick off'. On one occasion, this became 'Whites this side, Blues that side, Whites kick off', which caused such confusion that the whole game became a complete shambles. The most dreaded moment of the week was at the end of Sunday supper. Mr Drought would announce: 'The following will wash up . . .' All miscreants during the previous week were liable to be on it, and the feeling of relief or despair was never so heightened.

T. P. Williams, known universally as 'Pope', ran the school almost single-handedly, and was *the* housemaster until the advent of the house system. His running of the tuck-shop, situated where the main classroom of the Music Block is now located, can only be described as idiosyncratic, but it was profitable. He dealt in stamps, postal-orders, cash, and looked after pupils' pocket-money, thirty shillings (£1.50) a term being the recommended amount. At the end of one term I had half-a-crown left, which could have bought me five bars of chocolate. However, I had the temerity to ask for two caramel creams and one and sixpence in cash. 'Five marzipans', said T.P., smashing them on top of the counter. Other delights were the wagon-wheels, and the family block ice-creams which we would share ('You cut, I choose'), and try and devour using our wooden rulers in the remaining seconds before second prep. One of my favourite stories concerning T.P. occurred at the start of a meal. He presided at almost all meals, and would say grace in his inimitable style; indeed, understanding what he was saying publicly was almost as difficult as reading his writing. At the start of one meal, he said to one of the nearby prefects 'Fetch a chair for Tommy', which the school assumed was grace, and immediately sat down!

T.P. used to teach arithmetic to Form One, but our Monday afternoon lesson would coincide with the arrival of the 'pop' lorry at the tuck shop. 'Open your books, and get on with your work', he would say, throwing his gown on the lockers. We never did find out what we were meant to do. The highlight of the week was the film show on Saturday evening in the gym, and the ultimate deterrent was being kept in during the film. T.P. detained some of our form one Saturday evening, and, not content with the normal detention, gave them a lesson on recurring decimals, which they had not encountered before. In a lesson during the following week, we were all instructed to do some problems involving recurring decimals. Needless to say, those of us who had seen the film did not know where to start. 'Hands up, those who can't do the work.' We dutifully owned up. 'Bring your books here next Saturday night instead of going to the pictures.'

In spite of occasional injustices, T.P. was very kind to me, both during my time as a pupil and after his retirement. He enjoyed receiving news about Old Llandoverians, and would always reply writing long letters in his best handwriting full of stories and reminiscences.

For many pupils, the sole sanctuary from the often oppressive system was to Tommy's flat. Tommy Jones taught music at the College from the late 40s to the early 70s, and writing his obituary in the September 1994 School Journal brought back poignant memories. Tommy was not a full-time member of staff, as his fragile health would not permit this, but he taught piano, and trained the chapel choir to the highest standards. He had to fight many verbal battles with colleagues who wanted pupils for games when they should be attending piano lessons or choir practices, and he learnt to give as good as he got, and quite enjoyed a certain independence. His room was always full of boys eating biscuits and making cups of tea, and for many of us Tommy went a long way towards replacing the parents whom we would not see for three weeks at a time. We could talk to Tommy, and his concern about our problems, his willingness to listen and his sympathetic and well-considered advice were valuable and consoling. Many a time an irate housemaster would be looking for pupils late at night, only to discover that they were with Tommy. I was especially close to him, and I did not realise at the time how much he was able to impart to me by way of musicianship and sensitivity. I visited Tommy regularly after his retirement, as my family home was also in Llandysul. He was still giving piano lessons to talented youngsters to the end, and we spent many hours discussing interpretative details in Bach fugues or Beethoven sonatas.

I found myself in the sixth-form at the age of 14, as the upper stream by-passed Form 4, taking 'O' levels after four years. Unfortunately, music was not an option in the sixth-form (nor was it for 'O' level), so I spent two years studying Maths, Further Maths and Physics. There was an immense change in the College around this time: staff became more approachable, and one was not afraid of talking to them, or asking questions in lessons. The house system created much more of a family atmosphere, and I was fortunate to have Revd. Neville Hughes as a housemaster. He was sympathetic and humane, and did not believe in visiting the studies too often. Several new activities were started, and the debating society, the sixth-form society and many others flourished. I learnt the art of bellringing from Timothy Lewis, and Christopher Bell's annual major Shakespeare productions were impressive, even if we did not always know what we were saying, or had to play ladies' roles. Many more trips were organised, several to cultural events, and the sports fixture lists widened to include far more inter-school matches. Careers advice was still very restricted,

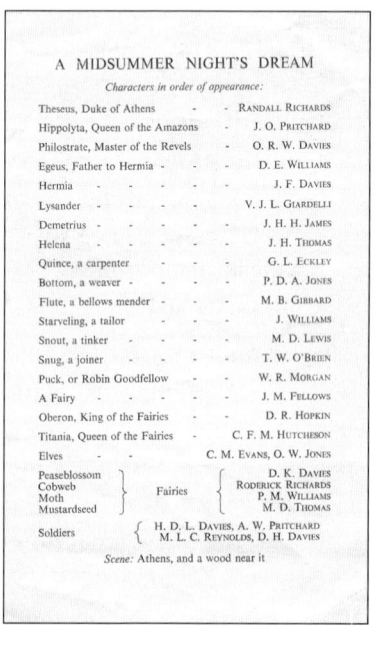

LLANDOVERY COLLEGE

A
Midsummer Night's
Dream
by William Shakespeare

★

FRIDAY, 17th FEBRUARY, 1961
at 6.0 p.m.

SATURDAY, 18th FEBRUARY, 1961
at 6.0 p.m.

A MIDSUMMER NIGHT'S DREAM

Characters in order of appearance:

Theseus, Duke of Athens	Randall Richards
Hippolyta, Queen of the Amazons	J. O. Pritchard
Philostrate, Master of the Revels	O. R. W. Davies
Egeus, Father to Hermia	D. E. Williams
Hermia	J. F. Davies
Lysander	V. J. L. Giardelli
Demetrius	J. H. H. James
Helena	J. H. Thomas
Quince, a carpenter	G. L. Eckley
Bottom, a weaver	P. D. A. Jones
Flute, a bellows mender	M. B. Gibbard
Starveling, a tailor	J. Williams
Snout, a tinker	M. D. Lewis
Snug, a joiner	T. W. O'Brien
Puck, or Robin Goodfellow	W. R. Morgan
A Fairy	J. M. Fellows
Oberon, King of the Fairies	D. R. Hopkin
Titania, Queen of the Fairies	C. F. M. Hutcheson
Elves	C. M. Evans, O. W. Jones
Peaseblossom, Cobweb, Moth, Mustardseed — Fairies	D. K. Davies, Roderick Richards, P. M. Williams, M. D. Thomas
Soldiers	H. D. L. Davies, A. W. Pritchard, M. L. C. Reynolds, D. H. Davies

Scene: Athens, and a wood near it

and taking a year off between school and university was virtually unknown in Llandovery. So it was that I spent a third year in the sixth form, studying my subjects at 'S' level, and a fourth year concentrating on music, when I was fortunate enough to receive a piano lesson and theory coaching from Tommy daily. I also found myself teaching some Maths to Form One during a teacher's absence, and actually got paid for it. Teaching as a career still had not entered my mind at that point.

Maths at university was very different from what I had previously encountered, and it was some relief that other undergraduates found the same difficulties. I did consider switching to a Music degree, as I really enjoyed the music lectures which I occasionally attended. What would I do with a music qualification? I realised that a career as a concert pianist was a non-starter, and all that was realistically left was teaching, which is why I persevered with Maths. A few days spent on a computing course grappling with the difficulties of languages such as Fortran and Algol, and not even seeing a computer, were to be a turning point: I had assumed that I would find a career in computing, but it all seemed terribly dull. I decided that I would prefer to deal with people rather than with machines, for which I could find little enthusiasm. During my third year at university, I did what many students do, and applied for the Diploma in Education course, as it was then called, to postpone decisions, and to remain in Oxford for another year. Out of the blue, one December morning, a letter arrived from Tommy. It also contained an advertisement stating that Llandovery College were looking for someone to teach Mathematics, to start the following September. The closing date was days away, so I hurriedly put together an application which in retrospect must have been very clumsily constructed: I had not so much as heard of a c.v. in those days, let alone written one. I was interviewed by Chris Bell, then Acting Warden, and was offered the job. At the tender age of 21, I started at Llandovery for the second time.

*　　*　　*

It is greatly to the credit of the staff that I was able to settle into my first job so easily. I was very apprehensive of walking into the Staff Common Room and talking to teachers who had been 'Sir' three years previously, but they made me feel so at ease that it was natural to call most of them by their Christian names within a few days. There were no problems in relating to the pupils or controlling lessons: those who knew me from my earlier time in school remembered me as a prefect, indeed head of school, and I particularly enjoyed teaching the sixth form, who found it easy to talk to me and discuss their problems.

*Chris Bell,
Dr Ernest Davies (Trustee)
and Josh Evans*

I spent two years living in Bank House, a house in Broad Street owned by the College at that time. This was a bachelor residence where Chris Bell, Josh Evans and John Sammons also lived. There were many parties and riotous nights out during those times. Colleagues would often ask me out to join them for a drink, and it was difficult to say no. The North Western Hotel, subsequently the Rugby Club, and now sadly boarded up, was our usual haunt where Carwyn James, Eifion Davies and I were regulars in the back bar, and we took many a visiting rugby team there for functions. We played Dulwich School in a mid-week fixture, and caroused late into the night. I dutifully appeared the following morning, but had to give up a sixth-form lesson when I could not utter the word *perpendicular*.

Another of our favourite haunts was the 'Black Ox'. This pub had changed little over the years, and it was a meeting place for local people from all walks of life. Sometimes we would decide to call on Josh Evans in Bank House after a night out. Josh was always welcoming, and we would suggest opening a bottle of wine. Josh would often ask for another bottle (the Common Room supply was kept downstairs), but the scene the following morning would always be the same. All the empties would be in the bin in my room next door, and Mrs Crayford, the cleaner, would say, 'I see that Josh Evans had another party last night'. Josh would say later, 'We were sharing the cost of the bottles last night, weren't we?'

Gerallt Jones started as Warden on the same day as I started teaching at the College, and his ideas were far more progressive than those of his predecessors.

He was the first Warden not to have been ordained, and he enjoyed active involvement in many activities, especially rugby, cricket and drama. Within a year of his appointment, girls were admitted into the sixth-form, which was a radical innovation. Llandovery was one of the first 'boys' public schools to admit girls, only Marlborough, who admitted sisters of existing pupils, having already made a similar decision. It took some time for pupils, and staff, to adjust to mixed classes, but it was certainly the right way forward. There were emotional problems, particularly with some sixth-form boys, but the girls more than held their own. It must have been very difficult for them, being in such a minority, but the first intake was a resilient group, full of personality and character.

After two years in Bank House, I moved into the main College building as Assistant Housemaster in Tŷ Illtyd, a house created the previous year and run by Dr Iwan Williams. This was far more convenient than walking back and fore to town, although there were far more duties and responsibilities. During my time as assistant, I lived in, and the housemaster lived in the town, which was an added burden, but it is certainly true to say that running a house was much more straightforward in those days than it is now. I learnt a lot from Iwan, and we spent hours discussing pupils and the house. He was always very caring, and he saw Tŷ Illtyd as a large family. Iwan was the first to admit that there were some pupils to whom he could not relate, and I remember him calling me in one evening. One of the boys in the house had run off, and his friends suggested that he was making for a house in Newtown, where his girlfriend lived. Iwan asked me whether I would mind going to try to fetch the runaway back, as the sight of the boy's housemaster would probably make him run even further away. I managed to complete the mission successfully.

It was inevitable that, in time, Iwan would leave to take up a headship. He moved to Ysgol y Berwyn, Bala, where he served as head with great distinction until recently. Iwan's successor was Eifion Davies, who was a close friend. He had done much to nourish my musical interests when I was a pupil, and we ran the chapel choir together. One of our most selfless acts was to leave the great Wimbledon tennis final of 1972, with Nastase and Smith at 5-all in the final set, to go to choir practice.

Eifion continued to run Tŷ Illtyd along the lines established by Iwan, combining firmness and fairness in equal proportion. He would never act rashly, but would spend hours discussing issues and how to deal with them justly. He was not one to contribute small-talk to meetings, but when he did speak, it was with great authority and rationality, and his advice was always sound. These qualities no doubt led to his being appointed Second Master in 1976, when I took over the housemastership of Illtyd for the next five years.

These were happy times, and we were certainly a mixed bunch. It was a refuge for the more cultured pupils, whose horizons extended beyond the sports field, although we more than held our own in inter-house competitions in spite of being the smallest house. I remember one parent rejoicing that his son was to join the 'academic' house, although the boy in question was far from a high-flyer.

There has been a relatively small turnover in teaching staff over the years, which says a lot for the morale of the staff and the health of the school. There were the inevitable cliques from time to time, but they soon collapsed. In the early years, teachers had far less paperwork to do than is now the case, and there seemed to be much more time to relax. The evening meal for the staff was a civilised affair in the Board Room, where we would often sit for an hour or two making conversation over good food and a glass of wine. Chris Bell would sit at the head of the table, with Josh Evans on his left. Their conversations would sometimes be monosyllabic, and Bell, fuelled by pre-prandial whisky, would sometimes speak his thoughts aloud. One of his more memorable utterances, while attacking a particularly tough piece of meat, was 'This, like marriage, is defeating me!'

The French department saw many a fledgling come and go, but the most eccentric, who stayed for a longish period, was surely Mike Wilson. He would arrive on his motor-cycle, and, if he was late, would ride to the side of the teaching block, leap off his bike and jump in through the window. His great love in life was building, for which he had great aptitude.

Harry Goddard certainly made his mark when he joined in 1970. His experiments in the Chemistry lab had a habit of going wrong, and he would often look harassed, especially after teaching 4B. He looked particularly flushed as he entered the Common Room one day. 'What's the matter, Harry?' asked one of the staff. 'I didn't realise until now that I could vault the bench in the lab', he replied. 'Who were you chasing, Harry?' we asked. 'I wasn't chasing anyone; they were chasing me!' It is greatly to Harry's credit that he learnt through his mistakes, became Deputy Head of Rougemont School, and, for the last 15 years has been the respected Head of Derby High School for Girls.

One of the first responsibilities which I inherited in 1967 was to organise school concerts. There had been a strong Music Club in the town, which attracted such artists as Dame Janet Baker and John Shirley-Quirk to the College. The first artists I engaged were a woodwind trio based in London, with a young flautist named James Galway. Little did we realise at the time how his career would blossom—and we paid £30 for the trio, including their travel. It was a joy to welcome musicians of the calibre of Jack Brymer, the well-known clarinettist, Alan Civil (horn), Hugh Bean (violin) and Bernard Roberts (piano). Generations of Llandoverians will remember Florence Hooton and her cello, and it was a great pleasure for me to accompany her in her last visit to College. Her husband, David Martin, gave violin recitals, and one of my first concerts involved accompanying their daughter, the violinist Nina Martin. The tradition of concerts and music-making has happily been maintained, and has been under the guidance of Richard Whitehead, the Director of Music since 1972.

One of my greatest joys was to see the College Chapel completely renovated, and this included the building of a 'new' organ. This consisted in part of an instrument from the Forest of Dean, to which were added some pipes from the previous organ, and some new parts, including a new pedal board. A group of us sat down to discuss the possibilities with Keith Jones, the organ builder, and the resulting instrument exceeded my wildest dreams. It is equally effective for choir accompaniment, congregational singing and for recitals. Many eminent recitalists have spoken highly of the new organ, and it gave me particular pleasure to arrange recitals given by Jane Watts, Roy Massey, Kerry Beaumont and Huw Tregelles Williams, to name but a few.

There have been many highlights over the last 40 years. The visit of HRH Prince Charles in 1985 was memorable, and a great honour for the College and the Warden at the time, Dr Brinley Jones. I greatly treasure the conversations I had with Viscount Tonypandy, who was a regular visitor while he served as a Trustee of the College. Such men are rare, and we mourn his recent passing. The Rt. Hon. David Hunt opened the new College Library in 1992, and greeted me like a long-lost friend as I was about to play the organ. I don't know why: I had never met him before! Professor Idris Foster was a regular visitor in my earlier years, and we were able to renew reminiscences of Oxford, although he never quite forgave me for one thing. The Dafydd ap Gwilym Society in Oxford is one of the longest surviving and respected, and is a natural focal point for Welsh students at Oxford; indeed, countless Old Llandoverians have been involved from its inception. During my last year at Oxford, I became *Caplan* of the society, and, after seeking the advice of my fellow officers, and noticing both the decline in attendance and the sudden influx of attractive Welsh girls to Oxford, I proposed that the constitution be amended to allow girls to join what had been an all-male society. Even the Oxford Union had taken this step some years earlier. Happily, the *Dafydd* flourished again, although Sir Idris, President of the Society, demurred.

On the sports field, the level of excellence has continued to rise, and the building of the Sports Hall in 1991 has enabled rigorous training programmes to be carried out. The quality of schoolboy rugby has never been higher, and the matches against Christ College rarely disappoint. Indeed, the centenary match of 1979 and the 100th match in 1988 were both superb matches, and many of the players involved have gone on to win major honours. The cricket field brings back many happy memories, particularly the fixtures against the Old Llandoverians, and the staff matches. I was looking forward to renewing acquaintance with the golf course during my 'retirement', but this has not happened yet. This is a superb facility, surely the envy of many a school, and the success of the Old Llandoverian Golf Society gives me particular delight. Tennis has become a major sport, a far cry from my student days when we were allowed two hours a week on the bumpy town courts under the shadow of the castle. We have produced many athletes of talent, and the number who go on to gain major honours is encouraging.

The Old Llandoverian Society has gone from strength to strength, and I was proud to be its secretary until my retirement. The address list of the 1970s consisted of barely 300 people, and the hard work of Owain Howell and Rhys Jones changed this dramatically. Now some 2000 Old Llandoverians receive the School Journal yearly, along with address lists and other news. It is important that they are kept informed of developments in the school, as many former pupils have never returned, imagining the school to be the Dickensian establishment they attended up to 50 years ago. I strongly urge them, if they have not been back recently, to come and visit, and witness the improvements which have gradually taken place over many years. I received enquiries almost weekly from Old Llandoverians, or descendants of O.Lls, asking for information. Several of the questions related to pupils at the College in the 19th century, many called Jones, inevitably, but it was rewarding to find their entries in the admission register, and references to them in the early journals.

As we celebrate the sesquicentenary of the College, we look forward to its continuing fame and success. We are thankful for all the opportunities it has given to countless generations of pupils, and for their interest and loyalty to the school. It occupies a unique position in the history of Welsh education, and long may it continue to do so.

(J. Hugh Thomas was educated at Llandovery and Corpus Christi College, Oxford where he read Mathematics, graduating in 1967 when he returned as a master to Llandovery. His contribution to the school was considerable—mathematics master, housemaster, rugby referee, cricket umpire, careers master, Director of Studies, organist, business-game organiser, archivist, secretary of the Old Llandoverian Society and Editor of the Journal. His musical talents have made him much in demand as an accompanist and repetiteur.

He left College in 1996 to direct his own company organising musical trips abroad.)

1968-1970

WENDY BASEY (NÉE THOMAS)

In September 1968 nine girls joined the college, seven boarders and two day girls. Seven studied arts subjects and two studied science. The girls were based in the Warden's house and occupied three study-bedrooms on the town-side of the house and a small sitting room adjoining the kitchen. The Warden, Mr Gerallt Jones and his wife and young family occupied the rest of the house. Mrs Jones was house-mistress.

The girls integrated rapidly into the academic and cultural life of the School—the boys accepted our presence readily and seemed to enjoy having us around and the staff were kind and welcoming. A number of the girls had parts in school productions such as Shakespeare's 'Hamlet', Edward Albe's 'The American Dream' and 'The Bear' by Chekhov which were all produced during the first two years of the girls being at the college.

Sporting facilities were limited for girls—some hockey was played in the winter, and tennis and canoeing were available in the summer. The mysteries and importance of 'colours' were not appreciated until one of the girls inadvertently wore red socks for a friendly hockey match against the staff—someone in the first XV took exception to the socks/colours!

The Duke of Edinburgh Award Scheme was introduced for the girls and all were encouraged to participate.

At one stage the girls were occupied on one afternoon a week with cookery classes. These were given by a number of masters' wives (and the bursar's wife) to three or four girls at a time, in their own kitchens.

The first winter uniform was not universally popular with the girls. It consisted of grey culottes, white shirt, grey jumper or cardigan and a short grey flannel cape which was neither serviceable nor attractive! (Grey duffel coats soon replaced the capes). The summer uniform was a royal blue long sleeved dress in a light Welsh woollen fabric and was worn very short! Straw boaters—identical to the boys' boaters—were optional extras.

In the summer of 1969 all nine girls joined senior boys on a 25 mile sponsored walk in aid of Kidney Research. The walk began in the hills and ended in Swansea. It was enormous fun and seemed quite an achievement in that time—before marathons were a common event.

We welcomed the second intake of eight girls in September 1969. Windermere House had been purchased by this time and was converted into the first boarding house for girls—the new girls moved into this accommodation, but the original intake remained based at the Warden's house.

The presence of the girls perhaps provided added competition for the boys (as well as being a distraction to some!) and there was much interest in new friendships and who was sitting with whom on Saturday night at the weekly film in the gym.

We all seemed to enjoy life at the college and most of the girls were successful in their academic work and went on to various universities after spending the 6th form at Llandovery.

(Wendy Thomas proceeded to the University College of Swansea where she read Biology and then took up a teaching appointment. She married Dr Colin Basey of Llandovery, a mathematician who is a Housemaster at Eton College).

1986-1988

Elinor Wyn Reynolds

On'd oedden nhw'n ddyddie da . . . Dydw i ddim yn gredwraig gref yn y dywediad hwnnw sy'n cael gorddefnydd braidd—dyddiau ysgol yw dyddiau dedwyddaf bywyd. Mae yna gymaint all fynd o'i le yn ystod y cyfnod tyngedfennol hwnnw fedr ddistrywio'r profiad o fod yn blentyn ac sy'n medru creithio'r cof yn ogystal. Rwy'n adnabod digon o bobl sy'n teimlo y buasent wedi cael gwell addysg pe na baent wedi camu drwy byrth sefydliad addysgol o unrhyw fath. Ond nid dyna fy mhrofiad i o fod yn yr ysgol, ac yn sicr nid dyna oedd fy mhrofiad i yng Ngholeg Llanymddyfri.

Des i Lanymddyfri ym 1986, i'r chweched dosbarth, yn ferch ysgol oedd yn barod am antur, rhywbeth newydd, annisgwyl, cynnwrf—yr hyn y mae pob merch ifanc yn chwilio amdano, mae'n debyg. Roeddwn i newydd gwblhau fy lefel 'O' ac yn awchu am gymryd y cam nesaf tuag at y gwagle mawr y mae pobl yn ei alw'n fywyd go iawn. Mae mynd i unrhyw le newydd yn medru bod yn anodd ar y gorau ond o'r cychwyn, teimlais yn ddigon cartrefol yn yr awyrgylch ddieithr yma. Roedd yna gymaint ohonom yn yr un cwch, a'r cwch hwnnw'n un hwyliog, llawn sŵn a ffrwst a baneri lliwgar oedd yn anelu am diroedd anghysbell.

Chofia i ddim llawer o fanylion am yr wythnosau prysur cyntaf. Cofiaf i ni gael cyfweliadau er mwyn asesu'n dewis ni o lwybr ar gyfer gyrfa, a minnau wedi 'nrysu'n llwyr gan yr holl wynebau newydd a'r drefn newydd. Ro'n i wedi 'nrysu hefyd o orfod gwisgo *blazer* i'r ysgol; do'n i erioed wedi gwneud y fath beth o'r blaen ac am fisoedd bu'r siaced ddu-las a'r bathodyn arfbais ac arni'r ddraig aur a choch cyfarwydd yn gorwedd yn anesmwyth ar fy ysgwyddau.

Cofiaf hefyd sut brofiad oedd bod yn y lleiafrif. Gwn ein bod ni'r Cymry yn hen gyfarwydd â theimlo felly, ac o orfod brwydro i osod ein stamp ar bethau, ond mewn sefyllfa fel Coleg Llanymddyfri roedd bod yn ferch yn beth anarferol a chyda dim ond pedair ar hugain ohonom ni sgert-wisgwyr a thua thri chant o fechgyn trowsysog, roeddem ni'n cael mwy na'n siâr o sylw! Efallai fod ysgol fel Coleg Llanymddyfri, oedd yn ysgol i fechgyn gyhyd, yn ei chael hi'n anodd i ddelio â merched o dan ei tho. Rwy'n gwybod roedden ni'r merched yn teimlo allan ohoni ambell dro; anodd tynnu cast oddi ar hen gi neu hen ysgol, mae'n siŵr. Er hyn cawsom ein derbyn yn weddol ddidrafferth i goridorau'r Coleg. Mae'n debyg fod cael llond llaw o ferched yn y dosbarthiadau yn gwneud lles i'r bechgyn (ac i'r merched hefyd) ac yn eu dysgu sut oedd ymwneud â'r 'rhyw deg' mewn ffordd ystyrlon a charedig. Diau ein bod ni fel criw bychan benywaidd wedi creu cwlwm cryfach na'r arfer â'n gilydd yn ein chwaeroliaeth, oherwydd ein nifer neu ein diffyg nifer. Ac mi gawsom ni hwyl, o do, mi gawsom ni hwyl.

Un canlyniad o fod mewn ysgol i fechgyn oedd bod rygbi yn gêm bwysig ar y naw i'r disgyblion a'r athrawon fel ei gilydd. Roedd y parchus, arswydus gêm yn ymylu ar fod yn rhyw fath o fuwch sanctaidd i'w haddoli, a'r ornest rhyngom ni a'r gelyn pennaf—Coleg Crist, Aberhonddu—pinacl y tymor rygbi—yn frwydr i'r eithaf. Roedd y sanau cochion a wisgai'r pymtheg gwron dewr yn y tîm cyntaf yn wobrau i'w trysori. Fel tipyn merched, roedd disgwyl i ni gefnogi'r tîm â'n presenoldeb pan oedd gêm yn digwydd, ac mi wnaethom ni hynny'n ddirwgnach gan mwyaf, chwarae teg i ni, ond pan oedd yr entrychion yn arllwys eu cynnwys ar ein pennau, roedd ein brwdfrydedd a'n bloeddio ni'n pylu braidd. Rhywsut, fedren ni ddim dychmygu'r bechgyn yn rhoi'r un gefnogaeth i'n tîm hoci ni, er gwaetha'r ffaith fod ein tîm hoci'n un anhygoel o wael. Pwy a ŵyr, efallai fod pethau wedi newid erbyn heddiw. Ydy'r merched yn cael gwisgo sanau cochion bellach?

O ran ei natur, mae pob ysgol breswyl yn cael ei siâr o blant sy'n dod o gartrefi lle mae'r sefyllfa deuluol yn un anodd ac, o'r herwydd, roedd llawer o'r disgyblion yn medru teimlo pethau i'r byw. A phwy fedr ddweud nad yw yntau wedi teimlo gwân drwy ei galon o glywed gair croes bob nawr ac yn y man? Byddai'r creadur sensitif oddi cartref yn medru bod yn ysglyfaeth hawdd i'r sawl a deimlai ei hun yn dipyn o foi. Nid lle i'r gwangalon oedd y Coleg, mae'n rhaid cyfaddef, gan fod plant yn medru bod yn greulon iawn. Ond, er hyn, roedd yna dynerwch mawr i'w gael yno a chyfeillgarwch fyddai'n para byth. Roeddem ni i gyd yn rhannu'r un profiadau, yr un teimladau ac yn tyfu, yn datblygu ac yn aeddfeddu gyda'n gilydd.

Un o'r llefydd lle roeddem ni'r disgyblion yn cael cyfle i brofi cwmni'n gilydd oedd wrth fwyta. Gyda phob pryd bwyd roedd stori neu'i gilydd i'w thrafod, dadl i'w thorri, jôc i'w rhannu, ac er nad oedd pob pryd bwyd yn fwyniant pur, gan fod trefn yn medru mynd yn drech na dyn, crëwyd sawl cyfeillgarwch dros blataid o datws a phys sy'n dal yn ei flas wedi'r cof am y pryd bwyd hen bylu.

Wrth gerdded ar hyd coridorau'r ysgol roddem ni'n ymwybodol iawn o hanes y Coleg a'r holl genedlaethau o blant fu'n rhedeg ar y lloriau cerrig, yn cyffwrdd â'r waliau, yn gweiddi hyd nes bod eu lleisiau'n diasbedain hyd y nenfwd, yn cau drysau derw'n glep. Ac o'r muriau hefyd roedd wynebau cenedlaethau o fechgyn (a bellach merched) yn syllu yn ôl. Roedd un peth yn fy nharo i wrth edrych ar y lluniau du a gwyn: er bod pob un o'r bechgyn yn edrych yn hynod drahaus a henffasiwn—ac ymhell o gyrraedd ein dyddiau ni ddisgyblion ar ddiwedd yr ugeinfed ganrif—o graffu'n agosach ar yr wynebau lliw lleuad, ro'n i'n medru gweld y llygaid yn pefrio a'r gwefusau'n ymffurfio'n wên wrth sylweddoli eu bod hwythau wedi cael yr un profiadau dryslyd wrth dyfu, yr un math o anawsterau a buddugoliaethau—eu bod nhw yn bobl gyffredin wedi'r cyfan. Dro ar ôl tro, roeddwn i'n cael fy nhynnu i edrych arnynt a cheisio syllu y tu hwnt i'r lluniau i mewn i'w heneidiau ac i ddyfalu sut fywydau gawsant wedi iddynt ymadael â'r Coleg. Ys gwn i a fydd unrhyw un yn holi'r un cwestiynau wrth edrych ar y lluniau ohonom ni?

Un o'm hoff bethau i ynglŷn â'r Coleg oedd y dramâu oedd yn cael eu cynnal yno. Bob yn ail flwyddyn byddai amryfal dalentau cudd yn dod i'r amlwg ac yn cyfuno i greu un sbloet anferth o liw ac egni dramatig. Yn ystod fy nghyfnod i, *Under Milk Wood* Dylan Thomas oedd y ddrama dan y chwyddwydr. Dydw i ddim yn credu i griw gael gymaint o hwyl ar fod yn Gymry gwallgo erioed! Unwaith eto, roedd ysbryd undod yn amlwg, a phawb yn cyddynnu i greu darlun reit agos ati o bentre'n berwi o bobl ecsentrig. Roedd y teimlad o gael gweddill yr ysgol yn gwylio ac yn cymeradwyo yn un heb ei ail ac yn un sy'n dal i fedru creu cynnwrf ynof i wrth gofio am ein perfformiad ysblennydd.

Ers gadael y Coleg, rwyf i wedi cwrdd â chyn-ddisgyblion y blynyddoedd cynt ac wedi fy nghyfnod i, a chael sawl egwyl bleserus yn eu cwmni. Yn weddol ddiweddar, roeddwn i'n cynnal darlleniad barddoniaeth rhywle yng nghanolbarth Cymru, a chyn mynd penderfynais—hyd yn oed os na fyddwn i'n medru swnio fel bardd—mi fuaswn i'n edrych fel bardd. Gwisgais siaced fraith amdanaf, trowsys brethyn a thei ysgol. O blith y gynulleidfa ymddangosodd cyn-ddisgybl a sylwi ar y tei yn syth; cawsom gyfle i sgwrsio a thrafod hanes yr ysgol a'r bobl fu'n rhan o'n profiadau ni ac er nad oeddem ni wedi bod yn yr ysgol yr un adeg â'n gilydd, roeddem ni'n teimlo fod gennym ni gwlwm gyffredin yn cysylltu ni y naill wrth y llall.

Soniais lawer tro yn ystod hyn o lith am y ffaith i mi wneud ffrindiau triw a ffyddlon tra oeddwn i yng Ngholeg Llanymddyfri ac nid celwydd mo hynny ychwaith gan fod mod i'n dal mewn cysylltiad agos â sawl un. Gan fod y Coleg yn fach o ran nifer, roeddem ni, yn ferched ac yn fechgyn, yn dueddol o gymysgu ar draws y blynyddoedd ac felly'n derbyn persbectif amlhaenog pan oeddem ni rhwng ei muriau. Roedd ceisio deall sut beth oedd hi i fod yn iau neu'n hŷn yn un dymunol a gwerthfawr, hynny yw, cael cyfle i flasu profiad rhywun arall am ychydig, cael bod mewn sawl lle ar un tro. Mae 'nghyfeillion a minnau'n trefnu i gwrdd yn aml ac rwyf i wedi darganfod fod rheol anysgrifenedig yn bodoli ynglŷn â'r Coleg; lle bynnag y cyferfydd dau neu fwy o gyn-ddisgyblion y Coleg, rhaid siarad yn huawdl—hyd at syrffed, medd rhai—am y cyfnod disglair hwnnw sy'n ymddangos mor bell yn ôl ac eto sydd ond fel ddoe hefyd. Y cyfnod hwnnw wnaeth gymaint i'n creu ni fel oedolion yn awr. Rwy'n gwybod fod gennyf ffrindiau am oes o 'nghyfnod i yng Ngholeg Llanymddyfri ac rwy'n gwybod 'mod i'n ffodus iawn o fedru dweud fy mod wedi bod yn rhan o'r profiad yno.

Rwy'n gwybod fod yna lawer mwy y dylaswn ddweud am y Coleg ond efallai, er mawr ryddhad i chi, ddarllenydd hoff, nid wyf am ddilyn y sgwarnogod hynny—mae gormod ohonynt. Mae gan bawb fu yno ei brofiad personol yntau o Goleg Llanymddyfri, dyna sy'n ei wneud yn lle mor unigryw —cymaint o bobl o dan yr un to. Mae yna werth cant a hanner o flynyddoedd o brofiadau yn hofran o gwmpas y muriau, y ffenestri a'r drysau, a channoedd, miloedd yn wir o fywydau ar ben hynny a dyna sy'n creu lle a'i wneud yn arbennig—pobl a hanes. Gwn nad oes unrhyw le tebyg i Goleg Llanymddyfri.

(Magwyd Elinor Wyn Reynolds yng Nghaerfyrddin lle mynychodd Ysgol Gyfun Bro Myrddin ac yna Goleg Llanymddyfri (1986-88). Astudiodd am radd yn y Gymraeg yng Ngholeg Prifysgol Cymru, Aberystwyth a symud ymlaen i wneud gradd ymchwil yng Ngholeg Iesu, Rhydychen. Bu'n gweithio am gyfnod fel cyfieithydd yn y Brifysgol ym Mangor ac yn ddiweddarach fel Warden a Threfnydd y Cyrsiau Cymraeg yng Nghanolfan Ysgrifennu Tŷ Newydd, Llanystumdwy, Cricieth. Bellach mae'n rhan o dîm rheoli Theatr Mwldan, Aberteifi. Mae'n ysgrifennu barddoniaeth ac yn cael ambell gyfle i ddarllen a pherfformio'i gwaith drwy Gymru yn ogystal â chynnal gweithdai barddoniaeth—bu'n ffodus i gael peth o'i gwaith wedi'i gyhoeddi mewn cylchgronau a chasgliadau barddoniaeth yn y Gymraeg ac mewn cyfieithiadau i'r Saesneg, yr Almaeneg a'r Gatalaneg).

1989-1997

CERITH REES

Schooldays for me in Llanwrda County Primary School had been extremely agreeable. It was small, friendly, caring and Welsh. Every pupil knew each other and the teachers knew every pupil. My only experience of Llandovery College at this time had been to watch the 1988 100th match between the College and Christ College, Brecon—I was one of thousands of spectators. On being asked whether I would consider moving to the College at the age of ten, I accepted without any fear or undue trepidation, but realistically I knew virtually nothing of the School, its history or traditions. The only feeling I was preoccupied with at this time was one of excitement.

However, before my time at the College was to begin there was an examination to sit with forty or so other 'hopefuls' and also an interview with the Warden (a term which I later discovered was synonymous with 'Headmaster'). I remember distinctly his asking me at which time I preferred to do my homework at the weekend—Friday or Sunday night . . . and I realized, then, that all would not be rugby and cricket for the next few years if I was to be accepted! And so, when the letter of acceptance arrived I knew that new doors had been opened for me: I began my school life at Llandovery as a day boy and 'converted' later to a boarder. But for the time being I enjoyed the best of both worlds in that Llanwrda was sufficiently close to family and school.

My first impression of College was one of awe—viewing this massive set of buildings, high, old . . . gargoyles looking down, paintings and portraits on the walls . . . long corridors, tall windows . . . and a chapel of its own! It really was an experience. And so term started and I nervously arrived in my newly purchased uniform to meet my new classmates and teachers. The first week was a struggle . . . to say the least. There were new subjects to tackle—Latin and Science being the most 'troublesome' . . . and there was also 'prep' to keep track of, along with the right books for the right lessons. At this early stage I wasn't sure how I was fitting in to the College but I could already detect an aura of warm friendliness permeating the whole place.

I had been brought up in church and so attendance at services was not a new experience for me, though for part of my early years the college chapel was being renovated. My previous church experience, however, had never taught me to sing and I knew early on that I was unlikely to be regarded as a potential choral scholar!

Llandingat—the junior house—was an island of refuge from the grown-ups the other side, as we were able to carry out childish pranks and play football at the back without a great deal of interference. Day-boys were not allowed into dormitories but there was a bated excitement at breaking the rules and sneaking up the wide staircase and view the line of beds and wardrobes. At that time, as far as I can remember, there were no overseas pupils at Llandingat, but once we went over to main school I realised that Llandovery College was a small world with pupils coming there from every corner of the globe—or so it seemed.

Because of changes in college organisation, I found myself belonging to four houses—Llandingat to start, Cadog then Teilo and Dewi for my VIth form. I realised that a couple of years earlier it would have been Llandingat and one other. And so, not only because of my 'belonging' to various geographical parts of the College but also being there for eight years . . . this gave me a very special feeling of attachment: it became my place. Of course, I did not enjoy every subject . . . or, indeed, my dealings with every master . . . any more than they enjoyed their dealings with me! I can see, now, on the majority of my school reports—'Could do better.'

I knew, too, that there were talents beyond my reach. I remember the concern and sly smile on Mrs Pat Davies' face in the Art Room when she declared— without saying it—that my sense of perspective was pretty hopeless!

I have to confess—rugby was my passion at school. As a young boy in Llandingat it was everyone's dream to represent the 1st XV and to venture a footstep on to Tredegar Close—something that was strictly disallowed by all the senior boys. The rugby team were truly held in awe by all the lower school—and rightly so—some boys, including myself put rugby rather foolishly above work on their list of priorities. We played rugby every day in school—be it official training with one of the junior sides or mass games of rugby league 'down the pitches'. What fun it was! The three Brecon matches I played in were the most special occasions that I experienced. Wearing red socks to bed the night before *the* game, the presentation of jerseys, the special Chapel service for the players, punching the 'monkey' as you ran on to the pitch—*all* added to the aura of mystery and history of 'Brecon day'. And then there were the celebrations at night when the college community gathered to discuss and to analyse 'yet again' . . . sending the Christ College boys home with their tails between their legs. And last year as captain I witnessed the 1st XV enjoying their most successful season for a number of years with victories over Brecon, Monmouth, Rydal, Colstons and Millfield!

But the most important 'gains' of College life for me were the friendships I made. Living as part of a small community, with people of your own age really does allow you to grow close to people whom you would otherwise never have met.

**Prize Day Ceremony
at the College
11.30am**

Introduction
by
Sir John Venables-Llewelyn, Bart, MA
Chairman of the Trustees

Report
by
Dr Claude E Evans
Warden

Address
by
Mr David G John
Old Llandoverian
Chairman, BOC Group

Presentation of Prizes
by
Mrs Gillian John

Vote of Thanks
by
Cerith Rees
Head of College

1.00 p.m.
Lunch at the College

2.00 p.m.
Old Llandoverians Tennis Match

And to crown it all for me was the great privilege of being selected as Head of School in my final year. In this I followed Rebecca Lillywhite, the first girl ever to be 'Dux'. She was able academically and socially—she was successful at the Duke of Edinburgh Award Scheme, at hockey and music. After almost one hundred and fifty years of unbroken male dominance she gained the respect of the School. It was not an easy act to follow and, for me, there were new challenges, new responsibilities and new confidences. Now I had to do things 'by the book' but what a fantastic honour it was!

Eight years have slipped by—working, playing, dreaming. I find it impossible to say what I owe to Llandovery College—in the instruction and encouragement I have had from masters and coaches. And I find it impossible to measure how much my own development has been formed by my being there.

Bellach mae'n rhaid ffarwelio dros dro ac edrych ymlaen i fywyd Prifysgol a'r holl sialens sydd yn fy wynebu. Credaf fod Coleg Llanymddyfri wedi rhoi'r cryfder imi wynebu'r sialens honno. Dyma ddiolch i bawb am hynny ac i'm rhieni am arwain y ffordd.

Now, I am off to university and a new life lies ahead. But I am so honoured to add my name—the youngest and the most recent—to those who look back over their years, with gratitude. Llandovery belongs to Wales and to the world beyond—but it is *mine* too.

Vale Landubrium

Now the term is waning,
'Vac' is getting near;
Glimpses of Board papers
Plunge us all in fear.

When the French is done with,
We enjoy some peace;
Baneful words and phrases
Have run out their lease.

When we try the Latin,
Oh, how hard it seems,
Working three whole hours
'Neath Apollo's beams.

Sophocles and Proses,
Grammar and Unseens,
Algebra and Euclid,
What a deal each means!

Then our object changes,
Packing is the thing,
All our toil is over,
How we shout and sing!

One more pompous meeting
In the old School 'Hall';
Speeches by the dozen:
Let the curtain fall.

In the early morning
Shaking of the hand;
Fifteen in one carriage,
Scarcely room to stand.

Three cheers for the Masters,
Three more for our friends;
Then the train glides onwards,
And our school life ends.

We Three

(From the School Journal Midsummer 1909).

SECTION III

SPORT AT LLANDOVERY

D. I. Gealy

RUGBY FOOTBALL

'As concerning football playing, I protest unto you that it may rather be called a friendlie kind of fight than a play or recreation, a bloody murdering practice than a fellowly sport or pastime.'

The game of football as described by a man called Stubbs in the sixteenth century continued to have a purely rough and tumble, even barbaric element in it, until the Victorians imposed a new kind of law and order upon the game; a game which had largely been played in the streets was driven into fields and other open spaces.

The arrival of Dr Arnold of Rugby School in 1827 to some extent coincided with the growth of football there. The interest taken by the famous headmaster in his pupils' sports saw 'a vast improvement upon the surreptitous brutalities, not to mention gambling and drinking, then so prevalent at the Public Schools.' As David Smith and Gareth Williams put in their admirable History of the Welsh Rugby Union 1881-1991—*Fields of Praise*—'Games, especially football, cricket and athletics, became moral correctives, instruments of character formation and social control.' John Williams, the first Warden of Llandovery and Dr Arnold were contemporaries at Oxford, both read Classics and both achieved First Class Honours.

Professor H. A. Harris in his book *Sport in Britain: Its origins and development* suggests that the first game of 'rugby' in Wales was played between Lampeter College and Llandovery College in 1856. The game had been introduced to Lampeter in 1850 by the Revd. Rowland Williams, who was vice-principal and Professor of Hebrew at St. David's College. Prior to this, Rowland Williams had been at Cambridge, both as undergraduate and Fellow of King's College, at which time Arthur Pell introduced the Rugby School game to the university. Unfortunately no written account of this first game survives. Professor Harris, it seems, had been told of the game by a certain William Davies, Lampeter College's manciple in the 1880s. The game played was most probably 'a hybrid twelve-a-side played at a point mid-way between both places'. [David Smith and Gareth Williams *Fields of Praise*].

In 1939, the then Warden, the Revd. Walker Thomas gave a talk on the radio on the History of the School. He refers to this match as follows:

'An interesting legend survives of the first match against Lampeter. It was played at Caio, mid-way between the two towns. On the day of the game there happened to be a hiring fair in a neighbouring field where the young men of the district assembled to hire out their services to the farmers for the coming year. Curiosity drew them over to the field of play. For the first ten minutes they were merely interested; then they came to the conclusion that this was a rough and tumble for all comers and joined in the fray. With much difficulty they were cleared off the ground and the match proceeded.' Apocryphal, maybe, nevertheless a wonderful story.

As far as Llandovery is concerned, it is highly likely that the game was introduced by a master who had learned the game in the English or Scottish public schools. Such a master was the Revd. Walter Price Whittington, former pupil of Cowbridge Grammar School, who had come down from Oxford in 1867 to become master at Fettes in Edinburgh which is where he had learned the Rugby School game. In 1868 the Revd. Whittington joined the staff at Llandovery and introduced both rugby and athletic sports to the school.

What is not often realised, of course, is that between the founding of the school and 1875 when the Revd. A. G. Edwards became the fifth Warden, the number of boys was never more than 80, ranging in age between eleven and twenty five. There were occasions when the numbers were as low as twenty: the third Warden the Revd. Evan Owen Phillips (1854-61) increased the numbers from twenty to eighty. Unfortunately, when the next Warden, the Revd. William Watkins [1861-75] left the numbers had declined to forty.

In June 1875 the Revd. A. G. Edwards, who was already Second Master at the school, was appointed Warden. He has been seen as the second founder and there is no doubt that we owe the organisation of a vigorous system of school games to him. Sport in the school was run by the School Sports Committee consisting of the senior master, other members of staff and senior boys. They were responsible for organising the games, keeping records of the income and expenditure incurred in sport. Captains of all the school sides were chosen by them. There were games played internally between teams which went by the names of Sharks, Penguins, Puffins, Slashers, Druids and Socii.

It was during A. G. Edwards' Wardenship that the first fifteen-a-side match was played between Llandovery and Brecon at Builth Wells on the last Saturday in November 1879. The Rev P. C. Cornish who played in the match recalls, 'I can remember the drive to Builth in an enlarged wagonette driven by C. P. Lewis and accompanied by a band of enthusiastic supporters who were all out for the kill'. Cornish played in three Brecon matches first as full back; then in the pack as 'dribbler' and finally on the wing.

A Breconian in his recollections 1864-1867 does refer to a match where he was 'bodily lifted up by a burly Llandoverian and landed on my face, luckily in the mud,' but these earlier encounters would have had teams of twenty-a-side.

The first Golden Era of 'Rugger' at Llandovery may be said to date from the days of the great C. P. Lewis. At Oxford he won a 'Blue' in 1876 in both cricket and athletics but though he played rugby for the Varsity he did not win his 'Blue'. C.P. returned as master to Llandovery in 1877 and in 1881 was asked to captain the Welsh XV in their first ever game against England. He refused as he did not believe the team was representative of Wales. However, C.P. did later captain Wales against Ireland in 1882 and Scotland in 1883, both matches being the first between the respective countries. When the Welsh Rugby Union was officially established in the Castle Hotel, Neath on March 12th 1881, it was C. P. Lewis who represented the College and most probably Llandovery Town at that meeting. He was later, in 1885, to referee the Wales v. England game at St. Helens, Swansea.

C. P. Lewis: A great pioneer of Welsh Rugby, and the friend and adviser of all Llandovery games players from the time of his return as a master in '77 until his death in '23. At Oxford he won Blues for cricket and athletics, and he captained Wales in their first matches against Ireland and Scotland in '82 and '83.

Two Old Llandoverians T. Aneurin Rees, the son of William Rees, The Tonn who was one of the first trustees of the school, and Dr E. J. Lewis played in the first Welsh team to play England in 1881. Furthermore, in 1885, W. H. Thomas won one of his eleven caps when he was still at school, and he won a 'Blue' at Cambridge in 1886-7. The Warden at that time, the Revd. John Owen was a very enthusiastic sportsman. 'He used to race up and down the touchline with the ardour of a boy, shouting the School's battle cry.' In his last year as Warden in 1889 there were 193 boys in the school, 'the highest it had ever been'.

The Team of 1877

In 1886 the Breconian-Llandoverian Football Club was formed at Oxford under the captaincy of W. W. Poole Hughes who, in the beginning of the following century, was to become the eighth Warden of the school.

Finally in the 1892 and 1893 seasons, the College provided a captain in both the Varsity matches: C. B. Nicholls captained Cambridge in 1892 and Conway Rees who introduced to the University the four threequarters and full-back system, captained Oxford. Both captains agreed to adopt the new system in the Varsity match of 1893 played at the Queen's Club.

Between the years 1881 and 1896, there was not a season without an Old Llandoverian donning the red jersey and there is no doubt that the influence of the college on the game in Wales was second to none.

The above successes are all the more impressive when one considers that in 1898 the editor of the School Journal refers to the fact that 'Football has to do without a permanent field much to its disadvantage'. Furthermore, it was not until the end of the Rev Owen Evans' wardenship (1889-1900)—that rugby and cricket were made compulsory. By the end of the century, there were 160 boys in the school. That such a small school was able to achieve such outstanding academic and sporting success was in itself remarkable.

On 1st of December 1900 the Revd. W. W. Poole-Hughes M.A. was appointed Warden. The appointment was to take effect from the following January 1901. At the time of his appointment he was a master at Sherborne School and had played for the Barbarians in 1892-3 season when he was a playing member of

London Welsh. The Rev T. H. Ward Hill described Poole-Hughes' Wardenship as 'Benevolent Despotism'. As soon as he arrived he curtailed the powers of the School Committee—no team could be published, no colours awarded and no captain chosen without his approval. However, it was during Poole Hughes' wardenship that a new gymnasium was opened in 1908—what is now the Performing Arts Centre—and Tredegar Close was acquired through the generosity of Viscount Tredegar and Poole Hughes' acute business acumen.

In 1901 the College XV played Sherborne for the first time at the Arms Park, Cardiff, no doubt a game arranged by the Warden himself; a system of House matches was introduced in 1903 where the Infernals, the Slashers and the Druids played against each other. This developed into a Senior League which was played in the Easter Term and a Junior League in the Christmas Term.

Old Llandoverians were at this time continuing to make a name for themselves at international level. In 1904 Harry Watkins, a local boy, won the first of his six caps; in 1912 and 1913 Ewan Davies and J. L. Morgan won caps for Wales, as did Dr H. Graham-Davies and the Rev J. D. Bartlett in 1921 and 1927 respectively. However, the Old Llandoverian who will always be remembered from this era was the Rev J. Alban Davies who led the 'Terrible Eight' against Ireland in 1914 in a game recognised as being one of the roughest ever played in the history of Welsh rugby. It was the last international played before World War I broke out, and the match account referred to 'those furies in red jerseys who fought to a standstill the militant Irish pack'.

During the wardenship of Poole Hughes, two Old Llandoverians returned as masters to the college, both of whom were to play a very significant part in the development of rugby in the school. In 1923 D. R. Williams returned as master in charge of rugby and in 1927, his brother T. P. Williams joined him. When D.R. died in 1979 Arthur Rees, in the obituary which he wrote for the School Journal, refers to him as 'rugby coach supreme, who set the standards which were followed by T.P. and Carwyn'. When D.R. left in 1930, T.P. became coach to the College First XV, a post which he held until 1964 when he was succeeded by Carwyn James.

It was in the 20s that the College XV played Monmouth for the first time. The first two matches in 1921 were played at Abergavenny, the first of which the College XV won 32-0 and the second lost 3-6. In 1928 the game was played at Cardiff Arms Park which the College won 37-0. In this match, V. G. J. Jenkins kicked off. Little did he realise then that he would be facing the formidable All Blacks on this very pitch in seven years time [1935].

Following the death of the Revd. W. W. Poole Hughes in 1928, the Revd. T.

246   *Floreat Landubriense*

Walker Thomas was appointed Warden, another Old Llandoverian, who had returned briefly to teach in the school from 1914-1916 before joining the army. During the years 1929-38 inclusive, the average number of boys at the school was no more than 100, yet one or more Old Llandoverian played in every Oxford and Cambridge game. Furthermore, between 1925 and 1934, the College produced a player for Wales in every position behind the scrum. In the 30s, there was an Old Llandoverian playing for Wales in twenty consecutive internationals. Three Old Llandoverians, Cliff Jones, Vivian Jenkins and A. M. Rees played a significant part in the victory of the Welsh XV over the New Zealand Touring Side in 1935.

Wales 1936: The team which beat the All Blacks. A. M. Rees is on the left of the front row, next to V. G. J. Jenkins. Cliff Jones is on the right of the front row.

After the Second World War, one of the most dominating forwards in Welsh rugby until 1957 was Rees Stephens who won 32 caps and toured Australia and New Zealand with the British Lions. In the early 60s K. D. Jones, the nephew of the great Cliff Jones, won ten caps for Wales and he also toured South Africa with the British Lions playing in all four tests. Furthermore, in the 70s Geoff Evans won seven caps for Wales and toured in 1971 with the victorious British Lions in New Zealand; the team which had Carwyn James as assistant manager and coach.

The tradition of winning 'blues' was still maintained during this period with Peter Davies and H. B. Griffiths in the early 50s and J. H. H. James in the early 60s representing the 'light' blues in the match against Oxford. Peter Davies in

1956 was selected to play for Wales against Scotland and Ireland but had to withdraw because of injury. In 1954 P. J. Y. Scott played for Scotland at Secondary School level.

1963 saw the end of 'The Second Golden Era of Rugby Football' as C. P. Sharpe, in his 'Llandovery's Achievements' describes the era 1927-1963, when T. P. 'Pope' Williams retired as master in charge of rugby. T.P. was to live until the ripe old age of 93, dying at his home near Penzance in February 1995. A Memorial Service in the College Chapel was held on the 14th September 1995 when Professor Tom ap Rees gave the address. In his address he posed the question: how was it that T.P. was able, year in, year out, to turn gifted players into brilliant ones and the ordinary players into seemingly gifted?' Tom ap Rees, who had been Head Boy and captain of rugby under T.P., believed that the main features of T.P.'s coaching were that he knew the rugby playing ability of every boy in the School and planned accordingly, not merely for the current XV but those for the years to come. He taught the basics to perfection: the backs were expected to catch and kick, take and give a pass at top speed, deliver the pass to the man outside in a single stride and in front of the taker 'at your finger-tips'. Finally backs were never to kick away possession. Forwards were taught to scrummage, to take the ball in the lines-out with both hands, to maul, ruck and dribble. Everyone in the team was expected to tackle and fall on the ball. The whole width of the field had to be used, so that the ball was constantly moved to the wings and when they were stopped the process was repeated the other way. Finally T.P. was a great motivator. He required and got 100% effort from everybody all the time. Praise had to be earned but T.P. knew the value of 'well played chaps'.

How fortunate the school was to have Carwyn James as T.P.'s successor. One of the great schoolboy coaches — T.P .— had retired and his place was being taken by one, who would later prove to be one of the greatest thinkers and coaches that the game had seen. Carwyn had joined the staff in 1956 and would later be the first to acknowledge that his apprenticeship under T. P. Williams had been invaluable.

'T.P.' and Carwyn

The College First XV fixture list had always included a large number of men's sides. In the 20s J. D. Bartlet and D. R. Williams regularly brought sides to play the school. In 1944 Graham Jones's XV appeared on the fixture list for the first time; a fixture which his son Phillip Jones, now a trustee of the College, continues to this day. In the 50s D. John Morris brought up a side to play the school and continued to do so until the mid 80s. Furthermore in the 50s-60s Rees Stephens' XV was a regular fixture. Tom Baxter Wright also brought up a side to play the school for a number of seasons and Sam Simon's XV and the Welsh Academicals continue to be permanent features of the rugby season.

On October 2nd 1929 Captain Geoffrey Crawshay brought up a side to play the school which included in it Rowe Harding—later Judge Rowe Harding—a Welsh international centre and many other talented first class players. The school side on that day included at centre V. G. Jenkins and Arthur Rees at open side flanker, both of whom would later become distinguished internationals and play against the All Blacks in the famous victory in 1935. The visit of Crawshays XV continues to be one of the highlights of the season and just as the school celebrates its 150th anniversary this year Crawshay's XV celebrates its 75th.

Monmouth and Brecon were the only two schoolboy sides which were played on a regular basis when Carwyn James took over as coach. Far more schoolboy sides were introduced onto the fixture list: Hereford Cathedral, Atlantic College, Rydal, Whitgift, St. John's Leatherhead, Merchant Taylor's Crosby, Belmont Abbey, Dean Close Cheltenham and in 1968 Millfield. Rugby was also played in the Easter Term where young players would be 'blooded' in preparation for the following season. A short, pre-term rugby course was introduced: 'there are new laws to be faced and new schools to be played'.

In his review of the first season Carwyn James analyses the effect the new laws would have on the game. 'The new laws and the concept of the modern game has laid far more responsibility on the forwards; gone are the days when forwards automatically feed the ball to the backs. The accent now is on forwards crossing the advantage or the attacking line, and when stopped they set up a platform for the secondary attack . . . Few first class clubs in Great Britain manage to play the modern game. The modern game calls for new skills and new skills take a long time to be mastered. They have to be taught at an early age'.

By the time Carwyn left in the Easter Term of 1968, many of the boys had mastered the skills and the First XV of those years played some of the most exciting rugby that has been seen at the school. In 1966/7 Ian Lewis gained his W.S.S.U. cap playing against England and went on to play with distinction for Bridgend. One would like to think that the seeds of Carwyn's success as assistant manager and coach of the British Lions in New Zealand in 1971 were sown on Tredegar Close.

Mr Goronwy Morgan, who had joined the staff as master in charge of Physical Education in 1968, succeeded Carwyn as coach. He had been a coach at Baslake School, Coventry after a very successful rugby career as scrum half for the Welsh Secondary Schools—scrum half to the great Cliff Morgan—and the All Whites when they played the All Blacks.

During the 70s and early 80s the College XV toured extensively visiting Romania, Italy, Spain, Scotland, France and Ireland. New state schools such as Llanelli Grammar and Cwmtawe appeared on the fixture list. Teams at all levels now played against other schools whereas up until the 60s, teams other than the First XV played very few games against opposing schools.

The rugby highlight of the 70s was undoubtedly the Centenary match played at Brecon on 27th October 1979. Brecon won by 19 pts to 10 but the real winner on the day was the game of rugby. In the match programme Vivian Jenkins refers to the best thumbnail description he had seen of a Llandovery-Brecon match as being the one in an article by John Mason in the Daily Mail: 'Fierce, Frantic, Wonderful'. This match certainly lived up to this description. Both sides had players of rare talent: Brecon's Robert Ackerman would in a very short time win his first full international cap. Llandovery's side included Rowland Rees Evans who won his Welsh Secondary Schools Cap and later played for Llanelli; G. Mayberry Wolfe who also played for the Welsh Secondary Schools and at fly-half the young Aled Williams. Aled, after winning his Welsh Secondary Schools Cap in 1982, would in the 80s and 90s become one of the brightest stars of Welsh rugby playing for Wales and the Barbarians. That only two caps has came his way, both as substitute against Namibia and Fiji is a mystery to the thousands of spectators who, over the years have been dazzled by his lightning acceleration and deft distribution. The one thing that is certain is that he will go down in the history of rugby at the college as one of the finest players produced by the school.

Finally on the 26th July 1980, the school was well represented at the Gala Opening of the Welsh Rugby Union Centenary Year at the National Ground. Cliff Jones O.B.E. was the President of the W.R.U. and John R. Evans, later Chairman of the Trustees, was Hon. Solicitor. Sixteen Old Llandoverians marched in the parade and as Mike Yeates so eloquently puts it in his account for the School Journal, 'We were the ones to symbolise the contribution Llandoverians have made to the Welsh Rugby Union over one hundred years and to the whole game of Rugby Football'.

There were periods during the late 70s and the mid 70s when it had proved particularly difficult to maintain the school's usual high standards on the rugby field. In the 1977 Journal, the rugby review reads, 'For the second year in succession we were to lose the whole of the previous season's 1st XV pack with most of the forwards from the 2nd XV'. Boys were no longer staying on for a third year in the VIth form so there were fewer experienced players 'to teach the youngsters the ropes'. Furthermore, a greater intake of girls, with no appreciable increase in the overall numbers, meant that there were fewer boys to choose from. The 1984/5 season was very disappointing with the First XV winning only three matches. There was an improvement in the following year when Mr Huw S. Thomas and Mr Randall Jones took the First XV on a successful tour of Belgium.

In January 1983 Mr Carwyn James had tragically died at the comparatively young age of 54. The world of rugby had lost one of its finest coaches and the school had lost one of its most loyal supporters. After leaving, Carwyn always spoke with genuine affection of his days at the college. A plaque in his memory was placed outside the pavilion and in 1987 on the initiative of the then Master-in-charge of rugby Huw S. Thomas it was decided to award scholarships, to be called the Carwyn James Scholarship, to three students who were gifted both in the classroom and on the sports field.

In 1987 Mr Robin Barlow took over the running of rugby football in the school, assisted by Mr Randall Jones to whom was given the onerous task of preparing the First XV for the 100th match to be played on Tredegar Close on Saturday 22nd October 1988 which the school won handsomely by 19 pts to 0. J. J. McPartlin writing about the game concludes his article with these words, 'I suspect that perhaps the finest coach of all, Carwyn James, watching from the Elysian Fields, would have nodded his approval'. He would certainly have been proud of the scholarship boys on that day.

On the morning of the match, in the absence of Colonel John Evans due to illness, a ceremony to unveil the 'T. P. Williams Sporting Honours Board' was held in the Main Hall. In his absence, Colonel Evans' speech was read by Mr Peter Davies and Mr Arthur Rees unveiled the board.

Finally, the 80s ended with Owain Lloyd, Luc Evans, Ian Jones and Matthew Lewis all playing for the Welsh Secondary School against the Scottish Secondary Schools in Melrose. In July 1989 the XV went on a tour to Canada and

M. J. A. B. Lewis toured New Zealand with the Welsh Secondary Schools. But a new era was also beginning for in the Easter Term of 1989 Mr Iestyn Thomas, an Old Boy of the School, who himself had been coached by Mr Carwyn James, took over as coach of the First XV. The successes of the last decade must inevitably lead one to conclude that it could justifiably be called the 'Third Golden Era of Rugby Football'. The old rivals of Rydal, Monmouth and Brecon have over the years been consistently defeated. But what is truly remarkable is that a school of fewer than two hundred boys has been able to defeat some of the most formidable of English schools such as Millfield, St. Josephs Ipswich and Colston's, Bristol; the latter had been undefeated for two seasons before losing on Tredegar Close.

There is no denying the fact that the Carwyn James Scholars have made a considerable contribution towards the success of the College XV over the years and one could say that the college is their finishing school: the talent which they possess is sharpened and refined over the two years so that they are well prepared to compete in the intensely competitive rugby of the 'professional' game which lies beyond the college gates.

'A modern line-out at Llandovery' 1997

The opening of the Sports Hall by Mr Gerald Davies—Cambridge, Cardiff, Wales, British Lion—on April 30 1991 has also been a contributory factor: the level of fitness of the students in general is now high and the well-equipped weights room and more scientific approach to fitness does mean that the college teams are always well prepared physically and mentally. However, without the high level of coaching that is given throughout the school, all the innate talent and superb equipment would be of little value.

Gwyn Jones

In the last decade Aled Williams, Luc Evans, Craig Quinnell, Nathan Thomas and Gwyn Jones have all played for Wales at Senior level with Gwyn Jones captaining the side on the Tour of America and Canada and against Romania at Wrexham in August 1997. In 1990 Luc Evans, Matthew Lewis, Ian Jones and Owen Lloyd were all in the Welsh Under 21 Squad preparing for the match against Scotland. Cerith Rees, Gary Powell and Jeremy Roberts all played for the Welsh Secondary Schools in 1996/7 season; Cerith Rees and Gary Powell toured New Zealand with the Welsh Secondary Schools and played in the test match at Eden Park.

SEVEN-A-SIDE

The College entered a team in the Public Schools Seven-a-Side tournament initially held at Richmond and then at Rosslyn Park, for the first time in 1949. Considering that 'sevens' was relatively new to the school, the team did well to reach the Fourth Round.

Over the years the School VIIs team have won the competition three times beating Bedford in 1952 by 13 pts to 5, Belmont Abbey in 1970 by 6 pts to 0, and Glantaf in 1992 by 24 pts to 4. They were also beaten finalists in 1957 and 1971. This is a truly remarkable record for such a small school.

School v. Bedford

Llandoverians who have played International games for Wales at Senior Level

(Date of First Cap in Brackets)

		No. of caps			No of caps
T. A. Rees	(1881)	1	H. V. Watkins	(1904)	6
E. J. Lewis	(1881	1	D. G. E. Davies	(1912)	2
C. P. Lewis	(1882)	5	J. L. Morgan	(1913)	2
J. H. Hudson	(1883)	2	J. Alban Davies	(1914)	7
F. L. Margrave	(1884)	2	H. G. Davies	(1921)	3
L. C. Thomas	(1885)	2	J. D. Bartlett	(1927)	3
E. P. Alexander	(1885)	5	G. G. Jones	(1930)	2
W. H. Thomas	(1885)	11	D. E. A. Roberts	(1930)	1
(First capped when a pupil at College!)			A. H. Jones	(1933)	2
E. M. Rowlands	(1885)	1	V. G. J. Jenkins	(1933)	14
A. A. Mathews	(1886)	1	C. W. Jones	(1934)	13
T. Pryse-Jenkins	(1888)	2	A. M. Rees	(1934)	13
W. H. Howells	(1888)	2	J. R. G. Stephens	(1947)	32
G. Rosser Evans	(1889)	1	K. D. Jones	(1960)	10
E. H. Bishop	(1889)	1	T. G. Evans	(1970)	7
D. W. Evans	(1889)	5	D. A. Williams	(1990)	2
C. B. Nicholl	(1891)	15	I. L. Evans	(1991)	1
R. L. Thomas	(1891)	7	J. C. Quinnell	(1995)	6
J. Conway Rees	(1892)	3	R. G. Jones	(1996)	10
D. W. Nicholl	(1894)	1	N. Thomas	(1996)	3
A. M. Jenkin	(1895)	2			

Total No. of Caps 1st September 1997 = 209

Llandoverians who have played for the Barbarians

(Each player's name is followed by his year of election to the Barbarians; his club at that time; and where applicable, the year of his first International cap.)

1890-91	D. W. Evans	Cardiff (1889)	1937-8	C. W. Jones	Cardiff (1934)
1890-91	*C. B. Nicholl	Llanelli (1891)	1941-42	H. J. C. Rees	Rosslyn Park
1892-93	W. Poole-Hughes	London Welsh	1947-48	*J. R. G. Stephens	Neath (1947)
1892-93	*J. Conway Rees	Llanelli	1962-3	K. D. Jones	Cardiff (1960)
1894-95	G. Lloyd Roberts	Cardiff	1970-71	T. G. Evans	London Welsh (1970)
1906-07	S. H. Lockyer	Llanelli	1992	D. A. Williams	Swansea
1909-10	T. P. Lloyd	London Welsh	1993	I. L. Evans	Bridgend
1932-33	*V. G. J. Jenkins	Oxford Univ. (1933)	1994	M. Lewis	Bridgend
1934-35	A. M. Rees	London Welsh (1934)	1996	J. C. Quinnell	Richmond
1936-37	H. O. Edwards	Cardiff			

Total = 15

*Committee Members.

CRICKET

Cricket was certainly being played at the school in the early 1860s. In the diary of William Rees, The Tonn, a trustee of the school, there is an entry dated 26th May 1861, 'A cricket match between the students of St. David's College and the pupils of Llandovery Institution who beat former 116 runs to 56'. Furthermore, the 'Cambrian News' of May 26th 1865 records the result of the game between Welsh Collegiate Institution and Town Club return match: College 49 and 74; Town 68 and 7 for 1 wkt.

Games in those early days were played on what was called the Union field. Curtis Morgan in his 'Reminiscences' says that, 'it was called the Union, because it was parallel with the Union or Workhouse, now the Hospital, the present row of council houses not then existing.' It was not until 1879 when John Jones M.P. of Blaenos offered the school the site on the banks of the river Tywi and a Pavilion was built near the river in 1882 that cricket was given a permanent home. The Old Pavilion was sited much nearer to Chain Bridge and the square was between what is at present Cerrig Cottage rugby pitch and the girls' hockey pitch. In the Journal of 1887 one reads that 'the cricket pitch has been greatly improved and enlarged last summer' and again in 1892 'a large new piece of cricket pitch laid'.

In 1911 the cricket field and the adjoining field came on the market. £1,500 had to be found at once—the modern day equivalent would be many thousands of pounds. Miss Thomas, one of the Ladies of Llwynmadoc, came to the rescue and advanced £1,000 on mortgage and the remaining £500 was borrowed from the bank, the Warden Canon Poole Hughes making himself responsible for the interest. Canon Poole Hughes's successor, the Rev Walker Thomas, in his 'Notes on Llandovery College 1899-1948' refers to the way, 'In 1937-9 two men with truck and rails filled two river beds and doubled the size of the cricket ground.' Finally the new pavilion was built and in 1937 was opened by Lady Dynevor. The occasion was marked with a cricket match between the school and T. P. Williams XI, an XI chiefly drawn from Old Llandoverians who had distinguished themselves in various fields of sport.

Now that a new pavilion had been built—which is the one that is there today—it only remained for a new square to be laid opposite it which was duly done in 1938. The review of the cricket season of that year refers to this new

The Pavilion

wicket as being, 'a little sporting but in time will undoubtedly rise to the standard of the old.' When the adjoining field came on the market in 1948 the Rev Walker Thomas purchased it for the school, then completing what is the present ground.

It was customary in those early days for masters to play for the First XI, except for games against other schools. The only two regular fixtures against school sides were the ones against Christ College Brecon and Hereford Cathedral School, the latter game usually played on the Christ College ground. The annual match with Christ College, had begun in 1865.

In 1877, C. P. Lewis returned to the college to become master of the junior school and assistant master-in-charge of athletics. The presence of C. P. Lewis, an Oxford double Blue and Welsh rugby international, gave an immense boost to the sport in the school, no more so than to cricket, so that in 1881 the College XI won the South Wales Challenge Cup, beating Swansea Working Men's Club in the final.

C. P. Lewis resigned as coach in 1887 to be succeeded by a man called Walker and then in 1891 E. Attwell 'a cousin of the Notts man'. However, in the early 1890s all was not well with cricket: the cricket captain was having difficulty getting people to attend nets and practices, 'barely one third play cricket regularly. There is a need to make cricket compulsory'. Furthermore, there was concern about having to pay the expenses of going to away matches which was the case in both rugby and cricket. It was also evident that there was danger to both life and limb at some of the away grounds. 'A lover of a good pitch and fair play' in the correspondence section of the 1889 Journal complains about 'the danger of losing an eye, a tooth etc. At Lampeter the home wicket-keeper had to be carried off the ground.' However, a radical change took place in 1895 when it was decided that only boys would play in the cricket matches for the school.

The year 1906 saw the arrival of Tom Soar, the old Hampshire professional and assistant coach at Winchester. As the new professional he soon made his mark. Time and time again reference is made to 'Soar's admirable coaching and also the excellent wickets which he has prepared'. He also began the tradition of presenting a bat to the best First XI cricketer and a ball to the best Junior player. Tom Soar was to remain at the College for thirty-three years. In that time he produced wickets 'of which any club could not be proud. If not always a joy to the bowler, not always a paradise for the batsman, it has always been interesting, nearly always true and almost certainly a ground on which it is a pleasure to field'. Furthermore, W. Curtis Morgan in his Reminiscences 1903-11, refers to the fact that boys were allowed to bring back bicycles for the summer term so that they could cycle to Brecon to watch the cricket match.

In the 20s the game continued to flourish but most of the matches were still against men sides. The brightest stars in the firmanent was undoubtedly a young man who in 1926 was described as being 'an excellent bat with every stroke. Should become very dangerous in a couple of years.' V. G. J. Jenkins certainly did become 'dangerous' both on the rugby and cricket field. He went on to win his 'blue' at cricket and to play for Glamorgan.

College v Town 1922 and the old Pavilion

It was not until the 30s and 40s that more schools were included in the fixture card. Indeed in 1938 a Junior XI played Craig-y-nos School in a two innings game. The summer of 1939 saw Monmouth introduced for the first time. In that team was a certain J. A. Gwilliam who later distinguished himself as Captain of the Welsh XV which won the Triple Crown and Grand Slam in 1950 and 1952.

During the Second World War, petrol rationing made it difficult for teams to travel very far. However, the school was fortunate in that Wycliffe College and Bromsgrove School had been evacuated to this area and were looking for fixtures. In the 1943 match Wycliffe scored 186 of which 120 not out were scored by a boy name W. G. A. Parkhouse. Gilbert Parkhouse would later play for England and become one of Glamorgan's most prolific batsmen.

After the Second World War, Chris Bell joined the College staff and took over the coaching of the XI. A year before his arrival, a very young P. M. Davies had begun playing for the First XI. Under Chris Bell, Peter Davies—the son of Emrys Davies, Glamorgan's opening bat, Test Umpire and later to coach at the school—flourished as a cricketer and went on to captain Wales in the first match between the Welsh and English Cricket Association. Schools such as Ruthin and Cardiff High School were added to the fixture list. In 1952 D. T. Jones took all ten wickets in the annual match against Christ College but was still on the losing side.

However, one of the most significant developments of the 60s was the better provisions made for cricket at Middle School and Junior level. New squares were prepared towards the Black Bridge end of the field so that Senior and Junior Colts and a Junior XI would have reasonable wickets on which to play.

In 1964 Mr Bell retired as cricket coach, having guided the fortunes of college cricket for eighteen years. In the School Journal of November 1966, J. G. (Jack) and W. E. P. [Tim] Protheroe-Beynon who for years had brought up teams to play against the school and often umpired the Christ College match, wrote an article. 'Memories of Llandovery College Cricket 1913-1966' where they refer to 'Chris Bell who always acted as Umpire and always with his famous shooting stick; during the great game, Llandovery v. Brecon, practically smoked himself to death while watching the game as far from the Pavilion as possible. Chris has been a wonderful coach and we will always remember him.' Sentiments, I am sure, echoed by hundreds of Old Llandoverians who were privileged enough to have been coached by him.

Chris Bell

The school was fortunate enough in having Mr Carwyn James to take over from Chris Bell in 1964. By the late 60s cricket was being played against other state schools at all levels. In the 1965 season W. D. A. Lloyd and P. H. Jones, and the 1968 season E. A. Jones and M. P. Jones, played for the Welsh Schools Cricket Association. 1968 was to be Carwyn's last season as coach but it was hoped that 'he would return to plague us with his own brand of unorthodox bowling'.

Carwyn James' successor as coach was D. I. Gealy, who himself had been coached by Chris Bell. When Mr Gerallt Jones was appointed Warden in January 1967, he was the first lay man to be made Warden of the College. He had spent some time in Jamaica and it was obvious from his first summer term in school that he loved the game of cricket. His enthusiasm was unbounded and he was never happier than when he was taking a net or even preparing a wicket. The retirement of Elvet Williams in 1970, meant that the school had lost one of its most loyal servants. Elvet had been groundsman at the college since the 1920s—only leaving the school for a few years in the 1940s to work on the council. He had served his apprenticeship with the legendary Tom Soar, in the days before the mechanised heavy roller, when they shod the school horse with leather-made shoes so that it could pull the roller without damaging the wicket or the field; in the days when as a punishment boys would form a long chain from the river to the square so that the square could be watered with the river water and the flat, true wickets could be prepared. Now that Elvet had retired it was proving difficult to find a worthy replacement. Therefore it was not unusual to see Gerallt Jones cutting the square or rolling the wicket.

His era as coach was a successful one: in 1971 David Samuel and Nigel Duncan played for the Welsh Under 15s XI and in 1973 Nigel Clarke, Nigel Rees and Paul Rees played for the Welsh Schools Under 16s XI. In 1975 the First XI went on a tour of Jamaica and also played at the College an Indian touring side which included the Indian Test player Chandrasekar.

When R. Gerallt Jones departed in 1976, Mr Tom Marks, who had joined the staff in 1974, took over as coach and has remained as coach to the present day. In this time Stuart Richards and Shaun Howells played for the Welsh Independent Schools and Shaun opened the batting for the Welsh Secondary Schools on their tour of Zimbabwe. In 1988 the First XI played against Central Club Barbados for whom the legendary West Indian opening bat Gordon Greenidge scored an immaculate 124 not out. Furthermore, in 1991 and 1992 the First XI participated in a cricket festival at Merchiston Castle School, Edinburgh and the Oratory School, Reading.

The School XI v. Old Llandoverian XI continues to be played. In the late 50s Mr Bell began an Old Llandoverian weekend. Games were played against the School, the Town XI and other invited sides. The Town XI game was played on the Sunday after which a sumptuous dinner was enjoyed at the Dolaucoed Hotel, Llanwrtyd, followed by an evening of singing in Mr Bells' rooms at Bank House.

In 1980 the Old Llandoverians arranged an annual fixture against 'Cobs', a side comprising Old Breconians, masters and friends of Christ College. Stalwarts like Huw Miles, Adam and Robert Hathaway have been returning every year to play against 'the old enemy'. These games have provided a feast of often tense, exciting cricket and of the 14 games played Old Llandoverians have won 6, Cobs 2 and 6 have been drawn. Stuart Richards for the Old Llandoverians has scored three centuries in these matches.

HOCKEY

The first mention of hockey in the School Journal occurs in the correspondence section in 1893 and 1897 where 'Quincunque' and 'Gal' suggest that hockey should be played in the Lent Term. However, it was not until 1900 that hockey was played for the last three weeks of the Lent Term 'after the football had finished'. The two games played were against Llandovery Town, which Town won by 4 goals to 1, and The Masters.

In the Lent Term of 1903, mainly through the enthusiasm and effort of a master, Littleton Powys, the School joined The South Wales Hockey Association and hockey was then placed on a firm footing.

Between 1906 and 1913 Old Llandoverians began to play a prominent part at international level: R. V. Johnson, J. H. Cannop, P. E. M. Richards, Rev C. Mostyn Davies and E. W. G. Richards all played for Wales at hockey; E. Richards eventually as captain.

However, a correspondent in the Journal of 1913 deplores the lack of support for the game: 'For some years the fate of hockey has hung in the balance owing to its lack of popularity. While admitting its inferiority to Rugger as a school game, I should like to point out that if played in the proper spirit, that is to say, with some amount of science, instead of the wild slashing, at man and ball which is the chief feature of 2nd and 3rd sets, it might become a most enjoyable game'.

1st Hockey XI 1920

It was the appointment of the Rev F. C. Stocks, a Blue and England hockey player, in 1922 which brought about a revival of interest in the game of hockey in the school. A fixture between the College and Christ College, Brecon was arranged but it was unfortunately rained off. Furthermore, between 1927 and 1930, T. Nevill, a master at the school, won six Welsh caps for hockey.

The captain of the School hockey XI in 1930 was none other than V. G. J. Jenkins and in the Easter Term of 1932 A. M. Rees and J. H. Hopkins represented the Welsh Secondary Schools Hockey XI against England.

During the Second World War because of petrol rationing and transport difficulties only a few hockey matches were played but well into the 40s the game continued to be played with enthusiasm. The introduction of 'sevens' in 1949, inevitably resulted in a decline in the numbers playing the game so that by the 50s very little hockey was being played.

In September 1968, girls were admitted into the school for the first time. At first there were nine Sixth Formers and by 1972, this number had increased to 13. Coached by Mrs Dwerryhouse, the girls' hockey XI, played against Llandeilo, Dumbarton, Amman Valley, Llandovery High, Brecon Convent and St. Michaels. As the number of Sixth Form girls increased and girls were admitted throughout the school, so hockey grew from strength to strength under the guidance of a succession of dedicated coaches such as Mrs Kendrick, Mr Snell, Mr Jennings and Mrs Davies. Girls now play hockey throughout the school in the Christmas and Easter terms. Success has been achieved by individuals and teams at county level. In 1995 Angharad John, captain and goalkeeper, represented Carmarthen County, West Wales and had a Welsh trial at both Junior and Senior level. In 1996 ten girls in all were chosen to represent the county. Moreover, not to be outdone by the rugby boys, the girls hockey team, has in the last few years toured London and Ireland.

The appointment of the Rev F. C. Stocks was responsible for the revival of hockey in the school in the early 20s, and the arrival of Father Simon Leyshon as Chaplain in September 1996 seems to have had the same effect. Boys' hockey, seemingly dead, is now alive again and its future seems assured.

Tennis

'Dear Mr Editor,

When so many improvements are being made in the shape of fives courts, gymnasium etc., it seems a pity that we are still without a tennis court. Objections have been made to it because it interferes with the cricket of the school and also tennis, unlike cricket and football, wins no glory for the School. The first objection might be met by the fact that in the good old days when we never lost a cricket match with Brecon, there was in existence a School tennis court. With reference to the second there is no reason why a tennis match could not be arranged with Brecon, where, I am told, they have a club. Trusting by next season we shall have at least one tennis court, if not more.

Yours hopefully,
Racquet.'

This letter appeared in the correspondence section of the School Journal of 1888. It can be seen that there had been a tennis court in the School prior to 1888 but it no longer existed; furthermore tennis was no longer being played at the school whereas the game was being played at Brecon.

In 1893 a student who goes under the name of Racket again deplores the lack of tennis courts: 'There is no reason in my opinion why a corner of the bank should not be converted into a tennis court.' Obviously no progress had been made since 1888. Furthermore W. G. Curtis Morgan, who played for the Welsh tennis team in 1931, in his Reminiscences of Llandovery College 1903-11, refers to the fact that, 'Fives were played in an indoor court and two outdoor courts. There was no tennis.'

It was not until the late 50s when Mr Carew Jones became master-in-charge of tennis and the Llandovery Council allowed the school to use the town

Tennis on the Warden's lawn

courts on Tuesdays and Thursdays that the game of tennis began to flourish in the school. A grass court had existed at the corner of the front lawn outside the present Warden's study since the early part of the century, but it was not generally used by the boys. Mr Huw S. Thomas, master i/c tennis from 1978-96, was Captain of the Llandeilo Grammar School tennis team in 1961 when the College side played them on the town courts, a game which the College lost 5-4. Captaining the College side was Clive Powell Williams who later became the Welsh Boys' Champion. Regular fixtures were made with schools such as Cardiff High School, Llanelli Grammar and Christ College and in 1968 Christ College was beaten for the first time.

School VI (Amer Arslanagic the Yugoslavian Junior International is middle of the back row).

Interest waned a little in the mid 70s though David James was selected to play for Wales' Junior tennis team. However, with the arrival of Mr Huw S. Thomas, who had been master i/c tennis at Blundell's School from 1971-77, the game of tennis was revived. New tennis courts were built in 1978-80 and by the mid 80s there was a strong Senior VI and Junior VI playing a full fixture list of matches against the likes of Monmouth, University College of Wales, Aberystwyth Town TC and Hereford Cathedral as well as Christ College Brecon. In 1992 under the captaincy of Chris Atkinson, the School VI had its most successful season ever. Included in that side was Amer Arslanagic, a Yugoslavian Junior International. This side only just failed to qualify for the last 16 of the All British Schools Glanvill Cup and in 1993, the First VI reached the semi-finals of the Midland Bank Senior Schools and Glanvill Cup. Furthermore, a regular fixture since 1987 has been against Newport Athletic Club, on their excellent grass courts, for the Ken Phillips Trophy.

Over the years, the School VI has played against an Old Llandoverian VI on Speech Day. The game has been organised by a former captain T. D. Williams, who presented the T. D. Williams Tennis Cup to the school when he left. When Mr H. S. Thomas retired in 1996 seven former captains returned to play in the match.

Mr John Brand took over as master i/c tennis from Mr H. S. Thomas. He inherited a sport in a veritably blooming state of health. There are tennis fixtures at several levels in the summer term and it will not be long before girls' tennis will be as flourishing.

ATHLETICS

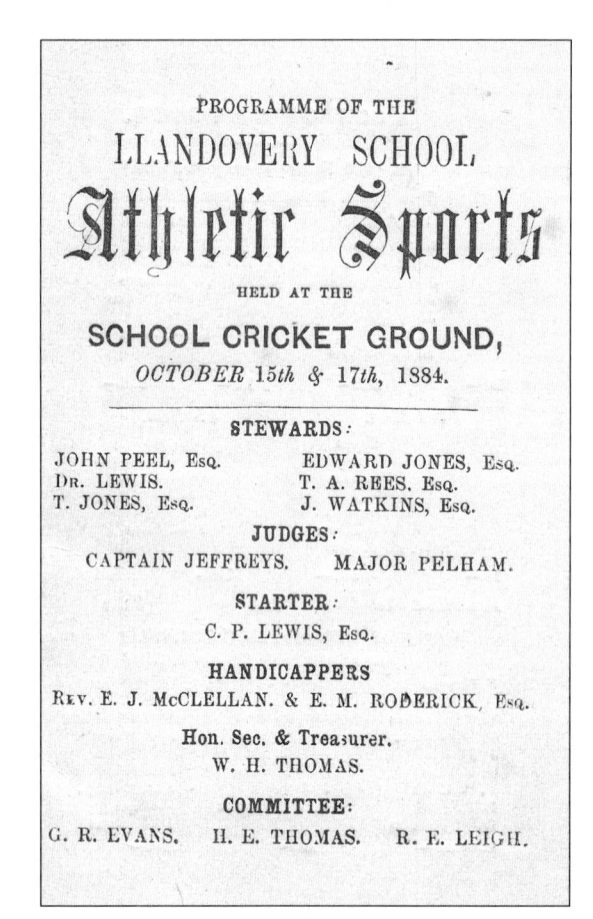

PROGRAMME OF THE
LLANDOVERY SCHOOL
Athletic Sports
HELD AT THE
SCHOOL CRICKET GROUND,
OCTOBER 15th & 17th, 1884.

STEWARDS:
JOHN PEEL, Esq.   EDWARD JONES, Esq.
Dr. LEWIS.   T. A. REES, Esq.
T. JONES, Esq.   J. WATKINS, Esq.

JUDGES:
CAPTAIN JEFFREYS.   MAJOR PELHAM.

STARTER:
C. P. LEWIS, Esq.

HANDICAPPERS
Rev. E. J. McCLELLAN. & E. M. RODERICK, Esq.

Hon. Sec. & Treasurer.
W. H. THOMAS.

COMMITTEE:
G. R. EVANS.   H. E. THOMAS.   R. E. LEIGH.

From the accounts given in the school journals of the nineteenth century, Sports Day was the one day when the college boys were able to show their prowess at 'Athletic Sports'. Sports Day was a grand occasion: in 1888 the Town Band played music to entertain 'the large attendance, including the leading gentry of the town and neighbourhood'. In 1890 when the Sports were postponed because of the inclement weather at the end of Easter Term and had to be held at the beginning of the Summer Term, 'The ladies did much by the bright and varied colours of the summer costumes, to brighten the prospect of the cricket field.' The prizes were presented by the wives of the trustees such as Lady Hills-Johnes.

Heats for the main events were held on the previous day and the sports' day programme included the usual 100 yards, 440 yards, half mile and mile, putting the shot, high jump and two mile steeplechase. However, so that the competition did not get too intense, one had the 'egg and spoon race which as usual created much merriment amongst the spectators' or the sack race 'suddenly there was a general tumble—a catastrophe which elicited a loud hum of pity from those present. Out of the heap, however, one boy, E. J. Price, came and amid cheers, cut the tape.' There was, too, the choir race, which assumed the form of a three-legged race where competitors had to dribble a football through one goal post and return to finish up at the starting point. There was an old boys' race and a half-mile race for the residents of the town which in 1889 was won by J. Jones of Victoria Arms with W. E. Williams, Station Hotel, second and a football race, restricted to members of the First and Second XV. In 1896 there was a competition for the best drop goal and place kick. Finally, in 1898 a fully fledged steeplechase of 3½ miles was introduced.

The beginning of the 1900s saw the introduction of inter-house competitions and in 1910 there was an athletics match between the School and the Masters in eight events: 100 yds, 440 yds, half mile and mile; throwing the cricket ball, long jump and high jump and putting the weight. The masters won by six events to two.

Most probably the first Old Llandoverian to win a 'Blue' in any sport was Rev R. J. James, who in 1866 gained his 'Blue' at Cambridge in the hammer event. Ten years later in 1876, C. P. Lewis gained a Blue at Oxford for the hammer and hurdles and C. B. Nicholl for putting the shot. 1896 saw C. R. Thomas winning his Oxford Blue for the 100 yds and representing Oxford and Cambridge in the athletics match against Yale and Havard. He was also at that time Welsh 100 yds champion.

Athletics continued to flourish under the wardenship of Rev W. W. Poole-Hughes. However the less serious events, such as the egg and spoon race, were done away with and the Warden's race, which was a 440 yds race for under 15s or 13s, was introduced instead. After the opening of the gymnasium in 1909 'a special gymnastics squad of 20 boys entertained the guests before prizes were presented to the winners'. This continued to be a feature of Sports Day certainly until 1936 when Sergeant Shellard, who was the first to be appointed as P.T. instructor, decided to award colours for proficiency in certain P.T. tests, and those successful formed the 'special squad'.

In the account of Sports Day in the Journal of 1913, it would seem that since

1909, in addition to the steeplechases, a point-to-point race from Cynghordy Station to Devils Bridge, had been a feature of the school's athletics. This was, most probably the beginning of cross country in the school. As well as individual winners, the school was divided into Houses and on this occasion Old Buildings and College House tied for first place. Sports Day, in 1913, was held on April 1st but the steeplechase on the 22nd March, postponed from the previous Wednesday, 'owing to the swollen state of the river'.

Old Llandoverians continued to make their mark with Goronwy Jones in 1912 winning a 'Blue' in the long jump and Evan Davies who played twice for Wales in rugby, becoming Welsh 100 yds champion. In 1924 D. R. Hughes was awarded a 'half blue' for the long jump at Oxford. He did not gain his full blue as he was unable to jump in the inter-University match because of injury.

A salient feature of the early 30s was the number of times C. W. Jones' name appears in the results. That Cliff Jones was a rugby genius no one would deny but his versatility in athletics in school was also remarkable: he won the steeplechase in 1930; the mile in 1932 and the open 100 yds and 440 yds in 1933. Speed and stamina, he obviously possessed in abundance.

The early 1960s to the mid 1970s was a most flourishing era for athletics in the school. Under the guidance of the Revd. Neville Hughes and John Sammons and later, in 1968, Goronwy Morgan, cross country matches were arranged against other schools such as Whitland, Gwendraeth and Christ College; in 1965 cross country became a feature of the Christmas term whereas before it had been confined to the Easter Term. Triangular Athletic matches were held involving schools such as Cyfarthfa and Lucton and in 1966 an athletics match, which the school won, took place against Christ College. In the journal of 1893, it was recommended by one of the students that an inter-school sports be held against Brecon. It had taken over seventy years for this recommendation to be translated into a reality.

T. C. Murray won the Welsh Secondary Schools Steeplechase in 1968 and J. C. Evans in the following year became Welsh Schools' Champion in both the 800m and 1500m. He was later to represent Wales in Holland. In 1970 Robert Squibbs won the Welsh Schools title in the javelin and Anthony Irving in the triple jump. Finally, in 1971 D. I. S. Stephens won the youth javelin in the Welsh Games and in 1973 H. L. Lewis became Junior Men Welsh Champion in the 400m hurdles. At Senior International level an Old Llandoverian D. Gwynn Griffiths represented Wales and Great Britain in the 400m.

The early 70s, however, saw a slight decline in interest which led to Mr

Sammons in his athletics report commenting on 'the lack of dedication and self discipline' evident at that time. However, by 1977 Sports Day, 'the first the College has held for years' proved to be a very successful day and the report of the day's events end with, 'I'm sure Sports Day is back with us to stay'. Sports Day flourished in the 80s and the inter-house rivalry was as intense as ever.

When Mr Iestyn Thomas took over in the late 80s, he continued to instil in both boys and girls an interest in and love of athletics which has been an inseparable part of the tradition of the school. Boys and girls continue to participate in the Brianne and Dyfed County Sports. In 1996 Martha Jones, Alex Leyshon, Jonathan Francis and Charles Madeira Cole represented the County in the T.S.B. Welsh National Track and Field Championship. In 1996 Charles Madeira Cole became Welsh Senior Men Triple Jump Champion and Junior Men 50m Champion. He also, in 1997, represented Great Britain U23 in an international competition.

FENCING

In the mid 70s fencing was introduced to the school. Mr and Mrs Bonney from Cynghordy were the coaches and the sport grew rapidly in popularity. In 1975 the School fenced against Christ College Brecon winning once and losing once. Paul Chmielewski reached the final of the Cardiff u19 Open. However, when Mr and Mrs Bonney left the area, there was no-one to take their place.

GOLF

In 1971 a narrow strip of bracken-covered land, lying between the railway line and the river was transformed into a golf course. The brain-child of the then master in charge of sport Mr Goronwy Morgan, the college could now boast a 9 hole course which over the years has proved an attraction to both the students and the golfing enthusiasts of the town.

Matches against other schools and the annual match against the Old Llandoverians have been a feature of the sporting calendar of the college. A golf professional has been employed once a week to teach the rudiments of the game.

The Old Llandoverian Golf Society under the inspiration of its honorary secretary Major T. Gwyn Davies has grown from strength to strength and the annual match against the Old Breconians played at Southerndown has the passion and commitment of the rugby match.

FIVES

Fives Court late 40s

Fives was a game similar in many ways to squash but using a gloved hand rather than a racket to hit the ball. The Western Mail of September 22nd 1896 printed an article entitled 'Reminiscences of an Old Boy'. 'I was sent to Llandovery School in 1848 when a lad of twelve years old. There was no cricket at Llandovery School in those days and no football worth mentioning. The game of the school was hand ball or fives. Fives was played in many parishes against church steeples. There were fives courts attached to public houses in parts of Breconshire. I feel sure Llandovery at this time could have beaten any school in England and Wales at fives as played there. This does not apply to Eton fives.' As the school was housed in the 'Depository Cottage' near Llandingat Church in 1848, the game was played against the pine end of the building.

When the school moved to its more permanent buildings later, fives courts were provided. Furthermore, in the Journal of 1878 there is reference to the Fives Court Fund, money subscribed for the building of the New Fives Court. Later in 1888 the Old Fives Courts were converted into a gymnasium and new courts, one covered and two open, were erected.

Fives were certainly a very popular game in the first hundred years of the school's sporting history. No matches were played against other schools but within the school, the 'singles' and 'doubles' tournament proved highly competitive.

The Fives Courts remained in existence until early 1970 when they were converted into what is now the Music School.

SHOOTING

The Shooting Team 1993

Shooting is first mentioned in the Lent Term Journal of 1935 where a parent is thanked for the generous gift of rifles for a miniature range. In 1936 the School Rifle Club, with Mr Stead in charge, became affiliated to the Society of Miniature Rifle Clubs. All boys above the 4th Form were allowed to shoot and a 20yds range was laid out inside the gymnasium—the present day Performing Arts building. The first match took place against Llandeilo Rifle Club.

Shooting remained popular throughout the 40s and in 1952 a Shooting Society was founded with the intention of forming a School Shooting VIII to compete in the Country Life Public Schools Small Bore competition and in 1956 the School Shooting VII won the bronze medal in the competition.

With the arrival of Mr Martin Clarke, shooting matches were arranged against schools such as Rydal, Royal Masonic School, Kings Taunton and Monmouth. In the late 80s and early 90s, with Mr Vernon Price and Mr Godfrey Williams as coaches, the shooting team has enjoyed immense success. William Thomas and Gareth Jones were in the Welsh team. In 1996 Jake MacAdam won the Welsh Schools Individual Shooting Cup and in 1997 Edward Mitchell won the 'Ashburton' competition at Bisley.

Since the opening of the Sports Hall in 1991 pupils at the school have been able to enjoy a greater variety of sports than at any other time in the history of the college. Badminton, indoor cricket and hockey, basketball, wall climbing and table tennis are all on the sporting menu. Furthermore, the squash courts, which the College shares with the town, have proved a real attraction.

The newly opened swimming pool in the town will provide an added sporting facility; no longer will the college pupils need to resort to swimming in The Shallows, Tonn Pool and The Deeps. Old traditions die hard and swimming in the Tywi doubtless will be one tradition that will survive.

In 1863 Richard Henry Morgan won a rowing 'Blue'; in 1908 V. Edwards obtained a soccer 'Blue' at Cambridge and Thomas Jenkins played soccer for Wales. A. W. M. Griffiths and J. P. Williams won 'half blues' for boxing in 1908 and after the First World War R. G. Rea captained Oxford University at billiards. With the wall climbing facilities in the new Sports Hall, the next fifty years could well see an Old Llandoverian planting the school flag on the top of Everest!

In 1854 a young man of twenty seven years of age, the Revd. Evan Owen Phillips became the third Warden of the College. He held very strong views on education: 'Man consists of mind, soul and body. We must not neglect to cultivate all these parts'. The academic and sporting successes enjoyed by the school over the one hundred and fifty years of its existence are ample proof of the prophetic wisdom of the Rev Evan Owen Phillips.

(David Irlwyn Gealy entered Llandovery in 1949. From there he proceeded to St. Edmund Hall, Oxford, University College of North Wales Bangor and the University College of Swansea. He taught at Gowerton and, then, returned to Llandovery in 1966.

His rugby playing as a pupil remains legendary. As a master he contributed enormously to many aspects of school life—Head of English, Housemaster . . . and took an active interest in rugby, cricket, choir, drama . . . His contact with the Old Llandoverian network reaped great results in recruiting for the College. He was Secretary of the Old Llandoverian Society for many years.

He retired in 1997. He was—and is—an avid collector of books and paintings. He is Chairman of Llandovery Civic Trust).

Ackowledgement

D. I. Gealy wishes to record his thanks to Mr W. I. Goronwy Morgan and Mr Huw S. Thomas. The photographs chosen are not intended to represent the history of sport at the College: such a collection would call for a substantial volume. The selection is arbitrary and its purpose is merely to give a 'taste' of activities.

SECTION IV

IN HONOREM LANDUBRIENSIS ACADEMIAE:
celebrating 1848, 1898, 1949, 1998

1848

OPENING OF THE NEW WELSH EDUCATIONAL INSTITUTION AT LLANDOVERY

On Saint David's Day the town of Llandovery exhibited a scene of excitement that will doubtless be held in grateful remembrance for ages yet to come. At an early hour the inhabitants were roused from their slumbers by merry peals of bells, and, as the morning advanced, the excitement increased, the shops were shut, and all business was suspended: the streets were filled with the inhabitants of the town and visitors from the country, who were anxious to participate in the pleasures of the day appointed for the opening of the institution, under the presidence of the Venerable Archdeacon Williams, late Rector of the Edinburgh Academy, of whose literary fame and acquirements it is superfluous to enlarge.

Soon after 10 o'clock the lively strains of the Llandovery band announced the assembling of the honourable fraternity of the Ivorites of the 'Vicar Prichard Lodge', who perambulated the town, and then drew up near the Town Hall, where the Mayor and Corporation, the Venerable Archdeacon Williams, the Rev J. Hughes, vicar, and several gentlemen of the town and neighbourhood, were in attendance to receive them. A procession was then formed, headed by the Mayor and Corporation, with the mace bearers, next followed the Venerable Archdeacon and the Vicar of the parish, then a band of music, and the Ivorites in their showy and appropriate costume, and several handsome banners, among which we noticed a splendid new banner, made expressly for the occasion, having thereon the national emblem, with the motto 'Gwell Dysg na Golud' at the top, and at the bottom the following englyn, expressive of the gratitude of the public to Mr Phillips, the founder, and the Venerable Archdeacon, as Principal of the Institution:

> I Phillips, hoff ei haeledd—y cluder
> Ein clod yn ddiddiwedd;
> Ac i Williams, am goledd
> Yn ein mysg loywddysg yn wledd.

From the Town Hall the procession moved off to Llandingat Church, where the vicar read the service, partly in English and partly in Welsh; after which the Venerable Archdeacon preached a most impressive and interesting sermon in English . . . After the close of Divine Service, the procession retraced its steps to the School-house, which soon became crammed to suffocation. The Rev Mr Hughes then briefly explained the occasion of their meeting there; Mr W. Rees, one of the Trustees of the School, next read the whole of the Deed of Trust, explaining the principles upon which the Institution was founded by Mr Phillips, after which the Venerable Archdeacon rose, and stated his views respecting the system of education to be pursued at the Institution; that his object, as well as that of the founder, was to give a complete course of education to the pupils committed to his charge; that he anticipated complete success in the undertaking, both from his own past experience, and from his estimate, not only of the natural talents, but also the studious habits of his young countrymen—that his practice was to influence his pupils more by exciting them to the diligent pursuit of their studies, by gentle encouragement and moral persuasion, than by influencing them by their fears . . . he would rather call upon all idle, disobedient, and contumacious pupils, to leave the establishment than to compel him to have recourse to any system of bodily punishments . . . But he hoped better of the pupils of the Institution—he hoped and trusted that they would be not only young gentlemen, but also young Christians . . .

   He must confess that in one respect a difficult task had devolved upon him—he had to choose fifteen pupils out of a considerable number of candidates who presented themselves as competitors for the free scholarships which Mr Phillips had endowed . . . he had to examine almost four competitors for every vacancy . . . many must necessarily be disappointed . . . Henceforward every vacancy would be supplied from the pupils of the establishment, and no one would be admitted to the competition except he had been a member for at least one half-year. The only test in future would be accurate scholarship, general information, and such conduct, both moral and religious, as would bear the test of the severest scrutiny. With such a system, wrought out by willing pupils, he did not despair of sending forth from the Phillip's foundation, scholars who would be enabled to compete with the very best which the great schools of England produced. He had already in Scotland been enabled to do *that* . . . Wales was comparatively a poor country . . . the children of the middle classes, the very hope and promise of the country did not in Wales possess those advantages which they ought to possess . . . he hoped to be able to remove their disadvantages, and enable them to procure the very best and highest education . . . at a very moderate expense . . . it would be necessary to close with reading a list of the fifteen free scholars selected after examination . . .

>   Owen Jones, Pontsenny, Breconshire.
>   William Hughes, Gwnnws, Cardiganshire.
>   John Morgan, Llwyn, Carmarthenshire.
>   Lewis Williams, Lampeter, Cardiganshire.
>   Stephen Brown, Haverfordwest, Pembrokeshire.
>   Edward Jones, Dol-Iago, Radnorshire.
>   Henry Williams, Talsarn, Cardiganshire.
>   William J. James, Llandilo, Carmarthenshire.
>   John Jones, Llangendeirne, Carmarthenshire.
>   Edwin Isaac, Malpas, Monmouthshire.
>   Nadolig X. Gwynne, Llandovery, Carmarthenshire.
>   Grafton Phillips, Haverfordwest, Pembrokeshire.
>   David Thomas, Trecastle, Breconshire.
>   John P. Griffiths, Cwmamman, Carmarthenshire.
>   David Saunders, Cefen, Carmarthenshire.

At 3 o'clock a large party, at least 130, of the clergy, gentry, yeomen, and members of the Ivorite society, sat down to dinner, at the Clarence Inn. We noticed several gentlemen and clergymen among the company who had come from a distance to be present on the occasion . . .

The Chairman gave the toast of 'Oes y Byd i'r Iaith Gymraeg', then followed the usual loyal and patriotic toasts of the Queen, Prince Albert, the Prince of Wales, and the Royal Family . . . The Chairman gave next *the* toast of the day . . . it was his act of munificence that had caused the present assemblage; he then proposed the health of Thomas Phillips, Esq. of Brunswick-square, London, the founder of the Welsh Grammar School . . .

Mr W. Rees rose on behalf of his esteemed and venerable friend, Mr Phillips . . . the advanced age of 88 years alone prevented Mr Phillips being with them. (Mr Rees) gave a very brief outline of the circumstances which led to the endowment of the Welsh Grammar School, as they were known but to a few.

About twelve months ago, Mr Phillips, whose princely munificence towards St. David's College (Lampeter), in the foundation of several scholarships, and in enriching it with a splendid library . . . deeply regretted that the cultivation of the Welsh language had fallen into desuetude in the College . . . and proposed to vest a sufficient sum in the public funds that would adequately remunerate a Professorship of the Welsh language and literature . . . After certain negotiations, an unforeseen difficulty arose, which prevented Mr Phillips's patriotic and liberal intentions from being carried into effect, so far as regarded St. David's College, and it seeemed to be the opinion of some in authority that a due knowledge of the Welsh language should be acquired by students previous to their entering upon their theological course at the College, Mr Phillips changed his original purpose, and after consulting some real friends of the Principality, upon whose judgment he could rely, he determined upon founding a Welsh Institution, wherein young men might have an opportunity of acquiring a grammatical as well as colloquial knowledge of the language of their forefathers, and at the same time should have the privilege of benefitting by a first rate course of classical and mathematical education. The next question which arose was, where to fix the Institution? Several places were proposed, but at length Llandovery was chosen (cheers) on account of its central situation, and the easy communication from thence to all parts of South Wales, and the public of the town and neighbourhood were greatly indebted to the Hon. Col. Trevor, M.P., and to Lady Hall, of Llanover, for their good services in obtaining the use of the building wherein they met that morning. (Much cheering). Those temporary premises having been secured, much time was necessarily taken up in settling upon the various provisions to be embodied in the Deed of Trust . . . which was duly executed by Mr Phillips and the Trustees in August last. Having thus secured a good foundation and a temporary building to commence operations, the appointment of a Principal occupied much of the attention of Mr Phillips and his Trustees. Amongst others whose advice was sought, was the worthy and respected Bishop of the Diocese, who gave his opinion that he knew only of one person whose qualifications were fully equal to those required by the Deed of Trust, and that person was the Venerable Archdeacon Williams, of Edinburgh. (Tremendous cheering) . . . Mr Rees added, respecting the premises now occupied by the Institution, although Mr Phillips had expended a considerable sum in repairs and fitting up, its occupation must only be considered as temporary, for Mr Phillips has, in the Deed of Trust, recorded his hopes that the leading men of property and influence in South Wales, and more particularly of the county of Carmarthen, would soon contribute a sufficient sum to procure a more permanent and suitable premises for the Institution, together with a fit residence for its Principal . . . Mr R then concluded in Welsh, by thanking the company . . . His thanks were especially due to the Ivorite Society, which came forward so warmly to welcome the establishment of the new Institution . . .

The Chairman then proposed the health of the Venerable Archdeacon . . . The Archdeacon then rose and said—

Mr Mayor and Gentlemen . . . This day's proceedings have given me the greatest delight, and I hail with pleasure the commencement of an institution, which, as I hope and confidently augur, will confer the greatest benefit upon the cause of sound education in the principality. It is not for me to undervalue the benefits of similar institutions, seeing that it was owing to the advantages derivable from the Free Grammar School of Ystradmeiric, founded by the learned and illustrious Edward Richards, I was enabled to receive as sound an education in classical learning as could be procured at the time, not only in the principality, but also in the kingdom. It would be difficult for you now to realise the extent to which scholarship was carried in that mountain district . . . I myself became at a very early period the immediate assistant of the second master of Winchester. So excellent was the training received in that school, under my father's auspices, of whose name Mr Symons, the Government reporter, has made honourable mention, although accompanied with considerable mistakes. But my father was conscious that there were certain deficiencies in his system, which required the aid of more polished and perfect scholarship, and was very anxious that I should enjoy those higher advantages, which had not fallen to his own share. He sent me consequently to Balliol College, Oxford, which had the reputation which it still enjoys of being one of the most efficient schools of instruction in the University. In these schools I had to meet the best scholars of England, and had the honour of being placed in the first class, with four others, one of which was the late Dr Arnold, the able, learned, and most successful head master of Rugby School . . . Although placed in the first class by the decision of the examiners, I was nevertheless convinced that I had much to learn before I could call myself a finished scholar; I eagerly availed myself of the opportunity of becoming the immediate assistant of the late Dr Gabrell, the second master of Winchester school . . . After spending two years with the Messrs. Richards, at Hyde Abbey School, I was selected to succeed the late Rev Eliezer Williams at Lampeter . . . some differences of opinion between me and his Lordship (Dr Burgess), respecting the intended institution, rendered me glad to avail myself of an opportunity of taking upon me the superintendence of the Edinburgh Academy, a new institution . . .

During the whole of my long absence from my native land, I had always fondly cherished the idea of returning thence, and conducting a great school among my own countrymen on the best and most efficient principles . . . I signified my intention to resign in the Autumn of 1846, resigned in August 1847, and soon after was consulted by Mr Phillips respecting the plans of his intended institution. I lost no time in proffering my own services as the active Principal of the Institution, and my services were willingly accepted . . . I hope . . . to dedicate myself heart and soul to the task which I have undertaken . . . The intentions of the Founder contemplate a much wider field of institution than is actually cultivated commonly in schools . . . Gentlemen, I again beg to return thanks for the honour you have done me.

The health of the Rev Joshua Hughes was then proposed, and . . . responded to . . . The 'Bishops and Clergy of the Principality' was the next toast . . . next 'The Dissenting Ministers of various denominations.' The Rev John Morgan, of Talrhyn, responded in Welsh . . . He said it was a day that betokened the dawn of a better tone of feeling between persons of various religious persuasions, with all the heart-burnings and jealousies that had been unfortunately suffered to exist of late on the subject of education . . . The Archdeacon had made his hearers . . . proud of their country—proud of their race—and still more and more thankful to the Almighty for having preserved their language and their pure Christianity, such as was professed and believed in Wales from the time of the apostles themselves. (Cheers).

A song by Mr J. Lewis was warmly applauded, being a national Ivorite Welsh song.

Several other toasts were proposed, and duly acknowledged . . .

The remainder of the evening was spent in convivial hilarity and enjoyment, when the company separated at a late hour, and all appeared highly gratified by the important proceedings of the day.

[In concluding our report of these highly interesting proceedings, we cannot refrain from noticing another proof of the paternal solicitude of the benevolent Mr Phillips, in furtherance of the grand object of Founding the Institution—he has commenced the establishment of an extensive Library, as an useful and instructive appendage thereto. The books he has already so munificently presented amount to several hundred volumes, one case of which already received arrived at Llandovery on the very day the Institution was opened.]

(From the Carmarthen Journal, March 10, 1848).

1848

ENGLYNION

Expressive of the general feeling manifested at Llandovery, on St. David's Day, towards the Venerable Archdeacon Williams, M.A.

    Clodforwn mewn clyd fwriad—y gwron
        Dyngarol ei deimlad,
      Llona' gŵr llawn o gariad,
      A doeth fel ei barchus dad.

    Chwi feirddion heirddion eu hurddas—cenwch
        I'r cynnor cyweithas;
      Ei enw myg pan el hwn ma's
      A erch iddo barch addas.

    Gŵr ydyw o fron garedig—gŵr doeth,
        A gŵr detholedig,
      Gŵr da yw, heb un gair dig,
      A gŵr dyddan, gwâr diddig.

    Ugeiniau a fo'n gweini—dwys godwr
        Dysgeidiaeth uchelfri;
      Lloned dwyfron Llandyfri,
      A gwenu'n awr oll gwnawn ni.

    Sŵn miwsig sy'n y meusi—i'r Llywydd
        Gwneir llawer o gerddi;
      A glyn tawel glan Towi
      Ar fyr fydd o erfawr fri.

    Anwyl bu gan Albaniaid—ei ddoniau
        A ddeuent benaethiaid;
      Atto bawb â'n plant heb baid,
      Awn ninnau o un enaid.

Os gwael hogiaid ei ysgolheigion—nawr
    Cyn hir dônt enwogion
Gwŷr ar dir ac ar oer don
Prawf ddoniau y Prif-Ddeon.

Y Roeg, Lladin, Cymraeg, Llydaw—glewion
    Blant glywir yn seiniaw;
Aruthrol ddysg yr Athraw
I droi anhawsderau draw.

Un ydyw tra hynodol—o gywrain
    I gario'n mlaen ysgol;
Llon oedd pob gŵr llenyddol
Ei wel'd 'nawr yn ei wlad 'nôl.

Ein Llywydd sydd ŵr mwyn llawen—mewn dysg
    Mae'n dasg cael ei amgen;
Gwŷr hwn iaith gŵyr hen Athen,
Amen byth, mae yma'n ben.

W. Davies
Frood Vale Academy, March 6, 1848.

(From the Carmarthen Journal, March 10, 1848. The Reverend Dr William Davies was tutor at the renowned Athrofa Ffrwd Fâl—Froodvale Academy, some eight miles distance from Llandovery. During its existence as a Nonconformist Academy it was much sought after, and the education given was classical (including Hebrew), mathematical and general. In 1849 there were thirty-four pupils on the books. It was closed in 1855).

1848

'The Christening of the Institution'

The sons of brave Cambria will have reason to bear in grateful remembrance the year of our Lord one thousand eight hundred and forty-eight, and more especially the day set apart in honour of their patron saint, St. David, as the day on which the Welsh Educational Institution was first opened, and still more should they bear in remembrance the time-honoured name of Phillips, the munificent founder and supporter of that Institution . . .

These remarks are occasioned by the very interesting proceedings that took place at Llandovery on Tuesday, when the first examination of the pupils, or as it has not inappropriately been designated, the christening of the Institution took place . . . When we reflect and consider that in the short period of twelve months, there have been established in this town and county so many educational institutions, we say we have just reason to feel an honest pride and gratification; we allude to the Training College, now nearly completed, the Model Schools, for the education of the poor, in an advanced state of completion, and last, though not least, the establishment of the Welsh Educational Institution. We feel assured that bright and glorious days are at hand, we therefore call upon all to assist in providing suitable buildings for the latter institution, so that it may in as short a time as possible be brought into full action, and that its benefits may be early developed. The examination took place at the temporary school-room . . . The attendance was very numerous, although the weather was any thing but favourable; we were glad to perceive a great number of the clergy present. The examination was most satisfactory to those who had the pleasure of hearing it, and great surprise was manifested at the astonishing progress that had been made in such a short time. The recitations in Latin and Greek were well delivered, and were the theme of much and deserved admiration. The following is the report of the Venerable Warden:

Report from the Warden to the Trustees, of the First Examination of the Pupils of the Welsh Educational Institution, Llandovery, on Tuesday, the twenty-seventh of June, 1848

Sir,—I have to make the following report concerning the examination to which my pupils were yesterday subject, which you will be so good as to communicate to the Trustees, and also to Mr Phillips, our Founder. Only two of the classes at the Institution had to undergo the ordeal on the present occasion, nor were those examined on all the subjects, which they will have necessarily to prepare during the course of the next session.

The first, or senior class, consisting of seven pupils, was examined in the presence of the Lord Bishop of St. David's, of the Very Reverend the Principal and of Professor Browne of St. David's College, and of other gentlemen, fully competent to judge of the scholarship and general proficiency of the pupils.

The class had read during the course of the session—

In Greek
The greatest part of the Oedipus Coloneus of Sophocles
The Sixth and Seventh Book of Homer's Iliad
Certain portions of the Anabasis of Xenophon
And the First Ten Chapters of the Acts of the Apostles.

In Latin
The Fourth Georgic of Virgil
The Ars Poetica of Horace
Cicero's Treatise de Amicitia
And portions of the Twenty-first Book of Livy

In Geometry
The First Sixteen Propositions of Euclid's First Book.

They were examined principally on passages selected by the Lord Bishop and Professor Browne, from the Oedipus, the Iliad and Livy, and displayed an intimate acquaintance with their work, and gave no small promise of future scholastic eminence.

The Examiners were pleased to express their satisfaction with the appearance made by the whole class, and especially by the following pupils:

Mr William Hughes, Cardiganshire
Mr William Jones, Pembrokeshire
Mr Henry Williams, Cardiganshire
Mr Stephen Brown, Pembrokeshire.

In the second class, comprising twenty-one members, the examination was confined to the work of the session, which consisted—

In Greek
Of the Two First Chapters of the Gospel of St. John
Of a part of the Anabasis of Xenophon

In Latin
Of a part of Caesar's Commentaries
And of all the Saphic and Heroic Odes of Horace

In Geometry
Of the First Twelve Propositions of Euclid's First Book.

The proficiency of some members of this class, whose previous advantages had not been very great, was highly praiseworthy, and such as gave me great pleasure. The Examiners were pleased especially to approve of the appearance made by—
Mr Thomas Rowlands, Meirionethshire
Mr Edward Jones, Breconshire
Mr Edward Williams, Montgomeryshire
Mr Lewis Williams, Cardiganshire
Mr John Jones, Llandovery, Carmarthenshire
Mr Nadolig S. Gwynne, Carmarthenshire
Mr Thomas Howell Evans, Radnorshire.

I have also to express my full approbation of the docility, diligence, and invariable good conduct of the great body of the pupils, of whose future prospects I augur most favourably.

        John Williams,
        Warden

Llandovery, 28th June, 1848
To the Secretary of the Welsh Educational Society.

The Public Meeting was held at the National School, and was particularly well attended . . . His Lordship took the chair and spoke as follows . . . Although I can have no doubt that those connected with Llandovery and the County will do all in their power to promote the success of the Institution; still it must not be forgotten that it is an object that intimately concerns the Principality of Wales, and it is on that account, and on that account alone, that it has been denominated a Welsh Institution; and not, as some people have thought, an Institution solely for the encouragement of the Language and Literature of Wales (Cheers) . . .

The Rev Joshua Hughes then moved the following resolution: 'That the meeting . . . is prepared to carry the object of the munificent founder into full execution; to erect buildings for the accommodation of the masters and scholars' . . . It was true that Institution was not formed for the purpose of giving education to the poorer classes, a work in which the National Society was engaged with so much success but he had always been of opinion that the education of the middle classes was of the greatest importance to the poor . . . It (the Institution) would do so much good, especially to the Church, and also to that large portion of the population that dissented from the Church . . . He rejoiced to find that the Principal and Professors of St. David's College (Lampeter) were present, as it showed the interest they took in the matter; and he was sure they would bear him out in saying that they had felt greatly the want of such an Institution . . .

The Rev Professor Browne . . . one of the examiners . . . was well aware that the object of this Institution was not to feed the college (St. David's), but he hoped that would be the result and that although many would undoubtedly go to the Universities of Oxford and Cambridge, he hoped that they should get some of them. (Hear, hear) . . .

The Venerable Archdeacon Williams—'I should state that when I resigned the situation of Rector of the Edinburgh Academy, I had no intimation of Mr Phillips's munificent intentions . . . I will not however deny that it was my intention, whether any public opportunity offered itself or not, to establish an Academy, not under such auspices as this, but at my own risk and establish something of the same kind of Institution as the one which I hope before long to see flourishing at Llandovery. (Cheers) . . . it is particularly gratifying to me that so many parties, distributed over so wide a portion of the Principality of Wales have entrusted their children to my care. (Cheers) . . . I am sure you will all agree with me in saying that the greatest gratitude is one to our estimable

Bishop (loud cheers), for the great trouble he has taken and the great zeal he has displayed in support of this Institution . . .'

The Bishop . . . said . . . the good likely to be done to the Church by the Institution . . . but . . . it will meet not only the support and encouragement of the Church but of the Dissenting body, who are as free to enter it as any class of the community (Cheers) . . .

The Chairman again rose and proposed the health of the trustees, Lady Hall, John Jones, Esq., the Rev Thomas Price, the Rev Joshua Hughes, and Mr William Rees . . .

Mr Rees then rose . . . He would not trespass upon their patience by discussing the benefits or evils that might possibly result from the extinction of the Welsh as a living language; but as long as it pleased the Almighty that the Welsh should be the present vernacular tongue of nearly a million of our fellow countrymen, there could not be the slightest doubt that it was a most sacred duty upon all who were interested in the education of those intended for the high and sacred calling of Spiritual Pastors in the Principality, to see that ample provision was made for their due instruction in that vernacular language, through whose medium alone they could hope to reach the hearts of the people (cheers). It had been often alleged, and he must confess not without some show of reason that the time spent in acquiring the Welsh language was lost to other higher and more important studies; but he could not forbear believing that the best learning was that which would prove most extensively useful and important as the medium of communication between a man and his fellow creatures in the district wherein providence had cast his lot. (Cheers) . . . It was well known that Mr Phillips had made provision in his Deed of Trust for the cultivation of the Welsh language as a part of the studies at the Institution . . .

The Venerable Archdeacon rose . . . They must allow him to make one observation he had omitted in his address that morning, and it was this, that he was aware that some persons were averse to the change of name from Grammar School to that of Educational Institution, and many would have preferred that he should have kept the honoured title of Head Master to that of Warden. He could assure them that it had not been done without due consideration. It was clear, that owing to circumstances with which he had no connexion, and to which he would not allude, the Grammar Schools had degenerated to such a degree, that the term did not now include all the studies which should be taught in an Academy, which was the name given to them in Scotland. There was something wanting in Wales which had been supplied in Scotland, and it was an Institution between a Grammar School and an

Academy. He felt proud in being able to state that in that Institution they would go beyond a Grammar School, and that they would have many things taught there that were not taught in any Grammar School in Wales. (Cheers). That was the reason he had submitted to the judgment of the Trustees, and that that Institution had been called an Educational Institution, and himself the Warden. (Cheers).

The Venerable Warden continued at great length, but we regret that our limited space compels us thus briefly to notice his able and eloquent address, as well as the remainder of the proceedings of the evening . . .

His Lordship then left the chair, and the meeting speedily broke up.

Thus ended a meeting, from which we cannot but hope the most successful results will flow, and if the inhabitants of Wales will have course to remember St. David's Day . . . as the day on which so much was done to place the Welsh Educational Institution on a firm and lasting foundation. May it prosper and flourish is our heartiest and most earnest hope.

We are glad to find that since the meeting additional subscriptions have been received. The total amount now is £1,354.

(From the Carmarthen Journal, June 30, 1848).

PROGRAMME OF THE
ORDER OF THE PROCEEDINGS,
AS INTENDED TO BE CARRIED OUT
AT THE LAYING OF THE FOUNDATION STONE,
OF THE
WELSH EDUCATIONAL INSTITUTION,
LLANDOVERY,
On Thursday, the 13th day of December, 1849.

To meet at the Town Hall, before half past Ten o'clock, and to move from thence in the following Order to Llandingad Church, where a Sermon will be preached by the Lord Bishop of the Diocese, after which a collection will be made in support of the funds of the Institution.

Band of Music.

Odd-Fellows
and
Ivorites' Societies,
with Banners, &c.

Tabernacle
Benevolent
Society.

Mayor and
Corporation
of Llandovery.

Warden,
Masters,
Trustees,
and Pupils of the
Institution, 2 abreast.

Clergy,
Preceded by the
Dean of St. David's.

Ministers of various
Denominations.

Architect & Builder.

Other Friends
Of the Institution.

Pupils of the National
School.

Pupils of the British
School.

From the Church to form in the same Order, and proceed to the site of the Institution.

The laying of the foundation stone of the new buildings

1898

THE LLANDOVERY JUBILEE

(a) *The background*

Today is being celebrated the jubilee of Llandovery College, the famous school founded by Mr Thomas Phillips and other patriotic Welshmen.

   It is the custom in these days of greater educational advantages and opportunities, in speaking of Wales of fifty years ago and upwards to look at the darker side of matters. We are so much in love with the results of our own efforts, with our intermediate schools and university colleges, that we seem to forget that our fathers and grandfathers enjoyed any educational advantages whatever. It must be admitted that, compared with those enjoyed at present, the advantages which fell to the lot of Welshmen two or three generations ago were meagre, but they nevertheless existed, and were largely utilised, as a glance at the list of those who rose to distinction up, say, to 1875, will show, Welshmen, that is to say, who received all their preparatory training within the borders of the Principality. Endowed schools then, as now, were few, but these were so geographically distributed as to keep the lamp of learning burning in every county in South Wales, including Monmouthshire. The chain reached from Abergavenny to Cardigan, the chief intermediate links being Cardiff, Monmouth, Cowbridge, Swansea, Brecon, Carmarthen, Haverfordwest, Lampeter, Ystradmeurig, and Aberystwith, not to mention several other endowments less known, which can scarcely be said to have been applied to the purposes of intermediate education, though in Welsh schools of fifty years ago it was difficult to draw the line between primary and secondary. Beside these, there was a large number of schools, equally efficient and equally serviceable, set up by private enterprise, several of which enjoyed a wide and well-deserved reputation, such as Talicsin Williams's well-known school at Merthyr Tydfil, the famous normal school at Swansea, the short-lived, but excellent, seminaries at Ffrwd y Fal and Neuaddlwyd, and the important institution set up by Davies of Castell Hywel, not to mention lesser lights at Llandyssil, Newcastle Emlyn, and in numerous other places, by ministers of the Gospel, chiefly Unitarians and Congregationalists.

At present, it is unnecessary to refer to those means of high education which existed in Wales—Lampeter College, and the denominational institutions at Carmarthen, Brecon, Haverfordwest, Pontypool, and Trevecca—which were primarily and chiefly intended to raise young men for the ministry, but indirectly were the means of diffusing much culture and learning among the laity. Nearly every clergyman and educated Nonconformist minister in days gone by performed more or less efficiently the duties of a teacher.

If one excepts the great English public schools and a number of secondary schools set up in towns, one does not find that the case of Wales in the earlier part of the century was much worse than that of England in the matter of intermediate education. Probably, in proportion to the population, it would be found that the number of Welshmen who then occupied posts of influence at home and from home was quite as large as that of Englishmen. This is saying a great deal, for in Wales we lacked that numerous middle class which is such a conspicuous feature of English social life, and is the main source of supply of the learned professions and other lucrative posts in England.

In writing thus of the educational condition of Wales up, say, to 1850, one is far from thinking that it was satisfactory or anything like it. The bulk of the population remained uneducated. A vast amount of ignorance prevailed, nearly half the farmers of Wales could scarcely write their names, as a reference to the marriage registers of the time will show. Education was very unevenly distributed. Speaking generally, the country fared better than the towns, owing to the majority of small schools having been established in rural districts. A school must necessarily chiefly influence its immediate surroundings. A lamp may draw people from a distance, but its light shows strongest to those who are close to it. A Royal Commissioner of the time has told us that fifty years ago the people around Ystrad Meurig were better educated than those hailing from Aberystwith and the immediate neighbourhood, a fact which, it is supposed, must be attributed to the influence of Edward Richards's school at the former place.

Wales in the forties was in a transition state. The agricultural classes were beginning to acquire political power, and, owing to the establishment of coal and iron works in Glamorgan and Monmouthshire, many a Welsh farmer waxed rich and fat. The country was ripe for the establishment of a school where Welsh youths might be equipped for any and every profession or trade. The flower of the youths of Wales in the joint counties and in Glamorganshire as yet had been sent to England preparatory to a university career, simply because Wales afforded not the necessary training. There was no reason why this state of things should continue, and, thanks to the founders of Llandovery College—not forgetting other institutions—the course of events was soon to be shaped otherwise. How much South Wales, irrespective of sect or party, owes to that great institution will be learnt from the following sketch, the facts mentioned in which have been obtained from absolutely trustworthy sources.

The 'Old Boys' and a host of the well-wishers of Llandovery School are to-day celebrating the jubilee of that institution. So large a part has that school played in the work of higher education in Wales during the last half-century that it is difficult to realise that it was only in 1848 it was established, and that from the point of view of age it is but a Cinderella among the endowed grammar schools of Wales. Llandovery occupies, moreover, the unique position of being the only endowed school that has been established in Wales during the whole of the present century. The great school-founding epoch of the Principality (as, indeed, of England also) fell within the hundred years following the Act of Union between England and Wales in 1535. During that time more than two-thirds of the Welsh grammar schools were established, including Brecon and Bangor, Carmarthen and Ruthin, Haverfordwest, Beaumaris, and Monmouth, and within the same period that Jesus College was also founded as a home for Welsh students at Oxford. A few more schools, such as Dolgelly and Swansea, were set up in the latter part of the seventeenth century, while, as to the succeeding century, Bala and Ystradmeurig were practically the only foundations which came into existence. In the present century Llandovery stands absolutely alone.

Fifty years ago Wales was, educationally, in a state of considerable ferment. The reports of the three Commissioners appointed in 1846 to inquire into the condition of the elementary education of the country had just been issued, and, whatever may have been the mistakes of the Commissioners in their treatment of side issues and questions only indirectly connected with education, their reports serve the purpose of enabling the public to realise in a manner previously impossible the neglected educational condition of large and, in some cases, thickly populated areas, the wholly inadequate supply of trained teachers, and the general absence of anything like method or organisation in the conduct of the existing educational agencies. At this juncture two gentlemen of the same name came forward to render, each in his own way, their patriotic services. One was Sir Thomas Phillips, a barrister (and subsequently a Q.C. of the Inner

Temple), who stated the case of Wales in respect to education in a volume which is still one of the chief authorities for the condition of the country at the time. His namesake, with whom he is almost invariably confounded, was plain Thomas Phillips, a retired Indian surgeon, who in his 88th year lived in Brunswick-square, London, and was 'Father of the College of Surgeons'. He belonged to a Radnorshire family, but though himself born in London in 1760 he had spent many of his earlier years among the hills of Brecon and Radnor, where, among other things, he served an apprenticeship with an apothecary at Hay. During his long life he had travelled widely, and had served his Queen and country in all the four quarters of the globe. His philanthropy and benevolence had taken many curious turns, but never a more practical one than when he directed his attention to the improvement of Welsh education. In Lampeter College he had since, about 1835, taken a special interest, and had founded there several scholarships, which still bear his name. In 1847 he submitted an offer to further endow the college, but the authorities demurred to the conditions of the proffered gift, and Phillips thereupon decided on devoting the money to the endowment of the new foundation of his own. When this became known there was a competition not unlike the battle of the sites, which more recently occurred in connection with the University College of Wales; the town of Rhayader was all but selected, though eventually the choice fell on Llandovery. This result was almost entirely due to the exertions of that public-spirited man, William Rees, of Tonn, the fame of whose printing press is known to all lovers of Welsh literature. It was he that also bore the chief burden of the difficult task of collecting funds towards the erecting of school buildings, for the endowment was given by Phillips on the express condition that no penny of it should be spent on buildings which should be supplied by local effort. The founder transferred into the names of five trustees the sum of £4,666 13s. 4d. three per cent. stocks. The foundation trust deed shows that the object of the founder was to establish a self-contained and independent collegiate institution rather than a school, which should form a link in a chain of educational agencies, and to provide within its walls such a full and adequate training in all the chief departments of learning as to equip men for public life and for professional work in Wales, and especially among Welsh-speaking people, such training to be so far as possible of a complete and final character, and not merely preparatory to a further course of study at any other college or university.

For this, however, a much higher ideal was at once substituted on the selection of the first head-master, or warden, as he came to be called. Among the men whose advice the founders sought as to a suitable person to place at the head of the new institution was the Ven. John Williams, Archdeacon of Cardigan, who, with an alacrity which surprised as much as it gratified the founder, offered his own services as master. It would probably be no great exaggeration to say that Archdeacon Williams was the most brilliant scholar Wales has ever produced, while his success as a teacher had drawn from Sir Walter Scott such high praise as to be characterised a 'heaven-born teacher' and 'the greatest schoolmaster in Europe.' His profound scholarship had left its indelible impress on higher education in Scotland, where for 22 years he had held the office of rector of the Academy at Edinburgh, being, in fact, not only its first rector, but also its intellectual founder. With a record second to no other living master of the time, he answered what he considered the call of duty, and came to Llandovery, where from the very first he set before the young school, not the somewhat limited, albeit useful, ideal of the founder, but the higher and nobler ambition of being content with nothing less than the best education possible, of preparing its scholars to compete for the honours and distinctions of the older universities, and, in short, of training them for the very highest kind of intellectual pursuits. Ever since his days this has been one of the most sacred traditions of the school, the opening of which practically doubled the number of Welshmen proceeding to the universities.

But to the outward eye the beginning of the school on its opening day, the 1st of March, 1848, was a very modest one. There were no school buildings available, so the old armoury or depot of the long since disbanded 'Carmarthenshire Fusiliers,' now converted into an ordinary cottage close to Llandingat Church, was fitted up as a school, and here in the upper storey did the archdeacon, in the first three years, teach his pupils, his assistants taking classes on the ground floor, while, after a term or two, a wooden shed was put up in the garden outside for the mathematical master. Meanwhile the public had been appealed to for funds towards the school buildings, and, in spite of the zeal and persistency of William Rees, anything like an adequate amount would never have been collected but for the prestige of the archdeacon's name, and, it should also be added, the irresistible appeals made to many people by his charming daughters. Lady Llanover (then Lady Hall), whose name stood first among the five trustees of the school, purchased a field which she presented for a site, the subscription list included £100 from the Prince of Wales, £200 from Bishop Thirlwall, £100 from the archdeacon himself, while the two M.P.'s for Carmarthenshire agreed to hand over an equal proportion— the money which they usually spent on election dinners. The new buildings were completed by May, 1851, but in the hurry to get them ready they had been so badly finished that for many years after they gave endless trouble to the trustees and successive wardens. Within less than two years from their opening the institution lost the services of Archdeacon Williams, who had to retire on account of failing health. Among the candidates who applied for the vacant post was William Basil Jones (afterwards Bishop of St. David's). He had come to an understanding, it is said, with his friend, Mr (afterwards Professor) E. A. Freeman, that if appointed warden Freeman should join him as assistant master, so that Jones and Freeman would then have collaborated in even a greater work than their 'History of St. David's.' Some of the trustees, however, felt that, although Jones was all that could be desired from the point of view of scholarship, it was almost more necessary for so young an institution to have at its head some well-known Welshman possessing popular qualities, which would help to draw to the school the tide of educational enthusiasm which was then beginning to flow in Wales. Such a man was found in one of the most eloquent and gifted clergymen Wales had ever had Dr David James ('Dewi o Ddyfed'), the vicar of Kirkdale, Liverpool, the father of Dr James, the present distinguished headmaster of Rugby School. Dr James, however, soon found school work less congenial to him than the work of the ministry, and on his resignation he was succeeded by the Rev Evan Owen Phillips, whom our readers will readily identify with the subsequent Chancellor and Dean of St. David's, who passed away less than eighteen months ago. Mr Phillips was a scholar of Corpus Christi College, Cambridge, and in the mathematical tripos of 1849 had come out as eighteenth wrangler. The following four years he spent as senior mathematical master at St. Peter's School, York, where he had among his pupils the present Bishop of Bristol. During his five years' wardenship Dean Phillips did a great work at Llandovery. He had real insight into character, a sympathetic nature, and a great capacity for realising the circumstances and difficulties of his pupils, taking the seniors for walks, and playing ball with them in the ball-court, which he saw erected in his time. It is also affectionately remembered by many of his old pupils that his interest in them did not cease on their leaving the school. Himself a strong personality, he attracted to him able assistants; and here we may, perhaps, interpolate a few words about the able assistant masters of the school. The archdeacon had been chiefly assisted by John Edmund Cheese, who afterwards became vicar of Boshury, Herefordshire, and by Thomas Rowlands, the author of the well-known 'Welsh Grammar.' For a shorter period he also had the help of a Scotch graduate, named Stewart, who had tried to teach mathematics in the shed, but left in disgust, because the boys did not know how ignorant they were of mathematics; of Leonidas Clint, who died only a year ago; of Henry Knight, who is remembered as a most excellent penman; and of John Rhys Jones, a promising Welsh poet, the author of a booklet called 'Yreosig.' All these left either before or at the same time as the archdeacon himself. Dr James brought with him from Liverpool, as mathematical master, a young Welshman of great promise, Robert Griffith Williams, who remained for two or three years under Mr Phillips, but then left for the Bar, where he rapidly gained distinction on the North-eastern Circuit, refusing a county-court judgship, and taking silk in 1874, but dying suddenly in the midst of a prosperous career in 1875. As both Phillips and Williams were mathematical men, a graduate of Worcester College, Oxford, Mr William Scott, afterwards headmaster of Haverfordwest Grammar School, and now vicar of Slebech, Pembrokshire, was appointed 'reader in geology and classical master.' This curious combination of duties is explained by the fact that the founder, who had died in June, 1851, had, by his will, left a considerable fund for the endowment of professorships (of chemistry, geology, and botany). Hence the necessity of having a 'reader.'

Several university successes—rich first-fruits, promising an abundant harvest—had been gained even before the archdeacon left, the very earliest being an open classical scholarship at St. John's College, Cambridge, in 1850, by Frederick Watkins, who was placed three years later in the second class classical tripos, and subsequently became one of her Majesty's inspectors of schools. He was followed in 1853 by T. M'Kenny Hughes, son of the then vicar of Llandovery (afterwards Bishop Hughes, of St. Asaph), who now occupies the post of Woodwardian Professor of Geology at Cambridge. So the efforts of the early readers in geology were not wholly spent in vain. Other pupils (or 'lambs,' as they were called) of the archdeacon went up to Oxford, and among names, which are sure to conjure up many memories, both sad and pleasant, are those of Owen Jones, who died vicar of St. Ishmael's, Carmarthenshire; William Hughes, of Gronnws; John Pugh Griffiths, of Cwmamman; the brothers Morgan, of Llewyn; Thomas Gwynne Mortimer, of Fishguard, St. David's; Herbert, vicar of Tremain, Cardigan, most of whom had scholarships or exhibitions at Jesus College, Oxford, while William Hughes, who was dux in 1850, also won the Powis Exhibition direct from school. Some boys, such as David Thomas, the present rector of Garsington, and T. Wolseley Lewis (afterwards a master at the school), left for other schools before proceeding to Oxford. Others remained on till Warden Phillips's time, and the most brilliant of these was William Watkins, a Brynamman boy, who was at the school from 1848 till 1857, when, with an open mathematical scholarship, he entered Caius

College, Cambridge, graduating as seventeenth wrangler three years later. For the next year or two he was engaged as assistant mathematical master at Eton, but when Dean Phillips, in 1861, accepted the living of Llanbadarn Fawr, all thoughts turned to young Watkins as the most fitting successor to carry on the work of the school. Both were old Cantabs, both mathematical men, so that in their successive wardenships mathematics became the forte of the school, and Cambridge the Mecca of its more successful scholars. Throughout all the ages that had passed since the union of Wales and England, and even still earlier, Oxford had been practically the only university to which Welsh students proceeded while it was something quite exceptional to go to Cambridge. Phillips and Watkins changed all this. In one continuous stream they sent the cream of the school to Cambridge, where Wales, previously all but unknown, came to be soon recognised as a country that had a rich store of mathematical geniuses. The average number of pupils at Llandovery in the later fifties and throughout the sixties was between 60 and 70, but it was no unusual thing for as many as twenty 'old boys' to be at the same time in residence at Cambridge during that period. To mention only a few of them at random, there were Morris Jones (scholar of St. Catherine's), David Lewis (now Canon of St. David's), and Evan Evans (both scholars of Emmanuel's), John Jones (afterwards a master of his old school, a scholar of Christ's), John Rogers, a scholar, and J. M. Jenkins, a prize man, of Queen's; John Hughes, of Clare; Melbourne David, of Pembroke; Octavius Davies, of Magdalen; Henry Rees (afterwards Canon of Bangor), of Lydney; and David Edwards and Rhys Bishop, of Corpus, of which college David Llewellyn and J. H. Protheroe, now Archdeacon of Cardigan, were also scholars, the latter passing as third senior optime in 1864. The year 1865 was a specially brilliant one for the school, for then William Griffiths, scholar of St. John's (afterwards principal of Hooghley College, Bengal), came out as the twenty-fifth wrangler, while Owen Jones, of Sydney Sussex and David Edwards, now headmaster of Denstone Grammar School, were respectively placed as second and twenty-fourth among the senior optimes, and on the river Herbert Morgan, of Emmanuel, rowed for his university, being probably the first Llandovery boy to win his blue as an oarsman. The chief successes of the following year marked a still higher level of distinction, for D. J. Davies, scholar of Emmanuel (now vicar of Benfleet), came out as thirteenth wrangler, this to be surpassed, however, a few years later by his own brother, Tom Davis, now a master at Clifton, who scored two first classes in mathematics at Oxford, and by G. J. Griffiths, who passed as fifth wrangler in 1875, and himself acted as one of the moderators in 1879. The list could be very considerably prolonged, but we shall be content with mentioning some two or three boys of Mr Watkins's later period, such as David Lewis, the late county-court judge, who graduated twelfth senior optime in 1872, and John Davenport Mason, who, after winning a high place in examinations of the Indian and Ceylon Civil Service, rose to be chief magistrate of Colombo. There were also, of course, many who went up to Oxford during this time, but they were not nearly so numerous as the Cantabs, for the study of classics occupied a decidedly secondary place in the school curriculum. It should be mentioned, also, that in the time of Mr Watkins, who was a good Welsh scholar, the school turned out several distinguished Welsh scholars, e.g., Thomas Powel, Professor of Celtic at Cardiff; Llywarch Reynolds, of Merthyr, and R. Morris Lewis, of Swansea. During his fourteen years' wardenship, from August, 1861, to midsummer, 1875, Mr Watkins had some eminent men on the teaching staff, especially Henry Thomas Edwards (afterwards Dean of Bangor), to whom the recent revival of the Welsh Church is so largely due. Among other masters of this period whom we can only mention here were T. Wolseley Lewis (afterwards master of Shrewsbury School); Trevor Owen, now Canon of St. Asaph; Llewellyn Thomas, the late genial vice-principal of Jesus College, Oxford, who got up the first dramatic entertainment for the boys, himself writing a prologue for it; G. W. Bloxam, an energetic science master, who formed and taught a college choir, and is still remembered as a most active member of the town Volunteer corps; David Melville Morris, himself an old pupil of the school, now vicar of Penally, and brother to the heroic chaplain of the ill-fated Victoria, and W. P. Whittington (now headmaster of Ruthin Grammar School), who first introduced Rugby football among the boys, and was instrumental in starting the college sports. When Mr Whittington left, at midsummer, 1874, he was succeeded as classical master by an old boy, Dr Edwards, present Bishop of St. Asaph, who had entered the school as a very young pupil in Warden Watkins's first term, when his elder brother, the late Dean of Bangor, was also joining the staff. When, in 1875, Mr Watkins accepted ecclesiastical preferment in Glamorganshire, Dr Edwards was unanimously elected his successor in the wardenship, and the phenomenal success of the school during the ten years he presided over it is still fresh in the memory of most readers.

Bishop Edwards may almost be called the second founder of Llandovery. With characteristic energy, he set before himself the high aim of making Llandovery for Wales what her great public schools are for England. For this purpose he found three things necessary—first, to bring down fresh from the

Universities of Oxford and Cambridge masters of first-rate rank in their several subjects, such as the late Principal Gent as classical master; Mr C. E. Williams, now of Wellington College, as mathematical master; and Mr C. W. Buckmaster, now one of the principal officers of the Science and Art Department of South Kensington, as science master. His second step was to create a strong esprit de corp among the boys, by abolishing the lodging-out system, and gathering all boys together from a distance as boarders under the personal care and discipline of the warden and his colleagues, and by organising a vigorous system of school games. Llandovery soon turned out football and cricket teams which won for themselves a leading position in South Wales clubs. For this the school has to thank the well-known athlete, Mr C. P. Lewis, who returned to his school as assistant-master under Bishop Edwards. In the third place, Bishop Edwards found it necessary to revise the position of Welsh in the school curriculum. Hitherto Welsh had been a compulsory subject for one hour every day for all boys, Welsh and English. Henceforth it took its place as an optional subject side by side with other languages, receiving such a place in the time-table as the general educational interests of the school required. The consequence of these three changes was that the number of boys soon became more than double the largest number Llandovery had ever seen before, and, with but slight temporary fluctuations, the school has for about twenty years steadily maintained this high level of numbers. The distinctions won by the school at the universities during Bishop Edwards's time showed that his conception of the future of Llandovery was not too lofty. A large number of scholarships were gained in classics and science, as well as in mathematics, and two of his pupils won the Balliol Scholarship, the blue riband of Oxford.

When Bishop Edwards became vicar of Carmarthen, in 1885, he was succeeded by the present Bishop of St. David's, who when he became Dean of St. Asaph, in 1889, was succeeded by the present warden, the Rev Owen Evans. Both Bishop Owen and Mr Evans worked the school on the lines laid down by Bishop Edwards. A staff of masters has been maintained at Llandovery which, in respect of strength and distinction, will compare favourably with that of any school of its size in the kingdom. During this period the school was confronted with two difficult problems. In Bishop Owen's time it had to face the establishment of three university colleges, while the present warden had to face the establishment of new intermediate schools all over Wales. At one time the friends of Llandovery feared that it would be crushed, first by the university colleges, and afterwards by the intermediate schools. Both these fears have turned out to be entirely groundless, and the school stands to-day stronger and higher than it ever did before. Both Bishop Owen and the present warden saw that the right policy for Llandovery was to trust to its own resources and rely upon the solid fact that with the development of Welsh education by the foundation of university colleges and intermediate schools, the need of public schools for Wales like Brecon and Llandovery would grow, and not diminish. Bishop Owen inspired others with his own confidence in the future of the school by taking every vacant house he could find in Llandovery for the accommodation of boarders, by building four new class-rooms, and by laying out all his plans on the assured conviction of success, and by the end of his four years at the school it became clear to everybody that Llandovery had nothing to fear from the success of the Welsh university colleges.

The school had to face a still more difficult crisis by the passing of the Welsh Intermediate Education Act. The Carmarthen Joint Education Committee were advised that it was their duty to bring the school under the operation of that Act. It took some years for the question to come to a decisive issue, when the Charity Commissioners definitely decided that the school was so clearly outside the scope of the Welsh Act that they could not legally so much as to allow the scheme to be published, much less sanctioned. No other scheme in Wales, we believe, was so peremptorily declined, and after this the friends of Llandovery may rest assured that nothing short of a new Act of Parliament can disturb the status of the school. It was also feared that the very large number of Welsh intermediate schools would draw away boys from Llandovery; but it has now become clear that the new schools, so far from hurting Llandovery, have greatly strenghtened it, by emphasising its higher public school character as a place of education for those who want a higher type of education all round than can possibly be found in intermediate schools. Most valuable as these are in their way for the class of boy for whom they were intended, they were not intended to train boys direct for the older universities, or to give them the social or moral character of the boarders of a public school. It was not a mere coincidence that soon after the intermediate schools set to work Llandovery beat every school in the kingdom in the number of distinctions gained from the Oxford and Cambridge Schools Examination Board, and has this year carried off ten scholarships at Oxford and Cambridge. The position which the school holds this year in open scholarships gained at Oxford and Cambridge comes out clearly in the public schools record published in the London 'Daily News,' July 20, 1898. It appears, bracketed with Winchester, ninth in the list of 76 successful schools, and of the fourteen schools which have gained more than five open scholarships each Llandovery is the only school with less than 400 boys, and it is singled out by the editor with special praise in the following words: 'There are some very obvious conclusions to be drawn from the above table in the direction of both praise and blame. We will content ourselves with merely calling attention to the striking success of Llandovery, a school of only 160 boys. Besides the seven open scholarships, which include one at Balliol and one at Trinity, Cambridge, this small school has gained three close scholarships, which are included in our last table. It will be seen that they have obtained scholarships in four different subjects.' One thing, however, is still required to make the future of Llandovery as a public school for Wales secure. At the celebration of its Jubilee to-day (Thursday) the trustees appeal for £10,000 to enlarge the school buildings. This, surely, is not too high a price to pay to provide for boys in Wales adequate public school education in their own country. The Welsh educational system would be disastrously incomplete without the public school element supplied by Llandovery and Brecon.

(From the Western Mail, 28 July, 1898. The un-named author was Daniel Lleufer Thomas.

He was born in 1863, the second son of William Thomas, Cefnhendre, Llandeilo. He was educated at Llandovery College and Oxford (when he was one of the seven original members of Cymdeithas Dafydd ap Gwilym). He was called to the Bar, Lincoln's Inn, 1889 when he joined the South Wales and Chester circuit. He was Stipendiary Magistrate for Pontypridd and Rhondda 1909-1933. He held many posts of distinction and was to be a member of the Court of the University of Wales, of the Court and Council of the University College of Wales, Aberystwyth. He was President of the Workers' Educational Association for Wales 1915-1919. He was a prominent member of the Welsh Library Committee in 1896 and a member of the Council of the National Library from 1907 to 1940: a bust of him stands at the foot of the main staircase there. He was knighted in 1931. Sir Daniel Lleufer Thomas M.A. (Oxon) Ll.D. (Wales) F.S.A., died 8 August 1940.

His contribution—barely acknowledged—to the 'history' of Llandovery College is immense. His papers, deposited at the National Library—have been a major source of reference, and inspiration, for this present book).

LLANDOVERY COLLEGE.

Jubilee Celebration.

THURSDAY, JULY 28TH, 1898.

President:—

The Right Hon. Lord Tredegar.

PROGRAMME.

8 a.m. Holy Communion at Llandingat Church.

11-35 a.m. School Service at Llandingat Church.
Preacher: THE LORD BISHOP OF CHESTER.

1 p.m. Luncheon in the Marquee.

After Luncheon—

PRIZE DISTRIBUTION AND SPEECHES.

4-15 p.m. Tea in the School Hall.
(Given by the Warden and Miss Evans.)

DISTRIBUTION OF PRIZES
(IN THE MARQUEE).

1. Speech by the PRESIDENT.
2. Official Statement by the TREASURER (Sir James Hills-Johnes.)
3. School Report by the WARDEN.
4. Examiner's Report by R. H. FERARD, ESQ., M.A.
5. Prizes Distributed by LORD CRANBORNE.

TOAST LIST.

1. The Queen and Royal Family
   by the President.
2. The Prosperity of Llandovery School and the Success of the Movement for New Buildings.
   Proposed by Lord Cranborne.
   Seconded by the Bishop of St Asaph.
   Supported by Dr. James, Head Master of Rugby.
   Responded to by Sir J. T. D. Llewelyn.
   Seconded by the Visitor, the Bishop of St David's.
3. The Warden and the Staff.
   Proposed by Sir James Hills-Johnes.
   Responded to by the Warden.
4. The Old Boys.
   Proposed by the Warden.
   Responded to by Rev. D. Lewis, Canon of St David's.
5. Lord Cranborne.
   Proposed by the Lord Lieutenant of Carmarthenshire.
   Seconded by Sir Joseph Bailey.
   Lord Cranborne responds.
6. The President.
   Proposed by the Lord Lieutenant of Cardiganshire.
   The President responds.

MENU.

Salmon Mayonnaise.
Rounds of Beef.
Roast Chickens.
Pressed Beef.
Roast Lamb.   Mint Sauce.
Savory Pies.
Galantine of Veal.
York Hams.   Ox Tongues.
Salads.

ENTREMENTS.
Fruit Tarts.
Jellies.   Creams.

Cheese.

R. Holland & Sons,
Purveyors, Chester.

(b) *The celebration*

A day long to be remembered in the history of Llandovery College was Thursday, when its jubilee was celebrated in a manner in all respects worthy of the great and prosperous institution it is and of the high status it has reached among its sister academies in this country. Preparations for the occasion had been made on an unusually large scale, the warden having scattered invitations broadcast, anxious, no doubt, to see around him on this occasion as representative a gathering as Wales could afford. In this respect his success was complete, Llandovery, probably, having never seen such a distinguished company within its walls; and this in spite of the inclement weather which prevailed in the morning.

The proceedings began by a celebration of Holy Communion at the historic Church of Llandingat, once the scene of the ministrations of the immortal Vicar Pritchard. Later on, at eleven, service was held in the college chapel, the preacher being Dr Jayne, Bishop of Chester. This was followed in due course by the luncheon, to which a very numerous company sat down, and the annual ceremony of distributing the school prizes, always an interesting function at Llandovery. During these events several important speeches were delivered, all of them taking their colouring from the event and the effort which the warden and the trustees are now putting forth to collect funds with a view to enlarging the premises. The sum aimed at is £10,000, and, judging by the enthusiasm observed on all hands on Thursday, the warden's idea at no distant time, will be an accomplished fact, and Llandovery will possess school buildings in all respects worthy of its great work and prestige.

The Lord Bishop of Chester, preaching at Llandingat Church, took as his text the words, 'Where is boasting then: it is excluded' (Romans, iii., 27) . . . It was moderate praise used with opportunity, and not vulgar boastfulness that did good . . .

About 400 guests were entertained at luncheon in a marquee in the college grounds. (There were many) 'old boys' present . . .

Lord Tredegar, chairman of the trustees, presided, supported by the Hon. Mrs Rice, Lord Cranborne, Sir James Hill-Johnes, Lady Hills-Johnes, Sir James and Lady Drummond, Sir Owen and Lady Scourfield, the Bishop of St. David's, the Bishop of St. Asaph and Mrs Edwards, the Bishop of Chester, Mr and Mrs St. Vincent Peel, the Very Rev James of Rugby, Sir Joseph Bailey, Sir John and Miss Llewelyn, the Bishop of Swansea and Mrs Lloyd, Colonel and Mrs Davies-Evans, Sir John Jones Jenkins, the Rev Chancellor Smith, Principal of Jesus College and Mrs Rhys, the Ven. Archdeacon Bevan . . . the Headmaster of Brecon . . . the Mayor of Swansea and Mrs Thomas, the Mayor of Carmarthen and Mrs White, the Mayor of Llandovery and Mrs Thomas . . . Mr and Mrs Pryse Rice . . . Mr and Mrs C. P. Lewis . . . Mr and Mrs Lleufer Thomas, Mr W. Ll. Williams . . . Mr Mrs and Miss McClellan . . . the Headmaster of Ystradmeurig . . . Mr and Mrs Ben Evans, Mr and Mrs Buckmaster . . . Mr Isaac Haley . . . The following members of the school staff were also present— The Warden (Rev Owen Evans) and Miss Evans, Messrs. Winter, Gregory, Richards, Knight, Calcott, the Rev T. Nicklin, the Rev E. H. Colville, Mr Roberts, Mr Williams, Miss Smit and Miss Norris.

After the luncheon and before the toast list, the presentation of reports and exhibition of prizes took place.

The treasurer (Lieutenant-general Sir James Hills-Johnes) reported—The Llandovery Collegiate Institution was founded in 1848 by Mr Thomas Phillips, a patriotic Welshman and a retired Indian surgeon. He left an endowment of about £700 a year for the salaries of the warden and three assistant masters. The endowment is the same now as it was 50 years ago, except that the late Mr Jones, of Cefnfaes, left £1,000 for improvements in calligraphy. There is one leaving scholarship of £27 a year, tenable at Jesus College, out of trust funds. There are three scholarships tenable at the school—The Golden Grove Scholarship of £25 a year, the Llewelyn Scholarship of £25 a year, and the Ystrad Scholarship of £10 a year. Welsh prizes were given by the late Lady Llanover of the value of £20 a year, and a scholarship of £25 a year was given by the late Mr Lloyd Jones, of Barwick, both have lapsed. There is at present accommodation for 52 boarders only, and the remaining 67 boarders now in the school have to be lodged in three additional houses rented in different parts of the town. This inconvenience places the school at a great disadvantage as compared with other public schools. A new kitchen and dining-hall and additional dormitories, with all modern equipments, are, therefore, urgently required. There is also a pressing need of more class-rooms, a sanatorium, new laboratories, and a workshop. It is estimated that £10,000 would be required to carry out these improvements, but the school should be provided, also, with a swimming bath, a new gymnasium, a new fives court, and with enlarged grounds around the buildings. The educational achievements of the school justify the trustees in appealing to the public for funds. I shall only call your attention in particular to two educational tests. The Oxford and Cambridge Schools Examination Board examines most of the English public schools, and in the analysis of the higher certificate examination for 1896, published in 'The Guardian,' the

9th of September, 1896, there are 79 schools represented as having had successful candidates. In this list Llandovery is bracketed in the seventh place in the number of higher certificates, and of the schools above it there is not one with less than double its number of boys, while it actually takes, irrespective of the number of boys, a larger number of distinctions than any other school on the list, gaining 38 distinctions. The scholarships result of the present year is no less remarkable in the list of public schools which have this year gained one or more open scholarships at the universities of Oxford and Cambridge, which list appears in the public schools record, published in the 'Daily News' on the 20th inst. Llandovery is bracketed with Winchester in the ninth place, with seven open scholarships, while of the fourteen public schools which have gained more than five open scholarships there is not one with less than 400 boys.

The Warden presented the school report as follows:—

The list of distinctions in the warden's report included H. R. V. Ball, junior university mathematical exhibition, Oxford; D. J. Lewis, first-class honours, mathematical moderations; D. J. Richards, £100 a year for mathematics at Trinity, Cambridge; A. J. Richards, £100 a year for classics, Brasenose, Oxford; I. O. Griffith, £80 a year for mathematics, Balliol, Oxford; Kingsley Jayne, £80 a year for classics, Wadham, Oxford; C. E. W. Jones, £80 a year for history, Brasenose, Oxford; and J. C. Crocker, £50 a year for natural science, St. John's, Cambridge . . .

(There followed speeches by Lord Cranborne, the Bishop of St. Asaph— former Warden—Dr James, Headmaster of Rugby—son of the second Warden, Sir J. T. D. Llewelyn MP, the Bishop of St. Davids, Sir James Hills-Johnes VC GCB and the Warden).

Sir James Drummond, lord-lieutenant of Carmarthenshire proposed the toast of Lord Cranborne, seconded by Sir Joseph Bailey, and the toast of 'The President', proposed by Colonel H. Davies-Evans, lord-lieutenant of Cardiganshire, concluded the proceedings.

Tea was afterwards served in the college hall.

(The Western Mail 29 July, 1898).

COLEG LLANYMDDYFRI
LLANDOVERY COLLEGE

Centenary Celebrations, July 2, 1949

PROGRAMME OF THE DAY.

8.0 a.m.—CYMUN BENIGAID (Holy Communion).
SCHOOL CHAPEL.

11.30 p.m.—CENTENARY SERVICE, Llandingat Church.
NOTE—Owing to the restricted accommodation, only ticket holders can be admitted; but the whole service will be relayed to loudspeakers placed outside the Church.

12.45 p.m.—CENTENARY LUNCHEON, Marquee.
NOTE—Admission to the Marquee will be by ticket only: but the Speeches after the Luncheon will be relayed to loud speakers in the School Hall.

2.0 p.m.—CRICKET. Old Llandoverians v. School.

2.15 p.m.—OLD LLANDOVERIAN SOCIETY.
LABORATORY LECTURE ROOM.

2.45 p.m.—OLD LLANDOVERIAN TRUSTEES.
LABORATORY LECTURE ROOM.

4.0 p.m. and 5 p.m.—TEA, Marquee.
NOTE—Admission will be by ticket only. Ticket holders are asked to observe the time shown on their tickets, as great confusion may be caused otherwise.

8.0 p.m.—INFORMAL CONCERT, Marquee.

10.30 p.m.—FIREWORK DISPLAY, Cricket Field.
NOTE—To avoid damage to the field and danger to themselves it is imperative that spectators keep to the banking at the Pavilion end.

1949

CELEBRATION

Next Saturday Llandovery College holds its centenary celebrations, unavoidably postponed from last year. Founded by Thomas Phillips to provide a liberal and humane education for Welsh boys, Llandovery had from the beginning a unique character, for by the express directions of the founder it was always to bear in mind the special needs of Wales and in particular the necessity of teaching boys to use the Welsh language not only as the medium of familiar conversation but also as the vehicle of serious study and scholarship.

The original arrangement by which the Welsh language and no other was used throughout the school for one hour each day was before very long found to hinder rather than promote this end and was discontinued; but the long list of Old Llandoverians who in their generation contributed richly to the welfare of their country proves that the trust reposed in the school was kept, and to-day Welsh may be heard in chapel and classroom, on the playing fields, and in the dormitories.

The centenary celebrations are to begin with a celebration of Holy Communion in Welsh. This will be in the school chapel, the anonymous gift of an Old Llandoverian. Later in the morning there will be a service of thanksgiving at Llandingat parish church. Canon Spencer Leeson, Bishop-elect of Peterborough, the former head master of Winchester, will preach in the presence of the Visitor, the Bishop of St. David's, who recently relinquished the Archbishopric of Wales. Dr Prosser, like the first archbishop and the present archbishop-elect, is an Old Llandoverian. There will be a cricket match in the afternoon between the school and an Old Llandoverian XI, and later a concert and a display of fireworks.

Although entirely independent of the State system of education, Llandovery has entered into a scheme with the Carmarthenshire education authority whereby six bursars are accepted at the school each year; and it is proposed, within the limits of the accommodation available, to accept bursars from other counties as well. Since the greatest strength of Welsh culture lies in the rich local life and traditions of the country's very diverse communities, it is important that

Llandovery should flourish as a place where in their common life and studies boys make their own definite contribution and learn from the contributions of others, so that after leaving school they may repeat in their generation the services of their predecessors to the country's life.

It is this circumstance, it is understood, that has encouraged the Thomas Phillips Trustees to appeal to the country at large to help them discharge their trust for the future by providing the additional buildings that will be necessary if Llandovery is to make its maximum contribution to Welsh education. They are reluctant to finance these developments by increasing the fees, for in keeping with the school motto, *Gwell Dysg na Golud*, 'Learning is better than Wealth,' it is from the homes of limited income that its boys have always come.

(The Times 29 June 1949).

A Guardian of Welsh Native Culture

Llandovery College, which celebrates its centenary this week-end with festivities postponed from last year, was founded in 1848 by Thomas Phillips, who until his retirement was a physician in the service of the East India Company and a member of the Calcutta Medical Board.

He and his associates had a very clear vision of the chief educational needs of their time, and Llandovery was set up to provide Welsh boys with a sound education on humane and liberal lines, designed to prepare them for the university, and afterwards for the ministry of the Church and for the other learned professions.

It was definitely intended that, as they progressed in the humanities and in science, they would learn to discuss these subjects in the Welsh language, so elevating the native tongue from the subordinate position it occupied in public life.

The subsequent history of the school falls into two main periods, the Jubilee in 1898 providing a convenient line of division. The first Warden and Headmaster, Archdeacon John Williams, and his immediate successors strove with varying success to give boys a thorough preparation for the universities while maintaining a strong emphasis on Welsh studies and on the constant use of the Welsh language, both inside and outside the classrooms.

From the first, the scales were heavily weighted against them, such were the conditions of their age. Boys usually came to Llandovery at 14 or 15, often from homes whose resources were exhausted even by the very small school fees of those days, and if they were to go on to Oxford or Cambridge they must pass through the narrow gate of the scholarship examination.

When A. G. Edwards became Warden he took, as was his habit, resolute action. With only three or four years in which to prepare them, he and his staff concentrated on this as the main object. Anything that would have interfered with it, including the Welsh language, had to go. That, it was thought, could be trusted to take care of itself.

The long record of scholarship successes gained partly as a result of this policy is widely known. For a school that in those days contained not many more than 100 boys to gain as many as seven university awards in a single year must approach an all-time record.

This policy had its grave educational defects; but it ill befits anybody in this age when the privileges of university education are more freely available to impute that it was out of indifference or hostility towards the Welsh language that Edwards and his successors took the course they did.

The Jubilee was celebrated at a time when Llandovery was thought to have been dealt its deathblow by the new Intermediate schools. Yet, despite the fact that secondary education was now available nearer home, the demand for places at Llandovery continued to increase, and this was met by the new buildings opened in 1903. The gymnasium and science buildings were added later on; and the chapel, the gift of an anonymous Old Llandoverian, was completed in 1934.

Despite the effects of the depression, there was a growing appreciation in the country of the educational and character-forming advantages of boarding school life. At the same time, the old concentration on scholarship work gave way to a broader and saner conception of education and during the past 20 years, especially the Welsh language has come more and more into its own in the general life of the school as well as in the classroom and chapel.

Now, there are large classes of boys learning Welsh as a second language and many children of Welsh parents living in England and abroad receive an education in which the native culture is carefully guarded.

Like their predecessors of the first period, men who have come out of Llandovery during this century have risen to positions of eminence not only in the Church where three out of four Archbishops of Wales have been Old Llandoverians, but in the Civil Service, education, law, medicine, science, industry . . . and sport . . . especially in rugby football.

Now that another period in the school's history has begun, coinciding once more with a further stage in the development of Welsh secondary education, it will be called upon to play a large part in the development of boarding school education. Though remaining as hitherto completely independent, Llandovery has already entered into a scheme with the Carmarthenshire Education Authority whereby six bursars each year are accepted by the school.

If it is to play the fullest part possible and provide for the many applicants who now have to be rejected for lack of room, Llandovery must be able to count upon the support of its friends, new and old, in providing the increased accommodation that will be required.

(Western Mail 1 July 1949 by Canon Gwilym Owen Williams, Warden and Headmaster of Llandovery College).

THE DAY OF CELEBRATION

This little town in the heart of rural Wales rubbed its eyes to-day and gazed in wonderment at the strangers. Yet were they strangers? Despite the fact that they were splendidly disguised in the robes of learning, they betrayed a familiarity with the place.

And then the town remembered! These grave, mostly elderly men, distinguished ecclesiastics, judges, teachers, all leaders of Welsh life in their own spheres, were old Llandoverians, back in the town to celebrate the centenary of their college.

The spirit of the founder, Thomas Phillips, must have rejoiced to see the splendid oak that sprang from the seed he planted. As an English clergyman said at the centenary service at Llandingat Church, 'a great enriching stream has flowed from the college for a century.'

The Bishop of Llandaff (Archbishop-designate of Wales) sounded a warning note at the luncheon, attended by 400 guests.

'It would be unreal and insincere if on such an occasion as this I betrayed no sense whatever of the precariousness of the future,' he said. 'The trend of legislation and, perhaps still more so, of local policy, in the last two decades undoubtedly has been towards uniformity and a certain flattening out in the educational scene.

CENTENARY LUNCHEON

July 2, 1949

Toast List

"The King"
  Proposed by The Visitor

"The School"
  Proposed by Sir Frederick Rees,
    Principal of the University College of South Wales and Monmouthshire
  Responded to by The Warden
    and His Honour Judge T. W. Langman

"The Guests"
  Proposed by The Lord Bishop of Llandaff
  Responded to by Professor Idris Foster,
    Jesus College, Oxford

"The Future"
  Proposed by The Visitor
  Responded to by The Head Prefect

Menu.

Mayonnaise de Saumon
Salade panachée
Tywi'n rhoi ei brenin brau,
Yr eog lân aroglau.

Charlotte Russe sur Biscuit de Savoie imbibé de Xérès
Glace Vanille
Gwin â misgeds gymysgwyd,
Neu felus ia gawn yn fwyd.

Fromage

Café
Bara a chaws, dim bîr, i chwi,
Caiff y sych yfed coffi.

'The tendency towards uniformity is neither positively good nor positively evil.

'May I voice for you all on this celebration of the centenary of one of our two Welsh public schools, the hope that when that uniformity is achieved, and when equality of opportunity is a reality and not a phrase, this value at least shall survive, that the two great re-acting forces of personality and community shall be triumphantly present, as they have been for the last 100 years at Llandovery.'

Sir Frederick Rees, Principal of the University College of South Wales, referred to 'Brad y Llyfrau Gleision,' the Blue Books that indicted Welsh culture and education more than a century ago.

Thomas Phillips, said Sir Frederick, had replied to that indictment by establishing a Welsh collegiate school, which later became known as Llandovery College. Its aim was to raise the standard of the Welsh language to that of the classical languages.

Insensibly the college became a public school for preparing boys for Oxford and Cambridge.

'I learned from the *Western Mail* that Llandovery College supplies the Church in Wales with archbishops,' continued Sir Frederick, 'and I would like to congratulate the Bishop of Llandaff on his promotion. This school has produced many distinguished men, and we thank the school for what it has done for the social and cultural life of Wales.'

Canon Gwilym Owen Williams, warden and headmaster of the college, said the most attractive feature of the college was that students met young people of their own age from all over the country. They all had different backgrounds, and the result was that a very fine type of character was developed.

The college was bilingual, and bilingualism was regarded not as a problem but an opportunity. It was the aim of the college to use the Welsh language as the founder intended, and the English language with dignity and grace.

His Honour Judge T. W. Langman, referred to the excellent work done throughout the years by the wardens and staff. In addition to the teaching of the art of learning they had also taught the art of living.

Bringing to the celebrations the congratulations and greetings of Jesus College, Oxford, Professor Idris Foster said the great opportunity of the college to-day was to produce Welshmen to help the cultural and spiritual life of Wales.

Dr D. L. Prosser, Bishop of St. David's, who recently retired from the Archbishopric of Wales, who presided, said the celebrations should mark, not the end of a century, but the beginning of a new century, a time for looking forward to what the school could achieve with the goodwill of a host of friends.

The head prefect of the college, Mr T. ap Rees, Penarth, said the college was maintaining the high standard of the past. The first XI were having an excellent season, Brecon having been beaten three times, and the Rugby XV had been equally successful.

Earlier, Llandingat Church was crowded for the centenary service. In his address, the Rev Canon Spencer Leeson, Bishop-elect of Peterborough, said the contribution of Llandovery College to Welsh culture was recognised throughout Wales and outside Wales.

The founder of the college was a man of great vision and his vision should be emulated by those looking to the future. They should build for the future as he had done. If he were present he would say, 'Look forward, as I have done . . .'

The service was conducted by the Warden, the lesson was read by the Bishop of Llandaff, and the Bishop of St. David's conducted the act of thanksgiving for the school.

In the cricket match the School beat Old Llandoverians by 71 runs.

(Western Mail 2 July 1949).

CELEBRATION

Llandovery College celebrated this week-end its hundredth birthday and can look back with pride to a century of valuable service to Wales, not less appreciated now than in the old days when few and narrow were the ladders by which an able Welsh boy could climb to the university and to all the liberal professions of which the university is the threshold. It has always been closely linked with the Church in Wales, and three out of the last four Archbishops of Wales have been old boys of the college; but it has never been narrowly ecclesiastical and its influence has been felt in many fields in Welsh life. In its early days great stress was laid on Welsh culture and the Welsh language. Some fifty years ago the fierce incentive of competition for university scholarships pushed Welsh aside in favour of more marketable kinds of learning, and the college was criticised for giving too little place to national studies. But the tide has turned, and to-day Welsh has again an honourable

The 'gathering' of 2 July 1949. In the front row, fifth from the left is Canon G. O. Williams, Warden, then Mrs Williams, Sir Frederick Rees, Canon Walker Thomas, Mrs Walker Thomas, Archbishop Prosser, Archbishop Morgan . . . . (The Western Mail 4 July, 1949).

place in the curriculum, not only for those who come from Welsh-speaking homes but for those who come newly to it as well. This is especially welcome to many Welsh parents living in England but anxious that their boys shall remain in touch with the stream of national culture. The college is, and means to remain, an independent school; but by a recent agreement with the Carmarthenshire Education Committee it now takes some of its recruits from the county schools, and so links the older with the newer systems of education and strengthens its claim to be thought of as a microcosm of the world of Wales.

(Manchester Guardian 4 July 1949).

DATHLU

Cynhaliwyd dathliad canmlwyddiant Coleg Llanymddyfri ddydd Sadwrn, Gorffennaf 2. Agorwyd yr ysgol (a urddwyd gan Thomas Phillips i fod yn Ysgol Gymraeg) ddydd Gŵyl Ddewi, 1848, eithr, oherwydd amgylchiadau anorfod, ni lwyddwyd i drefnu cyfarfod y llynedd i ddathlu'r achlysur.

Cafwyd tywydd godidog, ac adlewyrchai'r holl drefniadau glod nid bychan ar y Warden newydd, y Parchedig Ganon G. O. Williams, gynt Pennaeth Hostel yr Eglwys ym Mangor.

I ddechrau'r dathliad cynhaliwyd gwasanaeth yn eglwys Llandingad, lle'r arferai'r ysgol addoli cyn agor y capel presennol.

Offrymwyd y gweddïau gan y Warden, darllenwyd y llith gan y Gwir Barchedig John Morgan, Esgob Llandaf ac Archesgob etholedig Cymru, a datganwyd y fendith gan y Gwir Barchedig D. L. Prosser, Esgob Tyddewi (y ddau'n hen ddisgyblion o'r ysgol). Y pregethwr arbennig oedd y Parch. Ganon Spencer Leeson, cyn-Brifathro Ysgol Caergrawnt ac Esgob-etholedig Peterborough.

Apeliodd ef am ymlyniad wrth y Ffydd Gristionogol er mwyn gwrthsefyll treigl llechwraidd Seciwlariaeth, ac anogodd y disgyblion presennol i ymroddi o ddifrif i'w holl weithgareddau yn y sicrwydd fod gan Dduw gynllun i bob un ohonynt.

Yna cafwyd cinio i'r hen ddisgyblion a'r gwahoddedigion mewn pabell fawr ar lawnt y coleg. Llywyddwyd gan Esgob Tyddewi, Cadeirydd yr Ymddiriedolwyr, a siaradwyd gan Esgob Llandaf, y Barnwr T. W. Langman, y Prifathro Syr Frederick Rees, Caerdydd; yr Athro Idris Foster, Rhydychen; y Warden (y

Parch. Ganon G. O. Williams) a phennaeth y disgyblion presennol y deëllwyd ei fod yn ŵyr i'r diweddar Brifathro Thomas Rees, Coleg Bala-Bangor.

'Yr ydym yn ystyried dwyieithogrwydd Cymru fel cyfle, ac nid fel problem', meddai'r Warden.

'Y mae llygaid Cymru ar Lanymddyfri,' oedd geiriau'r Athro Idris Foster.

Ymhlith y gwahoddedigion a oedd yno gwelwyd yr Athro W. R. Williams, Prifathro-etholedig Coleg Diwinyddol yr Eglwys Bresbyteraidd yn Aberystwyth; y Parch. Athro J. Vernon Lewis y Coleg Coffa Aberhonddu; Syr William Ll. Davies, Llyfrgell Genedlaethol Cymru, Aberystwyth, a'r Athro Evan John Jones, Coleg y Brifysgol, Abertawe, ynghyd â nifer o wŷr a gwragedd eraill sy'n amlwg ym mywyd Cymru Gymraeg.

(Y Faner 6 Gorffennaf 1949).

CANMLWYDDIANT YR HEN GOLEG

Dathlwyd canmlwyddiant Coleg Llanymddyfri ddydd Sadwrn, ar ôl gohirio'r ŵyl llynedd. Gweinyddwyd y Cymun Bendigaid yn Gymraeg yng nghapel yr ysgol, ac yn ddiweddarach yn y bore pregethwyd gan y Canon Spencer Leeson, cyn-brifathro Winchester, yn y Gwasanaeth Diolchgarwch yn eglwys blwy Llandingat. Cymerwyd rhan yn y gwasanaeth gan gyn-Archesgob Cymru, Esgob Tyddewi, a'i olynydd, Esgob Llandaf, y ddau, fel yr Archesgob cyntaf, A. G. Edwards, yn gyn-ddisgyblion o Lanymddyfri.

Cynrychiolwyd y Prifysgolion, y Weinyddiaeth Addysg, a gwahanol agweddau bywyd cyhoeddus Cymru yno, a bu llu o fechgyn Llanymddyfri o bob cyfnod o'r wyth-degau ymlaen yn treulio'r dydd yn eu hen gynefin.

Ychydig o ysgolion preswyl a geir yng Nghymru; a pherthyn diddordeb a phwysigrwydd arbennig i Lanymddyfri gan ei bod yn ôl bwriad ei sefydlydd, Thomas Phillips, a dymuniad y llywodraethwyr presennol yn fagwrfa i Gymreictod iach a hoenus. Clywir yn y dosbarthiadau a'r ystafelloedd cysgu bob acen Gymreig o Fynwy i Fôn.

Fynychaf, rhaid aros hyd ddyddiau coleg i gyfarfod â Chymry o ardaloedd dieithr; ond yn Llanymddyfri caiff bechgyn yr addysg ymarferol hon yn eu blynyddoedd cynnar a sylweddoli, nid yn unig pa mor werthfawr yw'r traddodiad y codwyd hwy ynddo gartref ond hefyd ramant a gwerth y traddodiadau eraill.

Ni allai bachgen o Gaerdydd fyw am dymor yn Llanymddyfri heb wybod mai gwlad ddwyieithog yw Cymru, na bachgen o Leyn beidio â sylweddoli nad yr un yw awyrgylch meddwl Tonypandy a Phwllheli.

Y canlyniad yw bod bri mawr ar y dosbarthiadau dysgu Cymraeg a bechgyn yn darganfod heb yn wybod iddynt hwy eu hunain eangder a chyfoeth y bywyd Cymreig.

Wrth longyfarch Llanymddyfri ar gerdded rhagddi heibio i'r cant oed, bydd llawer yng Nghymru yn dymuno'i lwyddiant cynyddol. Bu aml dro ar fyd yn gyfundrefn addysg yng Nghymru er 1848, ond er pob newid, cynyddu a wnaeth ei chyfraniad hi.

Bellach, a'r Weinyddiaeth Addysg yn dymuno gosod addysg breswyl o fewn cyrraedd plant y werin, amlygodd Llanymddyfri ei pharodrwydd i hyrwyddo hyn drwy gytuno â Phwyllgor Addysg sir Gaerfyrddin i dderbyn chwe bachgen bob blwyddyn ar draul y pwyllgor.

Hyd y caniata ei hadeiladau, sydd eisoes yn rhy fychan i'r galw mawr sydd arnynt, deallwn fod yr ysgol yn barod i groesawu bechgyn Cymru gyfan os tybir y gallant fanteisio ar ei haddysg a'i bywyd.

(Y Cymro 8 Gorffennaf 1949).

LLANDOVERY COLLEGE

Coleg Llanymddyfri

1848-1998

Sesquicentenary Celebrations

Programme of Events

1997

September 9th 7.00 pm — Launch of celebrations as the Michaelmas term begins with a jazz band, street theatre, and lamb roast on the front lawn of the College

October 25th 2.30 pm — Rugby: 1st XV v Christ College, Brecon (A)
7.30 pm — Old Llandoverians Re-union Dinner at the College

November 8th 11.30 am — Service of Remembrance - during which Llandovery College Books of Remembrance will be dedicated

November 8th 7.30 pm — Fundraising Dinner at the Coal Exchange, Cardiff for College Rugby/Hockey tour in August 1998

November 15th 5.00 pm — "'Nabob', Wealth and Welsh education: The benefactions of Thomas Phillips". A Lecture by Gwyn Walters arranged by The Honourable Society of Cymmrodorion, at the College

November 21st 7.30 pm — Organ Recital by Geraint Bowen, Organist of St. David's Cathedral in the College Chapel

December 3rd 2.30 pm — Rugby: 1st XV v Crawshay's Youth XV - followed by a formal dinner

Sunday Half Hour (Radio 2), Dechrau Canu, Dechrau Canmol (S4C), and a Celebratory Service for Radio Wales will be recorded at the College during October and November and will be broadcast during the year.

Further information can be found in the School Journal and, nearer each event, on the College website: http//freespace.virgin.net/llan.coll

For further details about event(s) you may wish to attend please contact the College: Telephone: (01550) 720315 Fax: (01550) 720168

1998

February 4th 2.30 pm — Rugby: 1st XV v Welsh Academicals XV

February 20th — Old Llandoverian Society Annual Dinner - Savoy, London

February 27th 7.30 pm — Presentation of ode written by Tom Cannock and lecture by Dr Byron Harries, in the College

February 28th 7.30 pm — Dill Jones Memorial Jazz Concert, in the College Sports Hall.

March 1st — Foundation Day "Thanksgiving Service" at Llandingat Church followed by Afternoon tea and launch of "History of Llandovery College" by Dr R. Brinley Jones. Unveiling of Tapestry plus other events.

March 20th 7.30 pm — Organ Recital by Carlo Curley in College Chapel

April 17th — Annual Old Llandoverian Golf Day, Southerndown

May 12/13/14th — Play

May 23rd 2.30 pm — Speech Day (Guest Speaker Sir John Meurig Thomas, ScD, FRS, Master of Peterhouse, Cambridge) followed by Garden Party and Beating Retreat

Launch of "Llandovery College Who's Who"

June 6th — National Orchestra of Wales Celebratory Concert at the Brangwyn Hall, Swansea

July 11th — Midsummer Ball, at the College

Registered Charity No. 525394

THE ENDOWMENT DEED

of
THOMAS PHILLIPS' FOUNDATION
WELSH GRAMMAR SCHOOL
at
LLANDOVERY
dated
AUGUST XXV MDCCCXLVII

This Indenture made this twenty fifth day of August One thousand eight hundred and forty seven Between Thomas Phillips of No., 5 Brunswick Square in the County of Middlesex Esquire of the one part and Dame Augusta Hall the Wife of Sir Benjamin Hall Baronet of Llanover in the County of Monmouth commonly called Lady Hall. John Jones of Cefnfaes in the Parish of Nantmel in the County of Radnor Esquire The Reverend Thomas Price the Vicar of Llanfihangel Cwmdu in the County of Brecon The Reverend Joshua Hughes the Vicar of Llandingad and Llanfairarybryn in the County of Carmarthen and William Rees of the Town of Llandovery in the same County Printer and Publisher of the other part Whereas the said Thomas Phillips is desirous of founding and endowing a Welsh School in the Diocese of St. David's for the study and cultivation of the Welsh or Ancient British Language and Literature not only as a medium of Colloquial communication but as a means of promoting antiquarian and philological investigation in combination with a good sound classical and liberal education fitting for young men destined for any liberal profession or scientific pursuit to be exercised and followed in the Principality of Wales and more especially for young men desirous of qualifying themselves to be efficient Ministers of the Church in that principality. And whereas the said Thomas Phillips hath with intent transferred into the names of the said Dame Augusta Hall, John Jones, Thomas Price, Joshua Hughes and William Rees the sum of Two thousand three hundred and thirty three pounds six shillings and eight pence. Three pounds per Cent reduced annuities and the sum of Two thousand three hundred and thirty three pounds six shillings and eight pence Consolidated Three pounds per Cent annuities. And whereas the said Thomas Phillips hath selected the said Town of Llandovery as a central and convenient place for the site of such Institution and where for the present the building lately used as a National School is available as a School house and it is proposed to use the same accordingly until a more fitting one is provided. And whereas the said Thomas Phillips anticipates that ample means will be provided by the wealthier Inhabitants of South Wales and particularly in the more immediate vicinity of Llandovery for the acquisition of a proper site and the erection thereon of a good and suitable School house with proper accommodation for the School Master. And whereas the said Thomas Phillips is desirous by these presents of declaring the trusts of the said several sums of stock so transferred as aforesaid and of declaring and establishing the constitution of the said School and the rules laws and ordinances for its good government and regulation.

Now it is hereby declared and agreed that the said Dame Augusta Hall, John Jones, Thomas Price, Joshua Hughes and William Rees their executors, administrators and assigns and the Trustees for the time being of the said Charity shall stand and be possessed of the said several sums of stock so transferred to them as aforesaid to the end and intent aforesaid and upon and for the trusts intents and purposes hereinafter particularly expressed and declared (that is to say), Upon trust out of the interest dividends and annual proceeds of the said sum of Two thousand three hundred and thirty three pounds six shillings and eight pence.

Three pounds per Cent reduced annuities to pay Five pounds per annum for or towards the expenses of procuring the use of the said School room or other School house or room for the time being and repairing the same and keeping the same in proper state until such new and permanent School house and buildings shall be procured as aforesaid and then in or towards the repair and sustentation of such new and permanent School house and buildings or any expenses connected therewith and to pay the residue of the interest dividends and annual proceeds of the said Two thousand three hundred and thirty three pounds six shillings and eight pence.

Three pounds per Cent reduced annuities and also the interest dividends and annual produce of the said Two thousand three hundred and thirty three pounds six shillings and eight pence. Consolidated Three pounds per Cent Annuities to the Master of the said school for the time being And it is hereby further declared and by the said Thomas Phillips constituted and ordained That the said School shall be called "Thomas Phillips' Foundation". And for the present management of the School it is provided and declared that the said school shall during the life time of the said Thomas Phillips be subject in all things to his direction and control and he shall have power to place therein and to displace therefrom the Schoolmaster as he shall see occasion And for the regulation of the School after the death of the said Thomas Phillips it is declared that 1st.

The management and control of the School and of the Charity shall be in the trustees for the time being and all resolutions and acts of three Trustees at the least evidence by some writing signed by them shall be as good valid and effectual as if all the Trustees for the time being had concurred therein.

2nd. The Bishop of St. David's for the time being shall be Visitor of the said School and shall exercise all visitorial power in and over the same.

3rd. The site of the said School shall be at or near the Town of Llandovery aforesaid where the said School shall be conducted unless and until such School shall be removed in manner hereinafter provided. But nevertheless if at any time the building in which it is now intended to conduct the said School or any other building hereafter to be substituted shall fall into decay or if in the judgment of the Trustees the same shall from any other cause whatever be insufficient unsuitable or inconvenient for the carrying our of the purposes herein intended by the Founder and no new respectable and permanent School house and buildings shall previously be legally provided at Llandovery or its immediate neighbourhood that then the Trustees shall be at liberty to conduct the said School at any other suitable locality within the above mentioned Dioceses of St. David's and Llandaff at which a School house with necessary buildings shall or may be legally obtained or provided. But on no account shall the said trust funds or any part thereof or the dividends income or annual produce thereof be employed either in erecting or otherwise procuring or furnishing any such School house or buildings.

4th. As and when any vacancy shall occur in the Office of Master the Trustees shall with all convenient speed proceed to appoint thereto some fit and proper person being a Clergyman of the Church as now by law established in full Orders thoroughly acquainted with the Welsh language in its colloquial and literary use.

5th. The Trustees shall have power if and as they shall see occasion to displace any Master who in their judgment shall be guilty of any misconduct or neglect or shall not maintain the School in an efficient state to their satisfaction. But such removal shall be subject to an appeal to the Bishop of St. David's for the time being as Visitor Provided always that such appeal shall be made to him by the Master within one month after notification of the removal shall have been given to the Master and the decision of such Visitor shall be conclusive and final. It being hereby declared that it is the wish of the founder that the Visitor shall not interfere with the decision of the Trustees as to such removal unless it shall be proved that they have acted from improper motives or without due consideration or in a manner injurious to the real interests of the School and in opposition to the objects of the founder.

6th. The Master shall undertake fully and impartially to instruct (without any fee or reward to be by him directly or indirectly taken from them or their Parents or friends.) Twenty free Scholars to be nominated by the Trustees for the time being and to be by them selected from amongst Natives of the District comprising the present Dioceses of St. David's and Llandaff.

7th. That one public examination shall take place yearly and that the Bishop of St. David's be requested to nominate the Examiners but in case of his failing or neglecting to do so within ten days after he shall have been requested to do so by the Trustees such Examiners shall be nominated by them.

8th. The Master shall devote himself assiduously and exclusively to the duties of his School and shall not undertake any weekly parochial duties or any pastoral duties excepting on Sundays.

9th. The Scholars shall be properly instructed in Welsh, Reading, Grammar and composition and in English, Latin and Greek, Hebrew, Arithmetic Algebra and Mathematics, Sacred English and General History and Geography and such other branches of education as the Trustees with the approbation of the Visitor shall for the time being appoint and require and the Master shall under the direction of the Trustees make the proper classification of the Boys for the due education of them in such several matters according to their respective capacities and acquirements—The Welsh language shall be taught exclusively during one hour every School day and shall during that time be the sole medium of communication in the School and shall be used at all other convenient periods as far as may be possible as the conversational language of the School so as to familiarize the Scholars with the use of it as a colloquial language and the Master shall at all convenient times give lectures in that language upon subjects connected with Philology upon subjects of Science and general knowledge fitting for a Ministerial or liberal education and so as to give to the Scholars examples of its use in its higher style as a Literary language and the medium of instruction on grave and important subjects.

10th. It is especially enjoined that under no pretence or plea of the study or cultivation of the Welsh language or literature being no longer useful or required shall the object of the Founder or the provisions aforesaid for the instruction and education in the Welsh language and the cultivation thereof be disregarded or neglected but that the same be at all times religiously and faithfully observed as the primary and chief intent and object of the Institution. But should the Welsh language entirely cease as a colloquial and literary language then the education to be still such as to qualify young men either for Lampeter College or for Commercial agricultural or other useful callings. And it is further recommended by the Founder that in such case the substitution for the disused Welsh language should be instruction in Geology Mineralogy and Chemistry particularly such portions of those Sciences as may be applicable to the soil and substrata of the Principality. The object of the Founder being the dissemination of useful and practical knowledge in Wales and the raising both morally and intellectually the character of its people.

11th. The Master is to be at liberty subject to the regulation hereinafter mentioned to take into his School for education any number of pay Scholars so that they do not interfere with the due and sufficient education of the free Scholars according to the intention of the Founder. And it is especially enjoined that as between the pay Scholars and free Scholars the system of education shall be in all respects equal and so that no distinction whatsoever be directly or indirectly made to the disadvantage or disparagement of the free Scholars.

12th. That the remuneration to be received by the Master for the two senior pay Scholars shall be paid by him to the Trustees or their Treasurer for the purpose of forming a fund to defray their expenses attendant upon the execution of the trusts hereby in them reposed.

13th. That an annual Statement of Account be sent to the Visitor and a Report by the Examiner of the state of the School in general and particularly of the progress made by the free Scholars with especial reference to the Injunction in Rule 11. And for the continuance and permanent management of the Trustreeship Charity and Institution it is hereby declared that 1. When and as any vacancy or vacancies shall occur amongst the Trustees by reason of any Trustee dying or resigning or going permanently abroad or becoming disqualified to act it shall be lawful for the other Trustees for the time being while there shall be three such Trustees or the majority of them to appoint some other fit and proper person or persons being a Member or Members of the Church as now by Law established and resident within the Dioceses of St. David's or of Llandaff to be a Trustee or Trustees in the place of the person or persons so dying or resigning or going abroad or becoming disqualified to act. And if from any neglect of this provision the whole number of Trustees shall become at any time reduced below three then and in every such case the Incumbent of the parish in which the School shall at the time be located and the Mayor of the Borough of Llandovery for the time being shall appoint some other fit and proper persons qualified as aforesaid to be such Trustees in the place or stead of the Trustees so dying or resigning or going abroad or becoming disqualified to act so as to make up the full number of five Trustees and the persons who shall be appointed in manner herein before mentioned shall be Trustees of the Charity together with the surviving or continuing Trustees or Trustee if any or be and become the sole Trustees of the said Charity in case there shall be no surviving or continuing Trustees thereof. And all such Trustees shall thenceforth have the same power of continuing the number of Trustees and in all other respects the same powers as are given to the Trustees hereby appointed and on the appointment of new Trustees the proper means are to be taken (as shall from time to time be necessary, to vest the trust funds in the existing body of Trustees. 2. The said Lady Hall notwithstanding coverture shall have the same powers in all respects as a Trustee as if she were a feme and unmarried. 3. The Trustees shall be answerable each only for his or her own acts and not for any loss occasioned by any means not being his or her wilful default or neglect and shall have full power to reimburse themselves himself or herself any expenses which they may respectively be properly put to in or about the execution of the trust and it shall be lawful for the said Trustees if they shall think fit to appoint any one of their own body or any other person to be the Treasurer of the Charity to have and make all receipts and disbursements on behalf of the Charity. 4. And it shall be lawful for the Trustees for the time being or the majority of them to alter or vary any of the regulations aforesaid and to add or substitute any additional new or other regulations which shall appear to them calculated more effectually to promote the prosperity of the Institution and to effect the object of the Founder but so as not thereby to alter or pervert the fundamental character of the School as a Welsh School or to diminish the Instruction hereby required to be given in the Welsh Language or the cultivation and use of that language—But none of such Regulations shall be altered or varied nor shall any regulations be added thereto or substituted for the same except at a Meeting of the Trustees to be convened by Notice signed by one or more of the Trustees and delivered or sent to all the other Trustees seven days at the least previous to the holding of such Meeting and which Notice shall state the object for which such Meeting is convened. In Witness whereof the said parties to these presents have hereunto set their hands and seals the day and year first above written.

Thomas Phillips.	John Jones.	Joshua Hughes.
Augusta Hall.	Thomas Price.	William Rees.

GREETINGS FROM THE BOROUGH OF LLANDOVERY

To Thomas Phillips of Brunswick Square
London, Esquire

We the Mayor, Aldermen, and Councillors of the Borough of Llandovery in the County of Carmarthen, respectfully beg leave to tender our sincere and grateful thanks for your munificent Endowment of a Welsh Grammar School in this Town: The establishment of so excellent an Institution, not only reflects the highest honour on the character and benevolence of its generous Founder, but also forms an invaluable medium of securing to the youth of the present and future generations a sound, liberal and finished education upon the best and most solid basis.

We cannot but feel that the youth of this Town and neighbourhood, and the whole of those of the Southern portion of the Principality will have great cause to bless the Friend who has so disinterestedly and liberally placed within their reach, the superior advantages of a good education and consequent improvement in their future prospects of respectability and usefulness in Life. May the Almighty of His merciful kindness extend your useful life many years, that you may enjoy the pleasure and satisfaction of seeing the noble objects of your benevolent intentions worthily and effectually carried out.

CARMEN LANDUBRIENSE

Fundata saxo cinctaque flumine
Stat nostra sedes, muneribus tuis
    Dotata, Phillipsi, per annos
        Rite tuæ memorande genti.

Cuius laborem respiciat Deus,
Iactumque semen rore riget suo,
    Fruges ut auctumno mentendas
        Arva ferant opulenta donis.

Nostris Iuventus exeat ædibus
Exculta mentes, artibus et bonis
    Instructa, quas artes Athenæ,
        Quas Latiæ coluere Musæ.

Verbumque Christri gentibus editum
Vivis Alumni fontibus hauriant,
    Quo sanctiorem disciplinam
        Percipiant animis paratis.

Reddant honores et sibi debitos,
Cultuque recto pectora roborent,
    Virtute præclaraque crescat
        Quisque puer venientis ævi.

Sic, cara Mater Landubriensium,
Te laude digna concelebrent tui,
    Conclamet assurgens beatam
        Te pia progenies parentem.

John Williams, Warden, 1848.

(The College 'song' composed by the first Warden).

Pen-Pictures

THOMAS PHILLIPS was born in London, in 1760, of Radnorshire parentage: he returned to Wales when he was young and received some education there and, maybe, a smattering of Welsh. He had further schooling at Kempston outside Bedford before going back to Wales as an apprentice to a surgeon and apothecary in Hay before joining—as a pupil—John Hunter of Jermyn Street, London, later surgeon to George III. In 1780 Phillips embarked upon a medical career and by 1782 had entered the East India Company: it was the beginning of a varied, distinguished, profitable and successful life in which he combined medical skill with shrewd business acumen. In 1800 he married the daughter of the rector of Cusop near Hay and in 1802 returned to India. He was back in London in 1817: he died in 1851 and is buried in St Pancras Church. There were no children of the marriage. His years of long retirement were spent in benevolence—in book purchasing for libraries and in the endowment of scholarships—and as 'father' of the London College of Surgeons. Of him, the distinguished historian Professor T. F. Tout declared, 'He deserves remembrance as the only Welshman of his day who made large sacrifices in the cause of the education of his countrymen' (D.N.B.). He was a major benefactor of St. David's College, Lampeter, founded in 1822 and it was Phillips who made Llandovery College possible. He gave £4,666 to set up the Institution, he presented 7,000 books and established 20 scholarships. (There is no evidence that he was a book collector for his own sake but it would seem that he purchased books with the express intention of establishing or enhancing libraries of his choice). In his will be bequeathed £12,300 for the establishment of professorships in Chemistry, Botany and Geology . . . and a bequest to Jesus College and Balliol College Oxford for the creation of closed scholarships: Balliol was to refuse the offer.

One who remembered him described Thomas Phillips as 'a short thickset Welshman, [who] used to wear a fine thin frock coat with velvet collar' (NLW D.Ll.T. Papers June 24 1898). There is a bust of him by E. J. Thomas of Pimlico at St. David's College (now the University of Wales, Lampeter) and portraits of him by Mornewick at Llandovery College, the original paid for by public subscription. The *Journal* of December 1970 reports 'A portrait of the Founder at the age of 90 by C. A. Mornewick, 1850, has been presented to the College by Miss Eleanor Lloyd, a great niece of Thomas Phillips. She also presented a portrait of his father of the same name'. One Mornewick hangs in the Library, the other above the high table in the Dining Room. The portrait of his father—in a top hat—also hangs in the Dining Room.

Despite his wide travels—Canada, India, Australia for example, and his being domiciled in London, Phillips had kept up connection with Wales. The correspondent of June 24, 1898 comments: 'He used often to visit Hay . . . He used to send parcels of goods for the poor of Hay—thro Mr Watkins, Carrier, and amongst the things old red soldiers coats wh. were worn about the streets to the great astonishment of the townsfolk. He used to send parcels of cloth, flannel &c. to some of his relations, and hidden among them ½ of a £5 or £50 bill, never intimating where they came from. Later the other ½ of the bill arrived'. This correspondence reported his end, too, 'He had a seizure while visiting his relative Mrs Dyke of Westbrook, wh. caused them great anxiety. They sent intimation to the Rev. Samuel Powell, Rector of Dilwyn Herefordshire, who brought a carriage, and removed him to his house in London, Brunswick Square, where he died'. The report continues, 'He was very lavish with his money, giving freely to all manner of charities' and added, 'The cause of his founding the School at Llandovery was that he travelled thro Wales and saw the great need of the establishment of some such institution, and he wanted to do some permanent good with his money . . .'

But, why Llandovery? In 1898 T. Aneuryn Rees M.A. (Oxon), Old Llandoverian, sometime Town Clerk of Tenby . . . and Merthyr, son of William Rees, one of the founding trustees, spoke of a particular relationship. [Aneuryn Rees incorrectly attributes a title to the founder: there were two others, contemporary, much of the same name, with overlapping interests. One was Sir Thomas Phillipps, Baronet, 1792-1872, antiquary and bibliophile extraordinary who actually offered his collection to Llandovery . . . and another Sir Thomas Phillips 1801-1867, barrister, author, educationist who expressed, among other things, concern about the lack of Welsh provision at St David's College, Lampeter, and indeed suggested that it had been a mistake not to have associated St David's with Christ College, Brecon! It is clear, however, that Aneuryn Rees was referring to 'our' man]: '[My] father [was a] great friend of Sir Thomas Phillips the Founder to whom he was introduced by Dr Carl Meyer, Private Secretary to Prince Albert, the latter being my Father's guest for many weeks during which my Father taught him the Welsh Language. Sir Thos. Phillips intended leaving his money to endow or increase the endowment of Lampeter College and informed my Father of his intention. My father then said to him, why not endow a school at Llandovery in order that the Farmers' sons and others might have the opportunity of obtaining a good Education? This idea struck Sir Thomas as a good one and he acted upon it. The details of the Scheme were prepared and carried out chiefly by my Father . . .' (NLW D. Ll. T. Papers 12 July 1898).

There were further connections, maybe. William Rees's brother, four years his senior, was Rice Rees, professor and librarian at Lampeter when Phillips visited there in the early 1830s by which time William and his uncle had set up a printing press in Llandovery. Rice Rees was a man of considerable academic promise: he died suddenly at Newbridge on Wye at the age of 35 in 1839 . . . but, clearly, he would have told his brother William of Phillips's great interest and benevolence, the 'warm and enlightened benevolence' which Bishop Connop Thirlwall acknowledged in 1849.

It was early in 1847 that Thomas Phillips had offered to re-instate the professorship of Welsh, on particular conditions, at Lampeter: the offer was rejected. It was a rejection that led, urgently, to the Llandovery foundation. Lady Hall records 'my friend [Thomas Phillips] has determined on appropriating his money in an independent manner and establishing an Endowed School . . . where the most thorough Welsh instruction shall be given as well as Greek, Latin, English etc.' [NLW Llanbadarn Fawr Chest Collection 11 April 1847]. Llandovery College was born. . .

There is no doubt that Thomas Phillips, having endowed it, wished to be informed of the progress of the Institution but after three years of its opening he was dead . . . and *that* a month after the School moved to its present site. It is a fitting tribute to his memory that, of late, the name of Thomas Phillips adorns the entrance to the Institution which he so generously funded.

(Sources: DNB (Dictionary of National Biography); DWB (Dictionary of Welsh Biography); D. W. T. Price *A History of Saint David's University College Lampeter* Volume One to 1898; D. W. T. Price 'Thomas Phillips of Brunswick Square', *Trivium* 29/30; A. J. Sambrook 'Thomas Phillips 1760-1851, *Province* XI No 4; D. G. Crawford *Roll of the Indian Medical Service*; NLW D.LL.T. (National Library of Wales), Sir Daniel Lleufer Thomas Papers; NLW Llanbadarn Chest Papers; *The School Journal*).

CONNOP THIRLWALL was bishop of St. Davids for thirty-four years from 1840. He was born in London in 1797, educated at Charterhouse and Trinity College Cambridge. He travelled abroad then entered Lincoln's Inn to read Law, but in 1827 returned to Cambridge as a tutor. In consequence of his advocating degrees for Dissenters he was required to resign, became Rector of Kirby Underdale, Yorkshire where he compiled his *History of Greece* completed in eight volumes in 1844.

Thirlwall was an extremely able man, was temperamentally cold, forbidding and distant. His episcopate was marked by diligence and generosity in the restoration of churches (including the cathedral), in repairing parsonages and contributing generously out of his own income towards Church schools. In 1848 he saw with great pleasure the establishment of Trinity College Carmarthen and Llandovery College. He was, from the start, concerned about the prominence given to Welsh at Llandovery but Warden John Williams reassured him. (Thirlwall had learned some Welsh though his conversational powers were not strong). Relations between him and the college cooled. The language policy, the strong feelings shared by Lady Hall and The Venerable John Williams concerning the appointment of non-Welsh speakers to high office in the Church distanced him: the appointment of Ollivant to the see of Llandaff in 1849 exacerbated the situation. Allied in sentiment with Lady Hall and John Williams was David James. When there was dissent among two of the trustees in respect of his appointment as second warden, Thirlwall as Visitor was invited to intervene. He was devastating in his criticism of James.

The warm expressions of national sentiment which informed those at the helm at Llandovery College in the early years were not to Thirlwall's taste.

Connop Thirlwall resigned from the see in 1874, died in 1875 and was buried in Westminster Abbey.

(Sources: D.N.B; D.W.B; Ewart Lewis 'Connop Thirlwall, Bishop of St. Davids 1840-1874 *Province* Vol. II No. 2 Summer 1951).

LADY HALL / LLANOVER. Augusta Waddington born on 21 March 1802 married Benjamin Hall in 1823: he enjoyed an active public life as Member of Parliament, becoming Commissioner for works in 1855. During his period of office as Commissioner the great clock of Westminster was erected—hence 'Big Ben'. He was created a baronet in 1838 and a peer in 1859 assuming the title Baron Llanover. He was embroiled in bitter controversy with Bishop Thirlwall regarding the state of the Church in the diocese of St. Davids and supported, strongly, the use of the Welsh language in religious services. He was to share such sentiments with his wife.

Though she was born in Llanover of English descent, Augusta Hall became passionately devoted to the cause of the language and things Welsh and her influence (and that of her husband) in the circles of the local and wider nobility was to give the cause enormous and prestigious support. She had learned some Welsh as a young girl, and early, came under the influence of Thomas Price (Carnhuanawc), another founding Trustee of Llandovery College. Augusta's sister had married Baron Bunsen, the German chemist and professor at Heidelberg: he invented several scientific instruments but is best remembered for the 'burner' which bears his name. Bunsen was to become German ambassador to Great Britain and Chemistry apart he, too, had a deep interest in Celtic studies. Augusta was an early and prominent member of 'Cymreigyddion y Fenni', a cultured society set up in 1833 by patriotic Welsh people living in the Abergavenny area: Thomas Price was its moving spirit. In 1834 she won the prize for an essay on the Welsh language and she was involved as patron in the Welsh Manuscripts Society established in 1836. The family of William Rees—another founding Trustee—was closely associated with the activities of the Manuscripts Society: little wonder that his daughter claimed how her father 'was a very intimate friend of Lady Llanover, that enthusiastic admirer of Welsh literature and customs.' Such 'enthusiasm' is illustrated in the reminiscences of A. G. Edwards (quoted in the section *Voices from Within*): when he appeared before her as a candidate for the wardenship she 'was greatly impressed with my knowledge of Welsh.'

Augustus Hare, author of *Memorials of a Quiet Life* and brother of Julius Charles Hare who had collaborated with Connop Thirlwall in a translation of Barthold Georg Niebuhr's *History of Rome* paints a telling picture of Augusta Hall: 'Lady Llanover is very small and has been very pretty . . . Her great idea is Wales . . . There is a good deal to admire in Lady Llanover; her pertinacity in what she thinks right, whether she is right or not.' He refers to a visit to Llanover to meet the young Grand Duke of Baden and describes a visit to Lady Hall's daughter's home in 1879: 'In three carriages we went to Llanarth for luncheon. I went with the royal carriage, which with its smart scarlet postillions certainly went slow enough: for the dear old lady, to do the Grand Duke more honour, had engaged for the occasion not only the two horses used for the weddings at Abergavenny but also the two used at funerals, and the steeds of death outweighed those of mirth, and kept us down at a funeral pace'. Hare also describes the Grand Duke's departure: 'On Monday, September 27th all Llanover was in motion for the Prince's departure . . . the Welsh harpers harping at the door, the Welsh housemaids in high hats . . . and every guest in the house compelled to go to the station to see the Prince off . . . I wished myself to have travelled to Windsor by way of Gloucester, which is two and a half hours less journey; but no, that was impossible; the Queen of England sometimes has her own way; the Queen of South Wales always.'

Lady Llanover—her bardic name was Gwenynen Gwent—was rich, clever, determined, talented. She compiled a six volume study of Mrs Delaney her great aunt . . . and wrote a charming medley on Welsh cookery. She promoted the triple harp as she did Welsh dancing. She was certainly not without artistic talent—there is a self portrait, she illustrated her cooking book, she painted watercolours and executed landscape prints and she was responsible for a fine full-length silhouette of Thomas Price, Carnhuanawc. She designed a volume of Welsh costume. She collaborated in producing a collection of Welsh airs, supported the publication of a Welsh dictionary and devoted time to a cause of temperance and her own brand of Protestantism. And very close to her heart were the aspirations and success of Llandovery College. From the start she was deeply involved. She witnessed the débâcle at Lampeter which precipitated the move to create the institution at Llandovery. She wrote a "private" letter to the Reverend David James of Kirkdale, Liverpool (who was to become the second Warden) on 31 March 1847: 'Lady Hall presents her compliments to Mr James and is intrusted with a confidential enquiry viz. If Mr James would accept a Welsh Professorship and to reside at Lampeter Coll: if such a situation were offered him on an endowment of £140 per annum without liberty to take Clerical duty unless close to the spot. There is an intention (as yet unannounced) by a private individual to endow a Welsh Professorship and have it attached to Lampeter Coll: where doubtless Mr James is aware there is a Professorship called 'Welsh'—already—but the Professor is not resident and does not lecture. The object of Lady Hall's friend is to have a bone fide Welsh Professor of his own institution in the hope of raising Welsh Scholarship to the place it ought to occupy. Would Mr James accept it—were it offered? Lady Hall has not forgotten her agreeable visit to Liverpool or Mr James' noble efforts on behalf of his Welsh countrymen there which she trusts have been entirely successful in their establishment of their right to their own services in their *own Church*. An early answer will oblige.' She was to write further on 4 May that the authorities had declared against the re-establishment of a Welsh professorship at Lampeter and continued, 'My friend has determined on appropriating his money in an *independent* manner and establishing an Endowed school where the Master shall be a Welsh Clergyman in full Orders and where the most thorough Welsh Instruction shall be given as well as Greek Latin English etc. to a certain number of Free Scholars . . . The Master's salary I believe will be about £140 per annum—but he will be allowed to hold a Benefice . . . The present idea is to fix the school at, or near Llandovery . . . Not a word of this is known beyond two or three persons—for there is a building with a cottage where the National school was held at Llandingad which is now abandoned and which we hope to obtain for a trifle—and if the Dean had an idea of it, he might outbid—or prevent—for nothing could be more distressing to his feelings than to have a flourishing Welsh Grammar School within 21 miles of his College . . . I have little doubt if the new school went on well, he (the Bishop) would ordain straight from it—but if he did not, the Llanbedr residence is very short . . . Have the goodness to keep this to yourself and send me your ideas upon it. We must have a Man invulnerable to Episcopophobia—and then he will do well'. Lady Hall was to criticize, sharply, the appointment of Englishmen to sees in Wales, as did her husband. In a tart letter defending him in this matter, she concludes 'Lady Hall is generally at home at three in the afternoon if Mr James wishes to see her.'

When Llandovery College was opened she was active, too, even when she was unable to attend Trustees' meetings. In 1857 she replies to resolutions of a meeting: '. . . I beg to give hereby my written sanction to the sums agreed upon for the repairs of the building . . . We all know that the building was in a dreadful state when the Warden took possession and until we put the whole building in a water tight and habitable state we cannot call upon the Warden to keep it so . . .' In 1880 she was offering the services of her own surveyor to supervise the project of supplying spring water to the College.

There were occasions when, on principle, she was not so cooperative. In 1898 W. E. T. Morgan recalls his experience: '. . . Athletic Sports were, as far as I know, originated in my time, about the year 1864. I was appointed Secretary, and was requested to write to Lady Llanover for a subscription. Unfortunately my letter was penned in the Anglo-Saxon language. To this I received from her Ladyship a characteristic reply couched in the vernacular expressing surprise that I had ventured to write to her from the Athrofa . . . Cymraeg in a strange tongue. The letter went on to rebuke the attempt to introduce Athletics into the School, suggesting that our parents had sent us there to train our minds, not to exercise our bodies. Needless to say this missive was not accompanied by a cheque.'

She died 17 January 1896, in her 94th year: her connection with school having extended for half a century. The *Journal* of Midsummer 1896 records its regret: 'By the death of Lady Llanover the School has lost its Senior Trustee, and one of its most devoted friends. It was mainly through her influence that the School was located at Llandovery, and she was one of the first Trustees at the time of the foundation in 1847. All through her life she never ceased to take the keenest interest in its work and welfare, and by her forethought and by prompt and vigorous action, she was instrumental on more than one occasion in rendering it most signal and lasting service. For many years she gave £20 annually to be distributed in prizes to the best boys in the Welsh form, which greatly encouraged the study of the language in the School. We have ever reason to congratulate ourselves very heartily that such a worthy successor to Lady Llanover has been found in Lord Tredegar, a nobleman who has done and is doing so much for higher education in the Principality'.

In 1989 a new girls' house was opened by Viscount Tonypandy: it was appropriately called Tŷ Llanofer in honour of her memory. It was she, who in 1849 had purchased the field known as 'Cae Brenin' the purpose of which was 'the erection of a School House, Master's House and other suitable buildings.' The new house overlooks Tredegar. Inside is a copy of the charming painting of her by Charles Mornewick—now in the Dining Hall—presented by Lord Llanover in 1861 to which the Trustees had responded with 'the high appreciation they entertain of the anxiety, zeal and active part Her Ladyship has ever evinced and taken for the interest and welfare of the school'. In the painting she is decked in 'Welsh' costume, mistletoe, gorse and other plants associated with Druidic lore. It is as she would be remembered.

(The quotations are derived from collections at the National Library of Wales—the Sir Daniel Lleufer Thomas Papers and the Llanbadarn Chest; also from minutes of the Trustees meetings and from the School Journal).

Tŷ Llanofer

(Sources: DNB; DWB; NLW DLLT; NLW Llanbadarn Chest; Trustees Minutes; *The School Journal*; Augustus Hare *Memorials of a Quiet Life*; Meic Stephens ed. *The Oxford Companion to the Literature of Wales* M. E. Thomas *Afiaith yng Ngwent*; Paul Joyner *Artists in Wales* c.1740-1851).

WILLIAM REES was born at Tonn, Llandovery in 1808 of a family well-established in the area. The headmaster of the National School was John Howell, weaver, poet, editor and musician; Howell had received very little education himself but was deeply immersed in Welsh culture and had a talent for inspiring an interest in others. Rice Rees, William's elder brother and a fine scholar was much inspired by Howell. Their uncle W. J. Rees, Cascob, had been at Wadham College Oxford and Rice was at Jesus College: both were ordained. William however took a different direction. He was apprenticed to the printer's trade at Hereford but returned to Llandovery and, in conjunction with another uncle—David Rice Rees—entered the printing business there in 1829. D. R. Rees had returned to Llandovery in 1811 having been a shop assistant in England: in Llandovery he became a bookseller, keeper of the post office, printer and banker and played a prominent part in the life of the town. It was he, too, who in 1851 arranged and compiled a classified catalogue of the books which Thomas Phillips had presented.

When D. R. Rees retired from printing in 1835, William continued with the press and it went from strength to strength: it would not be too much to say that it became the finest in Wales. He printed works of outstanding merit—content-wise and design-wise: the three volumes of Lady Charlotte Guest's translation of the *Mabinogion* in 1848-1849 demonstrate this. He was to print many many more (apart from ephemera such as the 'Rules and Regulations' of the Institution). When William Rees was made founding trustee in August 1847, the Reverend Thomas Price—Carnhuanawc—was elected too: it was Rees, jointly with Longmans of London, who published Carnhuanawc's *Literary Remains* between 1854-1855. Another title published by him was Ieuan Gwynedd's work *A Vindication of the Educational and Moral Condition of Wales*, 1848. It was a study of great interest to him—printing apart. Rees himself had contributed to the debate on the condition of the Welsh people for the Report of the Commissioners of Inquiry into the state of education in Wales (Blue Books), 1847. His description of the life of the poor in Llandovery shows the social conditions prevailing at the time of the foundation of the College:

> 'The poor are mostly agricultural labourers, even those living in the town; though this class is less numerous than formerly owing to their being drained away to Merthyr and the manufacturing districts. Wages are now 9/- a week for a labourer; but this has hitherto been above the average. Wages are still advancing. The women can earn about 4/- per week. They eat but little meat of any kind and drink chiefly water. Their principal food is barley-bread, cheese and porridge. Coals are about 18/- a ton . . . The clothing is chiefly home-made and is cheap. The rent of a cottage (single room) was 40/- per annum; two rooms about 70/-'.

And he has further comment:

> 'The general character of the people is honest and industrious. Among farm-servants the chastity of the women is low, in consequence of the farmers conniving at young people meeting in their houses after the family has retired to rest. They observe Sunday well: most of the labourers appear in Church or Chapel well clad. The mother of the family is generally thrifty and tidy and the inside of the houses as neat as can be expected.'

Little wonder that as a trustee William Rees was able to 'inform' his fellows: 'bounds' from the start were clear and the 'Rules and Regulations' precise on lodging conditions!

William Rees's distinction as a printer and publisher is matched only by his immense contribution to life in Llandovery. He was Town Clerk from 1836 to 1867, Justice of the Peace, keen churchman, archaeologist. He was appointed Secretary to the Trustees of the Institution and was responsible for the Building Fund. His diligence and attendance at Trustee meetings is noteworthy.

His daughter, Angharad Corrysmith, wife of Colonel Corrysmith RMA wrote from Bedford on 15 July 1898:

> 'My dear Father was an indefatigable worker, and although not a robust man was most energetic in any matter concerning Wales and the Welsh. He . . . helped Lady Charlotte Guest (afterwards Schreiber) very materially with the 'Mabinogion', and was a very intimate friend of Lady Llanover that enthusiastic admirer of Welsh literature and customs . . . [He possessed a] collection of rare books in his library. I was particularly impressed as a child with the visit of Prince Louis Lucien

Bonaparte, being very disappointed that he looked like an ordinary mortal instead of being arrayed in grand robes and having a crown on!"

(NLW D.Ll.T. Papers).

(It is interesting that Napoleon's nephew should have visited Llandovery! He had lived in England until 1848 when he returned to France—to come back to England again in 1870. Public duties apart he was deeply interested in the Celtic languages: no doubt it was for this reason that he visited Rees).

William Rees's son T. Aneuryn Rees who attended the College and Sherborne before going to Oxford, was to play in the first Welsh International Rugby team against England in 1881 (together with another Old Llandoverian, E. J. Lewis). Aneuryn Rees was Town Clerk of Tenby . . . and Merthyr: he died in 1932. In the pen-picture of Thomas Phillips, reference is made to Aneuryn Rees's version of the association between the Founder and his father. He confirms his sister's reference to William Rees's diligence: 'My father gave all this time and labour free, and he was never remunerated for his work as Secretary of the Trustees' (NLW D.Ll.T. Papers 12 July 1898).

William Rees's attachment to Llandovery was total and there is no doubt that his contacts and the distinction that the press had brought helped to make the town the ideal place for the College. He died in 1873 and was buried in Llandingat churchyard. The Trustees meeting of 28 May 1874 'resolved that the vacancy which has occurred by the death of Mr William Rees has been filled up by the unanimous election of John Jones of Blaenos Esq. MP for the County of Carmarthen.' Between them—Rees and Jones—they gave half a century of service to Llandovery College.

(Sources: DWB; *The School Journal*; Trustees' Minutes; NLW, D.Ll.T; Ifano Jones *Printing and Printers in Wales and Monmouthshire*; A. T. Arber-Cooke *Pages from the History of Llandovery*).

THE REVEREND JOSHUA HUGHES was born in 1807 at Nevern, Pembrokeshire. He was educated at Ystrad Meurig in the new schoolroom built between 1810 and 1815 by John Williams, headmaster, father of Warden John Williams (who had preceded Joshua Hughes at Ystrad Meurig). From there he proceeded to St. David's College, Lampeter. In 1845 he was appointed vicar of Llandovery and was consecrated Bishop of St. Asaph in 1870. He was an ardent Welshman, committed to the language, deeply interested in education and well-disposed towards Nonconformists. He took a very keen interest in the foundation and subsequent success of Llandovery College. It was he who took the service at the opening of the Institution on 1 March 1848: in June he pronounced 'it was imperative on all who loved their country to do all in their power to aid and further the great and good cause' of its establishment. He was a trustee for forty-two years and on occasion disagreed vehemently with the decisions of his fellow-trustees: he expressed strongly an objection to the appointment of David James in 1853 (as did John Jones, Cefnfaes) and of William Watkins in 1861.

Two of his sons, both educated at the College, achieved considerable distinction. One, Thomas McKenny Hughes was highly regarded as a pupil: he was born in 1832, proceeded from Llandovery to Trinity College, Cambridge. He was secretary to the British consul, Rome, 1860-1861 and succeeded Adam Sedgwick as Woodwardian Professor of Geology at Cambridge: he remained there until his death in 1917. He had been elected F.R.S. in 1889.

The Minutes of the Trustees' meeting held on 17 December, 1862, in which Joshua Hughes was present records, '. . . Mr Thomas McKenny Hughes has presented to this Institution a collection of Geological Specimens. The Thanks of the Trustees be conveyed to Mr Hughes for his kind recollection of the scene of his early Education.'

The other, Joshua Pritchard Hughes, born in Llandovery vicarage in 1847 was educated at Llandovery, Shrewsbury and Balliol College, Oxford. He was an active, deeply-loved incumbent of Llantrisant, Glamorgan, for twenty-one years during a period of considerable industrial development—the parish extended from Miskin almost as far as Pontypridd. He was consecrated Bishop of Llandaff in 1905, retired in 1931 and died in 1938.

(Sources: D.N.B; D.W.B; J. Vyrnwy Morgan *Welsh Religious Leaders in the Victorian Era*, 1905).

THE REVEREND THOMAS PRICE (Carnhuanawc), historian and antiquary was the son of the vicar of Llanwrthyl: his grandfather, on his mother's side, was also ordained. Carnhuanawc—his bardic name—was born in 1787 and died nine months after the College was founded. A splendid bust of him, presented in 1877 is to be seen in the Warden's entrance.

He was ordained in 1811 and became vicar of Llanfihangel Cwmdu, Brecon, in 1825 and curate of Tretower, too, from 1839. He was well regarded as a historian and antiquary and ranks as one of the best Celtic scholars of the day: he had travelled in the Celtic countries and mastered Breton. His *History of Wales to the Death of Llywelyn ap Gruffydd,* in Welsh, published in fourteen parts between 1836 and 1842 was one of his important works of scholarship. He was a talented illustrator as may be seen in his drawings in *History of Brecknockshire* by Theophilus Jones and he demonstrated deep interest in the triple harp. He was a frequent attender and competitor at *eisteddfodau*.

Price shared antiquarian interests with Lady Hall, William Rees and with the Warden . . . and like them he was critical of the church's neglect of the language. He argued for its use in Sunday and day schools.

His death at a relatively early age deprived the school of a trustee who possessed a remarkable combination of literary, historical, musical and artistic talent: he had been much in evidence in the drafting of the Trust Deed.

(Sources: D.N.B; D.W.B; R. Brinley Jones 'References to Welshmen in 'The Critic' 1843-1863, 1962).

JOHN JONES (Cefnfaes). A brief biography of John Jones appears in correspondence held at the National Library of Wales (D.Ll.T. Papers 21 June 1898 Penralley, Rhayader):—

'Mr John Jones, Cefnfaes near Rhayader died April 25th 1865 aged 73 years; he was the son of a Mr John Jones . . . who was proprietor of the Oak Hotel in this town. Mr Jones of Cefnfaes married Joanna, eldest daughter of Rev. Jonathan Williams (author of the *History of Radnorshire*) . . . Mr John Jones early in life obtained an appointment as a Clerk in the Bank of England, where he rose to a position of some importance, and eventually retired on a good pension, he purchased the Cefnfaes property, and built a very nice residence thereon and was High Sheriff of the County in 1854, died without issue, leaving his property to his wife, who at her death left it amongst several relations.

Jones was an old friend of Phillips the founder of Llandovery School. I always understood that Jones was anxious to have the School established at Rhayader, but through the influence of Rees of Tonn it was established at Llandovery, the latter was I believe backed up by the late Lady Llanover . . .

T. W. Williams.'

John Jones took an active part in the early negotiations, was concerned about an over-emphasis on 'Welsh' at the Institution; he dissented (with Joshua Hughes) from the appointment of David James as second warden. In 1857 he was advising on building: 'Until the Lime and Sand in the Walls of the Institution crystallises, wet will continue to penetrate and the more so from the want of flatness in the Stones. With our flat Slate Stones it does so in a less degree. Time is the cure, if the Old adage be correct.

"When 100 years are passed and gone
Then Lime and Sand become a Stone"

. . . We had better follow Shakespeare's advice. "If it were done, when tis done, then 'twere well it were done quickly".'

It was a warning of concerns to come! By his will of 10 April 1865 he left £1,000 to promote the teaching of handwriting at Llandovery College.

JOHN WILLIAMS (1792-1858), Archdeacon of Cardigan, first rector of the Edinburgh Academy and first warden of Llandovery was born at Ystradmeurig. His father, John Williams 'Yr Hen Syr' was vicar there and master of the school, a school which had gained a fine reputation since its foundation in the middle years of the eighteenth century. The terms of the original Indenture of the school in 1757 speak of its intentions: 'to erect a grammar school in the village of Ystradmeyrick . . . for educating twelve poor boys of the parish': 'to nominate a schoolmaster, who was also required to read prayers and preach at the parish church of Ystradmeyrick as often as he conveniently could' and 'to actually teach and instruct twelve poor boys . . . in the Latin tongue, and in the principles of the Church of England as by law established'. For some half-century it became the leading school in Wales and rose to the position of a divinity school, supplying a considerable number of candidates for holy orders. John Williams was educated there.

After an interval of three years spent in teaching at Chiswick, John Williams went for a short time to Ludlow school and from there he proceeded to Balliol College, Oxford: he graduated in 1814. Like Dr Thomas Arnold, who was one of his four companions in the first class, Williams chose for himself the career of a public-school master. For four years he was at Winchester—and then two years at Hyde Abbey school in the same city. In 1820 Thomas Burgess, bishop of St David's offered him the vicarage of Lampeter with the expressed hope that he would carry on the school established there by the previous vicar, Eliezer Williams. He accepted, and through his influence Lampeter was selected as the home of the divinity school since known as St Davids College (now University of Wales Lampeter) the foundation-stone of which was laid in 1822, but, owing to some subsequent differences of view with the bishop, Williams was not appointed Principal.

Presumably at the suggestion of John Gibson Lockhart (son-in-law and biographer of Sir Walter Scott) who was one of Williams' closest friends, Charles, the second son of Sir Walter was sent to Lampeter in the autumn of 1820 as a private pupil. So inspired was Sir Walter with confidence in John Williams that he induced several of his Scottish friends to follow his example. In 1824 Colin Mackenzie (whose son also went to Lampeter) and Sir Walter invited Williams to become headmaster of a proprietary day school, to be called the Academy, which they were then promoting at Edinburgh, with the view of raising the standard of classical education and especially of Greek learning. The school was opened, with Williams as rector on 1st October 1824. His success at Edinburgh was in many respects even more remarkable than that of Arnold at Rugby, for apart from the difficulties incidental to a day-school, he had to overcome the native Scottish bias in favour of purely utilatarian education as against the more liberal training of the classics and other higher branches of learning. The Academy became famous for its oustanding standard of scholarship. In 1857 a former pupil Archibald Campbell Tait (later archbishop of Canterbury) ascribed to Williams 'more than to any man living the present movement in Scotland indicating a wish for a higher standard in the classical department of the universities'. Another Tait, no relation, Peter Guthrie Tait, who was at the Academy between 1841 and 1847, a brilliant mathematician and for thirty years professor of Natural Philosophy at Edinburgh wrote movingly in 1898 to Daniel Lleufer Thomas of his regard for John Williams: '. . . I have still a very vivid recollection of the genial old man, and of the real interest which he threw into our classical work. This was, no doubt, in part traceable to the fact that when we reached his hands we were emancipated from the horrors of pedantic syntax &c. and taught to look on Homer and Horace as literary treasures, not as instruments of torture: but also, and more especially, to the hearty way in which he seemed to regard us as his fellow workers in the search for knowledge.'

In August 1827 Williams rashly accepted the post of Latin professor at the London University, then in course of being organised, but with equal precipitation resigned in some nine months later, before entering on its duties, because of the opposition which its secular policy had aroused among the high-church party. After a twelve month break in his connection with the Academy, during which he devoted himself to literary work, he was re-elected rector in July 1829 and continued to hold the post until his retirement in July 1847.

His reputation had been high. Sir Walter Scott was to eulogise him as 'a heaven-born teacher' and 'the best schoolmaster in Europe'; he described Williams as a man 'whose extensive information, learning, and lively talent made him always pleasant company.' It was their conversations on Welsh history that prompted the writing of *The Betrothed*, Scott's Welsh romance. On Scott's death it was Williams who read the burial service over his remains at Dryburgh Abbey.

During his long sojourn in Scotland, Williams's connection with Wales had never been wholly severed. He continued to be the non-resident vicar of Lampeter till October 1833, when he was instituted Archdeacon of Cardigan. He, however, longed for some suitable opening for undertaking educational work in Wales. Within a few weeks after his retirement from the rectorship Williams was appointed the first warden of the new institution at Llandovery. The school was opened in very incommodious premises on 1 March 1848, pending the erection of permanent buildings which were completed by May 1851, the prestige of Williams's name being largely instrumental in raising the necessary funds. The warden desired to develop the school into a collegiate institution which might perhaps in time supersede the theological college at Lampeter. He and Sir Benjamin Hall openly attacked Lampeter College for the inefficiency of its training and its systematic neglect of Welsh studies. Llandovery was succeeding: in 1849 he was writing to David James who was to become his successor, 'We are getting on well here and hope that nothing may arise to cloud the very promising scene.' Ill-health, however, compelled Williams to retire from the wardenship at Easter 1853, but not before he had raised Llandovery to a foremost position among the schools of Wales. His concern would not end: he wrote to the secretary of the Trustees: 'I shall take a most lively interest in the welfare of the Institution, and will not cease to benefit it as far as I can by advice, recommendations, and active exertions'. The remaining years of his life he devoted chiefly to literary work, living at Brighton then at Oxford. In 1857 he moved to Bushey, Hertfordshire, where he died on 27 December 1858 and was buried on 4 January 1859 in Bushey churchyard. While at Lampeter, he had married Mary, only daughter of Thomas Evans of Llanilar, Cardiganshire: they had six daughters.

Besides being one of the outstanding educators of the nineteenth century he was a fine classical scholar. He had read several papers before the Royal Society of Edinburgh and published a number of works. He also made a special study of the early history of the Celtic races, and particularly of the language and literature of Wales. He was to expound on the pristine purity of the ancient British Church . . . and his correspondence shows deep concern about the appointment of English clerics to sees in Wales (a concern he shared with the 'Halls' for example). Maybe his return to Wales encouraged him to think of his own preferment. In 1849 he writes to David James, 'My Scottish friends, men of great weight and power are anxious in an attempt to press my claims to the vacant Bishoprick.' But it was not to be.

At his death he left behind him several unfinished works. These included some slight portions of an autobiography. His eldest daughter, Mrs Colquhoun-Grant, subsequently, as his literary executrix, collected further materials for biographical purposes; but these, together with most of Williams's papers and correspondence, were lost off the coast of Spain, near Ferrol, in the wreck of the steamship Europa on 17 July 1878, in which Mrs Colquhoun-Grant was returning to England from India.

An oil painting of John Williams by Colvin Smith, executed in 1841 on the commission of some former pupils hangs in the great hall of the Academy at Edinburgh. A portrait was copied from it and hangs in the Library at Llandovery. A marble bust of him by Joseph Edwards is on loan from Balliol College Oxford and stands in the newly designed concourse area. He composed the College song, the 'Carmen Landubriense' in 1848. In it he speaks of 'cara Mater Landubriensium'. He was to serve it with great, great distinction.

(This profile is mainly the work of Sir Daniel Lleufer Thomas which appeared in the *Dictionary of National Biography*: it appeared a century ago and remains the standard biography. Here it has been edited and there are annotations deriving from papers in the Llanbadarn Chest and also from the papers of Sir Daniel both in the National Library of Wales. The background to Ystrad Meurig School comes from the *Outline History* by W. M.

Davies. For this reference I am indebted to my friend Dr Glyn Rhys who lives in the house where John Williams was born. The identity of the Scottish references derives from *The Clacken and the Slate*, the story of the Edinburgh Academy 1824-1974 by Magnus Magnusson, 1974, which includes chapters on Williams' appointment and rectorship there).

RULES AND REGULATIONS

WELSH EDUCATIONAL INSTITUTION, LLANDOVERY.

Thomas Phillips' Foundation.

RULES AND REGULATIONS.

I.
That no Pupil of the Institution be permitted to lodge at any Inn or Public House.

II.
That no Pupil be allowed to enter an Inn or Public House without special reason.

III.
That if any Lodging House Keeper will suffer any of the Pupils to be out at improper hours, or to be guilty of improper conduct, without informing the Warden or such Master as he may name, of such impropriety, the Pupils of the Institution be not allowed to lodge at such House.

IV.
That no Pupil be allowed to change his Lodgings without Permisson of the Warden; for which, application must be made through the Acting Master.

V.
That every Pupil be required to attend Divine service at Church twice on Sundays, unless some other place of Worship be named by the Parents or Guardians.

VI.
That none of the Pupils be allowed to go beyond Three Miles from Llandovery, without special Permission from the Warden or one of the Masters.

VII.
That all the Pupils be required to attend a Roll Call at the Institution on the evening of every Holiday, unless special leave of absence be previously granted.

VIII.
That each of the Masters be requested to exercise as much superintendence as is practicable over all the Pupils out of School hours.

IX.
That one of the Masters shall visit each of the Lodging Houses as often as convenient, in each week, at uncertain hours.

London, April 8, 1851.

T. PHILLIPS.

Minutes: 1852

THOMAS PHILLIPS' FOUNDATION

At a meeting of the Trustees of the above Institution held at Llandovery the Eleventh Day of August, 1852. Present Lady Hall, Rev. Joshua Hughes, John Jones and William Rees. It was resolved—

That John Johnes of Dolaucothy, Esquire be appointed Trustee of the above Foundation in the room of the late Rev. Thomas Price deceased.

That Mr Leonidas Clint A.B., Trinity College Cambridge, late Principal and Professor at Martinere College, Lucknow, be appointed Reader in Chemistry and Botany, and Teacher of Mathematics and such other branches of Education as may be required by the Warden—at a salary of Two Hundred Pounds per annum. Such appointment to terminate at the end of Three years from the 30th day of June last.

That Mr Henry Knight be appointed Reader in Geology and Teacher of Writing, Arithmetic, Drawing and such other branches of General Education as may be required by the Warden, at a salary of One hundred Pounds per annum—Such Appointment to terminate at the end of One year from the 30th day of June last.

That the Rev. Edmund Cheese be appointed Librarian.

That the sum not exceeding Five Pounds be applied in erecting fixtures for the Library.

That the appointment of Scholars be according to merit, and that an adequate knowledge of Scripture be deemed indispensable. Such appointments to be made in Committee and in due form by the Trustees.

That any free Scholarships which may happen to be vacant at Christmas, be filled up at the commencement of the following Session and be open to general competition from the whole Principality.

That the habit of smoking, leading to so many evil consequences, particularly to that of intemperance, be effectually put down.

Ordered that the sum of £9.9.10 the amount due to Mr William Jones of St. Mildred's Court, London for legal advice be paid out of the proceeds of the Preston and Wyre Shares bequeathed by the Founder such advice being required respecting the said Bequest.

That Caleb Lloyd of Radnorshire be elected Free Scholar in the room of Edw. Williams who has left.

That Lewis Lewis of Carmarthenshire be elected Free Scholar in the room of Nadolig X. Gwynne who has left.

That Owen Thomas of Glamorganshire be elected Free Scholar in the room of David Davies who was expelled.

Aug. Hall, Joshua Hughes, John Jones, William Rees.

TRUSTEES OF THE COLLEGE
1847-1997

Lady Llanover, 1847-96
William Rees, 1847-73
John Jones, 1847-65
The Reverend Thomas Price 1847-48
The Reverend Joshua Hughes, 1847-89
John Johnes 1852-76
The Reverend E. O. Phillips, 1866-97
John Jones M.P., 1874-86
H. Campbell Davys, 1877-86
Lt. Gen. Sir James Hills-Johnes, 1886-1918
The Earl of Cawdor, 1886-1911
D. Lloyd Jones, 1889-93
Sir J. T. D. Llewelyn, 1893-1927
Lord Tredegar, 1896-1914
The Bishop of Llandaff, 1897-1905
Arthur Lewis, 1906-10
The Earl of Plymouth, 1910-23
Benjamin Evans, 1911-13
Lord Tredegar, 1914-34
F. W. Gilbertson, 1914-29
Lord Kylsant, 1919-32
Lt. Col. Sir Charles Venables-Llewelyn, 1928-48
Col. W. Bickerton Edwards, 1930-34
Lord Merthyr, 1934-57
Judge Frank Davies, 1934-42
Judge Lewis, 1935-50
Colin Mason, 1937-65
The Bishop of Llandaff, 1943-44
Capt. Geoffrey Crawshay, 1948-54
The Reverend Canon T. Walker Thomas, 1950-57
Brigadier Sir Michael Venables-Llewelyn, 1954-76
Lt. Col. A. H. D. Smith, 1954-60
H. Llewelyn Williams, 1954-64
D. Lawrence Jones, 1954-60

D. Harold Davies, 1954-76
Ewan G. Davies, 1955-79
H. Wyn Jones, 1955-66
The Most Reverend G. O. Williams, 1957-73
Sir Daniel Davies, 1958-65
Sir Grismond Phillips, 1959-65
Sir Cennydd Traherne, 1958-85 (Chairman 1972-81)
Dr D. Ogmore Williams, 1962-72
A. M. Rees, 1964-1997 (Trustee Emeritus 1997-)
Dr M. Ernest Davies, 1965-88
The Very Reverend W. Ungoed Jacob, 1966-78
Sir Ben Bowen Thomas, 1966-73
Professor Thomas ap Rees, 1966-94
Lt. Col. J. R. Evans, 1973-92 (Chairman 1981-92)
Professor Sir Idris Foster, 1974-84
The Honourable Sir Tasker Watkins, 1974-89
P. M. Davies, 1976-92
O. M. R. Howell, 1977-
Sir John Venables-Llewelyn, 1977- (Chairman 1992-)
Dr Emrys Evans, 1982-93
Rt. Hon. Viscount Tonypandy, 1984-91
Rt. Hon. Lord Aberdare, 1984-91
I. G. Price, 1984-94
Sir David Mansel Lewis, 1985-
Mrs Susan Morris, 1986-
Mrs Kathrin Thomas, 1986-94
A. M. James, 1986-94
Dr Gwyn Jones, 1990-92
B. K. Thomas, 1990-94
P. W. Ll. Morgan, 1990-93
Major-General P. R. Davies, 1992-
A. Daniel, 1993-96
S. A. Simon, 1993-
T. G. R. Davies, 1994-
Mrs Loveday Gee, 1994-
D. E. Gravell, 1994-
D. R. Jones, 1994-
P. H. Jones, 1995-
Professor R. E. Mansel, 1997-

'An Heritage They Must Maintain':

The Dillwyn-Llewelyn connection of a century and more

Sir John Venables-Llewelyn

Sir John Michael Dillwyn-Venables-Llewelyn 4th Baronet, landowner and farmer was educated at Eton and Cambridge. After university he did his National Service in Cyprus then worked as a land-agent and later as a vintage car expert: he still regards vintage car racing as his main recreation. He succeeded to the baronetcy on the death of his father Brigadier Sir (Charles) Michael Dillwyn-Venables-Llewelyn M.V.O. in 1976: within a short time Sir John was elected Trustee of Llandovery College. The connection of the family with the College extends over a hundred years and more. It is a connection which has been marked by generosity and an extraordinary blend of education, concern, experience and enterprise.

The Venables family derived from a Norman ancestor, who followed the Conqueror to England in 1066. Centuries later—in 1811—Bishop Burgess of St Davids was to nominate Richard Venables, sometime Fellow of Clare College Cambridge to the living of Clyro: in 1816 he was Prebend of Llansantffraed in the Collegiate church of Christ College Brecon. In 1847 he resigned the living of Clyro in favour of his son Richard Lister, a graduate of Emmanuel College Cambridge who succeeded his father not only in the living but as Chairman of Radnorshire Quarter Sessions and owner of Llysdinam House. When moves were afoot to transfer some of the border parishes to the diocese of Hereford, Venables thought hard—the Bishop of St Davids was not entirely to his liking: 'I have rather less taste for Thirlwall who is a very unsatisfactory man; and with the present humbug of assuming that everybody who lives in a Welsh diocese must speak Welsh it is perhaps as well to belong to an English diocese'. As luck would have it, Clyro remained *pro tem* in the diocese of St Davids. Venables was to acquire a new curate in 1865—Francis Kilvert. The years Kilvert was to spend at Clyro were to inspire the now famous diary which he compiled. For 29 March 1870 he recalls, 'Home at 6 dressed for dinner. At 6.30 Charles with the mail phaeton and the two mares, grey and bay, dashed up to the door in grand style. I was ready and away we went to the Vicarage to pick up the Vicar who took to the reins . . . It was refreshing to see the Vicar's stylish equipage driven by himself with two servants behind dashing past the small humble turn-out of the Squire'. In December 1871 Kilvert was to write a letter to Venables enclosing 'a Christmas card for Minna', his nineteen month old daughter. On 23 August 1893 Katharine Minna was to marry Charles Leyshon Dillwyn-Llewelyn (who, on marriage was to assume the Venables name).

This was the family which had bought the Cambrian Pottery in Swansea. When William Dillwyn of Walthamstow (of Quaker and Welsh family connections) visited in 1801 he recognised that the works would provide his son, Lewis Weston Dillwyn, with a profitable, agreeable and worthwhile interest. The Dillwyns were wealthy and it would seem that money was always available when Lewis wished to embark upon a business enterprise. But the Cambrian was only part of Lewis Weston Dillwyn's interest. He was a gifted naturalist—indeed his ideas were productive of new designs in ceramics at Swansea. He published a distinguished botanical book, *The British Confervae* which helped to elect him as a Fellow of the Royal Society and as a Fellow of the Linnean Society. And in 1807 he had married Mary, daughter of John Llewelyn of Ynysgerwn and Penllergaer. Dillwyn became active in his father-in-law's estates. The union of the Dillwyn and Llewelyn families made him one of the richest and most influential men in South Wales. By 1817 Dillwyn ceased to be active in the Pottery and became more involved in public life. He was High Sheriff for Glamorgan in 1818, Member of Parliament 1832-1837. He was prominent in Swansea life being one of the founders of the Royal Institution . . . and indeed he published a book on the history of Swansea in 1840.

There were two sons of the marriage—Lewis Llewelyn Dillwyn (1814-1892), industrialist and Liberal MP who was engaged in railway and banking business and who was a major figure in Swansea's industrial development. From the start he was a strong supporter of the movement for Welsh Church Disestablishment.

The other—and elder—son was John Dillwyn-Llewelyn (1810-1882), educated at Oriel College Oxford: he inherited his maternal grandfather's name (and lived at Penllergaer) . . . and his father's scientific interests. He was elected Fellow of the Royal Society in 1836, collaborated with Charles Wheatstone in his work on the electric telegraph and with Fox Talbot (related by marriage) contributed to the advancement of photography. He married Emma daughter of Thomas Mansel Talbot of Margam. Their son, John Talbot Dillwyn-Llewelyn (1836-1927) was educated at Eton and Christ Church Oxford. He was to become High Sheriff of Glamorgan in 1878, Mayor of Swansea 1891, and Conservative Member of Parliament for Swansea 1895-1900. He was created a baronet in 1890. J. T. D. Llewelyn was deeply interested in secondary and higher education—St Davids College Lampeter, the university college at Cardiff and Llandovery College were among his concerns. He was Trustee of Llandovery College from 1893 to 1927. When he was invited, in December 1898, to preside at an Old Boys' Dinner he remarked: 'I think it would be more in consonance with the proprieties of an old Llandovery Boy—one educated at the school itself were Chairman rather than myself who tho' an ardent admirer am a Trustee only and have no claim to call myself an 'Old Llandoverian'. In the event he took the chair at the dinner held at the Royal Hotel Swansea on 6 January 1899: tickets were '6/-'! His ardour in respect of the School was never wanting. He distributed the prizes in July 1901 commenting 'the boys must look upon the great traditions of Llandovery as an heritage they must maintain'. He presided at the Prize Day in July 1902, assembled in the School Hall, now the Library. He referred to the fact that the Trustees 'had now a very important work to perform. They had undertaken

Sir J. T. D. Llewelyn

great responsibilities in the new buildings, which were so essential to the success of Llandovery. They were determined that Llandovery should not suffer for want of accommodation or opportunities to continue the wonderful work it had done in the past . . . As to the character of the by-gone students in all branches of life, Llandovery boys had been highly successful. In medicine, law, Church, army . . . and now in the higher branches of the Civil Service . . .' The 'great responsibilities' and concern for opportunities were matters close to the hearts of his descendants, too.

The title passed to his younger son Charles Leyshon Dillwyn-Venables-Llewelyn in 1927. It was he who had married Katharine Minna to whom Kilvert had sent the Christmas card. He was educated at Eton and New College Oxford. He was High Sheriff of Radnorshire 1924, Lord Lieutenant 1929-1949 and sat as Conservative Member of Parliament from January to November 1910. He was Trustee of Llandovery College from 1928 to 1948 . . . and it was he who presented the painting of St Peter attributed to Guercino (1592-1666) to the School in 1936.

Colonel Sir Charles Dillwyn-Venables-Llewelyn was succeeded by his son Charles Michael in 1951. He was educated at Eton and at the Royal Military College and rose to the rank of Brigadier. It was he who presented to the College 'The Turn of the Tide', that splendid seascape by Neuman which adorns the Dining Hall. Sir Michael had married the Lady Delia Mary Hicks-Beach, only daughter of Viscount Quenington and sister of Earl St Aldwyn. They had two children—Mary (Mrs Elster) and John, the present baronet. It was Sir John, his sister and the Lady Delia who commissioned the fine stained glass window for the newly furbished College chapel. It was presented by the Llysdinam Trust in 1991 'in memory of Brigadier Sir Michael Dillwyn-Venables-Llewelyn Bart. M.V.O., a Trustee of the College 1954-1976 and to commemorate the association for one hundred years of the Llewelyn family with the College'.

The East Window

Sir John Michael Dillwyn-Venables-Llewelyn Bart, M.A., was appointed Chairman of the College Trustees in 1992.

(Sources: D.N.B; D.W.B; Owain Jones 'Llysdinam and Newbridge' Brycheiniog XX 1982/83; Helen L. Hallesy *The Glamorgan Pottery Swansea* 1814-38; N.L.W, D.Ll.T; The School Journal; personal knowledge).

The Wardens 1847-

The Venerable John Williams M.A., F.R.S.E. (1847-1852)

The Reverend David James M.A., Ph.D., F.S.A. (1853-1854)

The Very Reverend E. O. Phillips M.A., D.D. (1854-1861)

The Reverend William Watkins M.A. (1861-1875)

The Most Reverend A. G. Edwards M.A., LL.D., D.C.L. (1875-1885)

The Right Reverend John Owen M.A., D.D. (1885-1889)

The Venerable Owen Evans M.A. (1889-1900)

The Reverend Canon W. W. Poole-Hughes M.A. (1901-1928)

The Reverend Canon T. Walker Thomas M.A. (1928-1948)

The Most Reverend G. O. Williams M.A., D.D. (1948-1957)

The Venerable R. J. Tree M.A., B.Litt. (1957-1966)

R. Gerallt Jones OBE., M.A., FRSA (1967-1976)

R. Brinley Jones M.A., D.Phil., Hon D.D., Hon D. Litt., F.S.A. (1976-1988)

Claude E. Evans B.Sc., Ph.D., C.Chem., M.R.S.C. (1988-)

John Williams

David James

E. O. Phillips

William Watkins

A. G. Edwards

John Owen

Owen Evans

W. W. Poole Hughes

T. Walker Thomas

G. O. Williams

R. J. Tree

R. Gerallt Jones

The Wardens

R. Brinley Jones

Claude E. Evans

TRUSTEES, STAFF AND PREFECTS 1997-98

Visitor—The Rt. Rev. D. Huw Jones MA, Lord Bishop of St David's

Trustees
Sir John Venables-Llewelyn Bart MA—*Chairman*
Mr O. M. R. Howell MA FCA
Sir David Mansel Lewis KCVO JP BA KStJ
Mrs Susan Morris
Major General Peter Davies CB FBIM FITD
Mr S. A. Simon
Mr D. E. Gravell MIME

Mr D. R. Jones
Mr T. G. R. Davies MA
Mrs E. J. Gee BA MPhil
Mr P. H. Jones FCA
Prof R. E. Mansel MB BS MS FRCS

Mr W. J. Morris BA—*Clerk to the Trustees*

Trustee Emeritus—Mr A. M. Rees CBE QPM DLMA

Warden Dr C. E. Evans BSc C Chem MRSC PGCE
Deputy Warden Mr D. S. Beck MA *Head of English*
Senior Mistress Mrs J. D. Kendrick JP Cert Ed *EFL Games*
Director of Studies Mr M. H. Edwards BA PGCE *Physics, Mathematics*

Academic Staff

Mr C. Andras BA PGCE	*French, Spanish*	Mr B. Lynas BA ATD	*Director of Art*
Mr G. W. J. Brand B Ed MA PGCE	*Head of Business Studies*	Miss V. Maes	*French*
Mr T. J. Cannock MA	*Head of Classics*	Mr T. G. Marks BA Cert Ed	*Head of Welsh*
Mr G. R. Evans BA MEd	*Head of Modern Languages*		*Tŷ Ddewi Housemaster*
	Tŷ Teilo Housemaster	Mr D. G. Morgan BSc Dip Ed	*Head of Mathematics Examinations Officer*
Mr C. E. Griffiths LWCMD Cert Ed	*Head of Drama*	Miss S. M. Northam BSc PGSE	*Mathematics*
Mr D. A. Griffiths BA PGCE	*Mathematics, Science*	Mrs A. J. Owen Cert Ed	*Dyslexia Unit*
Mrs M. Griffiths BA	*History,*	Mr V. A. Price BSc PGCE	*Head of Physics*
	Tŷ Llanover Housemistress	Mr A. T. Rees BSc Dip Ed	*Head of Geography*
Miss R. E. Harrison	*Information Technology*		*Tŷ Llandingat Housemaster*
Mrs C. S. Hopkins BA PGCE Adv Dip Ed AMBDA	*Head of Dyslexia Unit*	Mr I. O. Thomas Cert Ed	*Director of Sport*
Mr C. N. H. Jennings BSc PGCE	*Biology, Chemistry, CCF*	Mr N. A. Watts AdDip Cert Ed	*Head of Design & Technology*
Mrs S. Jones Cert Ed	*Welsh*		*Tŷ Cadog Housemaster*
Mr J. M. Kendrick MSc MI Biol	*Head of Biology*		
Miss C. G. Ladd MA PGCE	*English*	Mr R. C. Whitehead MA	*Director of Music*
Fr. S. Leyshon BA B Th PGCMS	*Chaplain, Head of Religious Studies*	Mr A. Wielochowski BSc MSc	*Head of Chemistry*
		Mr A. G. Wood BA Dip Ed	*Head of History*

Visiting Music Staff
Mrs V. Couch ARCM ATCL LTCL
Mr I. Davies FLCM
Mrs M. Iliff LRAM GRSM

Mr M. E. Lewis Cert Ed
Mr P. M. Nicholas Cert Ed
Mrs E. Perfect ARCM

Mrs M. Stephens
Mr S. Stowell RCM
Mr P. M. Thomas Cert Ed

Bursar Major W. J. Evans MBIM
Development Director Mr S. A. Richards BSc

Support Staff

Mrs A. Hughes Cert Ed	*Warden's Secretary*	Mrs J. Marks HND	*Domestic Bursar*
Mrs R. Waters SRN	*Nursing Sister*	Mr H. D. Morris	*Bursary Officer*
Mrs C. Hughes	*Bursary Officer*	Mrs W. Rees	*Technician*
Mrs C. Watts	*Junior Boys' Matron*	Mrs C. Rees	*Junior Girls' Matron*

College Prefects

Dafydd Rees (Head of College) Martha Jones (Senior Girl Prefect)
Edmund Bailey Natalie Burrows
Sara Davies Rhiannon Hall
Simon Hutchings Jodie Milne
Freddie New Jamie Roberts
Tom Walker Arfon Williams

Pupil Numbers at November 1997
Male: 103 boarders 47 day
Female 36 boarders 36 day
Total number of pupils 222

SELECTION FROM THE YEARBOOK
(1997-1998)

Llandovery College
(Coleg Llanymddyfri)

Llandovery, Carmarthenshire SA20 OEE
Tel: Warden (01550) 720315
Bursar (01550) 720315
Fax: (01550) 720168

Llandovery College was formally opened on St David's Day 1848. Founded and endowed by Dr Thomas Phillips, sometime doyen of the Royal College of Surgeons, it occupies a fine site amidst magnificent countryside in the small market town of Llandovery. The extensive grounds and playing fields run alongside two miles of the river Towy.

Motto: *Gwell Dysg na Golud. (Better Learning than Riches).*

College Organisation. Pupils are accepted from the age of 11. Boys in the first three years are housed in Tŷ Cadog and move to Tŷ Teilo for Forms 4 and 5 (Years 10 and 11). Sixth Form boys are accommodated in single study-bedrooms in Tŷ Ddewi. Junior girls live in Llandingat whilst the senior girls occupy Llanover—a purpose built girls' boarding house opened in 1988.

Currently there are 170 boys and 70 girls divided almost equally between full boarders, weekly boarders and day pupils.

The College employs a catering company and high quality food is served from a modern kitchen.

Curriculum. The following subjects are taught through to GCSE and A-level: Art, Biology, Business Studies, Chemistry, Classical Civilization, Design and Technology, Drama, English, French, Geography, Greek, History, Information Technology and Computer Science, Latin, Mathematics, Music, Physical Education, Physics, Religious Studies and Welsh.

English as a Foreign Language is available as an optional extra.

The College also welcomes pupils of high intelligence but with moderate dyslexia. Special classes are taught by experienced dyslexia teachers who are always available to offer advice both to pupils and parents.

Entrance Examinations and Scholarships. Examinations for places and awards are set at the ages of 11, 13 and 16 although entrance can be gained at other ages by special arrangement. Pupils from Preparatory Schools would normally be expected to sit the Common Entrance Examination. Dates of the examinations are available from the Warden.

Scholarships. Scholarships up to the value to half-fees are offered as well as bursaries for the sons and daughters of members of the Clergy and Officers serving in the Armed Forces. Carwyn James Sports Scholarships are available in the Sixth Form for pupils showing superior sporting skills particularly in Rugby Football and Cricket. The College also participates in the Government Assisted Places Scheme and a number become available each year.

Buildings. The original buildings now contain the Dining Hall (which houses a remarkable collection of paintings) and Library and resource centre, the Warden's Study and administration offices, the Masters' Common Room and dining room, and two of the boys' houses.

Around the campus are the new girls' house, the senior boys' house, the teaching, science and music blocks, the sanatorium (staffed by fully-qualified nurses), a multi-purpose hall, the CCF headquarters, the Design and Technology Centre and the Warden's residence. The new Sports Hall completed in 1991 also houses the Sixth Form Club.

Chapel. The Chapel which was built in 1934 was the gift of Dr D. L. Prosser, formerly Bishop of St David's and Archbishop of Wales. In 1990 it was completely refurbished and dedicated to the memory of the donor. The pipe organ, now a fine instrument was completely rebuilt and a specially commissioned stained-glass East window installed. All pupils attend a short act of worship four mornings a week. There is a weekly celebration of the Eucharist. The Chaplain prepares pupils for Confirmation which is administered annually in the College Chapel by the Visitor. Pupils of other denominations are free to attend Sunday Services in Chapels and Churches in the town. The Michaelmas Term ends with an Advent Carol Service.

Music. As well as being a subject in the school curriculum, music also features prominently in the life of the college. Most instruments can be taught privately either by members of the Music Department or by visiting peripatetic teachers. There is a termly concert as well as a series of recitals throughout the year. Pupils are also encouraged to join the Chapel choir.

Career Service. There is a comprehensive Careers Service supported with regular visits by the Regional Director of the Independent Schools Careers Organisation, the Forces Liaison Officers and the Dyfed Careers Service. The department is well equipped to give advice on higher education.

Games. All pupils are required to participate in games unless medically unfit. The College has a long and distinguished reputation in sport particularly in the field of Rugby Football. For boys there is a comprehensive programme of Rugby matches against other schools in the two winter terms and the College also participates successfully in national Seven-a-side tournaments. In recent years boys have regularly won Welsh Schoolboy International Caps. Girls play competitive hockey at both school and county level. In the summer term, cricket, tennis and athletics feature as the main sports.

With the advent of the new Sports Hall a whole range of sporting activities is made available including squash, badminton, netball, volleyball, bowling and table tennis.

The College has its own golf course and riding, swimming and clay pigeon shooting are offered at nearby locations.

Archaeology, bridge, chess, photography, model-making and fishing are available for those who wish to participate. Plays performed by pupils and by visiting companies are staged in the College Theatre. A school journal produced regularly since 1886 perpetuates a continuous record of College events.

Outdoor Activities. There is a College contingent of the Combined Cadet Force to which pupils in Forms 3 and 4 belong and which is also open to senior pupils. Field days are held throughout the year and annual camps take place in the Easter and Summer holidays. The superb countryside within striking distance of the College lends itself magnificently to outward bound activities such as canoeing, rock-climbing and general expedition work.

The College's indoor shooting range is extensively used. Pupils are coached by the College's SSI and regularly represent Wales in international competitions.

The College participates extensively in the Duke of Edinburgh's Award Scheme. 25 pupils have secured the Gold Award in the last two years.

Regular visits to the theatre are offered throughout the winter season and both skiing and foreign tour holidays are also available. The French department arranges an annual Form 2 holiday and extensive use is made of the twinning arrangement between Llandovery Town and Pluguffan in Brittany.

Parents' Association. An active Parents' Association assists the College by providing such items as minibuses, video cameras and outdoor pursuit vehicles.

Old Llandoverian Society. There is a parent body (Secretary: Mr S. A. Richards, Llandovery College, Llandovery, Carmarthenshire SA20 0EE) and branches centred in Cardiff and London.

Charitable status. Llandovery College is a Registered Charity, number 525394. It exists for the purpose of educating children from the ages of 11 to 18.

(This is part of the 'insert' that appears in the 1997-98 list of schools in The Headmasters' and Headmistresses' Conference, published by A. C. Black, London. The 'insert' also includes the name of the Visitor, Trustees (and their Clerk), Teaching Staff, Medical Officer, Bursar, Development Director as included here in Appendix J).

'TAKE ONE LONG LOOK . . .'

'The corridors are crowded with boys, all laughing and chattering as they pour out from their classrooms, for lessons are ended for the morning. Numerous are the topics which they discuss; we can hear them talking over what has been done in the past, and what ought to be done in the future. Here, one who is playing in a rugger match to-morrow is wondering in what state the ground will be; there, another is delighting the ears of an encouraging audience, by giving the full particulars of an amusing incident which has occurred in form during the course of the morning; another is ruminating on the chances of a half-holiday. So great is the hubbub, so varied the conversation, that one has little opportunity to record the talk, and, we may say, little stomach too, for their chatter would fill volumes.'

Christmas 1927

'It had been a long and tiresome train journey from the Airport to Llandovery. On the way to Swansea I found myself among middle-aged men in dark suits discussing a difficult trade union meeting which they had attended in London. There was a break in Swansea before taking the Heart of Wales line: it was early September and the compartment was full of shoppers. Some were speaking Welsh—a language I had never heard before. Most of the passengers had left the train by the time we got to Ammanford. At long last we arrived at Llandovery. It was drizzling. I had lived in a big city all my life—the lights, the sounds, the hustle and bustle was the world I had known. And now I was in a small town . . . and the quiet hit me. My heart sank as I trudged my way with a heavy case, crossing the road to the College. It was going to be my home for the next two or three years!

I remember it all, vividly, now. When I left, on that Speech Day, three years later, I had made *so* many friendships. And I had stored up *so* many impressions—Roll Call, Chapel, Lunch, the Games, the Music, the expeditions, the Plays, the long, long conversations . . . and, of course, the lessons and the three weekly 'orders'. As I departed on that Saturday in July and said 'Goodbye' to the Warden, he said, 'Take one long look before you go'. I did . . . and even now, those buildings and corridors, those secret and sacred corners . . . the grass on Tredegar and the views across the Playing Fields come flooding back. And I see, in every part, so many faces and hear so many voices. How great it is to look back! Coleg Llanymddyfri will always be a very special part of my life'.

August 1985

(Just to recapture 'those buildings and corridors, those secret and sacred corners . . . the grass on Tredegar and the views across the Playing Fields' there follows a brief pictorial selection. On the whole the images are un-peopled for the faces, the laughter, the chatting, the concerns, the triumphs and the disappointments belong to the reader. Some 'corners', like the dining hall, the main hall/library appear as they were and as they are so that Old Llandoverians may rehearse the secrets of their ways when they were young and there.

Many of the photographs that follow were taken, at my request, by Mr Barrard Lynas. I am deeply grateful to him).

'Take one long look . . .'

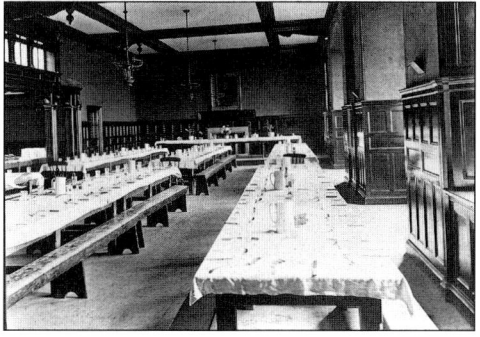

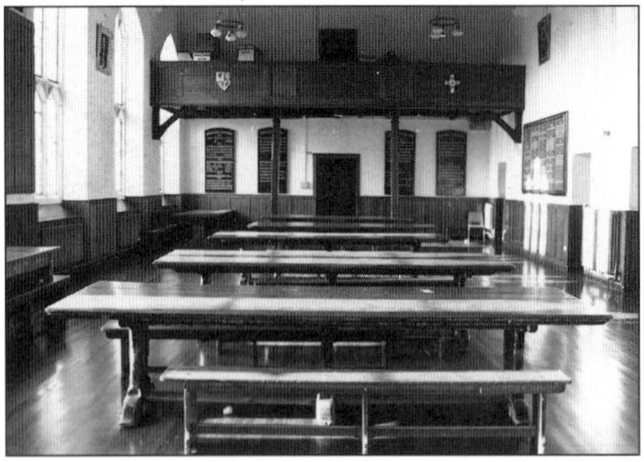

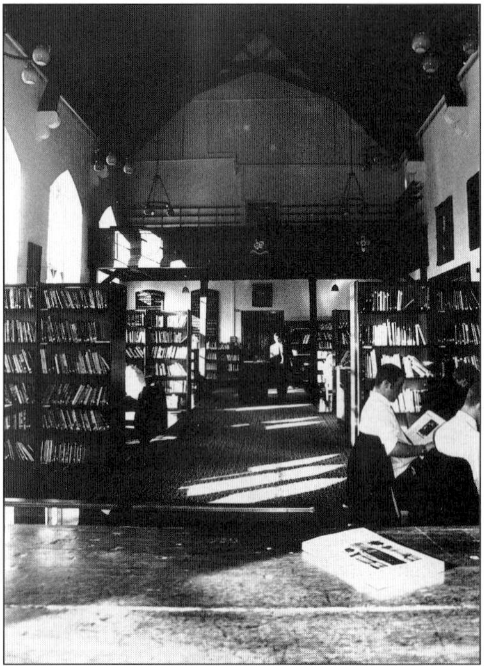

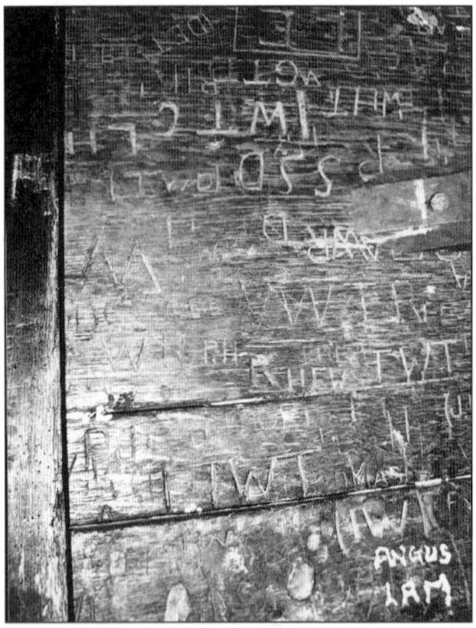
ANGUS
LAM

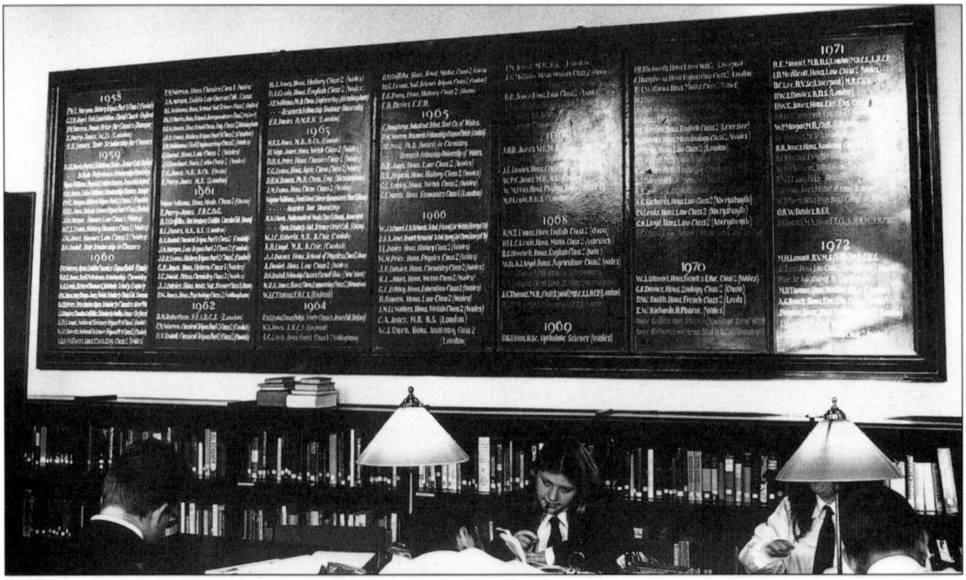

'Take one long look . . .'   363

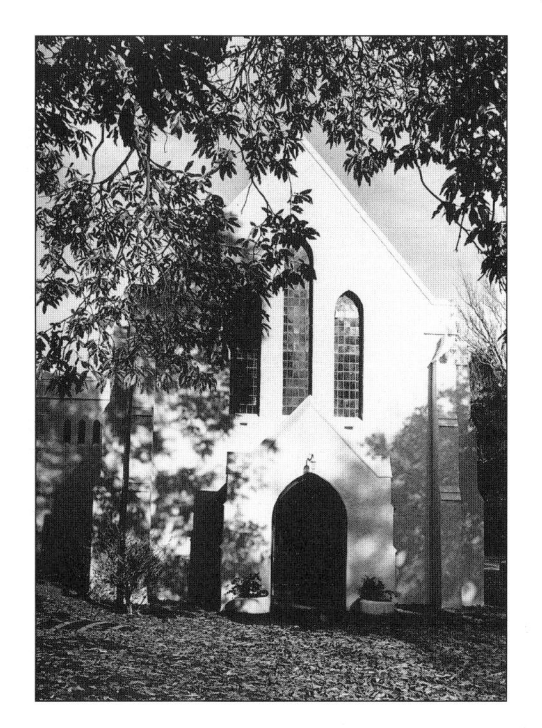

Floreat Landubriense

'Take one long look . . .'

366 *Floreat Landubriense*

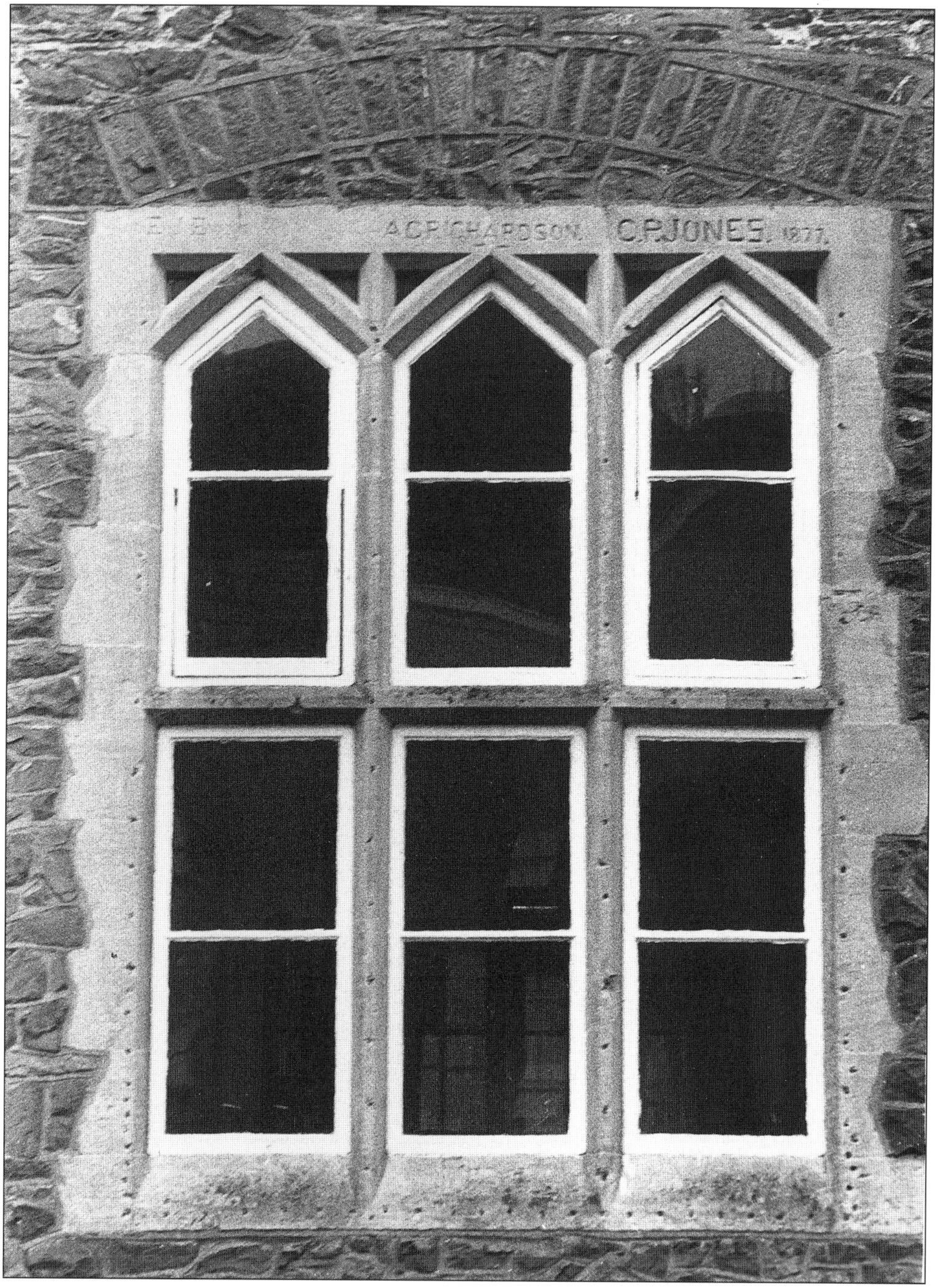
A.C.RICHARDSON.
C.P.JONES. 1877.